Not so much a pot, more a way of life

Current approaches to artefact analysis in archaeology

edited by

C. G. Cumberpatch and

Oxbow Monograph 83
1997

Published by
Oxbow Books, Park End Place, Oxford OX1 1HN

ISBN 1 900188 38 4

100334 5888
100349997X

This book is available direct from
Oxbow Books, Park End Place, Oxford OX1 1HN
(Phone: 01865–241249; Fax: 01865–794449)

and

The David Brown Book Company
PO Box 5111, Oakville, CT 06779, USA
(Phone: 860–945–9329; Fax: 860–945–9468)

Printed in Great Britain at
The Short Run Press, Exeter

Contents

Introduction

C.G. Cumberpatch and P. W. Blinkhorn

The origins of this book lie in two sessions organised by the editors at the Theoretical Archaeology Group conferences at Durham and Bradford in 1993 and 1994 respectively. The content of these sessions, and the discussions which followed them, revealed that there is a widespread feeling of frustration amongst those archaeologists working with artefacts arising from a perception that the current theoretical and practical orientations of artefact analysis are both restrictive and of questionable validity. This collection of papers is intended to articulate some positive responses to those frustrations and to demonstrate that there is more to artefact analysis than chronology and provenance.

The analysis of artefacts in field archaeology is dominated by the chronological calibration of stratigraphic sequences, which, combined with ritualised obeisance to the god of typology, generally results in studies which can be regarded as purely monotheistic (Blinkhorn and Cumberpatch, in press). In academia, the infatuation with novel analytical techniques (institutionalised until recently through SERC funding criteria) has resulted in displays of methodological virtuosity which are all too often 'full of sound and fury, signifying nothing': science for science's sake. More recently the reduction in the scale and scope of PhD theses in response to the grotesque imperatives of professional bureaucrats and managers poses new threats to the development of innovative intellectual responses to increasingly complex datasets.

Contextual archaeology first saw the light of day in the 1980s with a series of programmatic and ground-breaking publications (e.g. Hodder 1982a, 1982b, 1986, 1987a, 1987b, Shanks and Tilley 1987a, 1987b). During the first half of the 1990s a considerable amount of attention has been devoted to putting these approaches into action. This collection of papers is an attempt to explore some of the implications of contextual approaches for the study of artefacts and thus for the study of material culture as it is implicated in the constitution of past and present realities.

While the majority of the papers deal with ceramics, the volume should not be seen as concerned with pottery at the expense of other artefacts. A number of papers (Allison, Meadows, Cumberpatch) deal explicitly with pottery as one element in the material culture worlds of both the past and the present (the latter represented by the concerns of the archaeologist) and throughout the volume the concern of the authors is with the analysis of material culture as a whole, rather than with ceramics in particular. For historical, logistical and institutional reasons the analysis of material culture has been separated and divided into categories defined by raw materials, but these divisions are increasingly seen by artefact analysts as irrelevant at best and actively counter-productive to a broader study of the past at worst. The advent of a contextual archaeology offers the opportunity to contest, challenge and dismantle these increasingly absurd distinctions (including the questionable distinction between 'small finds' and 'bulk finds'). It is to be hoped that specialists in other categories of material culture (including landscape and environmental archaeology) will recognise within this volume issues which are of mutual concern. It is to be hoped that, in future, the focus of work will move more towards the connections between objects rather than being concerned solely with their distinctive characteristics.

The chronological and geographical span of the papers included is broad, from the Mesolithic of southern Italy to contemporary Peru via medieval England. Unity however is provided by the common concern with historical and archaeological context.

Penelope Allison has been studying the artefacts from what is arguably one of the most famous archaeological site in the world, Pompeii. Her paper expresses the frustrations of attempting to use the artefacts from the settlement as tools for the interpretation of social interactions when inhibited by the restrictions of the traditional excavation report. As a result of her experiences she suggests a method of publishing artefacts which will result in such catalogues being a useful data source for non-chronological analyses rather than the routinised presentation of art-historically derived taxonomies which have their roots in 18th century science.

Paul Blinkhorn attempts to explain Anglo-Saxon pottery. The material has never fully responded to traditional typological analyses, and despite Julian Richard's (1987) convincing demonstration of the symbolism of decorated pagan-period cinerary urns, other, non-decorated vessels are generally dismissed as being purely functional. In his paper, using some basic theoretical principles, he presents an interpretative model which suggests that such ceramics were loaded with 'meaning', and were a vital part of the identity of the people of Anglo-Saxon England from their time as a collection of disparate pagan peoples to the coming of Christianity and the first concept of the English as a nation.

Ann Woodward and Paul Blinkhorn's paper is a presentation of how, using simple statistical analyses, ceramic data can be linked with theory to demonstrate the ways in which apparently functional artefacts can be reflectors of social changes which do not appear in the stratigraphic record. The paper shows that there is a strong correlation between the rim diameter and volume of later Iron Age hand-made pottery in both Wessex and the south-east midlands of England, but that the same does not apply to the wheel-made pottery of the period in both locations. When the findings are placed within a wider context, it can be demonstrated that they are a material manifestation of changes in social practice.

Chris Cumberpatch uses a phenomenological perspective to set later medieval pottery from Yorkshire and Humberside into a context which acknowledges the emic reality of local conceptual and classificatory schemes and attempts to derive some of these from physical characteristics of the pottery itself. He stresses the importance of seeing pottery not simply as a chronological marker, or even an indicator of inter-regional trade, but as a component of the world-as-experienced by medieval people, implicated in the categorisation of activity, space and time which made that world a viable and workable one. From the perspective of archaeological practice such a view is predicated upon an open-minded approach to archaeological data and its potential for interpretation from a variety of perspectives, no one of which can be considered as having *a priori* methodological or conceptual primacy over others.

Kevin Andrew's contribution sets out an interpretative model of ceramic fineware production derived from the integrated archaeometric study of the surface coatings and treatment of Late La Tène slip decorated pottery from the Auvergne region of Central France. His study emphases the importance of directing physico-chemical analyses towards specific archaeological questions and the significance of the results for our understanding of practices of production within given social contexts.

Karen Meadows considers the process of Romanisation from the perspective of practices associated with cooking, eating and drinking on the late Iron Age and early Roman settlement at Barton Court Farm in Oxfordshire. Romanisation, for long a mainstay of attempts to explain the radical discontinuities consequent upon the Roman invasion of Britain, is viewed as partially constituted of changes in the fundamental practices of everyday life rather than simply as a set of political or emulative imperatives.

Following the recent rise in concern with studies of material culture consumption (e.g. Miller 1987, 1995, with references), Duncan Brown uses ceramic and other data from excavations in Saxon and Medieval Southampton to examine the patterns of use of locally manufactured and continental goods. Using quantitative analyses, differences in patterns of consumption over time are discussed in terms of the changing requirements of the consumer and the position of the town as a major port and point of contact with the European mainland.

Elizabeth Musgrave uses a combination of archaeological and documentary data to examine the organisation of the pottery industry of the Saintonge region of south-western France. Medieval pottery production began here around 1250 and continued into the 18th century, a time-span which offers an unusual opportunity to trace long-term trends in the manufacturing practices. Three aspects of industrial organisation are discussed; the capital and technological basis of production; the organisation of social relations of labour within and outside the workshop; and the changing patterns of consumer demand and the impacts on the industry. As with Duncan Brown's paper the importance of consumer behaviour, in this case the rise of a consumer ethic in 18th century France, is given detailed attention.

Bill Sillar's work in the south-central Andes investigates how and why modern potters maintain their community-based styles and the circumstances under which certain potters can challenge such styles. Through a close study of Andean communities he emphasises the extent to which production is situated within a social context and the articulations between the 'economic' and 'social' spheres.

In his paper Mark Pluciennik questions the use of pottery as a chronological and ethnic marker in the debate over the spread of farming across Europe. In place of the conventional view of the use of pottery as characteristic of 'the first farmers' Pluciennik emphasises that the processes of pottery acquisition, production and consumption were closely involved in the construction of new temporalities and spatialities; different understandings of time and space, history and landscape and in the formation of intra- and inter-societal identities and relationships.

Bibliography

Blinkhorn, P.W. and Cumberpatch, C.G. in press The interpretation of artefacts and the tyranny of the field archaeologist. In: H. Dalwood (Ed.) *Proceedings of the sixth Interpreting Stratigraphy conference* Worcester 1995.

Hodder, I. 1982a *Symbols in Action*. Cambridge University Press.

Hodder, I. 1982b *Symbolic and Structural Archaeology*. Cambridge University Press.

Hodder, I. 1986 *Reading the Past*. Cambridge University Press.

Hodder, I. 1987a *The Archaeology of Contextual Meanings*. Cambridge University Press.

Hodder, I. 1987b *Archaeology as Long-Term History*. Cambridge University Press.

Miller, D. 1987 *Material Culture and Mass Consumption*. Blackwell.

Miller, D. 1995 *Acknowledging Consumption*. Routledge.

Richards, J. 1987 *The significance of the form and decoration of Anglo-Saxon cremation urns*. British Archaeological Reports British Series 166.

Shanks, M. and Tilley, C. 1987a *Reconstructing Archaeology*. Routledge.

Shanks, M. and Tilley, C. 1987b *Social Theory and Archaeology*. Polity Press.

Reputable pots and disreputable potters: Individual and community choice in present-day pottery production and exchange in the Andes

Bill Sillar

Introduction

One of the most widely recognised phenomena in the archaeology of ceramics is the similarity of a particular pottery paste or fabric, deposited within a restricted area over a period of time. The identification of pottery wares relies on this, and yet the social practice that accounts for it is rarely questioned. In this paper I wish to consider the social causes of this material practice amongst several communities of peasant potters currently working in the South-Central Andes.

The Andean highlands of Southern Peru and Bolivia are a rugged area with many communities at 4000 metres and above. I worked in the department of Cuzco in Peru, and the departments of Cochabamba and Potosi in Bolivia (see Map 1). The wide scope of this survey combined with more intensive work in two of the communities has helped to alter my understanding of the relationships within and between these pottery producing communities.

In many areas of the world the recognition of distinct fabric groups seems to become easier for later periods when specialised pottery producers develop their own particular paste recipes. For instance in the Cuzco region the Chanapata and Pacalomoco pottery traditions, which cover a wide region, have a remarkably consistent fabric, characterised by the crowded speckles of white rounded quartz, for several centuries (C14 dates are still rare but broadly similar traditions may last from about 800 BC to almost 600AD). It is not until the Middle Horizon (600–900AD) and particularly the Late Intermediate period (900–1450AD) that a real diversity of fabrics emerges (Lunt 1987, Kendall 1990). The ability of what is assumed to be widely dispersed pottery producers to maintain such similar fabrics over a long time period is, I think, only explicable by a strong cultural agreement over how to make pottery. Rice (1981, 1991) argued that as pottery production becomes more specialised variation will be reduced and the pottery (including fabric, form and decoration) will become more standardised. What the Cuzco material shows is that the development of community specialisations may see the development of internal 'standardisation' but this is achieved at the same time as a rising differentiation between the various production centres. In this paper I am not concerned about the prehistoric breakdown in the coherence of the region's pottery fabrics; I am concerned with discussing how and why today's potters maintain their community based styles, and what circumstances can cause certain potters to challenge their community practices.

The distribution of prehistoric pottery in the Cuzco region is still relatively under-studied and is usually considered within a cultural-historical framework. According to Murra (1972, 1978), in pre-Hispanic periods pottery would have been made by one or more communities within each ethnic group (*ayllu*) and this pottery would be circulated largely within the group. As prehistoric ethnic groups are partly mapped by the distribution of ceramics the application of this hypothesis has resulted in circular arguments of somewhat self-fulfilling interpretations (c.f. Shennan 1989). Today ethnic affiliations are still important in many regions of the Andes, but I hope to show that the organisation of pottery distribution has developed as a part of the re-orientation of the Andean economy and its articulation with world capitalism. Pottery distribution is embedded in local socio-economic structures within which ethnicity is only one amongst many factors.

Andean pottery technology: the basic grammar

Pottery production in the South-Central Andes, although requiring great skill and a good knowledge of raw-materials and tools, is relatively simple and surprisingly consistent both in the techniques and in the organisation of production. All the pottery production I have observed is organised at the household level in a few communities where anything between six to a hundred households specialise in making pottery during the dry season. Pottery forming usually involves the use of a flat slab of clay to make the base, and large thick coils that are further thinned by drawing the clay up to form the sides (Figs. 1 and 2). The firing normally involves stacking the pots on a flat surface, then constructing a low protective wall around the base of the

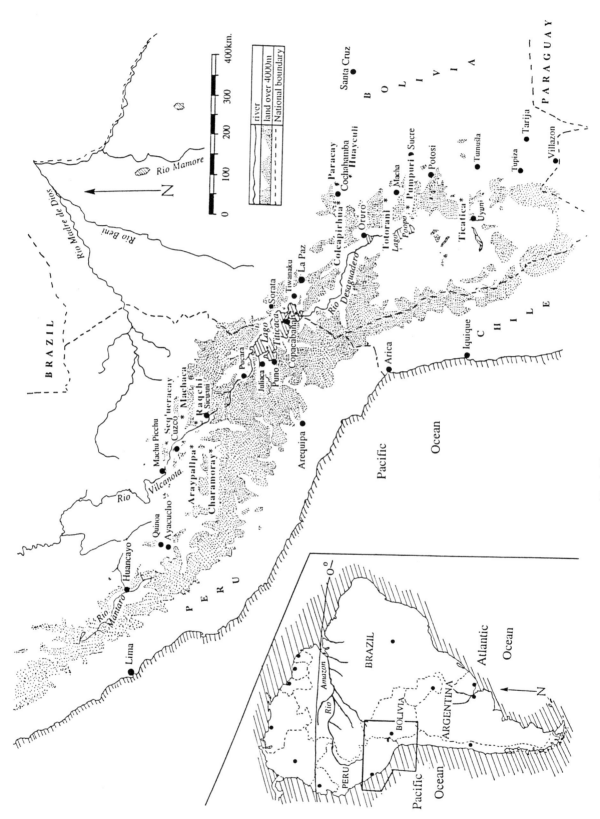

Map 1. The South-Central Andes.

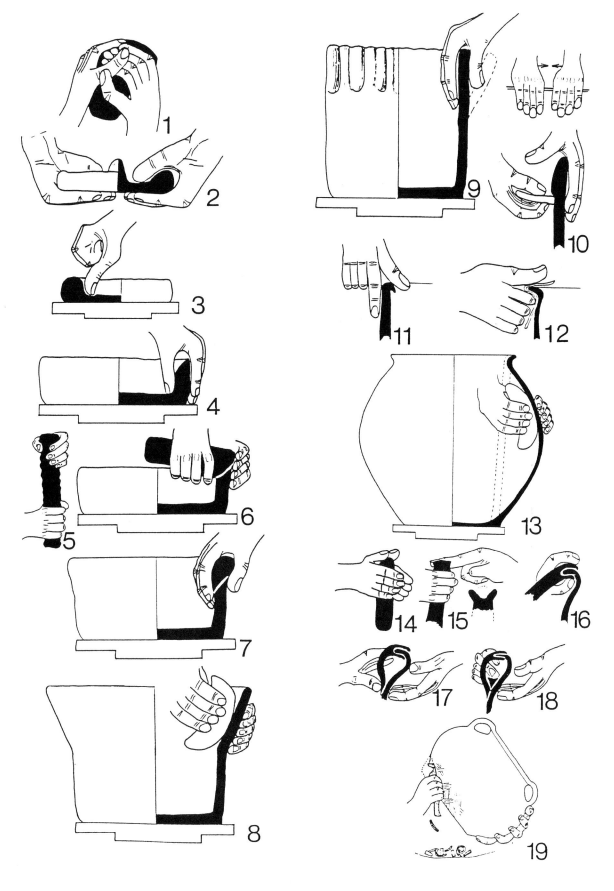

Fig. 1. The formation process for a cooking pot (manka) *in Machaca.*

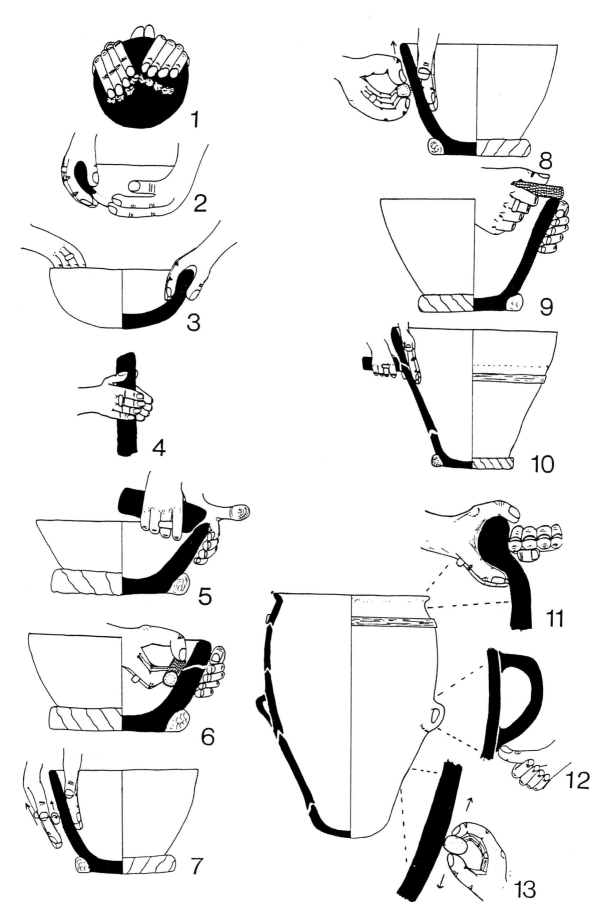

Fig. 2. The formation process for a larger jar (raki) *in Araypallpa.*

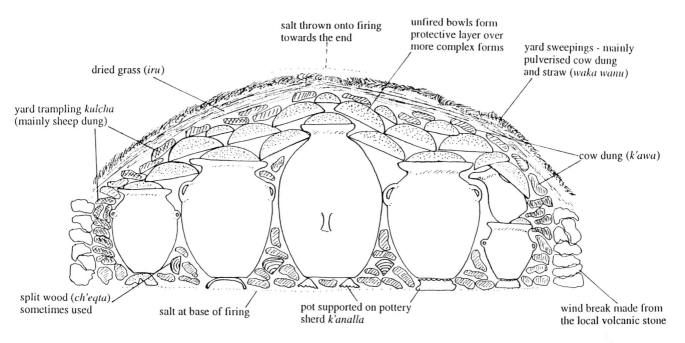

yard trampling *kulcha*
(mainly sheep dung)

dried grass (*iru*)

salt thrown onto firing
towards the end

unfired bowls form
protective layer over
more complex forms

yard sweepings - mainly
pulverised cow dung
and straw (*waka wanu*)

cow dung (*k'awa*)

split wood (*ch'eqta*)
sometimes used

salt at base of firing

pot supported on pottery
sherd *k'analla*

wind break made from
the local volcanic stone

Fig. 3. The firing arrangement used in Raqchi.

pile and then covering the vessels with fuel (most commonly animal dung) (Fig. 3.). This is not to say that alternative methods are not known and used (Sillar 1994, 1996) but the underlying grammar of pottery-making technology, described above, appears to be characteristic of the South-Central Andes and has consistently been reported by a number of authors (e.g. Tschopik 1950; Donnan 1971; O'Neale 1977; Ravines 1978; Hagstrum 1988; Ravines and Villiger (eds.) 1989; D. E. Arnold 1993).

Raw materials; sacred sources and community access

With reference to the potter's choice of raw materials Dean Arnold has re-worked a form of 'site catchment' model (e.g. Jarman 1972) to suggests that most non-industrial potters exploit clay and temper resources within an upper threshold of 7 km of their home (Arnold 1985, 56). The majority

of the communities I have worked in would conform with Arnold's model (Table 1), the few exceptions being due either to the availability of modern transport, or to the demand for what are considered particularly desirable materials – such as clay or temper for cooking pots and pigments for decoration. However, although Arnold's model suggest the outer limits beyond which few potters will go to exploit resources, it does little to explain how the potters conceptualise these resources. Also, while his argument supposedly includes the "social and psychological costs" (Arnold 1985, 33), it is a generalising model and is not concerned with the particular cultural understanding or socio-economic set-up within which these resources are collected. Clay collection is heavily embedded in the potter's social and economic relations and cannot be explained solely with reference to the economics of pottery production.

Table 1. Distance, by path or road, to clay and temper sources

Location	Community	Clay	Temper
Department	Arayallpa	0.1–0.3 km	+
	Charamoray/Urubamba	1.5 km	3.0 km
of Cuzco,	Machaca	2 km	0.1–0.3 km
	Raqchi	3 km	0.3–0.5 km
Peru	Seq'ueracay	2–3 km	0.1–0.3 km
Department	Colcapirhua	2–14 km*	+
of	Huayculi	1–2.5 km**	+
Cochabamba,	Paracay	1–3 km	+
Bolivia	Sarumi Rancho	5 km	1.5 km
Dept. Potosi,	Pumpuri	2–3 km	+
Bolivia	Totorami	3 km	1km

+   In these cases the choice of clays with naturally occurring non-plastics negates the need for a separate tempering material to be added.

*   The more distant clays are now always collected by truck.

**   Another clay, used by two of the potters in Huayculi and those in Vilaque for making cooking pots, is collected by donkey from near Anzaldo, 8km away.

In the Andes the choice of a particular clay source may be heavily influenced by the particulars of local land ownership and/or political control. For instance, there is some evidence that there was a fundamental change in the use of clay sources during the colonial period as changes in land ownership (particularly the setting up of haciendas), and agricultural practices (with the abandonment of Inka terrace systems, and the use of the ox-drawn plough, placing increasing emphasis on the use of flat river valleys) forced indigenous potters away from clay sources located in the river valleys to the exploitation of hillside sources (Ravines and Villiger 1989, 10). To justify this kind of suggestion requires the combination of detailed surveys of surface geology and an analysis of a large number of pottery fabrics from well-provenanced sources. Sadly this type of work is still lacking for much of Andean archaeology (exceptions are Hagstrum 1986; Lunt 1987; D'Altroy and Bishop 1990). However, all the modern potters that I know of around Cuzco, with the major exception of the Raqchi area, use hillside rather than river valley clays.

Payment for the rights to use clay or tempering material is quite common (e.g. Charamoray, Seq'ueracay, Raqchi, Totorani, Colcapirhua) but such payments have, at least since the agrarian reforms, been made to the potter's own community, or to the community which owns the lands, not to individual land-owners. In the case of Raqchi, the potters volunteered to pay for the temper source themselves as a way of raising funds for community activities, such as building a school-house and holding religious festivals. This illustrates how important it is to consider the potter's commitments which go well beyond those of their pottery-making but which must be taken into account if the economics and organisation of their pottery production is to be properly understood. This is perhaps most clearly seen in many potters' recognition of another 'owner' of the clay who must be paid for permission to dig it. By considering the supernatural owners of the clay mines, it is possible to recognise that, for the potters, their procurement of raw materials is thoroughly embedded in their social relations with these beings.

Clays are just one mineral for which the Andes have been exploited. Quarries for stone and mines for gold, silver and copper were in use long before the arrival of the Spanish, and the exploitation of these resources, and, more recently, tin, lead, and zinc, form an important part of the 'Andean moral economy' (Sallnow 1989). Sallnow uses this term because resource exploitation cannot be separated off from the cultural setting in which it takes place. The 'value' of such minerals and the 'cost' of their extraction cannot simply be measured in terms of energy expenditure, because their extraction is conceived of as the removal of a material that belongs to the mountain gods (the *Apus* and *Wamani*). "Typically, these notions cast gold mining as an illicit, amoral and ritually dangerous activity, in which the successful prospector may well pay for his new-found wealth with his life" (ibid., 209). The Andean landscape is 'animated' and people conceive themselves in a reciprocal relationship with it.

The mountain gods 'own' the flocks of grazing animals and the mineral wealth, and *Pachamama* 'owns' the earth and the crops that grow from it. People may take from these resources but in return they must feed the deities with offerings. "The fertility which the *Apus* and the *Pachamama* bestow on the soil and the protection they extend to humans and livestock are conditional, given only in return for periodic offerings" (Sallnow 1989, 211). In the case of mining these ideas are best illustrated by Nash's (1979) study of the tin miners of Oruro, who make a daily offering to *Tío* (the spirit owner of the mine) consisting of coca, alcohol and cigarettes, and the sacrifice of llamas at major festivals.

In many communities clay is also conceived of as belonging to a local spirit, and the extraction can only be justified through the making of an appropriate offering. In Pumpuri, Northern Potosi, Bolivia, an offering is made to the clay mines on the first of August. This is a *misa blanca* for *Tío* and consists of alcohol, coca, *q'oa*, a llama foetus and *misterios*. These offerings are given by the male potters, often before leaving on a second itinerant pottery making trip. The offering is made 'so that we may continue to use the clay, and it will not run out'. In Raqchi a major offering (*k'intuqwi*) is made on the night of San Luis, (August 24th/25th). Participants (men and women of the household) chew coca, and make libations over a ritual cloth with miniature animals, as well as stones from the *Apus* (Sillar 1996a). This offering is to ensure abundant agricultural production and the protection of the sheep herds, as well as being directed towards the clay and temper mines, the work areas of the house and the roads – all to do with the productivity of the household. Hernández Príncipe's account of 1622 describes the offerings made by the community of Olleros in Recuay, which consisted of two groups of potters who had been resettled there by the Inkas. The people of Olleros worshipped the deity *Huari* in underground caverns, and each year they made two *capac huchas* (human sacrifices) of children who were sealed into deep shaft tombs. This offering was explicitly made to ensure good clay for their pottery (Zuidema 1989, 130–5 and 149–150).

In both Pumpuri and Raqchi these offerings are given in August, which, throughout the Andes, is considered to be the month when the earth and mountains open up (Allen 1988). This remains a propitious time to make offerings, as it was at the time of the Spanish conquest (Guaman Poma [1584–1615] 1988, 225), as at this time the earth literally cracks open from the long dry months that have gone before. However, the dangers of mine collapse during the rainy season, and the let-up in agricultural work during the dry season combine to make the period from June till August the most favourable for mining and quarrying activities, providing another reason why this time of year may have been considered appropriate for making these offerings.

Clay mining is not seen *just* in terms of maximising effort. Rather, like tin and gold, clay is conceived of as a resource that belongs to the regional spirit, and its extraction cannot be accomplished without first asking permission and giving appropriate offerings. This ritualised relationship with the deified source of these raw materials serves to promote the idea that only community members should be allowed access to them. In Pumpuri, it is understood that only members of the same extended community should use the clay mines. In Raqchi continued residence in the community and participation in community projects is obligatory for those wishing access to the raw materials, and there is sometimes said to be a prohibition against potters continuing their craft if they leave (Chávez 1992, 83). Although it has been suggested that the Inkas "restricted access to the raw materials used to make imperial pottery, thus controlling its circulation at the source" (D'Altroy and Bishop 1990, 133), present-day evidence suggests that local, rather than state, ideology may have been responsible for such restricted access.

Itinerant potters

Most models of resource procurement are concerned with a world in which fired pots are acquired at markets by consumers who transport them back to their own homes. However in some areas, like the rugged environment of the Andes which, prior to the Spanish conquest used no wheeled transport and had no pack animals capable of carrying a person or an awkward bundle of pots, another solution has been for the potters to take their clay to the consumer's household and make the pots there, at locations up to and beyond a distance of 100km from the clay source and the potter's home community.

In the case of all the itinerant potters I know of, it is always highland groups who go down to lower-lying communities to exchange their pots for resources. Highland people own the llamas necessary to transport their sacks of dried clay and with which to return the newly-gained produce to their home community. Due to the climate, and a lack of irrigation, highland residents also have an extensive period of reduced agricultural work during the dry season, making it easier for them to organise long-distance exchange trips (Custred 1974). The itinerant potters from the highlands choose to go to warmer lower lands to make their vessels, thus promoting exchange between the ecozones that permits highland residents access to lowland resources. This is significant as the lowland valleys do not lack the necessary raw materials for pottery production, indeed many of the river valleys have good clays. Such exchanges are often facilitated by forming fictive-kin ties between the people carrying out the exchange or at least with one member of the community they are visiting (e.g. Burchard 1974). This was the case with the itinerant potter I met from Ticatica (Dept. Potosi, Bolivia) who was prepared to wait till next year to collect payment for some of the vessels he made because he knew he would be returning to the same lowland community, and he knows many of the residents in addition to his *compadres*. This type of relationship is not always the primary mechanism for inter-zonal exchange, and some exchange is carried out between people who do not previously know each other. The itinerant potters from

Pumpuri rarely have any fictive-kin ties with people in the communities they trade with. This is partly due to the limited demand for their produce. The large brewing jars that they make are a significant outlay for any household and, as they normally last for a number of years, the demand is not enough to sustain the regular visits necessary to form and foster fictive-kin relationships. The demand for cooking pots which are used daily and rarely last a year, and the smaller jars that frequently break when they are used to collect water or to take maize beer to the fields, is much higher, and can sustain the regular yearly visits of the Ticatica potter. It is partly the dynamics of supply and demand, as well as the different specialisations of the producers, that foster particular social relations. However the nature of these demands and the way people chose to satisfy them are cultural choices that have helped to shape social interaction.

Production as Community Specialisation

The continuity of community specialisations is further encouraged by the way that production has been organised. In many communities the complimentary roles performed by men and women makes this partnership central to the formation of new household. In Raqchi for instance men make the large brewing jars whereas women make smaller jugs and bowls using slightly different techniques (Chávez 1987). As a traditional firing requires the large brewing jars to be covered with a protective layer of bowls (Fig. 3) cooperation between male and female knowledge is made essential for ceramic production. A single man or woman may feel unable to produce successfully with an unknowledgeable partner, especially when removed from the support of other community members who could supply the missing vessel forms or help to teach their partner. As at the larger level of community specialisation the culturally constructed division of labour in the household supports the formation of particular social relations.

Some potters do leave their community in order to marry, normally to someone they met at a local festival, or while working outside the community. The newly-married couple usually set up their new house in the husband's community but this is easily modified if the wife's family is able to provide them with more land. Although pottery-making does not have any derogatory associations, it is not considered a prestigious activity, and most potters' primary commitment is to agriculture. This is due to the highly sentimental attachment people have for agriculture in the Andes, i.e. the way it is 'represented' in Andean perception. For this reason if potters are successful they frequently seek to invest in land, and if they gain sufficient land, particularly irrigated land that can be worked most of the year, they tend to give their time and energies preferentially to agricultural activities. Perhaps, as David and Hennig (1972) suggested for the Fulani, the mark of a successful potter is to have stopped potting! Thus there are strong social, practical and economic reasons for potters who leave their community to give up their craft, and this helps to perpetuate the uniqueness of the specialised pottery-making communities.

There are two major factors that facilitate community-based specialisation in ceramics:

1) Rathje (1972) has argued that control of localised scarce resources was responsible for the initial elaboration of specialised communities in the lowland Maya area. In the case of the Andes, while clays vary in quality over the area they cannot be considered a scarce resource. However, the continuing use of the same resources permits the development of appropriate techniques for creating particular forms. This is encouraged today by community-controlled ownership of the raw materials and strengthened through ideological links between the source of these materials and ancestors and/or deities.

2) Equally important is the localisation of technical knowledge (cf. Perlès 1992). The community and the household are the locus for the passing on of the technological knowledge of how to form vessels, and in some areas there are cultural prohibitions on continuing to produce after leaving the community. The skill necessary for competent work is as much a localised resource as the raw materials.

The link between raw materials and the potters' knowledge also serves to inhibit the movement of potters, as the production skills learnt by young potters are evidently appropriate for the particular paste prepared by them, and vice-versa. The informal sharing of tools and labour (for instance when mining clay or preparing a pottery firing) may encourage nucleated production, even when individual households maintain independence in the control of their production and exchange (Costin 1991, 14). The nucleation of groups of potters who share the same technologies and decorative traditions also concentrates the demand for any materials (such as fuels, tools, and pigments) which the potters themselves do not make or acquire. This means that they can support trading links for these resources which might not be worth gathering and transporting to them if they were more dispersed. This promotes the maintenance of a pottery-making tradition inside a restricted locality. Indeed, one Raqchi potter returned to his community after 10 years in Lima, precisely to start making pottery again even though his family were not prepared to give him any agricultural land. Thus it is the combination of local resources, the way these resources are perceived, local social organisation, and the reproduction of people's social and technical knowledge that can cause community specialisation.

Recipes for Success

When archaeologists identify a particular pottery paste as a fabric or ware this may be due to any one of several factors. By far the most common assumption is that the fabric group is the result of a clay paste recipe that was consistently used by a particular group of potters (whether a household, a community, or an industry) and in part this may be due to

their sharing access to the same raw materials from a restricted geographical area (e.g. Peacock 1969a/b, Fulford 1975, Lunt 1987). Alternatively the fabric may represent a more widespread 'idea' shared over a larger cultural area as to how a particular class of pottery should be made, (such as shell or flint tempered wares in British prehistory). Finally different fabrics may be determined by environmental restraints to do with the pottery forming techniques or the intended function of the vessel (e.g. Bronitsky 1986; Schiffer & Skibo 1987).

I would like to consider these three possibilities in the context of pottery production in the Cuzco region where there appears to be a common perception that particular pastes are appropriate for particular pot types. This does not mean that a potter will make a different paste for each type of pot s/he makes. On the contrary, throughout the Andes potters tend to prepare only one paste recipe that they use for all the pot forms which they make (c.f. Chávez 1992, 85). But communities which have specialised in a particular range of pots seem to share a common idea of what is a suitable pottery paste. For instance, the communities that are best known for making large *chicha* jars (Raqchi, Araypallpa and Seq'ueracay) all use a fairly coarse paste with abundant, somewhat spherical, inclusions (of quartz, gypsum, blocky mudstone and volcanic sand), whereas in communities better known for the production of cooking pots (Machaca and Charamoray, and the majority of cooking pot manufacturers in the Puno area) the paste includes abundant laminar inclusions of talc (Sillar 1988; Chávez 1992, 82). These choices are partly made in relation to the environment in which the vessels are intended to function: A coarse/open fabric is less likely to crack and more likely to fully oxidise in a bonfire firings, particularly in the Andes where fuel is scarce, so it is not surprising that all fabrics are fairly coarse with a lot of tempering material. The platy paste used in Machaca and Charamoray allows for the production of thin-walled vessels such as cooking pots (Figs. 1 and 4), where as the coarser, grainy paste used in Seq'ueracay and Araypallpa is less malleable, enforcing the production of thicker walled vessels such as large jars and toasting pans (Figs. 2 and 5). Thin-walled vessels have advantages as cooking pots, due to their refractive properties, and the saving of paste also makes the fired vessels lighter to transport. Whereas the thicker walled vessels may retain heat better, the more blocky inclusions permit easier evaporation, and are prone to chipping rather than shattering. The thick-walled form is also well suited to toasting maize, wheat and beans as it retains a steady heat even when removed from the fire for a short time – this is useful as it is common to make several loads of toasted grains at one time. The same property of heat retention (a lack of conductivity) also means that the handle of the vessel does not get too hot and can be held while stirring the toasting grains. Such suggestions fit with my own experience and observation but might be tested using material science techniques (e.g. Bronitsky 1986). If the physical effect of talc is similar to the laminar structure of burnt shell, then my suggestion of the way this would react to impact, in comparison to coarser rounded particles (such as sand), is similar to those of Bronitsky and Hamer (1986, 94–6), although talc's chemical structure, which is very similar to that of clay, would make it more resistant than crushed shell to thermal shock (ibid., 96–7).

This relationship between fabric, form and function is not simply a question of efficiency however. All the villages studied, with the notable exception of Raqchi, make the whole range of forms necessary for a 'fully furnished' kitchen. Potters in Araypallpa make perfectly adequate cooking pots in their usual coarse-grained-fabric (fig 5.),

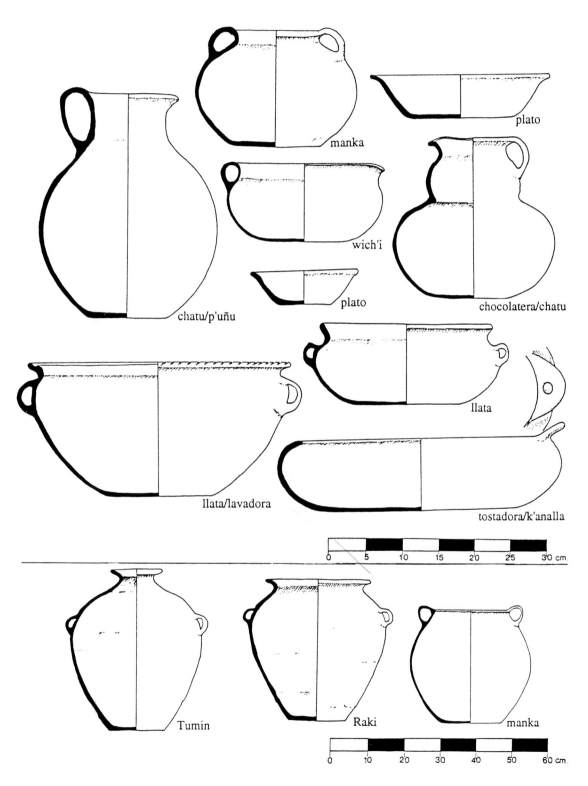

Fig. 4. A range of pot forms made in Machaca.

and Machaca potters make occasional *chicha* jars in their usual talc-tempered fabric (fig 4.). These 'hybrids' are not, however, usually traded outside their community of origin. Ken Hefferman (pers. com.) has noted a similar feature in Choquemarka where coarse fabric thick-walled pots are made but only the large jars and toasting pans are traded out of the community. Nor is it simply a question of avail-

able raw materials. There is a wide range of clays and tempering materials available throughout the Andes. Fourteen different clays were located within a day's walk of Cusichaca, all of which were demonstrated to be successful in the making and firing of pottery (Lunt 1987, 242), and I know of some alternative clay and tempering materials available to most communities. What is most striking is the apparent

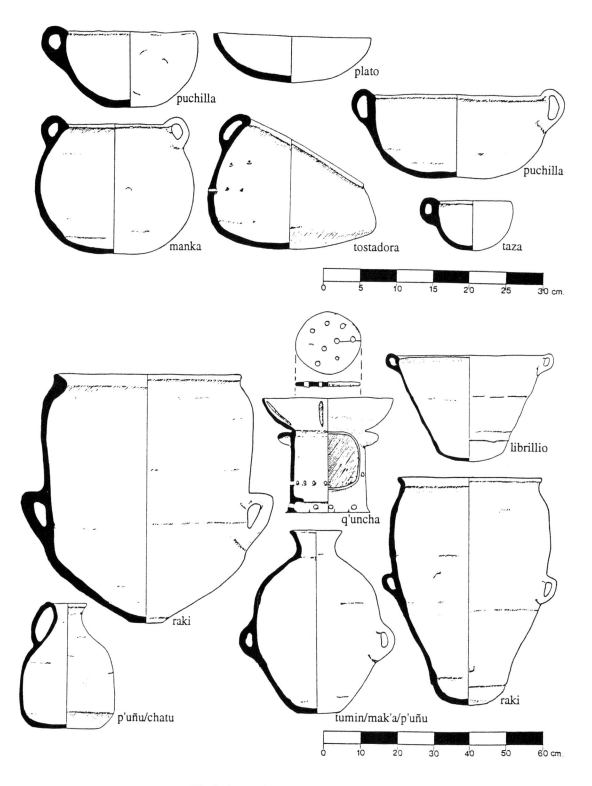

Fig. 5. A range of pot forms made in Araypallpa.

agreement amongst the potters and consumers of the Cuzco region over their perceptions about what materials are needed to make a suitable pottery paste. For instance Raqchi potters say they cannot make cooking pots because they do not have the talc temper, even though the archaeological record shows that pots made with similar volcanic temper to that used in Raqchi today were made and used as cooking pots in the past (Chávez 1992, 82). "Potters' technological explanations for their inability to make certain forms, seem artificial" (ibid., 82). But this perception of appropriate technology serves to promote village specialisation in the *exporting* of a restricted range of pot types (see Table 2).

Continuity and change in pottery fabrics

The survival of a pottery-making tradition relies on the potters' ability to modify their practice in the light of changing circumstances. For instance, forced to abandon valley clay deposits by the Colonial authorities, potters used their ability to re-evaluate their traditional behaviour and conceive of new solutions to new problems, these decisions being made according to cultural perceptions of materials and technology (c.f. Sillar 1996b). The Pumpuri potters sometimes have to modify their choice of clays if a mine has collapsed or is inaccessible due to flooding. In this case they use a classification of the clays as either strong or weak which appears to combine both the plasticity of the clay and the nature of any non-plastics, with weak clays being the very plastic ones which crack easily on drying. The Pumpuri potters use this classification when collecting clays from six or seven different mines, and they seek to maintain an even balance of weak and strong clays in the mixture they prepare. Two Raqchi potters who objected to the amount they were being charged for the use of community clay sources, have also begun to use new clay sources within their own fields, but they have found it necessary to alter the proportion of temper they put into the mixture to ac-

commodate this change. Another Raqchi potter went and collected some *ch'alla*, the talc temper they know to be used by potters in more distant communities who make cooking pots. She collected this *ch'alla* and mixed it with the Raqchi clay and the traditional *aqo* (volcanic sand) to try and make toasting pans. These were shunned by most community residents (although some close kin did acquire them) and were not considered to be good quality. She made no attempt to trade them outside the community. While this reinforces the idea of 'cultural recipes' for the paste, it also demonstrates that individuals can challenge the current practice of paste use in the community and that they do so by drawing upon culturally defined ideas about what makes a suitable pottery paste.

The ethnographic literature and local archaeology help to show the near infinite number of ways that clays can be modified to produce efficient pastes, so I do not think it is a 'coincidence' that certain materials are consistently sought after by potters working in the region. I suggest that, particularly in the case of talc, there is a common 'cultural' viewpoint that a particular ingredient in the paste is most suitable for the formation, firing, and functioning of certain vessel types. Interestingly the Inca period is characterised by a large amount of pottery with somewhat different pastes but many of the large jars use andesite as a temper, and it is a long running tradition to use talc as a temper for cooking pots. I suspect that these materials were considered to be particularly appropriate within the cultural traditions of the area. The use of coarse flint flakes as a tempering material in the British Neolithic and early Bronze age reveals a similar 'cultural choice' (Lemonnier 1993) which appears extraordinary within my cultural expectations of what makes a suitable pottery paste. In the case of andesite, as with flint in Britain, the explanation may partly lie in the raw material's role in other technologies; andesite was used as the major building stone of the Inca and petrographic work suggests that much of the pottery temper was col-

Table 2. *Pottery forms made in each community and whether or not they are commonly exported.*

Community	large jar	medium jar	jug	toasting pan	manka	stove	small bowl	large bowl	deep bowl	tourist pot	flower pot	miniature
Araypallpa	X	X	O	X	(X)	(X)	O	O	O	-	-	(X)
Charamoray/ Urubamba	-	O	X	X	X	-	O	X	O	-	-	(X)
Machaca	-	(X)	X	X	X	-	(X)	O	(X)	-	-	O
Raqchi	X	X	X	-	-	-	X	X	X	X	X	O
Seq'ueracay	X	X	O	X	(X)	-	O	(X)	O	-	-	O
Colcapirhua	X	X	O	O	(X)	-	O	X	O	-	(X)	-
Huayculi	-	-	X	-	**	-	X	-	-	X	X	X
Paracay	X	X	X	O	(X)	X	O	X	O	-	-	?
Surumi R.	X	X	O	-	O	-	O	X	-	-	-	?
Pumpuri	X	X	O	-	(X)	-	O	X	O	-	-	O
Ticatica	O	X	X	?	X	-	O	X	X	-	-	?
Totorani	O	(X)	X	(X)	X	(X)	X	X	O	-	-	?

O = made largely for own use; X = a substantial number are made for export; (X) = occasionally exported; - = not made at all; ? = uncertain.
    Naturally these are rather gross statements, but they provide a general picture of differences between what is made and what is traded.
By medium jars I mean *tumins* and *p'uñus* that have a volume up to about 40lt and can still be carried on someone's back when full of liquid. Large jars are bigger than this and difficult to move when full.
** *mankas* (cooking pots) are not normally made in Huayculi, but those made in nearby Vilaque are widely exported.

lected from the same quarry as the building material perhaps as a by-product of the construction work (Hunt 1990, Lunt 1988, pers. com.). Given the Inca reverence for stone, particularly that used in construction work, this may not only have been efficient, but also reflect a ideological link with the raw material. It is also interesting that the Inca potters occasionally used grog as a tempering material. When they did so they (like the potters in Seq'ueracay today) only used grog from their own wares and not from other contemporary or ancient pots (Lunt pers. com.). It is possible that this is expressing similar sentiments to the use of the communities, deified mines and we see a need to use home produce only; the community essence must be maintained within the pottery fabric (c.f. Lechtman 1984, 30). It would be interesting to conduct excavations (and archive research) at some of these pottery making centres to see how the fabric and range of forms has developed over time. Raqchi, which was already renowned for its large *chicha* jars by 1846 (Marcoy 1873, 126), has surface sherds and large ash piles, revealed by the modern road cutting, which suggest that pottery production may have been taking place here since the Inka period or earlier.

Many authors have investigated the choice of raw materials and techniques used in terms of environmental restraints and maximising efficiency (e.g. Arnold 1985; Bronitsky 1986; Schiffer & Skibo 1987). The choice of raw materials and techniques may be better understood as 'cultural choices' that are as dependent on local 'representations' as any ultimate scientific measure of functionality (Lemonnier 1993; Latour 1993). The concept of 'cultural choice' is intended to highlight the fact that while there are frequently a wide range of alternative techniques that could be used to overcome a particular problem, within the vision of a particular culture's understanding, they will only consider a very much more restricted number of alternatives (c.f. van der Leeuw et. al. 1991). The technical alternatives available to each individual potter are constrained by their culture's perception of the world and the 'choices' that have been made in the past. This certainly does not prevent invention and change as novel ideas are drawn into the craft from other spheres of cultural activity which provides a vast range of experiences and technical knowledge beyond that normally used in pottery making itself (Sillar 1996). What it does mean is that the choice of raw materials and techniques can be studied as expressions of cultural concepts (c.f. Lechtman 1977). In the case of the talc tempered pottery described above, chemical characterisation methods (e.g. Bishop et. al. 1982) could probably differentiate between pottery made in Machaca, Charamoray and Pucara, even if this was difficult to do by visual examination of the sherds. However the ability to differentiate between production centres should not blind us to the apparent cultural agreement over appropriate pottery making techniques.

Pottery-making 'colonies'

Nonetheless, some potters who leave their home community may start to make pottery at their new home. In such situations they will have to make efforts to find new sources of raw materials. A few Raqchi potters have moved to Cuzco and Pisac, where they continue to make pottery using the excellent river valley clays in the area, and another was just starting to work in Lima, prior to his untimely death from cholera. When I was told of these potters, there seemed to be no resentment that they had continued to work after leaving the community, but it was pointed out that they all made 'tourist pottery' rather than traditional forms, and it was thought that they all fired in kilns. It may be that this was a sufficient departure from traditional production in Raqchi not to be considered a threat, or to be breaking the prohibition that Chávez (1987; 1992) has mentioned. Some Quinoa potters who have left the Ayacucho region (partly due to the disruptions of Sendero Luminoso) continue to acquire their usual clays and tempers by truck from Quinoa. By 1988 there were 20 Quinoa pottery workshops in Lima (Arnold 1993, 240). These potters used their position in the cities to participate in the political, legal, and ritual activities of their birthplace partly through sponsoring major festivals there (Mitchell 1991). When this continuity of social relations and ritual obligations is maintained, the non-resident is permitted to own fields and is still considered to be a member of the community to which s/he may return (Mitchell 1991, Skar 1995). Without this continuing commitment to their home community it is unlikely that the emigrant potters would be permitted to exploit community resources. Potters from Huayculi have also moved to Cochabamba, La Paz, Santa Cruz and northern Argentina where they now make very similar pottery using local clays. This is seen as desirable by most Huayculi residents who say that there are now too many potters working in the Huayculi area. The Huayculi potters also find these 'colonies' convenient when they occasionally go to annual fairs in these areas and can then rely on the support of their relatives. The potter I worked with in Surumi Rancho was originally from Colcapirhua but moved to the village of his wife because her family owned more land than his. He has since returned to pottery-making during the dry season, and his vessels appear identical to the vessels still being made in Colcapirhua. He continues to use some of the same clays as the Colcapirhua potters, although he has also searched out other new sources of raw material closer to his home. It would be a mistake to see the establishment of pottery 'colonies' as only the result of recent social changes. The Machaca potters came to Machaca over 70 years ago from the Pucara region (Percy Paz Flores pers. comm.), and it is well documented that the Inka relocated large groups of potters to work in recently conquered areas in order to produce relatively standardised pottery forms and decoration (D'Altroy and Bishop 1990).

These examples demonstrate that with some effort potters are able to set up new 'colonies' of pottery production. Unless exactly the same materials can be imported this will require some modification to the technology and the organisation of production. But, when knowledgeable social actors (i.e. the potters) are re-located they will usually be able to transform the available raw materials and their technical practices to produce pottery in their new location. Rye and Evans (1976, 127) also conclude that pottery production in Pakistan was primarily located by the potter's choice of where to build a home, only after this does the potter search for available raw materials. Particularly in the Andes which, almost by definition, is an area of high erosion with abundant clay sources, the potter's skill is by far the most important resource in determining the location of pottery production. Nonetheless, the pressures are such that the maintenance of localised pottery-making communities is strongly favoured. The emergence of new pottery-making 'colonies' requires the combination of a reason for individuals to leave their birth-place (some perceived pressure, a strain in family relations, lack of land, too much competition), an attraction to a new location (a partner, availability of work or land), as well as reasons to continue to make pottery (relaxing of any prohibitions, access to raw materials, demand for the produce) which outweighs the commitment to other income-generating activities, particularly agriculture.

Community specialisation from a regional perspective

The Andean potters I have described are all examples of household-based production that, unlike their agricultural production, wherever possible only uses labour from the immediate family living in that household (Sillar 1994). But this production is also organised on a community basis with different communities specialising for part of the year in the production of distinctive and to some extent complementary products.

Shimada (1987) points out that community specialisation creates a form of 'horizontal interdependence' that contrasts with Murra's (1972) model of exchange between environmental zones at different altitudes, by creating the need to exchange goods even within the same ecozone. This is further encouraged by pottery-making communities specialising in the production of different vessel forms with different functions. For instance, Raqchi, Paracay, and Pumpuri are better known for trading larger jars and containers, whereas Totorani, Charamoray, Ticatica, and Machaca are all better known for their cooking pots, and Huayculi and Pucara are known for their lead glazed bowls and other wheel-made forms (Table 2). In the same way that people see potatoes, maize, beans, and llama products as all being necessary for their subsistence, these different vessel types are all perceived as complementary parts of a household's tool-kit, thus perpetuating 'horizontal interdependence' between communities.

Community specialisation has developed around the production of many different products such as; baskets, cloth, furniture, tiles, agricultural tools, musical instruments, raw materials such as; salt, metals, or gypsum used for plaster, and agricultural products including; coca, maize, freeze dried potatoes, wood, medicinal herbs, and llama wool. The Kallawaya, for example, have specialised as itinerant medical and ritual specialists (Girault 1987). Tschopik (1946, 537)

also mentions community specialisation in certain crafts, for instance in Chucuito two communities make pottery, two make felt hats, and another makes lime for chewing with coca, and the towns of Yunguyo and Copacabana import cane to make musical instruments. Indeed Mishkin (1946, 434) comments that localised "specialization in agricultural production as well as in handicraft and manufactured goods is characteristic of the entire Quechua community." While community specialisation in some products may in part be due to Spanish influence in setting up *obrajes* as well as their taxation policies, there is also ample evidence that this was a pre-Hispanic form of organisation. The Inka set up craft production communities often moving large numbers of artisans to do so (Murra 1978, 1980), and there is also evidence of specialised pottery production during the Middle Horizon such as at Tiwanaku (Franke 1992) and in the Moquegua valley (Goldstein 1993).

What is clear is that localised specialisation in the production of different crafts, raw materials, or agricultural produce acts to maintain a complementarity at the regional level due to the interdependence of communities on each other's specialisations. This interdependence is partly imposed by environmental factors, but it is also culturally constructed through the regional organisation of the division of labour, and a perception that the goods produced by other communities are necessary and/or desirable.

Reputable pots and novel forms for communication

Although many communities make a wide variety of pots for their own use, they have a *reputation* for producing and distributing a more limited range of forms. While there has been a great deal of discussion about standardisation in craft products in relation to emerging specialisations and reorganisation of production within complex societies (e.g. Hagstrum 1988, Rice 1981, 1991), this discussion has tended to ignore the important effect that consumers will have on the dynamics of standardisation. Indeed to understand pottery production and exchange we must also take into account the consumers' perceptions. "The appropriateness of standardization as an indicator of specialist production is contingent in part on what is motivating consumption choice in each particular case." (Costin 1991, 34)

A consideration of cultural perceptions of what makes a 'good pot' is vital for understanding consumer strategies in acquiring pottery, and the potter's strategy for supplying that demand. The concept of a 'good pot' incorporates several inter-related factors including serviceability, aesthetics and exchange value. It is important to emphasise that a 'good pot' may not be the same for all people and will depend on the context in which the pot is intended to serve. As noted above thin walled cooking pots are more normal but thick walled ones are made and can be utilised efficiently.

Acquiring a pot is not just a question of 'pot luck' as consumers use several strategies to reduce their risks. One of the most important qualities is that the pot should be strong, or what we might term 'well fired'. This is partly assessed by colour, and it is commonly thought that a well fired vessel should be red. The word *hanku* meaning raw or uncooked is applied to white pots (Chávez 1987, 173), and it is partly for this reason that many Andean potters apply a red slip to their wares, the Raqchi potters sometimes throw salt onto the firing which may promote the red 'blush' that appears on their pottery. Similarly potters frequent splash a small amount of glaze on to vessels which is intended as an assurance to the consumer that the vessel has been fired well rather than serving any practical function (Sander van der Leeuw pers. com.). The consumer also checks that the vessel is not cracked by striking the rim with her/his finger to hear if it rings. The word *t'inka* used to describe the sound made when a un-cracked vessel is struck is also the term for a ritual libation, often made by flicking the drink with one's finger. The potters themselves take great care in checking for cracks while making their vessels, and one of the stated purposes of the rough burnishing and slipping of the pots is to cover up any cracks that may appear. These are techniques for checking the quality of individual vessels, however, when the consumer is confronted by millions of pots at one of the annual fairs it is by drawing upon their cultural knowledge of appropriate forms and styles of pots that they decide what to acquire.

A certain degree of standardisation can act as a kind of trade-mark of pot quality which consumers use to recognise a 'reputable' pot (naturally a culturally defined value judgement). As the pottery makers I have been describing are not from the same community as most of their consumers, there is rarely any prior personal bond between them. However, knowledge of 'reputable' pots is itself a kind of contact. The goods themselves create a bond through the consumer's knowledge of the producer's wares. When a group of itinerant potters from Pumpuri, went to Lyncha, where they had never been before, a few Lyncha residents were somewhat hostile to them. Nonetheless they were in a sense 'known' by their produce as other Pumpuri potters had been there before (the last ones had visited some 5 years previously) so that they were permitted to come and live in a semi-abandoned house for three weeks while they made and traded their wares.

Although potters may make a much wider range of vessels for their own use, they do not exchange many of these beyond their own community (table 2). Instead they stick to marketing a restricted range of forms for which their community has a reputation. This reputation is not by the name of the community, as frequently consumers don't know where their pots come from, rather it is the way the pots look that reminds the consumer of similar vessels they have used and seen used before. Pottery styles are recognised by vessel form, decoration and paste (in as much as the latter affects the vessel's surface appearance, wall thickness and weight). Although potters make a wider range of forms for their own use that may be exchanged locally, the potters, and/or the consumers, seem to avoid the wide-scale distribution of these untypical fabric and form hybrids that are not 'reputable' pots (Sillar 1988, 55, Chávez 1992, 80). Instead potters are encouraged to maintain a fairly standard range of vessels for exchange outside the community and the way they learn how to pot teaches them to reproduce these traditional forms. Standardisation of paste, form and decoration of pots to some extent represents an economy of practice by the potters, who are able to repeat the same actions frequently, without investing energy in renewed experimentation. But it has further implications in that the consumer can recognisable 'reputable' forms which they know how to use. Standardisation also allows the consumers, who do not make their own vessels, to attach symbolic meaning to recognised forms and decorative features that recur within different households.

This certainly does not mean that no new forms will be tried and potters do take 'new' forms to the market occasionally. I have seen Raqchi potters with elaborately painted and novel forms of jugs and a potter from Pucara made an innovative form of a pottery bread-oven that was for sale at the Señor de Wank'a fair in 1989. But these forms are tentatively tried, and potters only risk making a very limited number for each fair. At the present time there are two major exceptions to these apparently conservative trends. One is the expanding importance of 'home improvement' vessels particularly for the urban market where flower pots, sugar bowls, candle holders, vases and some decorative pieces are an important area for innovative design. The other is that of ritual vessels particularly drinking cups which are some of the most elaborate pottery made in the Andes and seem to be the area in which innovative new forms are most appreciated. The majority of highland Andean pottery is relatively simple and lacking in much decoration, but when it comes to vessels for the consumption of home-made beer (*chicha*) it is considered appropriate and desirable to use a wide range of elaborately decorated pots. This preference partly relates to the sociable use of the vessels, as chicha-drinking is always a communal activity usually involving several people sitting around and drinking for a few hours. But it is also because chicha is used as a form of communication with the dead and the deities. Prior to drinking, a small libation is poured on the ground or flicked in the air, if this gift (from the drinker, but ultimately from the person who provided the drink) is received, then it serves to perpetuate a reciprocal relationship with the dead and deities who will hopefully promote the protection and productivity of the household, the crops, the herds or the community. Thus chicha, and the festivals at which it is drunk, forms one of the major routes of communication between living people and the world of the dead and the deities. The form of the drinking vessels (many of which depict animals or have forms, like double vessels, that express ideological concepts) is a part of this communication. Similarly Sterner (1989) comments that the majority of the symbolic messaging, expressed by the form and decoration of the pottery she studied, was directed at the spirit world.

At present, consumption patterns support the maintenance of 'traditional' styles (of form, decoration and fabric) for the more 'practical' vessel functions, whereas innovative vessels (in form and decoration but not in fabric) tend to be appreciated where their primary 'function' is in communication (either with people or with the deities). This division should not be accepted to uncritically however as the day to day 'practical' vessels still carry some symbolic meaning (e.g. a cooking pot can be symbolically compared with the womb). It is more a case that those vessels whose primary purpose is to communicate (including plant pots that express suburban ideals of the household) are partly valued for their novelty. But 'practical' vessels (mainly linked to preparing food and drink) appear to be judged on their adherence to more conservative norms.

Pottery trade and the wider Andean economy

In the Andean highlands most potters trade their own wares. The method of trade partly depends on what pottery forms are being traded (table 4). Large jars for making chicha are more likely to be acquired at annual fairs or from itinerant potters. Cooking pots are commonly sold at weekly and daily markets as well as annual fairs. Flower pots and decorated forms are more likely to be sold at daily city markets or at annual fairs (particularly some of the more recent annual fairs which are now held during the wet season at which cash sales predominate). Potters partly choose what to make, and where to exchange it, by deciding what they want in return – for instance going to the valley to get maize, choosing fairs known for barter rather than cash, or making flower pots for cash sales in urban markets. However, the potters are not entirely free agents in these decisions as the spatial and seasonal ordering of exchange relationships that has emerged historically provides the framework through which they must act.

The fact that the itinerant potters from Pumpuri do not rely on the creation of fictive-kin ties between them and their host community shows how the type of commodity and way it is used will affect the frequency of trade and the nature of the relationship between the trader/producer and the consumer. The type of goods or services, and the frequency with which they need to be replaced partly relates to (and partly creates) the depth of the social relationships involved.

The particular method of trade used by any one pottery-making household partly depends on the historic nature of the relationship between different areas, what agricultural goods they produce, how they evaluate their need for externally-produced goods, and what forms of trans-

Table 3. Forms of pottery trade and how commonly they are used.

Community	Production for own use	Exchange within the community	ad hoc trade from potter's house	Weekly markets	Annual affairs	Itinerant production	Sell in bulk for re-sale
Araypallpa	some	**	***	****	***	-	-
Charamoray/Urubamba	some	**	**	****	****	-	*
Machaca	some	***	**	****	**	-	-
Raqchi	some	*	**	**	****	-	***
Seq'ueracay	some	***	***	**	**	-	-
Colcapirhua	some	**	***	-	****	-	-
Huayculi	some	*	**	***	****	-	****
Paracay	some	*	***	****	****	-	-
Surumi R.	some	**	***	-	****	-	-
Caca Pata	all	-	-	-	-	-	-
Pumpuri	some	**	**	-	-	****	-
Ticatica	some	**	**	-	-	****	-
Totorani	some	**	**	-	*	-	****

**** = major forms of trade   *** = secondary form of trade   ** = occasional form of trade   * = very occasional form of trade   - = not used at all

Table 4. Forms of pottery trade: who normally trades what pots for which produce.

Community	Method of trade	Who does this trading	Main forms traded this way	Traded for
Araypallpa	weekly, annual, ad hoc	F	large jars, *tostadoras*	barter, cash
Charamoray/Urubamba	weekly, annual	F (M)	*mankas*, small jugs, bowls	barter, cash
Machaca	weekly	F, M	*mankas*, jugs, bowls	barter, cash
Raqchi	annual	F, (M)	large jars, bowls, jugs	barter, cash
	bulk purchase	F, M	tourist forms, flower pots	cash
Seq'ueracay	local, ad hoc	M, F	large jugs, *tostadoras*	barter, cash
Colcapirhua	annual, adhoc	F (M)	large jars	barter, cash
Huayculi	bulk purchase, annual	F, M	flower pots, decorative wares	cash
	annual, weekly	F (M)	bowls, jugs	barter, cash
Paracay	weekly, annual	F, M	large jars	barter, cash
Surumi R.	annual, ad hoc	F, M	large jars	barter, cash
Pumpuri	itinerant, ad hoc	M	large jars	barter
Ticatica	itinerant, ad hoc	M	*mankas*, jugs, small jars	barter-
Totorani	bulk purchase for travelling traders	M, F	*mankas*, jugs, bowls	barter

I have shown the sex in brackets if the task is normally performed by one sex but another sex (in brackets) occasionally performs the same task.

port are available. Dean Arnold (1993, 133) notes that Quinoa pottery is traded up the political hierarchy of Ayacucho, through the district, provincial, and departmental hierarchy and into the centres that have larger and more permanent markets, and a similar distribution pattern is mentioned by Hagstrum (n.d.) for the Mantaro valley. These political centres were partly located to take advantage of existing transportation routes which have been further developed according to the socio-political and economic importance of the centres themselves. Similarly in the Cuzco Region and in the Cochabamba valley, pottery trade is dominated by the use of weekly markets and annual fairs both of which now depend on mechanised transport. In Northern Potosi and Southern Oruro, however, where routes for mechanised transport are less developed, the importance of itinerant potters and to a more limited extent travelling traders is very much greater.

According to Murra's (1972) research pre-Hispanic pottery would have been made by one or more communities within each ethnic group (ayllu) for distribution within it. In some areas today, particularly Northern Potosi and Southern Oruro, such ethnic affiliations remain important and have major social, political and economic dimensions (c.f. Platt 1982a & b). Within some of these groups, particularly those which have access to a wide range of natural resources, there appears to be an understanding that produce should be acquired from inside the ethnic group whenever possible Amongst the Laymi of Northern Potosi, for instance, there is an obligation to acquire many goods, particularly agricultural produce, from inside the ayllu (Harris 1982). However, it is unclear whether pottery exchange would ever have taken place entirely within an ethnic group. Although some of the itinerant potters from Pumpuri trade within Ayllu Macha many trade extensively outside it (Map 2.) including into Laymi territory. Harris (1982) comments that the Laymi have no salt or potting clay within their territory and that it is for this reason that they trade with people from outside their own ethnic group for these resources. "Salt and pot traders come from areas where agriculture is much poorer than in the fertile territories of the Laymis. With outsiders, Laymis feel under no obligation to exchange and only do so if they specifically require what the other side is offering. Between Laymis, however, the definition of wants is affected by social obligations to circulate their produce" (Harris 1982, 78). I would be surprised if there were actually no potting clay available within the Laymi territory. Given the geography and geology of the area it is highly likely that there are some clay sources, for instance the pottery-making community of Totorani is on the border of the Laymi territory. I suspect that this perceived lack of raw material is, like the Raqchi potters assumed inability to make cooking pots, a cultural construct that is used to justify a long-standing trading pattern which has structured social relationships through a regional division of labour.

It may be that the taboo on exchange of produce from outside the ethnic group was largely centred on agricultural produce, and that pottery has always been a 'free trade' material. This would explain a large part of the difference between the interpretations of pre-Hispanic trade in the Andes offered by Murra (1972, 1975) (who describes the redistribution of agricultural produce within the ethnic group which seeks to own or control a range of ecological levels) and Rostworowski (1977; 1978) (who concentrates on a description of craft specialisation and exchange between independent polities). Undoubtedly part of the difference between these authors' descriptions is the cultural difference between the areas which they study, but another is that Murra's model, and most of his data, concentrates more on the distribution of agricultural resources, whereas Rostworowski's work is more concerned with craft products. Such a situation would obviously have important archaeological implications for how we should interpret the distribution of material culture with reference to social, political and economic relations in the past. Today pottery crosses over ethnic boundaries as a common trade item and neither pottery forms nor styles of decoration appear to be confined to particular ethnic groups, although clothing and hats are knowingly used as emblems of ayllu affiliation. However the context in which pottery is *used*, in the household's daily and ritual practices as well as for community festivals, does play an important role in developing local cultural identities.

Because Andean potters have largely retained control of the sale of their own produce, they have managed to avoid being dragged into debt dependence. It is by no means impossible for Andean people to be drawn into such dependent relationships. Indeed the *repartimiento* system which was in operation in the colonial period created just such debt-bondage. But the potters I have worked with have, so far, avoided long term debt dependency in spite of its overarching presence in many other areas of Latin America (e.g. Papousek 1981). I believe that the Andean potters resilience to these dangers of third-world capitalism are in part due to the way that production is organised within the peasant households. The division of labour within the household facilitates the families ability not only to be involved in a range of different production strategies (e.g. arable, animal herding, craft production, paid labour) but also to utilise a wide range of trade and exchange strategies (exchange of labour within the community, cash and barter transactions, markets, fairs, travelling traders etc.). The seasonal organisation of production further encourages households to participate in multiple income generating activities. This preference to maintain several types of productive work and several methods of trade facilitates the household's ability to withdraw from any part of their income generating activities that is proving unfavourable. Thus risk-spreading acts to buffer the household from being drawn into a situation of dependence.

There is a danger of circularity in almost any discussion of peasant economics, and Deere (1990) cautions against seeing class structures and poverty as 'traditional'. One could equally well argue that Andean peasants are unable to depend on any single product or any single form of trade due

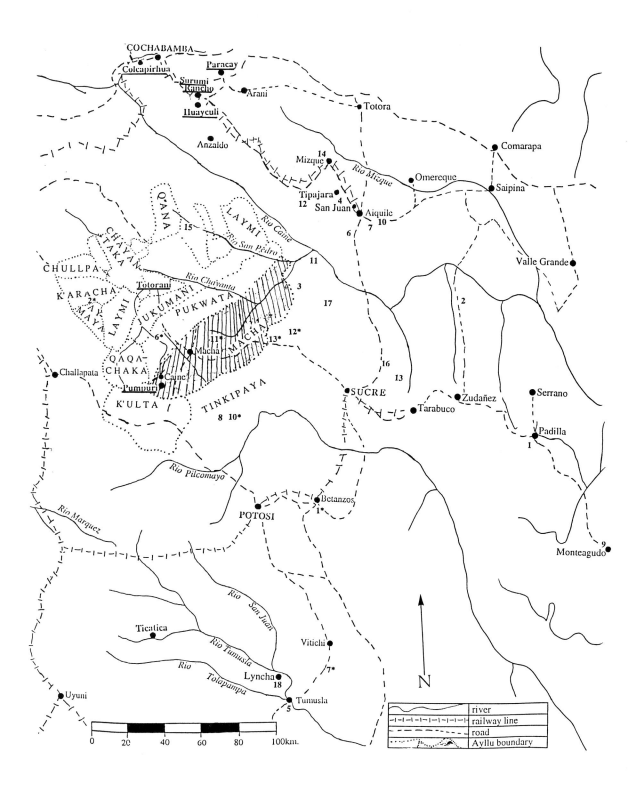

Map 2. The Ayllus of Northern Postosi showing the destination of some Pumpuri potters in 1991.

The demarcation of these Ayllus (ethnic groups partialy based on kinship) is based on the maps of Harris and Platt in Platt (1982b, 31). The numbers refer to the destinations of individual potters from the Pupuri area in Ayllu Macha. Some potters made two trips during the year (Sillar 1994).

to the instability of the Peruvian and Bolivian national economies. Within this interpretation it is understood that the peasants have been forced into the exploitation of their own families labour. Certainly peasants do not exist in isolation from their national and world economies, they are in constant articulation with urban groups and the labour market, they also require cash for many goods and services they consider central to their life-style. Even the existence of barter has undoubtedly been encouraged by the insecurities of massive inflation. However the seasonality of production, a gendered division of labour, community specialisation, inter-household barter, and household diversification in multiple activities all appear to be elements of Andean social and economic organisation that have existed at least since, and probably prior to, the Spanish conquest (Sillar 1994). It would be wrong to describe these characteristics as a product of recent capitalism; rather, they are features of Andean social organisation that people have found expedient to continue, within the present day socio-economic system. It is partly due to the poverty of most families that they lack the resources and capital to mechanise and increase production. But, it is also due to the campesinos commitment to a diversity of resource procurement methods, their use of reciprocal labour exchange within the community and their ability to turn to a wide range of trading methods, that these communities have been able to adapt and survive the ravages of the colonial encounter and the onslaught of the capitalist system.

To view the social and economic structures of the Andean peasants as simply a continuity from the past is plainly historically inaccurate, but we should also avoid constructing a monolithic viewpoint of 'the market'. While capitalism is a world-wide phenomenon, it is experienced and interpreted differently in different settings and it is individual people, each of whom pursues their own particular economic strategies, who together shape the nature of their local economy. Andean ethnohistorians have tended to seek signs of the durability of Andean cultural forms, whereas economic historians have emphasised the power of the market, the State, and capitalism to transform Andean practices (Harris et al 1987, 21). We must not fall into the trap of seeing a division between an exploitative market imposed by the Europeans and some form of benevolent Andean morality based upon reciprocity. Rather, we should seek to understand how the Andean peasantry has chosen to act within a developing framework which their actions have helped to create.

Conclusions

Dean Arnold (1993, 234) has suggested that the focus of ceramics research should be the community of potters which will have 'tangible correlates' in the ceramic products, one of which would be the choice of raw materials which the potters classify, select and use in community defined ways. Although the work discussed in this paper supports that conclusion, I have tried to emphasise some of the social

practices and cultural understandings that have contributed to the perpetuation of community specialisation in present day pottery production by Andean peasants. This is by no means the only way that pottery production can be organised. For instance, at Warren Fields in Colchester many different kiln types and several different fabrics were in use. The potters there shared some of their tools including stamps used on Samian vessels that were also used on colour coated wears (e.g. hunt-cups) and mortaria (Swan 1984). This was a group of people living together and co-operating with each other as a community, but the 'tangible correlates' that they produced show evidence of many different ceramic traditions. Rather than accepting the assumption that one fabric type suggests a single production source archaeologists should be trying to investigate the social organisation that supported such a set-up and considering the cultural choices that each fabric tradition represents. The choice of raw materials and the way they are processed represent cultural perceptions about what makes a suitable pottery paste. Archaeologists and ceramic analysts who wish to understand prehistoric pottery production must consider these issues as well as the physical properties of the materials. In considering aspects such as the colour of the paste and the type, shape, size and orientation of the inclusions we are, correctly in my view, integrating the materials and the effects of the paste preparation techniques within our concept of fabric. The use of characterisation methods to differentiate between raw material sources is enormously important in studying aspects of the economy such as the organisation of pottery production and exchange. But, as these characterisation methods continue to become ever more important in archaeology, we should not lose the social information which the choice of materials in a pottery fabric represents as this is at least as important an expression of cultural perception as the form, decoration and use of the vessels.

The wide variety of forms of production and trade in the Andes today shows the diversity that can and does flourish even within the capitalist world of the late 20th century. Barter, reciprocal labour exchange, itinerant potters and gift exchange do not just survive alongside waged labour and market trade, they are all part of a interactive whole. No economic system can be described by a single type of exchange, every economy involves a complex mix of exchange strategies each of which helps to maintain different social relations. For archaeologists, it is particularly important to consider how socio-economic forms have changed through time, and how these changes have affected different parts of the population. We should seek to understand this as the result of historical processes in which particular culturally defined economic and social practices may come to dominate for a period, but complex social relations rely on a range of exchange mechanisms for their expression.

Acknowledgements

This research would not have been possible without financial support from the following: Fitzwilliam Trust Research Fund [1990, 1991]; The Anthony Wilkin Fund [1991]; Crowther-Beynon Fund, Museum of Archaeology and Anthropology [1990, 1991, 1995] and The McDonald Institute for Archaeological Research [1995] all at the university of Cambridge. I have received permission to carry out my research, essential letters of introduction and support from the Instituto Nacional de Cultura's offices in Lima and Cuzco and the Museo Nacional de Etnografia y Folklore in La Paz. By far my largest debt goes to the communities in Peru and Bolivia who permitted me to live amongst them, who fed me, and gently educated me. Some aspects of this paper have been presented previously in two sessions of the Theoretical Archaeology Group Conferences organised by Chris Cumberpatch and Paul Blinkhorn at Durham (13th-16th December 1993) and Bradford (14th-16th December 1994), and at an archaeomaterials workshop, organised by Peter Day at the Department of Archaeology, University of Sheffield (29th April 1995). I am grateful for the chance to discuss my work and for participant's comments made on these occasions. Finally, in this paper it is particularly appropriate to thank Sara Lunt for her critical comments, insight and encouragement over a number of years.

References

Allen C. J. 1988. *The hold life has: coca and cultural identity in an Andean community.* Smithsonian Institution Press.

Arnold D. E. 1985. *Ceramic theory and cultural process.* Cambridge University Press.

Arnold D. E. 1993. *Ecology and Ceramic Production in an Andean Community.* Cambridge University Press.

Bishop R. L., R. L. Rands and G. R. Holley 1982. Ceramic compositional analysis in archaeological perspective. In M. B. Schiffer (ed.) *Advances in archaeological method and theory 5.* Academic Press: 275–330.

Bronitsky G. 1986. The use of materials science techniques in the study of pottery construction and use. In M. B. Schiffer (ed.) *Advances in archaeological method and theory 9.* Academic Press: 209–276.

Bronitsky G. and R. Hamer 1986. Experiments in ceramic technology: the effects of various tempering materials on impact and thermal-shock resistance. *American Antiquity* 51(1): 89–101.

Burchard R. E. 1974. Coca y trueque de alimentos. In G. Alberti and E. Mayer (eds.) *Reciprocidad e intercambio en los Andes Peruanos* Instituto de Estudios Peruanos: 209–51.

Chávez K. L. Mohr 1987. Traditional pottery of Raqch'i, Cuzco, Peru: a preliminary study of its production, distribution and consumption. *Ñawpa Pacha* 22–23 (1984–5): 161–210.

Chávez K. L. Mohr 1992. The organisation of production and distribution of traditional pottery in South Highland Peru. In G. J. Bey III and C. A. Pool (eds.) *Ceramic production and distribution: an integrated approach.* Westview Press: 49–92.

Costin C. L. 1991. Craft specialization: issues in defining, documenting, and explaining the organization of production. In M. Schiffer (ed.) *Archaeological method and theory 3*: 1–56.

Custred G. 1974. Llameros y comercio interregional. In G. Alberti and E. Mayer (eds.) *Reciprocidad e intercambio en los Andes Peruanos.* Instituto de Estudios Peruanos: 252–289.

D'Altroy T. N. and R. L. Bishop 1990. The provincial organisation of Inka ceramic production. *American Antiquity* 55(1): 120–37.

David N. and H. Hennig 1972. *The ethnography of pottery: a Fulani case seen in archaeological perspective.* Module 21. Addison-Wesley.

Deere C. D. 1990. *Household and class relations: peasants and landlords in Northern Peru.* University of California Press.

Donnan C. B. 1971. Ancient Peruvian potters' marks and their interpretation through ethnographic analogy. *American Antiquity* 36(4): 439–46.

Franke E. R. 1992. *Chiji Jawira: a case for attached specialisation at Tiwanaku.* M.A. Thesis, University of Chicago.

Fulford M. G. 1975. *New Forest Roman Pottery* BAR 17 Oxford.

Girault L. 1987. *Kallawaya: curanderos itinerantes de los Andes.* UNICEF/Quipus.

Goldstein P. 1993. House, community, and state in the earliest Tiwanaku colony: domestic patterns and state integration at Omo M12, Moquegua. In M. S. Aldenderfer (ed.) *Domestic architecture, ethnicity, and complementarity in the South-Central Andes.* University of Iowa Press: 25–41.

Guamán Poma de Ayala, F. [1584–1615] 1988. *El Primer Nueva Crónica y Buen Gobierno.* Siglo Vientiuno editores.

Hagstrum M. B. 1986. Ceramic production in the central Andes, Peru: an archaeological and ethnographic comparison. In C. C. Kolb and L. M. Lackey (eds.) *A pot for all reasons: ceramic ecology revisited.* (Special publication of Ceramica de Cultura Maya et al): 127–145.

Hagstrum M. B. 1996. Household autonomy in peasant craft specialisation. In T. N. D'Altroy and C. A. Hastorf (eds.) *Empire and domestic economy.* Smithsonian Institute Press.

Harris O. 1982. Labour and produce in an ethnic economy, Northern Potosi, Bolivia. In D. Lehmann (ed.) *Ecology and exchange in the Andes.* Cambridge University Press: 70–96.

Harris O., B. Larson and E. Tandeter 1987. Introduction. In O. Harris, B. Larson and E. Tandeter (eds.) *La participación indígena en los mercados Surandinos: estrategias y reproducción social siglos XVI a XX.* CERES: 17–50.

Hunt P. 1990. Inca volcanic stone provenance in the Cuzco province, Peru. *Papers from the Institute of Archaeology* University College London. 1: 24–36.

Jarman M. R. 1972. A territorial model for archaeology: a behavioural and geographical approach. In D. L. Clark (ed.) *Models in archaeology.* Methuen: 705–733.

Kendall A. 1990. The Cusichaca archaeological project, Cuzco, Peru: a final report. *Bulletin of the Institute of Archaeolgy, London* 28: 1–98.

Latour B. 1993. Ethnography of a 'high-tech' case; about Aramis. In P. Lemonnier (ed.) *Technological Choices: transforations in material cultures since the Neolithic.* Routledge, 372–198.

Lechtman H. 1979. Issues in Andean metallurgy. In E. P. Benson (ed.) *Pre-Columbian metallurgy of South America.* Dumbarton Oaks Research Library, Harvard University: 1–40.

Lechtman H. 1984. Andean value systems and the development of prehistoric metallurgy. *Technology and Culture* 25: 1–36.

Lemonnier P. 1993. Introduction. In P. Lemonnier (ed.) *Technological choices: transformations in material cultures since the Neolithic.* Routledge: 1–35.

Lunt S. W. 1987. *Inca and Pre-Inca pottery from Cusichaca, Dept. of Cuzco, Peru.* Unpublished PhD thesis, Institute of Archaeology, University College London.

Lunt S. W. 1988. The manufacture of the Inca aryballus. In N.J. Saunders and O. de Montmollin (eds.) *Recent studies in pre-Columbian archaeology.* BAR International Series 421: 489–511.

Marcoy P. 1873. *A journey across South America; from the Pacific Ocean to the Atlantic Ocean.* Blackie and son.

Mishkin B. 1946. The contemporary Quechua. In J. H. Steward (ed.) *Handbook of South American Indians, Volume 2: The Andean Civilisations*. Smithsonian Institution, Bureau of American Ethnology Bulletin 143: 411–470.

Mitchell W. P. 1991. Some are More Equal than Others; labor supply, reciprocity, and redistribution in the Andes. *Research in Economic Anthropology* 13, 191–219.

Murra J. V. 1972. El 'Control Vertical' de un máximo de pisos ecológicos en la economía de las sociedades andinas. In J.V. Murra (ed.) *Vista de la Provincia de León de Huanuco en 1562, Tomo II*. Universidad Nacional Hermilio Valdizan, 429–76.

Murra J. V. 1975. *Formaciones económicas y políticas del mundo Andino* Instituto de Estudios Peruanos.

Murra J. V. 1978. Los Olleros del Inka: Hacia una historia y arqueología del Qollasuyu. In *Historia Problema y Promesa – Homenaje a Jorge Basadre*. Univesidad Católica del Perú, 415–23.

Nash J. 1979. *We eat the mines and the mines eat us: dependency and exploitation in Bolivian tin mines*. Columbia University Press.

O'Neale L. M. 1977. Notes on pottery making in highland Peru. *Ñawpa Pacha* 14: 41–59.

Papousek D. A. 1981. *The peasant potters of Los Pueblos*. Van Gorcum.

Peacock D. P. S. 1969a Neolithic Pottery Production in Cornwall. *Antiquity* 43, 145–9.

Peacock D. P. S. 1969b A Contribution to the Study of Glastonbury Ware from Southwestern Britain. *Antiquaries Journal* 49, 41–61.

Perlès C. 1992. Systems of exchange and organisation of production in Neolithic Greece. *Journal of Mediterranean Archaeology* 5(2): 115–64.

Platt T. 1982(a). *Estado Boliviano y ayllu Andino: tierra y tributo en el Norte de Potosí*. Instituto de Estudios Peruanos.

Platt T. 1982(b). The role of the Andean ayllu in the reproduction of the petty commodity regime in Northern Potos (Bolivia). In D. Lehmann (ed.) *Ecology and exchange in the Andes*. Cambridge University Press: 27–69.

Rathje W. 1972. Praise the gods and pass the metates. In M. Leone (ed.) *Contemporary archaeology*. Southern Illinois University Press: 365–392.

Ravines R. 1978. Cerámica actual de Ccaccasiri, Huancavelica. In R. Ravines (ed.) *Tecnología Andina*. Instituto de Estudios Peruanos: 447–66.

Ravines R. and F. Villiger (eds.) 1989. *La cerámica tradicional del Peú*. Editorial los Pinos E.I.R.L.

Ravines R. and F. Villiger 1989. Introducción. In R. Ravines and F. Villiger (eds.) *La cerámica tradicional del Perú*. Editorial los Pinos E.I.R.L.: 9–16

Rice P. M. 1976. Rethinking the ware concept, *American Antiquity* 41: 538–43.

Rice P. M. 1981. Evolution of specialised pottery production; a trial model. *Current Anthropology* 22, 219–240.

Rice P. M. 1991. Specialization, Standardization, and Diversity: a retrospective. In R. L. Bishop & F. W. Lange (eds.) *The Ceramic Legacy of Anna O. Shepard*. University of Colorado Press, 257–279.

Rostworowski M. 1977. *Etnia y sociedad: costa Peruana prehispánica*. Instituto de Estudios Peruanos.

Rostworowski M. 1978. *Señoríos indigenas de Lima y Canta*. Instituto de Estudios Peruanos.

Rye O. S. and Evans C. 1976. *Traditional pottery techniques of Pakistan: field and laboratory studies*. Smithsonian Contributions to Anthropology 21.

Sallnow M. J. 1989. Precious metals in the Andean moral economy. In J. Parry and M. Bloch (eds.) *Money and the morality of exchange*. Cambridge University Press: 209–31.

Schiffer M. B. and Skibo J. M. 1987 Theory and experiment in the study of Technological change,. In *Current Anthropology* 28(5): 595–622.

Shennan S. 1989. Introduction: Archaeological approaches to cultural identity. In S. Shennan (ed.) *Archaeological approaches to cultural identity* Unwin Hyman, 1–32.

Shimada I. 1987. Horizontal and vertical dimensions of prehistoric states in north Peru. In J. Haas, S. Pozorski and T. Pozorski (eds.) *The origins and development of the Andean state*. Cambridge University Press: 130–44.

Sillar B. 1988. *Mud and Firewater; Making pots in Peru*. Unpublished MSc. dissertation, Institute of Archaeology, University of London.

Sillar B. 1994. *Pottery's Role in the Reproduction of Andean Society* Ph.D. dissertation, Department of Anthropology and Archaeology, Cambridge University.

Sillar B. 1996a. Playing with God: Cultural perceptions of children, play and miniatures in the Andes. *Archaeological Review from Cambridge* 13.1.

Sillar B. 1996b. The Dead and the Drying: techniques for transforming people and things in the Andes. Paper submited to *Journal of Material Culture* SAGE Publications, Vol. 1 no. 3: 259–89.

Skar S. L. 1994. *Lives Together – Worlds Apart: Quechua colonization in jungle and City*. Oslo Studies in Social Anthropology Scandinavian University Press.

Sterner J. 1989. Who is signalling whom? ceramic style, ethnicity and taphonomy among the Sirak Bulahay. *Antiquity* 63: 451–59.

Swan V. G. 1984. *The pottery kilns of Roman Britain*. Royal Commission on Historical Monuments Supplementary Series 5.

Tschopik H. Jr. 1946. The Aymara. In J. H. Steward (ed.) *Handbook of South American Indians Volume 2: The Andean Civilisations*. Smithsonian Institution, Bureau of American Ethnology Bulletin 143: 501–73.

Tschopik H. Jr. 1950. An Andean ceramic tradition in historical perspective. *American Antiquity* 15: 196–218.

van der Leeuw S. E., D. A. Papousek and A. Coudart 1991. Technical traditions and unquestioned assumptions: the case of pottery in Michoacán. *Techniques et Culture* 17–18: 145–73.

Zuidema R. T. 1989. *Reyes y guerreros: ensayos de cultura Andina* (collected essays of R. T. Zuidema). Grandes Estudios Andinos.

Much ado about nothing:
the social context of eating and drinking in early Roman Britain

Karen I. Meadows

Introduction

Many aspects of the "romanisation" of Britain, including the use of the term itself, are currently under scrutiny (cf Hingley 1996; Freeman 1993; Clarke 1996; Cooper 1996; Barrett forthcoming). The scope of my own work – the effects of imperialism on Early Roman Britain – has evolved in accordance with my own uncertainties regarding the concept of romanisation. Principally, I have been motivated by what I see as a lack of emphasis on the diversity of romanisation, on the imperial experiences of the non-elites, and on localised responses to the Roman presence. Underlying my approach have been nagging doubts about the cultural evolutionary tone of the discourse on romanisation which equates romanisation with 'progress' (see articles in Webster & Cooper 1996). Barrett (in reference to definitions of ritual) has also been critical of approaches to the past whereby a phenomenon is first defined and then applied to a particular set of circumstances: "such studies give the unfortunate appearance of knowing already what it is they are attempting to discover" (1991:1). Indeed, I am already unhappy with my initial attempts at defining romanisation (Meadows 1994:133). The current round of dialogues on 'romanisation', largely instigated by those who believe the concept is ill-conceived and outmoded, forces us to justify and explain our usage of the term. However tempting it is for me to give up the language of romanisation (because I agree with many of the criticisms of its usage) I do believe that, unchallenged, traditional concepts of romanisation would survive, albeit incognito. I will suggest instead, in this paper, that our current understanding of 'romanisation' is too simplistic an explanation for social change.

In an earlier publication (Meadows 1994) I outlined the relevance of studying dietary and culinary practices of households to studies of Roman Britain. I pointed out that what are (often) considered to be the principal material indices of romanisation are in fact the remains and artefacts associated with eating and drinking. While these remains have received much study in their own right, attempts to integrate the various artefacts and remains within the social context of eating and drinking have been rare, and have not been undertaken on any significant scale for Roman Britain. Through a series of anthropological and historical case studies I further emphasised that diet and culinary practices are inextricably linked to all aspects of social, political and economic life, and that the structure of these daily and ritualised acts are particularly sensitive to the more incipient aspects of imperialism. This paper aims to illustrate the potential of such an approach, through specific reference to the Late Iron Age and Early Roman period eating and drinking practices at Barton Court Farm in the Upper Thames valley, Oxfordshire.

Barton Court Farm
Late Iron Age and early Roman occupation *(see fig. 1)*

Barton Court Farm was excavated in the 1970s by the Oxford Archaeological Unit under the direction of David Miles. My own interpretations are based on the site report and micro-fiche (published in 1986) and the site archive held at Standlake, Oxfordshire. My interest in Barton Court Farm derives from the fact that it is a site which spans the Late Iron Age – Early Roman period transition. The Early Roman period settlement is viewed as a non-romanised settlement which conveys a strong sense of native continuity. The present discussion is an exploration of the theme of romanisation versus native continuity, rather than an exhaustive synthesis of data from the two settlements at Barton Court Farm.

There is a tendency in Romano-British studies to equate 'change' with romanising urban/villa-owning indigenous elites and 'continuity' with rural non-romanised natives. This imposed dichotomy is also used to describe the nature and extent of romanisation, which is currently the principal model used to describe social change during the pre/post conquest period (Scott 1993, Webster 1996:5; Hingley 1996:41; Clarke 1996:71). The exploration of social conditions during this period of imperial domination have consequently been sidelined by efforts to allocate particular cultural 'achievements', such as urbanism, to either the Late

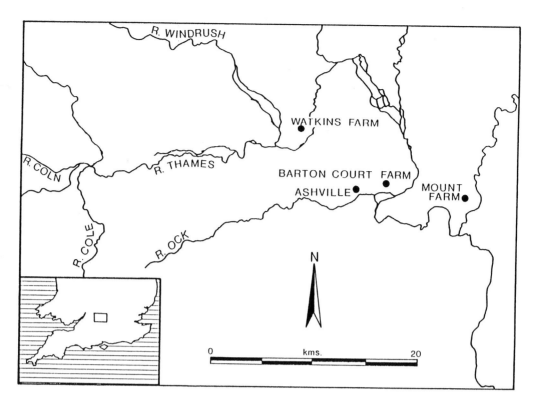

Fig. 1. The Upper Thames valley (drawn by Colin Merrony).

Iron Age or Roman periods (Woolf 1993:213). This tug of war across the lines of history and between 'natives' and 'Romans' has served its purpose by exposing the cultural evolutionary tone of many of the arguments, but the time has come to move on.

Freeman (1993) and Cooper (1996), for instance, have argued that the adoption of Roman-like accoutrements could have more to do with availability and access, than with a desire to emulate 'Roman' practices (although, as Hingley has pointed out, we must not negate the "active role of native society in defining the function, value and role of its own possessions" 1996:42). Equally, we need to consider the cultural implications and social context of 'Roman-like' material culture (see Deitler 1990; Sharples 1991; Woolf 1993; Willis 1994 for rare examples). What is becoming increasingly apparent is that the 'shopping-list' approach to the study of social change in Roman Britain requires a radical rethink.

Barton Court Farm is a multi-period site, inhabited during the Neolithic, Late Iron Age, Early Roman, Late Roman and Anglo-Saxon periods (see fig. 2). The Late Iron Age settlement appears to have had two occupational foci, one situated inside the main enclosure, the other just outside it. David Miles has suggested that these contemporary occupation areas may indicate the expansion of a single household over time, separated functional areas or possibly two households of differing status (1986:28). The Early Roman settlement had only one occupation focus, but the size of the principal rectangular structure – "five times that of an average Iron Age house" (Miles 1986:30) – suggests that it

may have accommodated a larger or more consolidated household (Miles 1986:30). The Early Roman period settlement was in the same general area as the Late Iron Age settlement, which may indicate a continuity of 'ownership' (Miles 1986:49). There is only minimal evidence of manufacturing at each settlement. Evidence is also lacking for the storage of a large surplus of agricultural produce in either period (Miles 1986:45). The artefacts and animal and plant remains are as such suitable for a study of consumption practices.

Towards an archaeology of consumption

Consumption has a direct effect on the configuration and contexts of animal and plant remains, and local and imported artefacts. The social practices which revolve around eating and drinking will be explored below through an examination of the implements and ingredients used in both the preparation and consumption of food and drink, together with the various processes involved in the distribution of these remains on the site.

The Artefacts of Consumption

At Barton Court Farm, the only implements recovered which related to the preparation and consumption of food and drink were ceramic. The present discussion will accordingly concentrate on pottery with the proviso that the use of glass, metal and especially wooden containers could have a dramatic effect on the repertoire of artefacts associated

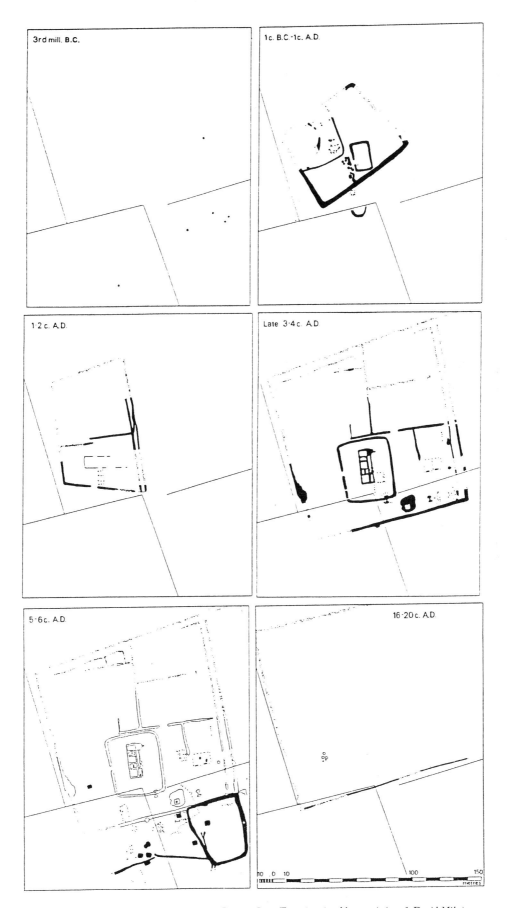

Fig. 2. The principal phases of occupation at Barton Court Farm (reprinted by permission of David Miles).

with eating and drinking and most importantly, the consumption practices associated with the use of vessels of different materials.

The relationship between vessel form, function and use is integral to studies of consumption. The current distinction between coarse ware (i.e. kitchenware) and fine ware (i.e. tableware) provides only part of the picture and is far from straightforward. Lambrick (1984), for instance, studied the residues of coarse and fine wares at Mount Farm in Oxfordshire and found that while there was a distinction between the use of the two types of fabrics, limescale residues on some fine ware vessels revealed a role in cooking as well as in consumption (1984:169). Allen (1990), on the other hand, found burnt residues on storage-type vessels at the Middle Iron Age site at Watkins Farm, also in Oxfordshire (1990:39). Large vessels could, for example, be used in beer production as well as storage (Vencl 1994:309).

Ethnographic examples can also be found to question the majority of our assumptions. In his study of African pottery, Barley (1994) has documented 'kitchen ware' that is better made than 'religious ware', 'imported ware' used in everyday contexts, and traditional 'native ware' used as high status table wares (Barley 1994:120, 73). These observations suggest that the association between vessel form and function is often more complex than has been suggested in the past. They also highlight our often ethnocentric approach to the study of vessel use. This is not to suggest that we attempt to assign a function to every category of pot; even if this was possible, vessels may have had multiple uses and their significance may have varied according to context and period. It is more that we need to recognise as Barley has done, that "pots are semantically promiscuous" (1994:76).

The Integration of Artefacts and Ingredients

> "...much of the variety which we study in pottery must relate
> to how the products of the fields were converted into the
> appropriate kinds of food and drink, and how these were pre-
> pared and served" (Sherratt 1987:83).

In the Late Iron Age and Early Roman periods general use vessels were gradually replaced by vessels with more specific uses (Millett 1979:39). The social link between more specialised forms, and eating and drinking needs, however, to be established. Modes of consumption need to be related to what is consumed. Deitler (1990) for example, has tied the storability of wine and hence the accumulation of alcohol, to the sponsorship of drinking events (1990:369). The Roman period butchery tradition of chopping the carcass into joints by cutting through bones, as opposed to the Iron Age tradition of separating bones through the cutting of ligaments (Grant 1989:141; Maltby 1985b:20), suggests a different attitude towards animals and how they were prepared for consumption. In the case of so called 'special' deposits involving animals, many of the Iron Age deposits

were not butchered, whereas in the Roman period, animals were invariably butchered, and presumably eaten (Grant 1989:146). Okun (1989), on the other hand, was able to demonstrate, through the plotting of rim diameters of particular vessel types, that the adoption of 'Roman' serving ware did not necessarily signify the adoption of 'Roman' dining customs. This was the case at a number of Early Roman period sites in the Rhine valley area where it was found that large – possibly communal – serving vessels were favoured over small serving bowls which was the more 'Roman' tradition (Okun 1989:123).

Artefacts and food at Barton Court Farm

The Artefacts

Vessel size, form and fabric were used to differentiate kitchenware from tableware for both the Late Iron Age and Early Roman periods. This type of distinction for the Iron Age pottery did not, however, satisfy the pottery specialist and while it was recorded in the archive it was not incorporated into the published report.

As with other Late Iron Age sites in the area, wheel-thrown jars and bowls were more common than the hand-made variety. The majority of the vessels were locally produced, although some pottery (butt beakers) was imported from the south-east. The bulk of the Late Iron Age assemblage consists of a variety of jars and bowls and vessels which fall in between the 'jar' 'bowl' categorisation. Large storage type vessels are distinguishable, although in light of Allen's findings at Watkins Farm (see above), their exclusive association with storage is at least questionable. It was not possible to confirm which of the jars served as cooking pots since evidence of residues or sooting – often the only means of specifying a cooking pot (Woods 1986:158) – was not evident in the archival record. Woods has observed, however, that Iron Age and Roman cooking pots generally had flat bases, were made out of a coarse fabric, and had pronounced, often everted, rims (Woods 1986:159–163). The two main fabrics found at the Late Iron Age settlement – calcareous and sandy coarse wares – were both used for vessels that fit the above characteristics (see also Woods 1986:163); in fact, most forms, including the rather high proportion of bowls, were made out of both fabrics.

My analysis, which I hoped would establish a range of small, medium, and large sized vessels (in order to incorporate identified vessels without rim diameters into the study), revealed instead a wide variability in size of the same form. For example, the rim diameters of a series of "large" storage type vessels ranged from 14cm to 30cm, a group of burnished globular bowls had rim diameters which ranged from 11cm to 30cm, and the rim diameters of a series of cordoned bowls (thought tentatively to be tableware by the pottery specialist) ranged from 11cm to 26cm. This obviously made any attempt to identify a specific pattern of consumption for particular types of vessels (such as large or small cooking-type pots or small or large bowls) extremely difficult.

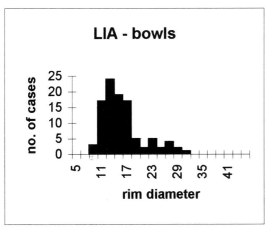
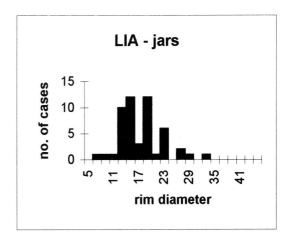

Fig. 3. Histograms of Late Iron Age bowls and jars.

Histograms of the rim diameters of jars and bowls (see fig. 3) revealed a range of small to large bowls, skewed towards the small to medium end of the scale, and medium to large sized jars. In addition to the bowls and jars, there were a number of beakers and dishes (also of differing sizes) and a variety of perforated bases suggesting the presence of vessels for cheese-making, distilling, steaming (D. Miles pers. comm.) and possibly flower pots and colanders. What is apparent is the sheer variety of forms and sizes of vessels which do not conform to one particular notion of kitchenware and tableware. Nor do they conform to one particular type of consumption practice, except possibly communal drinking although, the association of beakers with drinking is also circumstantial.

The Early Roman pottery assemblage was much smaller than the Late Iron Age assemblage, because of fewer pits and enclosures at the settlement, in addition to manuring, and practices governing their deposition. The assemblage consisted of some Roman-like pottery and a few imports: small numbers of amphorae, mortaria, and decorated and plain samian cups, bowls and dishes. The majority of the assemblage was made up of locally made bowls and jars

over half of which were of the form and fabric found at the Late Iron Age settlement. The distinction between jars and bowls is less blurred than in the earlier period, which suggests a more clearly defined specialisation of vessel form and possibly function. Some of the earlier forms were probably residual but the quantities and contexts suggest that these wares continued to be used (Miles 1986:microfiche 7:B4).

Although the sample is small, the range in size of the different types of indigenous vessels is less dramatic. This was confirmed through histograms of the rim diameters of bowls and jars (see fig. 4). The rim diameters of the jars show peaks of small, medium and large jars, demonstrating an increase in narrow-necked jars. The distribution of the rim diameters of the bowls is no longer skewed; the range is narrower, although, as with the Late Iron Age bowls, they are concentrated at the small to medium end of the scale. The significance of the Early Roman histograms, given the sample size, is debatable, but they do not appear to indicate a dramatic shift in the sizes of the vessels used to prepare, cook, and, at times, serve food. The presence of mortaria does signify the adoption of a distinctive type of food prepa-

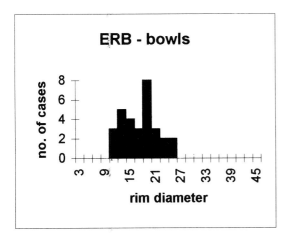
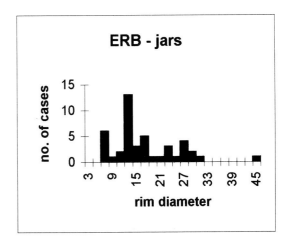

Fig. 4. Histograms of Early Roman bowls and jars.

ration vessel – although not necessarily a distinctive type of practice.

There were, however, a number of potentially significant differences between the two assemblages. There was a significant reduction over time in the number of vessels with perforated bases, which mark a decline in cheese making and/or distilling and/or different types of cooking practices. There was certainly a contrast between the types of vessels used for the consumption of liquids (see fig. 5). In the Early Roman period the presence of samian cups and wine amphorae, together with beakers and narrow-necked vessels, suggests a more varied drinking practice, possibly involving communal passing of beer-filled beakers as well as individualised drinking of wine. An increase in locally produced shallow bowls and dishes (designated as 'dish' in fig. 5), and samian bowls and dishes could imply a different emphasis on the serving or presentation of food at the Early Roman period settlement; however, the ambiguity in specifying serving-type ware at the Late Iron Age settlement remains.

The ingredients

The animal bones recovered from the various phases at Barton Court Farm were well preserved but quite fragmented. 37% of the hand-picked bones and 3% of the sieved bones were identified to species. The bones in the majority of the features are believed to represent butchery and food refuse (Miles 1986:29)

At the Late Iron Age settlement the proportions of the four main species put cattle and sheep vying for top position, depending on whether their abundance is measured by M.N.I or N.I.S.P. (see fig. 6). It has been suggested that the age and sex ratios of the cattle could indicate a propensity towards dairying (Wilson 1986), which might explain the prevalence of possible cheese-making vessels at the Late Iron Age settlement. However, it should be stressed that in addition to the many taphonomic factors that may effect species population and abundance ratios, cultural practices such as feasting, animal sacrifice and butchery techniques

have a direct affect on the configuration of different species (Gilbert and Singer 1982; Grant 1991:111; Hayden 1990). Schuster Keswani, for example, has suggested that herds dominated by young animals could signify "an intensification or heightened frequency of ritual consumption" (1994:261). These are important considerations, especially if the abundance of a particular species, such as cattle, is thought to indicate a 'romanised' diet.

Most body parts of the main domesticates were represented, which suggests that whole carcasses were present and butchered on site. Butchery marks on these species were characterised by knife cuts and chop marks (although the implements were not recovered from the site). Marks on the three main domesticates – cattle, sheep and pig – indicate the cutting and chopping of particular joints of meat and the stripping of meat from the bone. A number of the long bones of cattle and sheep were chopped mid-shaft, which could result from the chopping of bones into sizes appropriate for cooking pots. Cut marks to the mandible and hyoid suggest that the tongue and cheek of cattle were removed and possibly consumed. Evidence of the butchery of horse and dog, on the other hand, was minimal, i.e. nicks and/or cuts to two mandibles and upper vertebrae (horse) and nicks and/or cuts to a single humerus, radius and ulna (dog). The few deer remains that were recovered did not display any butchery marks – in contrast with other parts of Britain, such as Scotland, the butchery of deer in the Iron Age is quite rare in the south of England (Hingley 1995:186).

Small quantities of fresh water fish (eel & pike), oyster (a supposed 'Roman' delicacy), domestic fowl and a wild birds were identified. Some of these species probably made a limited, though not necessarily incidental, contribution to the diet.

The animal bone sample for the Early Roman period was quite small. The significance of the proportions of the represented main species, especially the increase in cattle, is notable, but questionable (see fig. 7). Cows were less abundant than bulls and steers, which together with the reduction of vessels possibly used in cheese-making, may

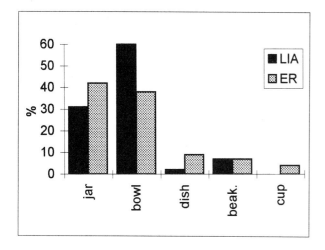

Fig. 5. Percentages of vessels within the 5 identified categories for the Late Iron Age and Early Roman period.

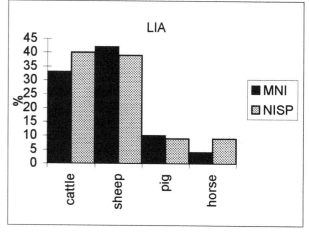

Fig. 6. Percentages of animal species for the Late Iron Age.

signify a shift in consumption habits at the Early Roman period settlement; however, as was stated above, the shifting animal population and husbandry regime could equally reflect the nature of deposition (most of the deposits were found in ditches) and socio-cultural practices.

The significance of the butchery patterns at the Early Roman settlement is also questionable in light of the small sample. There are, however, some similarities between the two periods in terms of the types of butchery techniques used (i.e. knife cuts and chop marks) and the major points of disarticulation of the main domesticates. The shafts of cattle long bones were frequently trimmed which could signify a taste for steak and/or dry roast cooking, or the stewing of larger joints in large cooking pots. Interestingly, sheep appear to have been more intensively processed with clear indications of tongue and cheek removal (not identified at the earlier settlement) and a higher incidence of bone splitting, especially the radius – probably for the extraction of marrow.

Horses, on the other hand, were more conclusively butchered as illustrated by butchery marks on a greater variety of bones including the pelvis, humerus, radius, and tibia. The butchery of horse in the region appears to have been site-specific during the Roman period. For example, horses were butchered at the Roman period settlement at Farmoor, Oxfordshire (Wilson 1979:131) but not at Roman Cirencester (Thawley 1982:211). No butchery marks were found on dogs – perhaps, as Thawley (1982) and Harcourt (1974) suggest, because dogs were also being used as pets. Fresh water oysters were recovered in a few contexts, as were small numbers of domestic fowl, a wild goose and a crow. The single incidence of a butchered humerus of a red deer, while suggestive, is inconclusive. The differing butchery practices and consumption of particular species and body parts at the Early Roman period settlement, may signify distinctive cooking preferences (roasting rather than one pot cooking), and possibly different types of food avoidance and delicacies.

Just short of 50% of the cereal grains recovered at Barton Court Farm were identified to species. Plant remains were

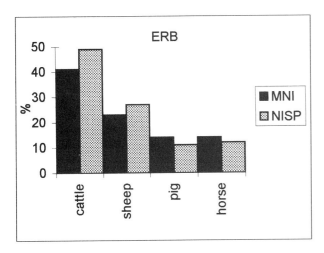

Fig. 7. Percentages of animal species for the Early Roman period.

not recovered for the Early Roman settlement and were only found in two contexts at the Late Iron Age settlement. The processing stages immediately prior to consumption are difficult to identify archaeologically (Jones 1991:25) and direct evidence for preparation and consumption, be it milling, rolling, or cracking, is absent. Additionally, the artefacts commonly associated with the preparation of grains for consumption were not found in either Iron Age or Early Roman contexts.

The two Late Iron Age assemblages are characterised primarily by cereals, with very small amounts of chaff, and a variety of weed species – many of which are thought to be edible. The types of edible species recovered include: celtic bean, fat hen, sorrel and knotgrass (both of which can be used as dyes), common orache, and black bindweed (Jones 1986a; Reynolds 1995:308). Spelt wheat was the most common cereal, followed by six-row barley; bread wheat was also prominent, and emmer was present in small quantities. A similar composition was found at the Late Iron Age site at the Ashville Trading Estate, Oxfordshire, although bread wheat was barely present in the Late Iron Age at this site (Jones 1978:103). Sites such as Barton Court Farm are thought to "mark the beginnings of [bread wheat's] rise from a minor crop in prehistory to prominence in the historical period" (Jones 1986b:120).

The social context of consumption

> "The main priority must be to gain information about the inhabitants of the site, not to study the pottery, finds or structures in isolation" (Darling 1989:98).

A study of the social context of the eating and drinking practices of households requires analysis of the remains and artefacts from associated features. Several archaeologists and specialists have commented over the years on the lack of discussion between specialists studying individual elements of sites, and how this affects the interpretations of sites as a whole (Hodder 1989:271; Maltby 1981:193; Payne 1972:80–1). The archaeological record is created by people with differing aims and objectives (and funding restrictions) and then recreated through subsequent interpretation or re-interpretation (also by people with differing aims and objectives). The Barton Court Farm excavation, for example, was a rescue project; its aim initially was "to elucidate the sequences of occupation and the main factors affecting change" (Miles 1986:xiii). As the result of a slump in the housing market, the excavation was extended and "modified to take account of the new circumstances and of the developing archaeological interests" (Miles 1986:xiii). The site report comes with an extensive micro-fiche in which the pottery report records finds in relation to individual contexts, but whose interpretation is for the most part not offered with reference to context. The bone report, on the other hand, records species and animal parts in relation to groups of similar features, but does not emphasise butchery practices or individual contexts. This is not a criticism of the report, which is comprehensive and together with the archival record provides a full account of individual contexts (rim diameters and butchery marks are recorded in the archive), but rather a qualification that my emphasis on the social context of consumption, which requires the integration of various types of 'data', does not necessarily fit with the original intentions of the excavation, the specialists and the resulting publication.

Reinstating the remains and artefacts into their excavated context, while laborious, is in many ways the easy part. The excavated context itself also has to be culturally defined. The majority of finds for the Late Iron Age and Early Roman period in the Upper Thames valley are recovered from enclosure ditches, gullies, post holes, and pits. These comprise both open features, subject to the accumulations of a variety of practices over time, and single event deposits (Hingley and Miles 1984). It is these types of features that provide the medium for the study of the social practices and cultural attitudes which led to the deposition of archaeological remains (Moore 1981).

Analysis of the deposition of finds and their social significance involves the examination of the diversity and frequency of species and types of artefacts across space. Various studies – primarily of bones and plants – have attempted to demonstrate the organisation of a settlement, through looking at the various stages of processing in relation to the location of refuse (see Halstead et al. 1979; Dennell 1974). Wilson, for example, has found on a number of sites in the Upper Thames valley that the bones of large species and other coarse bones do not tend to be situated around the more domestic areas of the site, which instead attract the bones of smaller species and burnt bones. He puts forward butchery practices, rubbish disposal regimes, and notions of acceptable hygiene or scavenging as possible explanations of the repeated inter-site patterns (Wilson 1989).

Most people recognise that the isolation of different types of activities is not straightforward. As Wilson (1989), Moore (1981), Maltby (1985a), Hill (1995), Lambrick (1984) and others have stressed, associations of specific remains may not bear any relation to areas of processing or use. Rather, they may reflect the differential states of preservation and types of deposition of remains in specific contexts (for example, pits versus ditches). The enclosures at the Late Iron Age and Early Roman period settlements at Barton Court Farm appear to have been open ditches, filled gradually over time. The gullies, pits and house slots, on the other hand, were probably 'open' at particular times during the lifetime of each settlement.

The distribution of pottery and animal remains at Barton Court Farm

The Late Iron Age Settlement (refer to fig. 8)

The pottery and animal remains at the Late Iron Age settlement were found in all types of contexts – pits, ditches and gullies – with the highest concentrations occurring in the enclosure ditches, especially the internal and main enclosures. The quantity of remains in the pits varied throughout the site, although the pits with the highest concentrations of both pottery and animal bones were situated within the internal enclosure. The northern gully contained a wide variety of vessel forms including a number of cordoned bowls. Of particular interest was a cache of 45 bases (21 were perforated) which was deposited at its terminal. The gully also contained a high concentration of animal bones, including 15 cattle mandibles and the remains of a huge pike. The southern gully, on the other hand, contained a smaller, and substantially less varied, quantity of pottery and fewer numbers of butchered animal remains.

The types of pottery recovered in each of the enclosures was comparable, although it were possible to identify a particular pattern of distribution for beakers. It was found that:

1) beakers were not generally situated in the main ditch (only one was recovered)

2) there was a higher concentration of beakers in the northern gully (six) than the southern gully (one)

3) the pits which contained beakers were situated within the internal ditch

If the beakers were indeed used for drinking, their distribution in particular areas of the site is quite suggestive (see discussion below).

The distribution of the butchered remains did not correspond with Wilson's observations at other sites in the Upper Thames valley, in that all types of body parts and species were found in a variety of contexts throughout the site. Distinct patterns were, however, observed with particular species: dog and horse bones were found in a number of pits and in the northern gully, but not together. (This differs from Grant's observation at Danebury where there was a statistical association of horse and dog bones (1991). Horse and dog bones were only found together in the ditches, and it was also in the main enclosure that evidence of butchered horse and dog occurred. Dog mandibles (and the mandibles of sheep and cattle in general) were especially prevalent in particular contexts within the settlement which could suggest that the deposition of the head was particularly significant (Hill 1995:103).

Only two plant assemblages, both carbonised, were recovered at the Late Iron Age settlement. The largest assemblage was found at the base of pit 311, within the internal enclosure. The second assemblage, recovered from a possible open hearth within the southern gully, was very small and contained fewer wild species and no chaff. The significance of the distribution of the plant remains, given the tiny sample, is unclear, although it does suggest that grains were possibly prepared for consumption (if not consumed) in the southern occupation area.

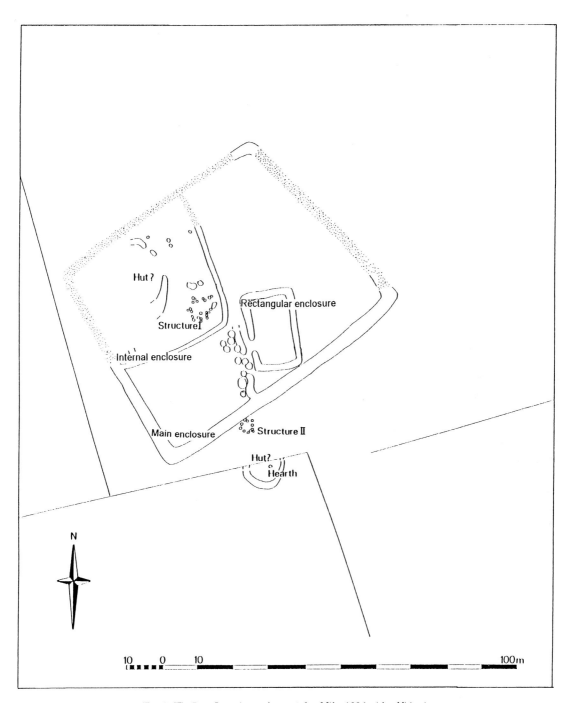

Fig. 8. The Late Iron Age settlement (after Miles 1986 with additions).

The Early Roman Settlement (refer to fig. 9)

The pottery and animal bones recovered from the Early Roman settlement revealed quite different distributions. The majority of the pottery was situated in the main enclosure at the periphery of the site with an especially dense accumulation in the northeast area of the enclosure. The small numbers of pits tended to contain distinct pottery groups: shallow bowls, dishes and samian ware versus narrow necked jars and cooking-type pots; and distinct types of butchered animals. Only two pits were situated close to the living area,

and the one located within the structure contained only serving type bowls. Beakers, samian cups and amphorae were also located away from the living area of the site, in the internal ditches, main enclosure and in pits positioned on the periphery of the site (except for one beaker in a foundation slot). Narrow necked jars, mortaria and large jars, were also concentrated away from the living area in the pits and enclosures at the periphery of the site. There was an especially dense accumulation of these pottery types in the northeast section of site.

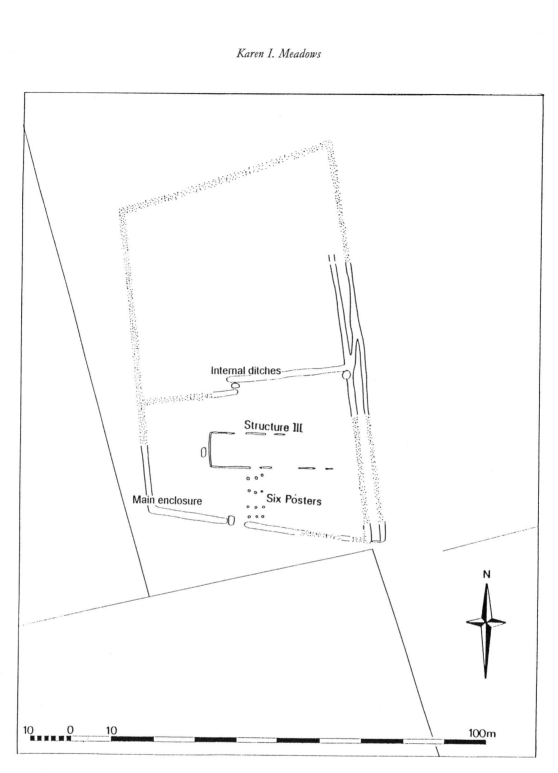

Fig. 9. The Early Roman Settlement (after Miles 1986 with additions).

Specific distributions of species and body parts were also observed. For example, two of the pits contained primarily cow and horse bones (these two contexts will be discussed further below). The foundation slots of the structure, and a small pit situated inside the structure, contained predominantly the head and foot debris of sheep, cow, and pig, and one dog skull, but no horse. In contrast to the Late Iron Age settlement, animal remains were not generally deposited within the domestic area of the site. With the exception of one pit situated outside the structure which contained highly fragmented and burnt bones, and the bones recovered within the structure, all other remains were deposited away from the living area – with an especially high concentration of butchered remains in the northeast section of the site. The distribution's of the butchered remains are therefore similar to Wilson's observations in that there is a distinction between the deposition of bones in domestic and non-domestic areas of the settlement, although both large and small species were found in the contexts within the domestic area of the site.

There were no plant remains recovered at the Early Roman Settlement.

The social context of deposition

Increasingly, archaeologists are considering the relatively small amounts of artefacts and remains actually found on archaeological sites in terms of their social context. Sharples, for example, has suggested that the distribution of imported Amorican ceramics at Hengistbury Head "was controlled in a manner that reflected, on a small scale, the pattern of the region: imports were restricted to areas apart from domestic activities" (1990:300). A similar pattern was also found at the Early Roman period settlement at Barton Court Farm. Hill (1994; 1995) has questioned the notion that Iron Age pits were receptacles for ordinary rubbish by revealing the sequential associations of certain types of animal remains and artefacts with depositional sequences which may have taken place over a number of years, even decades. Grant (1991; 1984) has linked distinctive animal deposits and the association of particular species to acts of sacrifice and/or feasting and ritualised behaviour. Similarly, Hingley (1990) has suggested that the placing of certain deposits within, and at the entrances of, enclosure ditches served to mark social relations within and outside the settlement. The cache of bases at the terminal of the Late Iron Age northern gully at Barton Court Farm could represent the deliberate deposition of these remains in an area of the settlement which, as will be shown below, was of particular significance. An acknowledgement of these entwined sequences of social practices is fundamental to the significance we place on the catalogues of remains and artefacts.

"Special" deposits at Barton Court Farm

While it is not possible to provide a detailed description of each deposit within the confines of this paper, comment on a few will help to illustrate the possible significance of the contextual association of certain deposits. It was tempting to take each context literally, and I had to remind myself that I too was 'observing' deposits which had been constructed and reconstructed by many people. The dividing of deposits into 'special' and 'ordinary' is also tempting, but not wholly appropriate. This has been illustrated by both Hill (1995; 1994) and Grant (1991), when each found that so-called ordinary refuse was structured, and as such incorporated into the rituals of everyday life. As was seen above, certain types of pottery and animal species and body parts were concentrated in specific areas and features for each period. The configurations of the deposits were appreciably different for both settlements.

There are on occasions, however, some deposits which appear to have distinctive associations not found in other contexts. The denotation of 'special' meals and/or events involving food and drink, is controversial (see Wilson 1992; and Hill 1995:13–5 for excellent discussions of this issue) and what is considered 'special' to one observer, may be quite 'ordinary' or taphonomic to another. I considered it significant when there were specific groupings of particular types of artefacts and/or particular species and/or body parts, or a specific type of butchery practice (or no butchery practice) in certain contexts.

The Late Iron Age Settlement (refer to fig. 10)

The Late Iron Age pit 379 – a possible hearth – was situated between structure one and the internal enclosure, lined with clay slabs and contained a single butt beaker, five butchered cattle mandibles and one dog mandible. Pit 338, located on the northern side of structure one, contained the non-butchered (non-consumed?) articulated remains of an ewe. This pit was attached to pit 311, which was lined with carbonised plant remains and large storage/cooking/beer preparation type vessels. Pit 415, also lined with clay slabs, burnt limestone and charcoal, contained a couple of large jars, a variety of cordoned bowls and a beaker, together with the articulated fore-limbs of two butchered sheep, butchered cattle crania and some burnt pig bones. These deposits were all located within the occupation area – a practice common at most Iron Age sites (Wait 1985:138). It is especially noteworthy that these deposits were all situated in the domestic area within the internal enclosure.

The Early Roman Period Settlement

The distinctive deposits recovered at the Early Roman settlement were found at the periphery of the site away from the living area. Pit 397, situated outside the main enclosure, contained a small necked bowl and the articulated lower right leg of a mature bovine and the lower right and left leg of a mature horse. The lower legs of cattle have been found in apparently ritual contexts at the religious complex in Uley, Gloucestershire (Ellison 1980:306). The bones in this pit were complete and displayed similar cut marks, indicating meat and/or skin removal. The grouping of cattle and horse together was also encountered in the cess-pit, where a single butchered sheep's skull and a variety of largely complete butchered horse and cattle bones including ten cattle mandibles, were recovered. The pottery in this pit was quite distinctive, including a samian dish, cup and bowl, four large jars, mortaria, and a beaker, as well as a bronze coin dating to AD 10–40 and a mid-first century brooch. It is also possible that the concentration of head and foot remains associated with the structure indicates the deliberate deposition of these body parts together. The association of head and feet in ritual contexts is quite common at other Roman period sites (Scott 1991:117).

Discussion

What is most interesting about the deposits and distributions of animal remains and pottery described above is the realisation that the different configurations of the settlements reflect directly on the social contexts of eating and drinking in the Late Iron Age and Early Roman periods.

The compartmentalisation of the Late Iron Age site is particularly suggestive. Miles hinted at the possibility of two

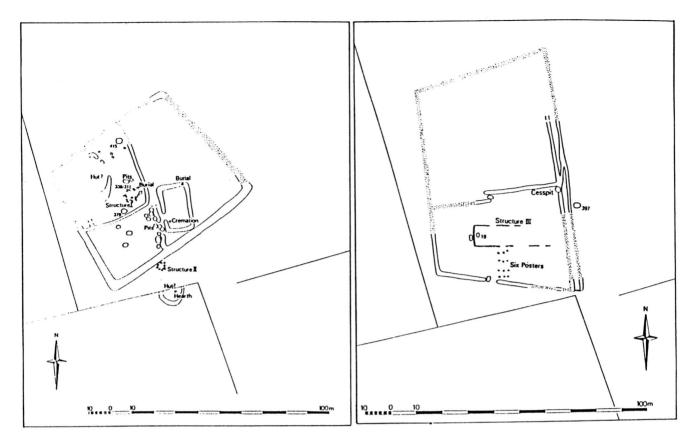

Fig. 10. The Late Iron Age and Early Roman Settlements (after Miles 1986 with additions).

different status areas within the site. As has been shown, there was indeed a contrast between the types of assemblages recovered in the northern and southern occupation areas. The northern occupation area was further distinguished by the presence of a human burial at the eastern entrance to structure one, an isolated piglet burial, and the concentration of possible hearths. Beakers were also concentrated in this area, as were the more distinctive animal deposits. This north-south divide, which accentuates the northern area, has been identified at a number of Iron Age and Bronze Age settlements in Britain (Parker Pearson 1996). The main collection of pits were located outside the internal enclosure. A number of these pits formed a line separating this area from a rectangular enclosure – thought by the excavators to have been an animal pen – which had a human cremation at its western entrance and an infant burial on the north-east corner.

It could be argued that there were two Late Iron Age groups, possibly related or of differing status, living side by side but within circumscribed boundaries of inclusion or exclusion (after Hingley 1990). The central area of the site which separates the two domestic areas, may represent a common area linking the two groups. It is particularly suggestive that two types of burial and a single animal enclosure were found in this area. It is also possible that the apparent compartmentalisation of the site marks the sequential movement of a single group over time from one area of

the site to another; or the use of different areas of the settlement for different types of activities. In either case, the northern section of the settlement was at various points in its history a focus for specific acts of commemoration.

The Early Roman settlement, on the other hand, had one central occupation area – situated intriguingly in between the northern and southern domestic areas of the Late Iron Age settlement. Of the few pits discovered, some appear to be situated at select points in the settlement: at the entrance to the main enclosure, at the point where the internal ditch meets the main enclosure, and at the passageway between the internal ditches. The two six-poster structures interpreted by the excavators as possible above-ground granaries served as a passage-way leading into the site from the south. There is also a possibility that there was some form of gate at the entrance, although the dating of the post holes is not secure. Nonetheless, entrances into the domestic area of the site and into the northern area of the site (interpreted as a paddock of sorts in light of the absence of any features) are conspicuous. The recovery of two iron door keys in the pit situated within the structure suggests that doors were sometimes locked. The eastern double ditch is thought by the excavators to have bounded a trackway or to have marked the construction of a substantial bank. The parameters around the site are as such well defined. The majority of the animal remains and pottery were deposited at the periphery of the site. The few distinctive pottery and animal deposits within the domestic area were recovered from within the structure or in the foundation slots. Enclosures and entrances to the settlement appear to have dictated the movement of people approaching the site. There may have been a distinction between private (behind closed doors) domestic practices and more public ceremonies away from the living area.

Romanisation as a concept for social change at Barton Court Farm

The Early Roman period 'native' settlement at Barton Court Farm does not fit into traditional models of native continuity. The concept of romanisation, as it is currently understood, does not account for the dramatic changes found at the Early Roman settlement. This study illustrates how 'native discontinuity' may be fundamental to considerations of social change in Roman Britain. The butchery practices at the two settlements revealed clear distinctions between the mores which governed the butchering and presumably consumption of particular species and body parts at particular times – distinctions which do not always conform to 'Roman' and 'non-Roman' categorisation. The vessels associated with cooking and containment were of similar form and size for both settlements. However, there was a marked contrast over time between vessels identified with drinking and possibly serving. The point at which the two pottery assemblages diverged was in the domain of public consumption of food and drink. Most importantly, the contrast in consumption practices is mirrored both in the distributions of the vessels and animal remains throughout the two settlements, and in the way the two settlements were organised.

I was particularly struck by the contrasting arrangement of the domestic areas at the two settlements. Ross Sampson, in a discussion on the socio-political implications of villas, considered whether the configuration of these types of buildings served to control the approach of strangers or outsiders (1990:175). The domestic structure at the Early Roman period settlement was not a villa (see Fulford 1992 for a critique of the emphasis on conventional villas in the Upper Thames valley). However, there is a definite sense that the restructuring and consolidation of the Early Roman settlement emphasised the approach and movement of outsiders rather than its inhabitants. Indications of public consumption events, in contrast with the Late Iron Age settlement, were identified away from the domestic area of the settlement. Indeed, the size of the Early Roman period structure and the absence of external hearths suggests that at times certain activities, such as cooking and eating, may have been taking place behind closed doors. Changes in the configuration of settlements and in social practice are often associated with periods of societal change. One explanation for the changes observed at the Early Roman settlement at Barton Court Farm, which convey the impression of an enhanced awareness of outsiders and of public/private consumption, could be that the inhabitants were re-

sponding to external conditions brought about by the arrival of the Romans. This may be an example of one type of experience of imperialism which has quite possibly been overlooked in the past because of our search for conspicuous consumption practices that fulfil our definitions of romanisation.

The time has come to challenge the inventories of 'Roman' and 'native' material culture, so that we can incorporate different types of settlements and the experiences of people of different socio-economic backgrounds into discussions of 'Roman' Britain. However, as this study of the social context of eating and drinking illustrates, we also need to develop paradigms for social change which account for the experiences of imperialism. An all-encompassing concept of romanisation may or may not ultimately have a place in such discussions. But, before we dispose of the term, we must deconstruct the concept and acknowledge the role it has played in the construction of 'our' Roman Britain.

Acknowledgements

I would like to thank Keith Branigan, Kathy Fewster, John Barrett and Kathryn Denning for commenting on an earlier draft of this paper. I would especially like to thank Jane Webster for enlightening discussions and her editorial wizardry. Bob Wilson has been extremely helpful in the translation of parts of the primary bone records. I am especially grateful to David Miles at the Oxford Archaeological Unit for his indispensable comments on an earlier draft of this paper, and for the use of the various illustrations of Barton Court Farm. Any errors or omissions found within are definitely my own.

Bibliography

Allen, T. G. 1990. An Iron Age and Roman-British Enclosed Settlement at Watkins Farm, Northmoor, Oxon. *Thames Valley Landscapes: the Windrush Valley 1*. Oxford University Committee for Archaeology, Oxford.

Barley, N. 1994. *Smashing Pots: Feats of Clay from Africa*. British Museum Press.

Barrett, J. C. 1991. Towards an Archaeology of Ritual. In: P. Garwood, D. Jennings, R. Skeates and J. Toms (eds.) *Sacred and Profane*. Oxford University Committee for Archaeology Monograph 32: 1–9.

Barrett, J. C. forthcoming. Romanisation: a critical comment. In: D. Mattingly (ed.) *Dialogues in Imperialism*.

Clarke, S. 1996. Acculturation and continuity: re-assessing the significance of Romanization in the hinterlands of Gloucester and Cirencester. In: J. Webster & N. Cooper (eds.) *Roman Imperialism: Post-colonial Perspectives*. Leicester Archaeology Monograph 3: 71–84.

Cooper, N. J. 1996. Searching for the blank generation: consumer choice in Roman and post-Roman Britain. In: J. Webster & N. Cooper (eds.) *Roman Imperialism: Post-colonial Perspectives*. Leicester Archaeology Monograph 3: 85–98.

Darling, M. J. 1989. Nice fabric, pity about the form. *Journal of Roman Pottery Studies*, 2:98–101.

Dennell, R. W. 1974. Botanical evidence for prehistoric crop processing activities. *Journal of Archaeological Science* 1:275–284.

Dietler, M. 1990. Driven by drink: the role of drinking in the political economy and the case of early Iron Age France. *Journal of Anthropological Archaeology* 9:352–406.

Ellison, A. 1980. Natives, Romans and Christians on West Hill, Uley. In: W. Rodwell (ed.) *Temples, Churches and Religion in Roman Britain*. B.A.R. British Series 77: 305–28.

Freeman, P. W. M. 1993. 'Romanisation' and Roman material culture. *Journal of Roman Archaeology* 6: 438–45.

Fulford, M. 1992. Iron Age to Roman: a period of radical change on the gravels. In: M. Fulford and E. Nichols (eds.) *Developing Landscapes of Lowland Britain: The Archaeology of the British Gravels: A Review* The Society of Antiquaries of London, Occasional papers vol. 14: 23–38.

Gilbert, A. S. & Singer, B. H. 1982. Reassessing zooarchaeological quantification. *World Archaeology* 14(1):21–40.

Grant, A. 1984. Survival or sacrifice: a critical appraisal of animal burials in Britain in the Iron Age. In: J. Clutton Brock & C. Grigson (eds.) *Animals and Archaeology 4. Husbandry in Europe* B.A.R. International Series 227: 221–227.

Grant, A. 1989. Animal bones in Roman Britain. In: M. Todd (ed.) *Research on Roman Britain – 1960–1989*. Britannia Monograph Series 11.

Grant, A. 1991. Economic or Symbolic? Animals and Ritual Behaviour. In: P. Garwood, D. Jennings, R. Skeates & J. Toms (eds.) *Sacred and Profane*, Oxford University Committee for Archaeology Monograph 32: 109–114.

Halstead, P., Hodder, I. & Jones, G. 1978. Behavioural archaeology and refuse patterns: A case study. *Norwegian Archaeological Review*, 11:118–131.

Harcourt, R. A. 1974. The dog in prehistoric and early historic Britain. *Journal of Archaeological Science* 1:151–175.

Hayden, B. 1990. Nimrods, Piscators, Pluckers, and Planters: The emergence of food production. *Journal of Anthropological Archaeology*, 9:31–69.

Hill, J. D. 1994. Why we should not take the data from Iron Age settlements for granted: recent studies of intrasettlement patterning. In: A.P. Fitzpatrick & E.L. Morris (eds.) *The Iron Age in Wessex: Recent Work*. Association Francaise D'Etude de L'Age du Fer, Trust for Wessex Archaeology Ltd.: 4–8.

Hill, J. D. 1995. *Ritual and Rubbish in the Iron Age of Wessex: A study on the formation of a specific archaeological record*. B.A.R. British Series 242.

Hingley, R. 1990. Boundaries surrounding Iron Age and Romano-British settlements. *Scottish Archaeological Review* 7:96–103.

Hingley, R. 1995. The Iron Age in Atlantic Scotland: Searching for the meaning in the substantial house. In: J.D. Hill & C. Cumberpatch (eds.) *Different Iron Ages: Studies on the Iron Age in Temperate Europe*. British Archaeological Reports, International Series 602 185–193.

Hingley, R. 1996. The 'legacy' of Rome: the rise and fall of the theory of Romanization. In: J. Webster & N. Cooper (eds.) *Roman Imperialism: Post-Colonial Perspectives*. Leicester Archaeology Monographs 3: 35–48.

Hingley, R. & Miles, D. 1984. Aspects of Iron Age Settlement in the Upper Thames Valley. In: B. Cunliffe & D. Miles (eds.) *Aspects of the Iron Age in Central Southern Britain*. University of Oxford: Committee for Archaeology Monograph 2: 52–71.

Hodder, I. 1989. *Writing archaeology: site reports in context*. Antiquity 63:268–74.

Jones, M. 1986a. The plant remains. In: D. Miles (ed.) *Archaeology at Barton Court Farm, Abingdon, Oxon*. Research Report 50, Council for British Archaeology. Fiche 9:E10–F8.

Jones, M. 1986b. *England Before Domesday*. B.T. Batsford Ltd.

Jones, M. 1991. Food production and consumption – plants. In: R.F.J. Jones (ed.) *Roman Britain: Recent Trends*. John Collis Publications: 21–27.

Lambrick, G. 1984. Pitfalls and possibilities in Iron Age pottery studies – experiences in the Upper Thames Valley. In: B.W. Cunliffe & D. Miles (eds.) *Aspects of the Iron Age in Central Southern Britain*. University of Oxford Committee Monograph 2: 162–177.

Maltby, J. M. 1981. Iron Age, Romano-British and Anglo-Saxon animal husbandry – a review of the faunal evidence. In: M. Jones & G. Dimbleby (eds.) *The Environment of Man: The Iron Age to Anglo-Saxon period*. B.A.R. British Series 87: 155–203.

Maltby, J. M. 1985a. Patterns in faunal assemblage variability. In: G. Barker & C.S. Gamble (eds.) *Beyond Domestication in Prehistoric Europe*. Academic Press: 33–74.

Maltby, J. M. 1985b. Assessing variation in Iron Age and Roman butchery practices: the need for quantification. In: N.R.J. Fieller et al. (eds.) *Palaeobiological Investigations: Research Design, Methods and Data Analysis*. B.A.R. International Series 266: 19–30.

Meadows, K. I. 1994. You are what you eat: diet, identity and romanisation. In: S. Cottam, D. Dungworth, S. Scott, J. Taylor (eds.) *TRAC 94: Proceedings of the Fourth Annual Theoretical Roman Archaeology Conference*. Oxbow Books: 133–140.

Miles, D. 1986. *Archaeology at Barton Court Farm Abingdon, Oxon*. Oxford Archaeological Unit Report 3. C.B.A. Research Report 50, Oxford Archaeological Unit and Council for British Archaeology.

Millett, M. 1979. An approach to the functional interpretation of pottery. In: M. Millett (ed.) *Pottery and the Archaeologist* Institute of Archaeology Occasional Publication 4: 35–48.

Moore, H. 1981. Bone refuse – possibilities for the future. In: A. Sheridan and G. Bailey (eds.) *Economic Archaeology: towards an Integration of Ecological and Social Approaches*. B.A.R. International Series 96: 87–94.

Okun, M. L. 1989. *The Early Roman Frontier in the Upper Rhine Area*. B.A.R. International Series 547.

Parker Pearson, M. 1996. Food, fertility and front doors in the first millennium B.C.. In: T.C. Champion and J. Collis (eds.) *The Iron Age – Recent Trends*. J.R. Collis Publications: 117–132.

Payne, S. 1972. On the interpretation of bone samples from archaeological sites. In: E.S. Higgs (ed.) *Papers in Economic Prehistory*. Cambridge University Press, Cambridge: 65–81.

Reynolds, P. 1995. The food of the prehistoric Celts. In: J. Wilkins, D. Harvey & M. Dobson (eds.) *Food in Antiquity*. Exeter University Press: 303–315.

Samson, R. (ed.) 1990. *The Social Archaeology of Houses*. Edinburgh University Press.

Schuster Keswani, P. 1994. The social context of animal husbandry in early agricultural societies: ethnographic insights and an archaeological example from Cyprus. *Journal of Anthropological Archaeology* 13:255–277.

Scott, E. 1991. Animal and infant burials in Romano-British villas: a revitalisation movement. In: P. Garwood, D. Jennings, R. Skeates & J. Toms (eds.) *Sacred and Profane*. Oxford University Committee for Archaeology Monograph 32: 115–121.

Scott, E. 1993. Writing the Roman Empire. In: E. Scott (ed.) *Theoretical Roman Archaeology: First Conference Proceedings*. Avebury: 5–22.

Sharples, N. M. 1990. Late Iron Age society and continental trade in Dorset. *Revue Archeologie Ouest Supplement* 3:299–304.

Sherratt, A. G. 1987. Cups that cheered. In: W.H. Waldren and R.C. Kennard (eds.) *Bell Beakers of the Western Mediterranean* B.A.R. International Series 331(I): 81–144.

Thawley, C. 1982. The animal bones In: J. Wacher and A. McWhirr (eds.) *Early Roman Occupation at Cirencester*. Cirencester Excavation Committee: 211–227.

Vencl, S. 1994. The archaeology of thirst. *Journal of European Archaeology* 2 (2):299–326.

Wait, G.A. 1985 *Ritual and Religion in Iron Age Britain*. B.A.R. British Series 149.

Webster, J. 1996. Roman imperialism and the 'post imperial age' In: J. Webster & N.J. Cooper (eds.) *Roman Imperialism: Post-colonial Perspectives*. Leicester Archaeology Monograph No.3: 1–17.

Webster, J. & N.J. Cooper (eds.) 1996. *Roman Imperialism: Post-colonial Perspectives*. Leicester Archaeology Monograph No. 3.

Willis, S. 1994. Roman imports into late Iron Age British societies: towards a critique of existing models. In: S. Cottam, D. Dungworth, S. Scott, J. Taylor (eds.) *TRAC 94: Proceedings of the Forth Annual Theoretical Roman Archaeology Conference*. Oxbow Books: 141–150.

Wilson, B. 1978. The animal bones. In: M. Parrington (ed.) *The Excavation of an Iron Age settlement, Bronze Age Ring-ditches and Roman Features at Ashville Trading Estate, Abingdon (Oxfordshire) 1974–76*. Oxford Archaeological Unit Report 1, C.B.A. Research Report 28, Oxford Archaeological Unit and Council for British Archaeology.:110–139.

Wilson, B. 1979. The animal bones In: G. Lambrick & M. Robinson (eds.) *Iron Age and Roman Riverside Settlements at Farmoor, Oxfordshire*. Oxford Archaeological Unit and Council for British Archaeology: 128–133.

Wilson, B. 1986. The animal bones In: D. Miles (ed.) *Archaeology at Barton Court Farm, Abingdon, Oxon. Research Report 50*, Oxford Archaeological Unit and Council for British Archaeology:Fiche 8:A1–G14.

Wilson, B. 1989. Fresh and old table refuse. The recognition and location of domestic activity at archaeological sites in the Upper Thames valley, England. *Archaeozoologia* 3: 237–260.

Wilson, B. 1992. Considerations for the identification of ritual deposits of animal bones in Iron Age pits. *International Journal of Osteoarchaeology* 2:341–49.

Woods, A.J. 1986. Form, Fabric, and Function: Some observations on the cooking pot in Antiquity. In: Kingery, W.D. (ed.) *Technology and Style, Ceramics and Civilization 2*. The American Ceramics Society: 157–72.

Woolf, G. 1993. The social significance of trade in Late Iron Age Europe. In: S. Scarre & F. Healy (eds.) *Trade and Exchange in Prehistoric Europe*. Oxbow Books: 211–218.

Historical, geographical and anthropological imaginations: early ceramics in southern Italy

M. Z. Pluciennik

Abstract

Pottery is one of the new forms of material culture which has been used to characterise the spread of 'the Neolithic' – the first farmers – across Europe. In much of the Mediterranean archaeologists have been content to use it as a chronological or 'ethnic' marker. There has been relatively little consideration of either its symbolic status, or its social and material role in the transformation of practices and identities when imitated, adopted or acquired by aceramic mesolithic hunter-gatherer societies, or used in the equally dynamic early neolithic societies of southern Italy. Despite poor contextual data for much of the area, it can be argued that various types of pottery, associated with new practices of burial, ritual and food preparation among others, and in contrast to the adjacent area of Greece, were linked with different arenas of power. The processes of pottery acquisition, production, use and consumption, and their associated knowledges, were intimately involved in the construction of new temporalities and spatialities – different understandings of time and space, of history and landscape – and in the formation of intra- and inter-societal identities and relationships.

Introduction

'... potters may be injurious to others. They cause diseases. Amongst the Dowayos, in men they cause piles, in women, a sort of ingrowing vagina. The worst thing that could happen is that a rainchief should come into contact with a smith/potter. Both would die. The smith/potter would swell up with moisture, the rainchief perish of a dry cough. Yet ... [s]ince the rainchief, too, needs pots to control the rain an elaborate series of arrangements must be made whereby the extreme ends of the Dowayo social world can be brought together and he can be supplied. It involves a post-menopausal potter baking the rainchief's pots, on a moonless night, in the shelter used to house dead male bodies and passing them to a ritual sorcerer for transport.' (Barley 1994: 64)

Compared with the rich Otherness evidenced in the ethnographic description above, archaeologists have been cu-riously reluctant to explore the wilder shores of ceramic interpretation, despite good examples which plead to be discussed in more theoretically imaginative terms reaching beyond either chronotypology or basic function as containers. In southern Italy (figure 1), in earlier prehistory, pottery is indeed taken as a signifier by archaeologists, but initially merely as one which, together with obsidian, polished stone and domesticated animals and cereals, signifies the presence of 'the Neolithic'. Pottery has been discussed in terms of exchange goods with symbolic status, and the presence of pottery has been noted in exotic contexts, yet only occasional hints are made about the potential wider roles and ramifications of ceramics. In the following, I shall argue that despite problems of poor contextualisation, the adoption of pottery in the early Neolithic in southern Italy was apparently within a different sphere of practices from those on the other side of the Adriatic Sea, in Greece. For most of the Neolithic, other symbolic roles and associations of pottery can also be demonstrated. Finally I shall argue that contrasting the results of recent petrographic analyses with the extent of style zones throughout the neolithic offer us a way of discussing the dynamics of changing temporalities and spatialities – the structuration of time and space in these prehistoric societies.

Pottery is the most widely studied and published artefact category from southern Italian neolithic sites, often to the detriment of other materials such as lithics. Although early descriptive typologies (Peet 1909; Stevenson 1947) blended easily with prevailing culture historical views, since the 1960s there has been a marked polarization in the interpretation of the material by Italian and British archaeologists. The pioneering work of Ruth Whitehouse (1968a, 1968b, 1969) has been followed by Caroline Malone (1985, 1986); both preferred to see variation in ceramic assemblages as partly controlled by access to exchange networks, which may thus vary not only in time and space but also by context. They have also produced synthesising works (but *cf.* Frangipane 1975) covering southern Italy (and beyond). Italian archaeologists, by contrast, generally have preferred to elaborate the culture-historical framework to produce a detailed chrono-

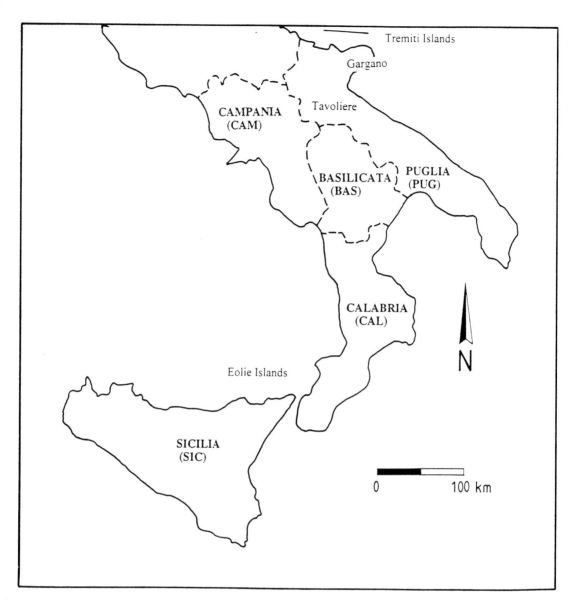

Fig. 1. The regions and areas of southern Italy discussed in the text.

typology in which each neolithic ceramic style was mutually exclusive in time and space (Tiné 1975, 1983; Bernabo Brea 1970, 1987; Bernabo Brea & Cavalier 1960, 1980; Geniola 1987), usually for a 'type region' but often attempting to extend the sequence for one area to much of southern Italy. The dividing line is not absolute (see Peroni 1967; Frangipane 1975; Tusa 1985, for example), but almost all published pottery reports are purely typological descriptions; interpretation is limited to discussion of the chronological position of the assemblages. I do not intend here to review or discuss the pottery chronotypologies at any great length, except for the question of the existence (or not) of any 'pure impressed ware' phase, which has been suggested as the marker of the earliest neolithic sites in southern Italy. The major chronotypologies, regional traditions and associated radiocarbon dates are briefly summarized. I shall argue that the Whitehouse-Frangipane-Malone view, which is more sympathetic to variability, contextuality, and the blurred and complex nature of the factors affecting ceramic assemblages, is

initially more productive than attempts to produce chronologies based on pottery alone, but still fails to address the sorts of issues raised by ethnographic understandings of the roles of pots and potters.

The most important ceramic chronotypology is Tiné's revised (1983) scheme which divides the neolithic ceramics of southern Italy (though based mainly on Puglian material) into 11 phases (*ibid*: 54–97; tavola 126). The second influential stratigraphically-based typology from southern Italy was based on the extensive work by Bernabo-Brea on the Eolie islands off north-east Sicily, particularly at Lipari, the source of much of the obsidian found throughout Italy from the neolithic onwards (Bernabo Brea 1970, 1987; Bernabo Brea & Cavalier 1960, 1980). Although the simpler sequence is broadly the same as that of Tiné, some of the pottery styles are suggested to represent exotic imports connected with the acquisition of obsidian.

By contrast Whitehouse (1969, 1986; see also 1992) has argued for much more overlapping distributions in time and regional or site differences in access to different styles. She describes the widespread generally decorated wares: impressed (IW) and Stentinello (St), red-painted (RPW), trichrome (Tr), sub-divided into Ripoli, Scaloria, Capri and Lipari wares, and Serra d'Alto (SdA); and a number of rarer or more localised wares including Materan scratched (MSW), various groups of plain burnished wares (BBW), and Diana and Bellavista wares (D). She also initially rejected the existence of a 'pure impressed ware' phase (see below), and although recognising chronological differences between some of the wares, argued that

> 'In place of the divisions into phases suggested by other authorities, I offer an overlapping series of wares, with regional differences tentatively suggested.' (Whitehouse 1969: 303).

This general approach is supported by Cipolloni-Sampo, who notes that, for example, according to the radiocarbon dates Tiné's phases IIa to IVa2 are chronologically inseparable (Cipolloni-Sampo 1987: figure 2, p.182). The chronological relationships of the ceramic styles of southern Italy are drawn from site reports and radiocarbon determinations are summarised in table 1.

Malone (1985, 1986) both developed and differed from Whitehouse's interpretation, though this is partly due to more excavations allowing better chronological and geographical resolution. One notable difference is her uncritical acceptance of the existence of an early and long-lasting pure impressed ware phase (see below). But her major contribution has been in the attempt to synthesise a vast amount of material and to interpret it in terms of a contextual and exchange-related analysis. She also points to regional facies of impressed ware styles as well as decorated and undecorated *figulina* (finewares); many of the latter, she suggests, would once have been painted (Malone 1985: 120–1).

Impressed ware: southern Italy in the Mediterranean context

The debate over the existence (or not) of a 'pure' impressed ware phase in southern Italy is of far more significance than

Table 1. Chronological relationships of the Neolithic ceramic styles of southern Italy from radiocarbon dates and excavation reports.

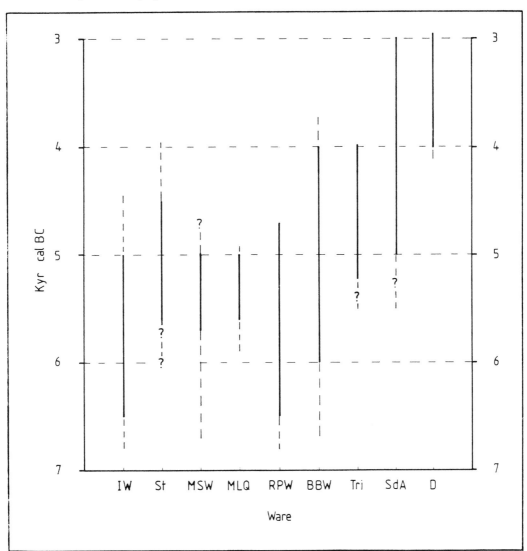

a regional issue of chronological priority. This is because impressed wares are one of the earliest (if not the earliest) types of pottery known in much of the central and western Mediterranean, and thus have become a signifier for 'the neolithic' in both a narrow and a broad sense. Its presence has been used to stand for the spread of agriculture, most notably in the work of Ammerman & Cavalli-Sforza (1971, 1973, 1984). The rapid but differential diffusion of impressed ware pottery in the central and west Mediterranean (Guilaine 1979, 1980; Lewthwaite 1981, 1985b) has also been instrumental in stimulating models of the spread of 'the neolithic', such as Lewthwaite's (1985b, 1986) 'island filter' model relating to the role of the Tyrrhenian islands, and arguments that 'the neolithic' spread into Liguria from the west (Biagi 1991). The complexity of the issue is also shown by recent finds of (non-impressed) pottery without any other 'neolithic' traits at Petriolo III in Tuscania (Donahue *et al.* 1992) at early dates; and a series of extremely early dates for impressed wares on Corsica (Cherry 1990; Lewthwaite 1985a, 1989). Further, southern Italy becomes crucial in interpreting these patterns given the very different patterns of ceramic production in the Aegean, from where 'the neolithic' is assumed to derive. The predominance (even if not chronological priority) of impressed coarsewares over finewares in southern Italian assemblages suggests that very different patterns of ceramic innovation, production, acquisition and diffusion may apply than in the Aegean (Hameau 1987; Perlés 1992: see below), and this in turn will affect our understanding of the adoption or acquisition of pottery and the mesolithic-neolithic transition.

The existence of a 'pure impressed ware' phase in southern Italy was most comprehensively questioned by Whitehouse (1968a,1969; but see e.g. Cornaggia Castiglioni & Menghi 1963: 149) although she recently admitted to feeling that the evidence was still ambiguous (pers. comm.). In her earlier article she pointed out that impressed ware was normally (77 out of 86 sites) associated with other types of pottery. Of the 'pure' sites, many were peripheral to the main (known) areas of neolithic settlement in peninsular southern Italy, that is, the Tavoliere (PUG) and the Materano (BAS). Further, some of the 'pure' assemblages were based on dubious stratigraphies and/or small samples. She pointed out that a large number of sites had produced predominantly impressed wares, with greater or lesser amounts of finewares, often amounting to only a few sherds.

> 'Apart from the presence of painted wares, the pottery from these sites is *indistinguishable* from that found on the 'pure' Impressed Ware sites. Likewise ... no distinction can be made between sites with 'pure' Impressed Ware and sites with both Impressed and painted wares on the basis of other cultural traits. This suggests that we are concerned not with two entirely separate groups ... but rather with a series of associations of Impressed Ware with varying quantities of painted pottery.' [Original emphasis] (Whitehouse 1968a: 189).

Nonetheless, Whitehouse still tends to follow Tiné and others by assuming a potential 'impressed ware only' phase

in her tabulated summaries (e.g. 1986: table 1, p. 38; 1992: table 2.2, p. 14). The two main (but undated) sites which are quoted as examples of early impressed ware sites are those of Prato Don Michele (PUG), which is placed earlier than Guadone, S. Severo (PUG); material from this latter site has been used to define a Guadone-style impressed ware.

The ceramics from Prato Don Michele on the Tremiti islands in the Adriatic to the north of the Gargano Peninsula, derived from survey and excavations in the 1950s (Fusco 1966). The excavated material came from two carbon-rich layers distinguished by colour, but in which no features or structures were definable. The vast bulk (80%) of the ceramic assemblage comprised coarse impressed wares, decorated with usually syntactically arranged motifs including shell-impressions, sometimes organised into bands or filled triangles (Fusco 1966: 78). These coarse impressed wares were distinguished from plain polished or burnished wares of a finer fabric.

The site of Guadone is in the very north of the Tavoliere, to the west of the Gargano peninsula. The material came from two artificial pits (assymetric bell-shapes: Tiné & Bernabo Brea 1980: figure 3) and from a section of a probable 'C-shaped' ditch of 20–25m diameter of a type common in the ditched Tavoliere settlements. The ceramic assemblage from all areas was similar and conflated. It comprised coarser and thicker fabric wares (70%) and finer fabric wares. More than half of the coarsewares were decorated with impressed (including shell-impressed) or incised decoration, generally covering the whole surface and showing little syntax.

The finer wares were harder, thinner and burnished inside and outside. Decoration was present on 40% of the sherds; although still impressed and incised and with similar or identical motifs, it was of a different character, with marked syntax to the decoration, often in parallel bands or in geometric shapes (*ibid*: 59). The decoration was also often limited to shoulders or rims, and had sometimes been infilled with red or white paste. The authors also noted the existence of 20 sherds (of a total of 2910) with red slips, and one fragment of plain figulina ware (*ibid*: 64).

These two sites serve to epitomise approaches to the published earlier neolithic sites of southern Italy: the first point is that pottery chronotypologies have tended (as elsewhere) to concentrate almost entirely on decorated wares, to the exclusion of considerations of other forms of variability, especially depositional context and spatial variation. At virtually all sites with published ceramic assemblages, however, there are both 'coarsewares' and 'finewares'. The former are thick-walled large vessels of coarse fabrics, often with rough impressed/incised decoration, and seemingly associated with storage and/or cooking. These usually dominate the assemblages. The variable amounts of 'finewares' are made in a finer fabric, are generally smaller and thinner-walled, more often smoothed or burnished both internally and externally, and are less frequently decorated. Secondly, even in terms of the decorated wares, and as Whitehouse (1969) pointed out, few of the early dated neolithic assemblages are devoid of all painted wares (I use this term to cover the brown-painted and impressed decorated Masseria La Quercia wares (MLQ), as well as the conventional so-called 'Middle Neolithic' red-painted wares). Thirdly, those few sites where only impressed wares are found (excepting tiny samples from surface collections) are both caves in the far west of the area: the Grotta dell'Uzzo in north-west Sicilia, and the Grotta Filiestru on Sardinia. The assemblage from the unpublished excavations at Kronio in south-west Sicilia, is also reported to conform to this pattern (see below).

The chronotypological insistence on adhering to the ideal of a non-overlapping ceramic sequence has had two effects. Firstly it has led to a tendency to overlook either sample sizes, context or 'inconvenient' material which cross-cut the ceramic phases. One of the most blatant examples is Geniola (1987), summarising the neolithic pottery sequence in central Puglia. He claims 12 sites as evidence of an 'Impressed Ware only' phase 1. The following phase 2 (of seven) is said to be characterised by impressed wares, burnished wares, scratched wares and small amounts of red-painted wares. However an examination of the original reports of the phase 1 sites shows that all his cited assemblages except four demonstrate the presence of other types of pottery; the four exceptions are from surface collections, of which the two with quoted sample sizes contained totals of 44 and 17 sherds (Pluciennik 1994: 220–224).

The second effect of these rigid chronotypologies has

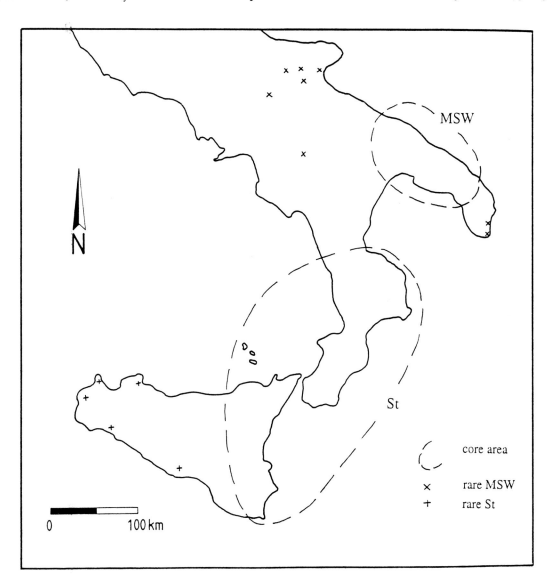

Fig. 2. The distribution of Materan Scratched (MSW) and Stentinello (St) wares in southern Italy.

In Sicilia and Calabria there are early coarse impressed and fine impressed (Stentinello) wares. In Puglia coarse impressed wares are associated with fine burnished wares. In both areas these may be associated with small amounts of slipped or painted (e.g. Masseria La Quercia type, or classic Red-Painted wares). Stentinello wares were produced for a long time and are also known associated with Trichrome wares in eastern Sicilia. In Basilicata scratched wares occur in association with coarse impressed wares, and their distribution extends into central Puglia. Stentinello wares are known from perhaps circa 5800 cal BC in Calabria and circa 5500 cal BC in Sicilia. Scratched wares are known from circa 5600 cal BC in Basilicata.

been to stultify interpretation of the (genuine) variability within ceramic assemblages, by assuming that the only cause of variation can be chronological. This has led, for example, in Sicilia, both to the search for an early pure impressed 'pre-Stentinello' phase (Tusa 1983, 1985; Tiné 1970; Gianni-trapani 1993), and its interpretation as a signifier of purely chronological interest. [The excavations from the Buco del Fico at Monte Kronio have not yet been published, but are said to demonstrate, like the Grotta dell'Uzzo, a sequence from the upper palaeolithic to neolithic, including an early 'pre-Stentinello' impressed ware phase.] The earlier excavations at Kronio (Tiné 1970; Maggi 1977) produced just 30 sherds of impressed ware from the lowest layers, which

is taken as the pre-Stentinello phase. While the existence of such a phase is individually quite possibly true for these (and perhaps other western Mediterranean and/or island) sites, that it does not demonstrate absolute chronological priority is demonstrated by the radiocarbon dates for Stentinello wares and coarse impressed wares from Calabria, compared with those from the Grotta dell'Uzzo in Sicilia (table 2). At the latter site Stentinello and Masseria La Quercia painted/impressed wares are said to be present in spits F1–4; 'syntactic impressed ware' similar to Stentinello pottery down to spit 9; again the 'pure (unsyntactic) impressed ware' level is predicated on a few sherds in spits 10–12 (Costantini *et al.* 1987; Piperno *et al.* 1980b; Tusa

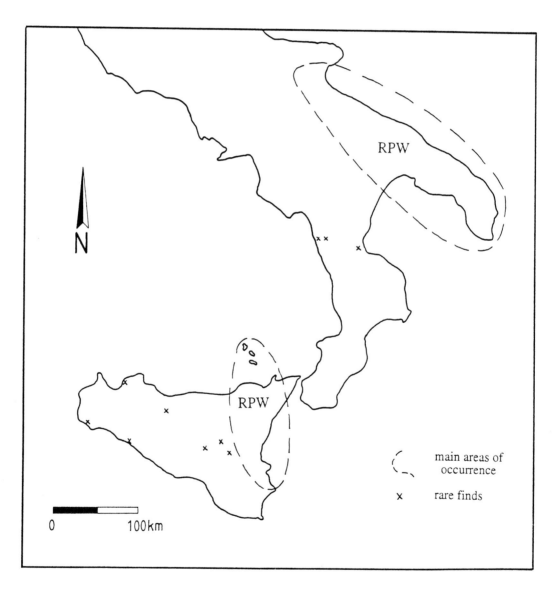

Fig. 3. The distribution of Red-Painted Wares (RPW) in southern Italy.

Red-Painted Wares, often taken as a sign of the 'middle neolithic' (e.g. Tiné 1983) are notably absent from central and southern Calabria, despite extensive surveys by Ammerman and others. In Puglia small amounts of RPW are associated with early dates and with coarse impressed and burnished wares, perhaps as early as the late seventh millennium cal BC. In eastern Sicilia and on Lipari RPW is found in association with Stentinello wares (unlike southern Calabria), but with no relevant dates.

Table 2. Dates for 'pre-Stentinello' wares (Grotta dell'Uzzo, Sicily) and Stentinello wares (Acconia, Calabria)

Site	Area/layer	Date (1 sigma)	Ceramics
Acconia	H	5950–5724 cal BC	IW, St
Grotta dell'Uzzo	F7–9	5711–5558 cal BC	IW
Grotta dell'Uzzo	W15 = F5	5648–5534 cal BC	IW
Acconia	n/k	5646–5508 cal BC	IW, St
Acconia	G	5438–5269 cal BC	IW, St
Acconia	M	4568–4464 cal BC	IW, St

Key: IW = Impressed Wares   St = Stentinello Wares

1985). These few sherds (e.g. three in spit 12) have been argued to be possibly intrusive (see Ammerman's comments and discussion in Guilaine *et al.* (eds.) 1987: pp. 443–445). The Calabrian sites in table 2, incidentally, contain no painted wares (Ammerman 1985; *cf.* figure 3).

This suggests that the nature of the ceramic assemblages at the Grotta dell'Uzzo (and other sites) is determined by modes of access, acquisition and consumption, rather than simply reflecting chronological variation.

The brief descriptions above show not only the ceramic variability present at these sites from the so-called 'impressed ware only' phase on, but also demonstrate that arguments over the *chronological* meaning of the presence or absence of red-painted wares at a particular site or at a particular time are, quite probably, in many cases irrelevant to our understanding of assemblage variability.

Contextual variability

Although Whitehouse (1969) had already suggested that ceramic variability was due to more than chronological change, it was Malone (1985,1986) who attempted to analyse the varying styles and their distribution in terms of exchange. She concentrated on the decorated finewares, and argued that the common occurrence of painted *figulina* pottery (i.e. RPW) on Puglian sites (figure 3) suggested that this was the centre of production. Its relatively common occurrence in eastern Sicily and on Lipari was argued probably to be connected with obsidian exchange. The Trichrome wares (figure 4), argues Malone (1985: 126) emerged 'in areas previously characterised by different Impressed Ware traditions.' In the later neolithic, the Serra d'Alto and then the Diana wares are widely distributed in southern and central Italy, although with concentrations in east Sicilia and Puglia (figure 5).

Examining not only finewares, but also obsidian and polished axes, Malone argued that

'the goods of long distance exchange networks are frequently found associated together and frequently in non-domestic settings, of ritual or symbolic character. At the same time there is regional variation in the patterning, showing that the more distant the areas were from south-east Italy, the more likely was the deposition of the imported goods in ritual contexts.' (Malone 1985: 143).

Malone investigated the quantitative relations between types of finewares and their contexts of recovery. She divided the latter into settlements without burials (A1), caves without burials (A2) and other sites (A3), and settlements with burials (B1), caves with burials (B2) and other burials (B3) (Malone 1986: 234*ff*). The overall distribution of these site categories for the neolithic is shown in table 3. She further quantified the distribution of finewares by site category at which each fineware type was present (table 4).

Malone (1986: 299*ff*) also attempted to approximate the longevity of each style in order to counteract imbalances in the number of occurrences (*ibid*: table 22, p. 301). I have preferred to express her data in terms of depositional preference from the 'norm' for the types of sites present in the Neolithic (table 5). Here I have compared the percentages of actual site occurrences of finewares for each ware, to the 'normal' overall distribution of contexts (A1–A3, B1–B3). I have then expressed the 'degree of preference' for each type in each context, in order to eliminate the effect of different sample sizes (i.e. {actual − norm}/norm × 100)

Given that the finewares are arranged in table 5 in approximate (though overlapping) order of chronological appearance there are a number of comments which can be made. The 'negative preference' for the deposition of *figulina* (F) and red-painted wares (RPW) in separate burials or

Table 3. Distribution of Neolithic site categories (After Malone 1986: table 7b, p. 236).

	Site type					
	A1	**A2**	**A3**	**B1**	**B2**	**B3**
%	59.2	20.3	-	9.5	7.1	3.9
(N)	225	77	0	36	27	15

Key: Sites without burials – A1 = settlements   A2 = caves   A3 = other
          Sites with burials – B1 = settlements   B2 = caves   B3 = other

Table 4. Distribution of finewares by site type (after Malone 1986: table 21). Settlement types as in table 3

Ware		A1	A2	A3	B1	B2	B3	TOTAL
				Site type				
F	(N)	79	28	-	16	12	4	139
	%	56.8	20.1	0	11.5	8.6	2.9	
RPW	(N)	48	31	-	3	13	3	98
	%	49.0	31.6	0	3.1	13.3	3.1	
Tr	(N)	10	-	4	7	-	37	
	%	43.2	27.0	0	10.8	18.9	0	
Tc	(N)	12	3	-	4	3	-	22
	%	54.5	13.6	0	18.2	13.6	0	
Ts	(N)	9	4	-	2	1	-	16
	%	56.3	25.0	0	12.5	6.3	0	
SdA	(N)	54	26	-	7	10	10	107
	%	50.5	24.3	0	6.5	9.3	9.3	
D	(N)	69	30	-	10	13	10	132
	%	52.3	22.7	0	7.6	9.8	7.6	

Key: F = figulina; RPW = red-painted wares; Tr = Ripoli trichrome; Tc = Capri trichrome; Ts = Scaloria trichrome; SdA = Serra d'Alto; D = Diana

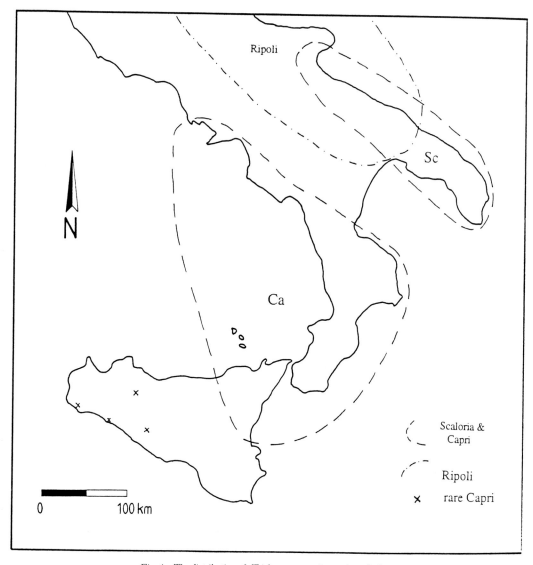

Fig. 4. The distribution of Trichrome wares in southern Italy.

The Scaloria, Ripoli and Capri wares, generically known as Trichrome wares, were thought to be a late addition to the southern Italian neolithic ceramic repertoire, but dates from the Grotta Scaloria suggest that it may be as early as the second half of the sixth millennium cal BC. These exotic painted wares are more common in atypical or 'ritual' contexts (see main text) and have been linked with the obsidian 'trade' from Lipari, where these types of vessels are fairly common.

Table 5. *Degree of preference of depositional context for each fineware. Settlement types as in table 3*

Ware	Site type					
	A1	A2	A3	B1	B2	B3
F	-4.1	-1.0	-	+21.1	+21.1	-25.6
RPW	-17.2	+55.7	-	-67.4	+87.3	-20.5
Tr	-27.0	+33.0	-	+13.7	+264.8	-
Tc	-7.9	-33.0	-	+91.6	+91.5	-
Ts	-5.1	+23.2	-	+31.6	-12.7	-
SdA	-14.7	+19.7	-	31.6	+31.0	+138.5
D	-11.7	+11.8	-	-20.0	+38.0	+94.9

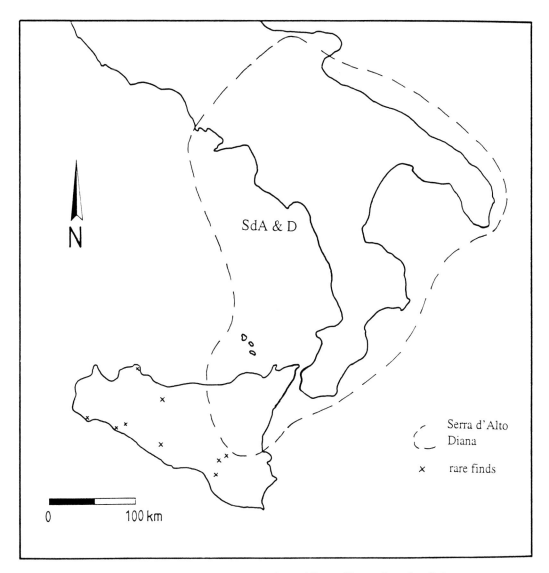

Fig. 5. *The distribution of Serra d'Alto (SdA) and Diana (D) wares in southern Italy*

The whole of southern Italy seems to participate in the later styles, including central and southern Calabria, where Ammerman's surveys have found large amounts of Diana wares in association with obsidian. In Puglia the variant (or copy) known as Bellavista Ware also occurs. Diana Ware is dated from circa 4000 cal BC and Serra d'Alto was thought to be similarly late, but recent dates from Stretto Partanna (SIC) in the mid-sixth millennium cal BC and from Santa Barbara (PUG) at around 5000 cal BC again produce problems for the simple chronotypological approach.

cemeteries (B3) probably relates to a chronological trend and shows the lack of these contexts in the earlier period rather than lack of deposition of wares in them. From her own analysis Malone concludes that the later neolithic (i.e. Serra d'Alto and Diana wares) 'are more frequently found in ... cult-cave-burial sites than the earlier finewares' (*ibid*: 301), and this can be seen in the negative preference for settlement-burial sites (B1) in this period. Her suggestions about the special contents of certain 'ritual caves' were followed up by Whitehouse (1992), who linked these and other features into an exploration of possible cult societies in neolithic southern Italy.

All finewares are less common than might be expected on 'normal' settlement sites (A1), and there is a generally strong preference for the deposition of finewares in caves (A2, B2) and with burials (B1–B3). There are anomalies in the patterns which may be due to regional differences, sampling biasses, over-generalisation and misunderstanding of the context of find (Grifoni-Cremonesi 1994) and poor publication, but the general pattern is convincing. Malone concluded that

> 'The relatively standardised pottery production suggests adherence to specific styles, and these could be interpreted as part of the symbolic apparatus used in Neolithic burial and ritual behaviour. ... We can infer that there was considerable interaction between widely-spaced Neolithic groups ... The maintenance of the exchange networks over the long distances probably involved a variety of symbolic actions, such as prestige gift-giving between exchange partners, as well as participation in ritual and social actions.' (1985: 146).

Material culture and exchange

Stimulating though Malone's treatment of southen Italian pottery has been, the difficulty with treating pottery in terms of long-distance material exchange networks is that published clay fabric analyses basically suggest that pots do not appear to be moving very far, in contrast to certain other materials such as obsidian and polished stone (see below). Although we can recognise differential deposition related to categories of pottery, and the existence of different scales of interaction in terms of shared or related styles, the equation of distance with status and prestige now appears too simple, and other models more able to deal with complexity are needed. At least two such models have been proposed for the neolithic items of material culture on the eastern side of the Adriatic (Perlès 1992; Chapman 1988).

In Greece Perlès (1992) examined the patterns of procurement, production and consumption for a wide range of materials throughout the neolithic. She argued that three types of exchange systems can be distinguished: utilitarian, social and prestige. The first relates to stone tool production and use. Lithic assemblages (including chipped and ground stone tools) seem to be produced for essentially utilitarian purposes. However a series of factors such as the 'absence of visible stylistic marking; homogeneity for Greece as a whole; large-scale circulation ...; even distribution;

[modes of] source-exploitation; and modes of production' (*ibid*: 148), including the technically difficult pressure-flaking of standardized blades, suggest craft specialization and the existence of 'middlemen' or specialized itinerant knappers (*ibid*: 136–7; *cf*. Perlès 1990). For ceramics, until the Final Neolithic, essentially non-utilitarian and non-cooking uses are suggested (*cf*. Vitelli 1989, 1993). The bulk of the ceramic vessels were locally produced, stylistically elaborate (individually and regionally), and show small-scale circulation in both quantity and distance, and sometimes uneven distribution (Perlès 1992: 149). Thus ceramics relate to localised social interaction and alliance. Stylistic similarities may be treated partially at least as markers of small-scale social interaction such as partner exchange (Cullen 1985), or perhaps as mutual recognition or meaning promoted by risk avoidance and the need for relatively short-distance alliances (Halstead 1989). Finally, certain stone, shell and metal ornaments and artefacts suggest 'essentially symbolic or ritual use' (Perlès 1992: 149), demonstrating some specialized production, low quantity but long-distance diffusion, and uneven distribution. Perlès suggests that

> 'All these observations ... bring us back to the notion that exchange networks and modes of exchange vary with the category of goods, but also to the idea that different exchange networks may fulfil different functions ... The raw materials and stone tools that were exchanged did indeed correspond to a regional shortage ... Conversely, [for pottery] it is the very process of exchange, with its social implications, which must have been prevalent. [Finally, for] prestige goods ... there is no way here that the producer groups and the receivers could have entertained direct relations. Repeated exchanges were the norm in this case, but they did not involve the population at large.' (Perlès 1992: 150).

Perlès also demonstrates change in the nature of procurement and exchange over time, and also changing regional – and broader – differences.

> 'But it also seems out of the question that, in other Neolithic contexts, exactly the same categories of goods participated in exchange systems having the same nature and socioeconomic role. Which goods were involved in which exchange system ... depended upon local resources and cultural traditions ... One may stress the contrast between fine wares, which predominate in Greece, and the much coarser utilitarian wares that characterize such areas as southern France [and southern Italy] from the earliest Neolithic times. It is *a priori* unlikely that both types of wares occupied the same place in inter-personal or inter-group relations, as well as in exchange networks.' [My insertion] (Perlès 1992: 152–3)

Thus Perlès argues convincingly that modes of consumption do not have to correlate with analogous modes of acquisition or production, nor is the nature of the articulation between these modes either static or inevitable. Nonetheless the model proposed by Perlès still remains within a predominantly functional and exchange-dominated interpretive framework.

Southern Italian pottery

Clay fabric analysis of samples from neolithic southern Italy (Dell'Anna 1986; Mannoni 1980; 1983; 1984; Skeates 1992; Williams 1980) suggests generally local and low technology (though not necessarily low quality) production. At Cassano San Matteo-Ciantinelle, in the extreme north of the province of Foggia (and hence to the north of the Tavoliere and west of the Gargano), the samples of coarse to 'semifine' impressed wares similar to the Guadone style, showed probably very local manufacture and firing temperatures of about 500°C (Dell'Anna 1986). In contrast to this localised production, however, there has been argued to be wide distribution of some finewares. The evidence from Lipari in the Eolie Islands (Williams 1980), often quoted as the recipient site of exotic pottery in exchange for obsidian, suggests otherwise. Locally-derived inclusions are relatively easily characterised here by virtue of the specific volcanic mineral suites present on the islands. Williams' analysis suggests that local production using local clays is important throughout the prehistoric and protohistoric periods. A second group of fabrics suggests either the import of whole vessels or manufacture from clays from mainland north-west Sicily. That the latter is plausible is suggested by a third fabric group which is interpreted as the result of local use of imported clays. Williams notes that this group includes samples of Serra d'Alto, Capri and Diana wares.

'It is considered that the volcanic matter entered into the clay when it was being fashioned into pottery. It is therefore implied that foreign clay was imported into Lipari and that these particular sherds could have been manufactured locally ...

There is one painted [SdA] sherd [whose fabric] clearly suggests that some painted pottery was made locally on the island ... Proof that clay was imported into Lipari is provided by Group C pastes ... There are seven thin sections ... showing that the tradition of importing clay was already in existence during the three earliest Neolithic stages ... These three points tend to suggest that some of the Group B pottery could have been made locally ...' (Williams 1980: 865–866)

Similarly, Mannoni (in Bernabo Brea 1984:70) suggests that thin section analysis of the fabrics for sherds including *figulina* and '*semifigulina*' wares argues for the use of very local deposits at Tirlecchia (BAS). His analysis of a selection of sherds from Guadone (Mannoni, in Tiné & Bernabo Brea 1980: see above) suggested that the bulk of the clays could have originated in the immediately surrounding area or nearby Appenine or Gargano deposits; only the unique *figulina* sherd contained minerals which suggested a a possible non-local source. This is basically the same conclusion reached by Mannoni for Puglian neolithic site of Passo di Corvo (in Tiné 1983: 94–97). After sampling all types of pottery present at the site (impressed wares, Masseria La Quercia, plain and painted *figulina* etc.) he concluded that

'all classes of ceramics at Passo di Corvo, like those from Guadone and Amendola, were produced with materials from the Tavoliere, even if not always from the same source. Some doubts remain only for [a few samples], but of the typologically more exotic ceramics (for example those with *pointillé* decoration), three samples fell in the [common local fabric] groups.' (*ibid*: 97)

A similar conclusion is reached by Skeates (1992) in his discussion of the Italian neolithic evidence: 'Thin-section studies indicate that few finished pottery artefacts were actually exchanged at an inter-regional scale' (*ibid*: 32). A similar conclusion has recently been expressed for the earlier neolithic in part of southern France, where both coarsewares and finewares are distributed at up to *circa* 70km from the clay source, but apparently not over longer distances (Barnett 1990).

In the Aegean, Vitelli (1993) discusses the meaning of the co-existence of regional styles of pottery in neolithic Greece, along with evidence for very local manufacture and consumption; only one per cent of the early neolithic wares at Franchthi are considered as of non-local origin, for example (*ibid*: 248). She notes that

'whether or not pots were circulated among sites, either potters or information about technology must have done so, to account for the parallel development of style and technology over many generations at each site' (*ibid*: 250)

In Italy there are both general regional styles or techniques (e.g. the red-painted wares, Materan scratched wares, Stentinello wares, trichrome wares) and more localised styles within these 'style zones' (e.g. Scaloria, Capri). Some of these overlap in time and space, and their relationship to the distribution of other materials (obsidian, greenstone) is not simple or direct, though some of the distributions may relate to both earlier and co-existing patterns of distribution of flint, for example. During the Late Upper Palaeolithic (LUP) and mesolithic there was probably movement between southern Basilicata and/or northern Puglia, and southern Puglia, in relation to flint procurement (Pluciennik 1994: 234–235; Skeates & Milliken 1989), and this possible axis is mirrored by the distribution of Materan Scratched Wares in the earlier neolithic (figure 2).

Beyond exchange

There have been some recent attempts to consider the meaning of pottery-making and pottery styles in far more imaginative and socially-interpretive ways. Cullen's discussion of stylistic differences and similarities among Middle Neolithic Urfirnis (fineware) pottery assemblages from five sites in the Northeastern Peloponnese, Greece, suggested that the observed patterns could plausibly be associated with the practices of exogamous communities and female potters.

'The hypothesized relocation of women from one community to another provides the necessary opportunity for close interaction and instruction among potters. Incentive for emulation among potters is also supplied by the model, as the stranger seeks social acceptance through conformance.' (Cullen 1985: 96)

Also referring to material in Greece, Vitelli argues that

> 'we should expand our concept of prestige and status beyond ownership of rare, exceptionally fine and exotic goods ... Pots (and other objects) must have been perceived as sometimes imbued with magical powers – to ward off particular fearsome happenings, ensure desired ones, and testify to the devout performance of sacred rites ... I suggest that the first potters in Neolithic Greece may have been in such a social category [of having "preferential access to supernatural power"] and that their pots may have been imbued with related powers.' (Vitelli 1993: 253)

Vitelli (pers. comm.) has also recently pointed out that the lack of obvious cooking wares in the earlier and middle Neolithic of Greece suggests a long-lived tradition of cooking which did not obviously demand fire-proof containers. It is also a strong argument against the often-cited purely utilitarian explanations of the spread of pottery (e.g. Arnold 1985; Brown 1989).

Another attempt to link the spread of pottery with other forms of social behaviour which moves beyond the functional or 'style as information' paradigms is that of Chapman (1988), looking at the Dalmatian coast in particular, as well as Greece and southern Italy. He argues that

> '... the introduction and differentiation of ceramic fabric, form and decoration have close behavioural correlates across a wide range of social activities (eating, drinking, feasting, gift-giving, storage and ritual).' (Chapman 1988: 4).

As well as identifying particular forms as perhaps related to the exchange and consumption of salt, he points out that '... it seems likely that the potential of clay vessels for a wide variety of household functions was at least as important in their widespread adoption as a symbolic role.' (*ibid*: 15). Following Malone (1985) he suggests that in southern Italy, 'new classes of containers ... in the form of fine ware bowls, cups and flasks ... [were] directly related to new habits of eating and drinking and possibly to new techniques of transporting liquids ... In addition, storage vessels such as salt-pots [were] adopted as part of a novel set of culinary habits' (*ibid*: 19). Although this might well be true, this once again concentrates on the minority component of most ceramic assemblages in southern Italy to the detriment of the bulk.

Throughout southern Italy, as suggested above, fragments of coarse large storage and/or cooking pots, often impressed-decorated, tend to dominate or form a large proportion of the assemblages. This is in contrast to early neolithic Greece where monochrome pottery predates coarse impressed wares by perhaps half a millennium (Hameau 1987), and finewares dominate the Early and Middle Neolithic assemblages (Perlès 1992; Vitelli 1993). In Italy one should note that at the carefully excavated struc-

ture at Piana di Curinga, Calabria (Ammerman & Bonardi 1985), however, seven coarseware vessels were associated with 21 fineware Stentinello vessels. In Greece, Vitelli (1993: 252) has argued that the dramatic increase in coarse wares in the Late Neolithic points to a 'significantly different kind of production, probably different producers and certainly different functions and roles for the pots.' She suggests that control of pottery production in the Greek Neolithic changed from 'specialists at the very beginning to non-specialists by the end of the period' (*ibid*.). Early Neolithic pottery in Greece, then, may have been related to shamans, sorcerers and healers and associated with music and 'medicines, debilitating poisons, and mind- or mood-altering potions' (Vitelli 1993:254). The situation is very different in southern Italy during the earlier Neolithic, with the predominance of coarse wares (on open settlements), but in co-existence with various finewares.

I wish to suggest that in southern Italy during the earlier neolithic (and perhaps in contrast to the Aegean), new foods and/or ways of food preparation and consumption were important in themselves, (recursively) embedded in changing social roles and practices, and that it was through these specific practices (among others) that pottery vessels became important constituters, and not just bearers, of symbolic meaning. Of course the association of pottery form and inter- or intra-household sharing and feasting, for example, has been made elsewhere, though usually in relation to finewares. However in neolithic southern Italy we see from the outset (however blurred in detail) *contextual* distinctions between ceramics associated with the utilitarian subsistence or 'domestic' sphere, and vessels at least partly reserved for other locations and practices. I wish to emphasise that though I am here concerned with imagining pottery as a novel resource within mundane practices as well as in what we may identify as cult or ritual contexts, I certainly do not wish in this way either to demystify, desymbolise or downplay the importance of its role. Rather I would argue that daily practices such as those of food acquisition, preparation, presentation and consumption are equally (or arguably more) important in the production, reproduction and transformation of habituses (*sensu* Bourdieu 1977, 1990), and consequent social roles and structures, than other apparently ritualised practices. These latter may in a sense be the crystallisation or legitimation of the cosmologies and ideologies which are practically instantiated in everyday life. Thus pottery as much as any other material culture is implicated in the construction and marking of those spatial and temporal rhythms and practices, and the production of both practical and discursive knowledges of social life.

Of course the apparently mundane function of (some) pots says nothing about the complexity or otherwise of understandings surrounding either the contexts of their production or use. To describe ceramics as either coarse or cooking wares tends to make us with our modernist and often utilitarian sensibilities downplay the possible proscriptions with which their production and consumption may be linked. Taboos and other forms of regulation may attend the process of extraction of clay from the earth, often perceived as mother or body (e.g. Barley 1994: 52; Gosselain 1992: 566); the making, firing and decoration of pots, including by whom, and when and where (e.g. Barley 1994: 63–64; David *et al.* 1988: 367; Haaland 1979: 57*ff*; Tobert 1984: 142); their use and categorisation, including by whom and for what purpose (e.g. Barley 1994: 59*ff*; Miller 1985; Müller-Kosack & Kosack 1988); and their disposal (e.g. Barley 1994: 73, 107, 112; Hodder 1982: 147, 166).

In southern Italy the 'arrival' of the Neolithic is often signified by an apparently more or less contemporaneous suite of elements including pottery, obsidian, polished stone artefacts, sheep and goats, and domesticated cereals – the traditional 'Neolithic package'. Nevertheless, this 'package' is introduced into an area, southern peninsular Italy and Sicily, at different times and into regions inhabited by hunter-gatherer societies with different traditions of, for example, hunting and fishing, flint procurement, lithic manufacture and artefact decoration, rock art, environments and landscapes; and by inference social structures and patterns of settlement and mobility (Pluciennik 1994: 336–340). The acquisition, preparation and consumption of food would have been one arena in which roles and practices may have been strongly structured by custom and tradition relating to age, gender and ascribed or achieved status, for example, defining who did what, where and when. The nature of relationships between groups or sections of communities may have been similarly defined, whether by 'exchange partners' or in other ways. In other words, neither the acquisition nor assimilation of novel resources – material and non-material elements of the 'neolithic package' – will have been adopted or otherwise spread within pristine, homogenous or unstructured social contexts, nor understood simply in functional or utilitarian ways.

If we assume that in some areas, at least, these novel resources (material or non-material, utilitarian and symbolic) were introduced into the existing hunter-gatherer communities, then the implication is that there may have been either differential access to, or claims or ability to manipulate the practical and symbolic capital associated with such elements. These new resources, including pottery, will inevitably, and both intentionally and unintentionally, have become implicated in the transformation (or maintenance) of existing practices, structures and understandings.

There is good evidence that one of those arenas may have been the gender roles associated with subsistence. Ethnographically, it is recorded that males are often actually and ideologically associated with hunting (especially for large-game), and women (and children) with gathering. Herded livestock may be associated with either or both, often depending on the location of the animals: those kept in close proximity to the settlement may be the responsibility of children and women, while those herded routinely further away from mixed-farming settlements are more often under the control of males (e.g. Almagor 1978: 91, 96; Galaty & Johnson 1990: 23–24; Khazanov 1984: 20). In Puglia, Whitehouse (1992) has argued plausibly that

the Grotta dei Cervi (Porto Badisco) may have been the site of a neolithic cult associating males with hunting, as a source of esoteric knowledge and power over females and/ or young males, in a society in which the settlement evidence shows little sign of consumption of wild foods. This is in contrast to the evidence from the Grotta dell'Uzzo, Sicily, for example, in which domesticated plants and animals represent a gradual addition and eventual substitution of wild species (Piperno *et al.* 1980b; Tagliacozzo 1993). It is possible that in the Puglian case the development of a male cult society may have been part of a reaction to changes in which the symbolic capital related to the use of novel plant resources and its associated pottery was appropriated by women, perhaps at the same time as such foods became in another sense 'mundane'. The baked clay female figurines known from neolithic settlement sites such as Rendina, Basilicata (Cipolloni Sampo 1983) and Passo di Corvo, Puglia (Tiné 1983) may also relate to these arenas of female control or power. Although Robb (1994a, 1994b) has argued that burial and other evidence points to binary gendering and an increasing ideology of male domination throughout prehistory, I would read the evidence differently for the earlier Neolithic. Noting the category of 'special burials' which Robb divides into (necessarily) already binarily sexed male-female categories (1994b: Figure 5, p. 47), I would argue that these demonstrate that in this sphere at least, the status or role that is symbolised is apparently open to males and females, though not equally (Pluciennik in press b; *cf.* Robb 1994a: 48). Gender relations too are dynamic, changing and contextually variable in the LUP, mesolithic and neolithic. Elsewhere, in different societies and different contexts in southern Italy and Sicily, both the modes and meanings of such appropriations of neolithic elements, including pottery, may have had different outcomes. At the Grotta di Sant'Angelo III in Calabria (see below), an unusual proportion of obsidian and fine pottery may signify the association of a certain restricted group with access to another 'exotic' resource.

Pottery and ritual

Examples from 'normal' settlement sites are sadly lacking due to the lack of contextual information, but from some of the 'cult caves' there is good evidence of special pottery used in atypical ways and circumstances. At the Grotta di Sant'Angelo III in Calabria, the lowest excavated stratum was dominated by painted *figulina* fabrics, with only a small proportion of coarser wares (Tiné 1964: 21–2). The ceramics were associated with, among other things, abundant obsidian, plus greenstone axes and numerous pestles and mortars. At the Grotta Latronico (BAS), albeit from chalcolithic and bronze age layers, vessels contained a mixture of wild fruits and cultivated cereal grains, interpreted as votive offerings (Rellini 1916). At the sealed Grotta Sant'Angelo (Quagliati 1931, 1934; Rellini 1934, 1935) and the Grotta dei Diavoli (Stasi 1906), both in Puglia, large quantities of neolithic pottery were found covering the floor and in a pool respectively: at the former Quagliati, who visited the site soon after its re-discovery, recalled that 'the broken vessels almost entirely covered the surface of the cave, so that on first entering one had to walk across them' (Quagliati 1934: 7). At the Grotta di Porto Badisco (PUG) and Grotta Scaloria (PUG), neolithic vessels had been placed to catch dripping water (*cf.* Whitehouse 1992; Grifoni-Cremonesi 1994). At Petraro di Melilli, Siracusa (SIC), a re-used karstic cavity was found (Sluga Messina 1988). At the rear was the lip of natural channel, roughly blocked. On the surface of the fill of the cave were ceramics, mostly ascribable to the early neolithic. There were also obsidian and flint flakes and two miniature stone axes about 5cm. long, and a number of river pebbles encrusted with ochre. Ochre was also thickly spread over the lip of the tunnel, containing numerous grindstones, and inside the blocking was a 'bed of red ochre in which were set fragments of bone' (*ibid.*: 83). The association of ?intentionally broken pottery with exotic materials and non-domestic or non-utilitarian practices strongly suggests that neither chronotypological analyses nor exchange models exhaust the potential of imaginative interpretations. The predominance of fine and painted wares at many of these cave sites argues for richly symbolic links between certain types of pottery and certain practices in specific contexts, at least. We can also see links between subsistence practices and the exotic which were structured and understood through cosmologies, cosmographies, and ritual and everyday social action. On many settlement sites anthropomorphic pots are common, while in many burials in neolithic southern Italy grave goods are 'limited' to pots or uncertainly associated broken sherds (Robb 1994a; Pluciennik 1994: 261–277). All these may offer us other connections between the body (individual and social), pottery, and life and death (*cf.* Barley 1994: 107; David *et al.* 1988; Hodder 1982: 166).

Discussion: pottery and other material culture

Primary materials, artefacts, ideas and styles are being transported by people in epipalaeolithic and neolithic southern Italy. How much of this is due to individual and group mobility, and how much to transfers between individuals or groups (i.e. 'exchange'), is uncertain. Such movement of materials is occurring (necessarily) by both sea and land. Perlès (1990; 1992) has argued in the case of the Aegean that sea-faring skills would have been confined to specialists, rather than being commonly held by members of virtually all communities. This seems plausible especially when considering the evidence of early island colonization (Cherry 1990). Such skills were necessary to reach Malta, Lampedusa, Pantelleria, Corsica and Sardinia by the early neolithic (at least). On the other hand we can note the widespread evidence for marine and coastal exploitation in the mesolithic (and pre-neolithic dates from Sardinia and Corsica; Cherry 1990), which at least implies a familiarity with these zones, as well as the possibility of 'coasting' in relation to the procurement of obsidian from Lipari. I have also suggested

that it was necessary to travel long distances from and to southern Puglia in the epipalaeolithic in order to procure flint. Nevertheless it seems likely that at least some of the material being carried the longest distances must have been moved via some process of exchange, whether generalized 'down the line' or by 'specialists', or a combination of the two. Skeates (1993) has suggested that certain sites (including caves) may have acted as 'regional foci for aggregation and ceremonial activities' in which 'inter-community alliances [were] ... accompanied by ceremonial exchanges of valuable gifts ...' (*ibid*: 110–111).

Other materials and stylistic zones seem to suggest interaction over lesser distances, perhaps generally less than 100km. This is the case, for example, for some other lithic materials found at the neolithic Tavoliere settlements: flint is being moved in blade form from the Gargano, and stone for querns, mortars etc. from Basilicata. Understanding the sorts of procurement and manufacturing processes involved is more difficult, though recent excavations at the flint mines of the Gargano (Galiberti 1987) may help. In Britain, for example, Edmonds (1993, 1995: 49–79) has recently discussed the social meaning of evidence that prehistoric flint mines were sites of intensive periodic use and deliberate backfilling; the nature and position of some of the stone-axe quarries also suggests that they must be considered as far more than purely functional extraction sites. Some procurement and production, then, may be better thought of as activity embedded in, or rather recursively involved in, practices undertaken by particular members or groups within communities, or perhaps temporary extra-community groups, and which would have explicitly or implicitly contributed to the construction of individual and/or group identities. Clearly, such activities were potentially just as necessary and likely in the epipalaeolithic as in the neolithic, but we have more archaeologically visible evidence in the latter period.

Finally, there is evidence of a whole host of materials moving over much shorter distances; the clays for daub (Ammerman *et al.* 1988) and for most types of pottery (Mannoni 1980, 1983; Williams 1980; Dell'Anna 1986; Skeates 1992); lithic production using local materials; and wood, other vegetable materials, animals (meat) and grain which are presumably deriving mostly from the immediate area.

From the little we know, the evidence suggests the existence of a series of various forms of interaction including 'exchange', partly related to but also cross-cutting material categories. For example, the wide distribution and abundance of obsidian in Sicilia and southern Calabria is not mirrored in the distribution of red-painted wares (see figure 3), though it is by the extent of the Stentinello ware tradition (figure 2). The nature of any particular mode of interaction seems to be potentially variable in space and time. However in terms of a general contrast between the mesolithic and neolithic we have evidence for an intensification or extension of the range of materials involved (pottery, obsidian, greenstone), and a tendency towards (archaeologically visible) expressions of local and regional differences through the medium of ceramics, at least, although there are also broad underlying similarities for the whole of the study area and beyond (e.g. the impressed/incised coarseware tradition in the central and western Mediterranean).

The distribution of styles and wares changes over time, with some types of wares becoming very widespread in the later neolithic (Serra d'Alto, Diana: figure 5). All this suggests a complex picture of function, meaning and interaction. Some of the differences across space and through time may relate to the contents and contexts of use of the vessels, rather than as objects in themselves (e.g. Lewthwaite 1981; *cf.* Chapman 1988). The apparently local nature of much pot production yet the existence of wide style-zones suggests that it was often ideas (styles and practices), rather than finished vessels, which were diffusing, whether by imitation, or via itinerant pot specialists (or other 'specialists' who were associated with pot – *cf.* Vitelli 1993), or by links between restricted sections of groups. It is tempting to link some unusual or exotic fineware pottery styles with 'cult caves' and hence perhaps in certain areas such as Puglia and in certain contexts, with males and mobility, for example (*cf.* Whitehouse 1992), and argue that pottery (and its associated practices) was certainly one medium through which gender differences may have been expressed and constructed.

Whatever the settings and practices involved, the procurement and production of exchange and other goods and participation in such practices may well not have been open to all within a community. As well as the physical objects such potentially restricted forms of social action and interaction also enables the acquisition of (or claims to) esoteric or exotic knowledge. Differential contact with other people, places and knowledges, may allow the consequent transformation of existing cosmologies and cosmographies. Different temporalities and spatialities offer ways of producing and manipulating geographical and historical imaginations, exercising social and political power, and reinforcing, reproducing and transforming social structures, roles and practices (see also Helms 1988, 1993). It is in this sort of anthropologically inspired approach to the mesolithic-neolithic transition that I see the richest interpretative possibilities. In general there is insufficient published contextual information for the southern Italian material to carry out the sort of analysis outlined above. However I have suggested that food preparation and food vessels (and perhaps the social roles and practices leading up to it) became one of those arenas of change. Here I saw a contrast to descriptions of the earlier Greek neolithic in which cooking practices perhaps remained more stable, and where pottery was apparently not used as a medium of expression in the same way. In southern Italy there is arguably continuity of mesolithic practices associated with wild animals (including the lithics), but which in the Neolithic become spatially separated from occupation sites. In neolithic burials and other practices we can also see at least a changed expression in ways of marking, and probably using and

moving through, as well as conceptualising, the landscape and settlement spaces. In the neolithic generally, and in contrast to the preceding societies, there is a greater concern with the marking of spatial boundaries (perhaps signifying other, conceptual boundaries too) and with the spatial separation of practices (Pluciennik 1994; *cf.* Robb 1994a: 50),. These different spatialities are expressive of different roles (though not necessarily by different individuals), and in one regional interpretation may be linked to gendered practices. For Puglia, Ruth Whitehouse (1992) has argued strongly that in fact male-controlled fertility cults may have been associated with an ideology of hunting and used to structure social relations in the southern Italian neolithic. She has also suggested (*cf.* Cullen 1985) that bride-exchange took place, one obvious mechanism for stylistic and other diffusion. I have also tentatively suggested that *if* males were linked with the cult caves and perhaps exotic materials which may sometimes include pottery, then the movement of (perhaps male) 'specialists', or at least restricted members of groups, may be another way to explain some of the widespread diffusion in material culture styles and practices (rather than items), which clay fabric analysis suggests. Of course, the two proposed modes are not mutually exclusive. Simultaneously, the (differential) possibility of the conflation of 'geographical' and 'historical' knowledges of other places, practices and people, partly evidenced in and through material culture, may have been a source for new strategies, social dynamics and (potential, actual, or at least altered) social differentiation and its expression.

At the same time, from examples of western Sicilian cave art, I have argued (Pluciennik 1996) for a reading perhaps expressive of the conjunction of 'human' and 'natural' time and concerned with the conceptual production of both in the Neolithic, compared with the previous emphasis on the marking of 'natural' time. Thus spatialities and temporalities both changed and drew on earlier practices and traditions. The widespread neolithic use of flexed burial positions (but very variable other burial practices), and the rapid spread of decorative styles in pottery, for example, both argue very strongly for non-material dimensions to neolithic diffusion too, as does the establishment of impressive ditched settlements in widely separated areas (the Tavoliere, eastern Basilicata, eastern Sicilia). Finally, one may note another change which participates in the mesolithic-neolithic transition: the diffusion of domesticated animals and plants. For example, at one the few sites which span the mesolithic-neolithic transition, the Grotta dell'Uzzo in Sicily, there is evidence of change and transformation, rather than revolution. The introduction of domesticated ovicaprines is gradual, and occurs in a setting of continuity in other spheres such as the lithics, wild fauna and even butchery techniques (Piperno 1978; Piperno *et al.* 1980a; Tagliacozzo 1995). This mixture of change and continuity may be argued to be mirrored by gradually increasing access to (or importance of) more varied types and styles of pottery. Rather than seeing the pottery sequence purely as a chronologically early phenomenon (the 'pure impressed' ware or 'pre-Stentinello' phase), it should be considered as evidence of changing attitudes, access to and perhaps integration with other communities. It is also from western Sicilia (albeit extremely poorly published) that we have a classic case of the seeming adoption of new ('neolithic') material culture within a 'mesolithic' context: the occurrence of two burials in the Grotta d'Oriente, both in similar (supine) positions, both with perforated shell necklaces, but the uppermost in association with pottery (V. Tusa 1977: 658; S. Tusa 1992: nota 21, p. 215)

A study of materials in Italy and elsewhere suggests that there was long-distance movement involving exchange before the neolithic (e.g Gronenborn 1990; Jochim 1990; Williams-Thorpe *et al.* 1979). Nevertheless there is evidence for changes in both the nature and scale of these movements. The sourcing of flint assemblages from sites in northern Italy suggests a change in procurement practices between the mesolithic and neolithic (Barfield 1987; Cremaschi 1981). The more local nature of the mesolithic site assemblages in conjunction with probably mobile communities suggests that procurement was to a large extent (and for this material) largely embedded (*sensu* Binford) or at least localized, and in relatively direct response to needs. By the neolithic period lithic materials are being obtained from greater distances from the sites. Although this is traditionally associated with exchange, one can argue that it is the *nature* of mobility which has changed. While this mobility may in a sense have been 'transferred' to some of the materials *per se* via changed exchange relationships, the evidence can also be interpreted as a changed distribution of mobility within the group or community. In other words the relative mobility among the *members* of each group may have altered. In line with my argument above about the diffusion of pottery *styles*, rather than necessarily pots, this may be used to suggest that both media and practices (and hence individual experiences and habituses) in the neolithic were potentially more various and separated in time and space at the local community level and beyond. The neolithic could then (generally) be argued to be a period with potential for increased social separation (of roles, mobility and other practices), or at least with more archaeologically visible expression of such potential differences. To consider merely whether new social perceptions arrived with new neolithic people, or as an entire ideology which was adopted (e.g. Thomas 1988, 1991), seems only to reproduce the simple mesolithic-neolithic dichotomy yet again. We have evidence for changing practices at all scales in both the mesolithic and neolithic. However, the exogenous techniques (ceramic technology), items (domesticates and cultigens) and practices (cultivation, herding and new forms of food preparation) associated with 'the neolithic' would certainly have offered new means and opportunities of expressing both existing and new statuses (*cf.* Armit & Finlayson 1992). They would *necessarily* have affected the construction of roles and identities for individuals and intra- and inter-community groups, and this may have included gender, age and other groupings.

Structures, spatialities and temporalities

I have been using the concepts of spatialities (which can be considered as structuration in space) and temporalities (structuration in time). Both are, of course, inevitably linked and implicated in each other. Spatiality can be considered as

> 'the organization, and meaning of space [which] is a product of social translation, transformation, and experience. Socially-produced space is a created structure comparable to other social constructions resulting from the transformation of given conditions ...' (Soja 1989: 79–80).

In an analogous way 'temporalities' refers to the specific and historical meaning(s) of time(s) which are constructed through the recursive relationships between cognition, perception, practice and experience in the material and in the social world. Spatialities and temporalities may thus be considered as historically particular, (though analytically-abstracted) structures emphasizing, respectively, space and time. Empirically, these can be approached both through an attempted straightforward description of past practices such as seasonal mobility, for example, or through more refracted instances such as the expression of concepts of time and space in art. Spatialities will be produced by direct experiences of both natural and built environments, and ways of using those environments. 'Direct experience' in the phenomenological sense in which I am using it here entails the sense of movement through space, which is defined through, for example, features in a landscape, buildings, and physical, social and conceptual boundaries which provide a constraint on movement. This (often habituated) constraint does not have to have a meaning *per se*. However, movement through space-time provides a sequence of experiences, which may generate meanings through the associations of those experiences or sequences of experiences. This is one of the senses in which I would wish to link the physical and social environment, social and physical landscapes, and temporalities and spatialities. Material culture is important because it may both objectify and symbolise these practices and concepts. That I have insisted on using these concepts in the plural is not purely an affectation: in the most undifferentiated society there are still likely to be differing concepts and experiences of both time and space according to different roles and practices (who goes where, when, and who does what).

We can see not only *different* temporalities, at least, in the LUP, but also suggestions of *changing* temporalities and spatialities in the LUP and mesolithic. However, in material terms there are also good arguments for both quantitative and qualitative changes in temporalities and spatialities in the neolithic. This concern with – or perhaps rather need to deal with – variable experiences is also perhaps reflected in the variety of movements, contacts, exchanges and practices. This is suggested by the evidence for different scales and locales of extraction, production, use, exchange and diffusion, for different classes and categories of material culture. This experience and awareness of different spatialities inevitably implied different temporalities. That there is a mixture of both patterns in both periods is a further argument for treating the LUP/mesolithic and the neolithic as 'equal' though different entities to be considered in their own right, in which communities/societies had their own (and own senses of) identities, histories and myths, and complex inter-relationships. This has profound implications for our perception of the 'mesolithic-neolithic transition'.

Pottery in the mesolithic-neolithic transition

The mesolithic-neolithic transition is often taken as synonymous with a change from hunter-gatherer to farming societies. Recent work in archaeology (Hodder 1990; Thomas 1988, 1991) has challenged this view. The problem has also produced a lengthy debate in anthropology: whether there are any necessary differences between these two categories of societies *beyond* our definition of their subsistence, such as ideology (e.g. Ingold 1986: 198–221; 1988), or social organisation (Lee & DeVore 1968; Murdock 1968; Bender 1985; Testart 1988; Bird-David 1990, 1992), for example (see Pluciennik in press a).

At the end of that paper, I suggested that 'the 'neolithic', far from (necessarily or invariably) being either a revolution or a package, may be 'just another' case of diffusion, but one which has been made special by our privileging of subsistence and economy as a classification within anthropology and archaeology, and of 'the farming way of life' in general. The mesolithic-neolithic transition may be considered on the one hand as part of a wider problematic of change, diffusion and interaction. Armit & Finlayson recently suggested that

> 'To Mesolithic groups, the elements which comprise our archaeological picture of the Neolithic would have represented a set of potentials. Material symbols associated with agriculture ... provided a range of new means of symbolic expression for Mesolithic groups' (1992: 674)

The nature of the evidence (poor temporal, spatial and contextual resolution) often makes it difficult to answer the question: What did the transition mean in southern Italy? Although I have suggested the outlines of a structural prehistory, I am unable to approach a detailed anthropologically-informed history. The contextual information, particularly from 'domestic' sites, is sadly lacking. No one model is likely to do justice to the potential complexity, and there was surely regional and chronological variability too. However, I believe that regionally different dynamic and historical societies came into increasing contact with one another from the early Holocene, at least. This is evidenced in the changing temporalities and spatialities I have proposed here. It suggests that there would also have been the development of new (intra and inter-societal) roles and senses of identity. The possibility of fragmentation and differentiation is supported by the local and regional variation in the natures, directions and scales of production, consumption and ex-

change in various material categories, including pottery, in varying contexts. Any changed conditions offer new possibilities, sources of social power, and new arenas for control. Pottery, as a material expression and archaeologically-surviving signifier of some of those conditions during the mesolithic-neolithic transition in southern Italy, partook of potentially changing cultural, historical and geographical imaginations in the past: if we can add our own anthropological imaginations, then the study of prehistoric pottery can become radically different to traditional understandings of what pottery means to archaeologists – and others.

Acknowledgments

I am extremely grateful to Chris Cumberpatch, Yannis Hamilakis, Louise Martin and Bill Sillar for discussion and references during the preparation of this paper.

References

Almagor, U. 1978 *Pastoral partners. Affinity and bond partnership among the Dassenetch of south-west Ethiopia*. Manchester: Manchester University Press.

Ammerman, A. (ed.) 1985 *The Acconia Survey: Neolithic Settlement and the Obsidian Trade*. London: Institute of Archaeology.

Ammerman, A. & Cavalli-Sforza, L. 1971 Measuring the Rate of Spread of Early Farming in Europe. *Man (N.S.)* 6:673–688.

Ammerman, A. & Cavalli-Sforza, L. 1973 A Population Model for the Diffusion of Early Farming in Europe. In *The Explanation of Culture Change: Models in Prehistory*, pp. 343–357 (ed. C. Renfrew). London: Duckworth.

Ammerman, A. & Cavalli-Sforza, L. 1984 *The Neolithic Transition and the Genetics of Populations in Europe*. New Jersey: Princeton University Press.

Ammerman, A., & Bonardi, S. 1985 Ceramica Stentinelliana di una Struttura a Piana di Curinga (Catanzaro). *Rivista di Scienze Preistoriche* 50:201–224.

Ammerman, A., Shaffer, G., & Hartmann, N. 1988 A Neolithic Household at Piana di Curinga, Italy. *Journal of Field Archaeology* 15:121–140.

Armit, A., & Finlayson, W. 1992 Hunter-Gatherers Transformed: the Transition to Agriculture in Northern and Western Europe. *Antiquity* 66:664–676.

Arnold, D. 1985. *Ceramic theory and cultural process*. Cambridge: Cambridge University Press.

Barfield, L. 1987 Recent Work on Sources of Italian Flint. In *The Human Uses of Flint and Chert*, pp. 231–239 (eds. G. de G. Sieveking & M. Newcomer). Cambridge: Cambridge University Press.

Barley, N. 1994 *Smashing pots. Feats of clay from Africa*. London: British Museum Press.

Barnett, W. 1990 Small-Scale Transport of Early Neolithic Pottery in the West Mediterranean. *Antiquity* 64:859–865.

Bender, B. 1985 Prehistoric developments in the American midcontinent and in Brittany, northwest France. In *Prehistoric Hunter-Gatherers. The emergence of cultural complexity*, pp. 21–57 (ed. T. Price & J. Brown). New York: Academic Press.

Bernabo Brea, L. 1970 Il Neolitico Mediterraneo Occidentale. In *Sources Archeologiques de la Civilisation Européenne*, pp. 40–60. Bucarest.

Bernabo Brea, L. 1987 Il Neolitico Nelle Isole Eolie. *Atti Della XXVI Riunione Scientifica del Istituto Italiano di Preistoria e Protostoria* 1:351–360.

Bernabo Brea, M. 1984 L'insediamento Neolitico di Tirlecchia (Matera). *Rivista di Scienze Preistoriche* 39:23–84.

Bernabo Brea, L., & Cavalier, M. 1960 *Meligunis – Lipara. Vol. 1.* Palermo: Flaccovio.

Bernabo Brea, L., & Cavalier, M. 1980 *Meligunis Lipara. Volume IV.* Palermo: Flaccovio.

Biagi, P. 1991 The Prehistory of the Early Atlantic Period Along the Ligurian and Adriatic Coasts of Northern Italy in a Mediterranean Perspective. *Rivista di Archeologia* 15:46–54.

Bird-David, N. 1990 The giving environment: another perspective on the economic perspective of gatherer-hunters. *Current Anthropology* 31: 183–196.

Bird-David, N. 1992 Beyond 'the hunting and gathering mode of subsistence': observations on Nayaka and other modern hunter-gatherers. *Man* 27: 19–44.

Brown, J. 1989 The Beginnings of Pottery as an Economic Process. In *What's New?* pp. 203–224 (eds. R. Torrence & S. Van der Leeuw). London: Unwin Hyman.

Bourdieu, P. 1977 *Outline of a Theory of Practice*. Cambridge: Cambridge University Press

Bourdieu, P. 1990 *The Logic of Practice*. Cambridge: Polity Press.

Chapman, J. 1988 Ceramic Production and Social Differentiation: The Dalmatian Neolithic and the Western Mediterranean. *Journal of Mediterranean Archaeology* 1(2):3–25.

Cherry, J. 1990 The First Colonization of the Mediterranean Islands: a Review of Recent Research. *Journal of Mediterranean Archaeology* 3(2):145–221.

Cipolloni Sampo, M. 1987 Problemes des Debuts de L'economie de Production en Italie sud- Orientale. In *Premières Communautés Paysannes en Méditerranée Occidentale*, pp. 181–188 (eds. J. Guilaine, J. Courtin, J.-L. Roudil & J.-L. Vernet). Paris: CNRS.

Cipolloni Sampo, M. 1983 Scavi nel Villaggio Neolitico di Rendina (1970 – 1976): Relazione Preliminare. *Origini* 11:183–354.

Cornaggia Castiglioni, O., & Menghi, L. 1963 Grotta Delle Mura – Monopoli. II: Paletnologia dei Livelli Olocenici. *Rivista di Scienze Preistoriche* 18:117–154.

Costantini, L., Piperno, M., & Tusa, S. 1987 La Neolithisation de la Sicile Occidentale D'apres les Resultats des Fouilles a la Grotte de L'Uzzo (Trapani). In *Premières Communautés Paysannes en Méditerranée Occidentale*, pp. 397–405 (eds. J. Guilaine, J. Courtin, J.-L. Roudil & J.-L. Vernet). Paris: CNRS.

Cremaschi, M. 1981 The Source of the Flint Artefacts for the Central Po Plain and Appennine Sites, Between the 7th and the 2nd Millenium (*sic*) BC. *Staringia (Third International Symposium on Flint)* 6:139–142.

Cullen, T. 1985 Social implications of ceramic style in the neolithic Peloponnese. In *Ancient technology to modern science*, pp. 77–100 (ed. W. Kingery). Colombus, Ohio: American Ceramic Society.

David, N., Sterner, J. & Gavua, K. 1988 Why pots are decorated. *Current Anthropology* 29: 365–389.

Dell'Anna, A. 1986 Applicazione Dell'analisi Mineralogica Allo Studio Della Ceramica Impressa di C.no San Matteo-Chiantinelle (FG). *Taras* 6:97–103.

Donahue, R., Burroni, D., Coles, G., Colten, R., & Hunt, C. 1992 Petriolo III South: Implications for the Transition to Agriculture in Tuscany. *Current Anthropology* 33:328–331.

Edmonds, M. 1993 Towards a Context for Production and Exchange: the Polished axe in Earlier Neolithic Britain. In *Trade and Exchange in Prehistoric Europe*, pp. 69–86 (eds. C. Scarre & F. Healey). Oxford: Oxbow Books.

Edmonds, M. 1995 *Stone tools and society*. London: Batsford.

Frangipane, M. 1975 Considerazioni sugli aspetti culturali neolitici a ceramica tricromica dell'Italia meridionale. *Origini* 9: 63–152.

Fusco, V. 1966 Resti di un Insediamento Neolitico Nell'isola di San Domino Alle Tremiti. *Atti Della X Riunione Scientifica del Istituto Italiano di Preistoria e Protostoria*:71–90.

Galaty, J. & Johnson, D. 1990 Introduction: pastoral systems in global perspective. In *The world of pastoralism*, pp. 1–34 (eds. J. Galaty & D. Johnson) New York: Guilford Press.

Geniola, A. 1987 Il Neolitico Della Puglia Centrale. *Atti Della XXV Riunione Scientifica del Istituto Italiano di Preistoria e Protostoria*:55–86.

Giannitrapani, E. 1993 Some Comments on Underground Religion. Cult and Culture in Prehistoric Italy, by Ruth Whitehouse. *Papers From the Institute of Archaeology* 4:91–97.

Gosselain, O. 1992 Technology and style: potters and pottery among Bafia of Cameroon. *Man (N.S.)* 27: 559–586.

Grifoni Cremonesi, R. 1994 Observations on the problems related to certain cult phenomena during the Neolithic in the Italian peninsula. *Journal of European Archaeology* 2: 179–197.

Gronenborn, D. 1990 Mesolithic-Neolithic interactions – the lithic industry of the earliest Bandkeramik culture site at Friedberg-Bruchenbrücken, Wetteraukreis (West Germany). In *Contributions to the Mesolithic in Europe*, pp. 173–182 (eds. P. Vermeersch & P. Van Peer). Leuven: Leuven University Press.

Guilaine, J. 1979 The Earliest Neolithic in the West Mediterranean: a new Appraisal. *Antiquity* 53:22–30.

Guilaine, J. 1980 Problèmes Actuels de la Neolithisation et du Neolithique Ancien en Mediterranee Occidentale. In *Interaction and Acculturation in the Mediterranean*, pp. 3–22 (eds. J. Best & N. De Vries). Amsterdam: B.C. Gruner.

Haaland, R. 1979 Ethnographical observations of pottery-making in Darfur, Western Sudan, with some reflections on archaeological interpretation. In *New directions in Scandinavian archaeology*, pp. 47–61 (eds. K. Kristiansen & C. Paludan-Müller). Copenhagen: National Museum of Denmark.

Halstead, P. 1989 The economy has a normal surplus: economic stability and social change among early farming communities of Thessaly, Greece. In *Bad year economics: cultural responses to risk and uncertainty*, pp. 68–80 (eds. P. Halstead & J. O'Shea). Cambridge: Cambridge University Press.

Hameau, P. 1987 Le Niveau a Ceramique Imprimee Dans le Neolithique Grec. In *Premières Communautés Paysannes en Méditerranée Occidentale*, pp. 329–334 (eds. J. Guilaine, J. Courtin, J.-L. Roudil & J.-L. Vernet). Paris: CNRS.

Helms, M. 1988 *Ulysses' Sail. An ethnographic odyssey of power, knowledge, and geographical distance*. Princeton: Princeton University Press.

Helms, M. 1993 *Craft and the kingly ideal. Art, trade and power*. Austin: University of Texas Press.

Hodder, I. 1982 *Symbols in action*. Cambridge: Cambridge University Press.

Hodder, I. 1990 *The Domestication of Europe*. Oxford: Basil Blackwell.

Ingold, T. 1986 *The Appropriation of Nature: Essays on Human Ecology and Social Relationships*. Manchester: Manchester University Press.

Ingold, T. 1988 Reply to Testart (1988). *Current Anthropology* 29(1):14–15.

Jochim, M. 1990 The Late Mesolithic in southwest Germany: culture change or population decline? In *Contributions to the Mesolithic in Europe*, pp. 183–191 (eds. P. Vermeersch & P. Van Peer). Leuven: Leuven University Press.

Khazanov, A. 1984 *Nomads and the outside world (Second edition)*. Madison: University of Wisconsin Press.

Lee R.B. & DeVore I. 1968 Problems in the Study of Hunters and Gatherers. In *Man the Hunter*, pp. 3–12 (eds. R. Lee & I. DeVore). Chicago: Aldine.

Lewthwaite, J. 1981 Ambiguous First Impressions: A Survey of Recent Work in the Early Neolithic of the West Mediterranean. *Journal of Mediterranean Archaeology and Anthropology* 1:292–307.

Lewthwaite, J. 1985a The Lacuna in the Lagoon: An Interdisciplinary Research Frontier in the West Mediterranean Holocene Palaeoecology and Prehistory. *Cahiers Ligures de Prehistoire et de Protohistoire (Nouvelle Serie)* 2:253–264.

Lewthwaite, J. 1985b From Precocity to Involution: the Neolithic of Corsica in its West Mediterranean and French Contexts. *Oxford Journal of Archaeology* 4(1):47–68.

Lewthwaite, J. 1986 The Transition to Food Production: a Mediterranean Perspective. In *Hunters in Transition*, pp. 53–66 (ed. M. Zvelebil). Cambridge: Cambridge University Press.

Lewthwaite, J. 1989 Isolating the residuals: the Mesolithic basis of man-animal relationships on the Mediterranean islands. In *The Mesolithic in Europe*, pp. 541–555 (ed. C. Bonsall). Edinburgh: John Donald.

Maggi, R. 1977 Gli Scavi Nelle Stufe di San Calogero sul Monte Kronio (Sciacca) e Rapporti fra la Sicilia e Malta Durante il Neolitico. *Kokalos* 23:510–518.

Malone, C. 1985 Pots, Prestige and Ritual in Neolithic Southern Italy. In *Papers in Italian Archaeology IV (ii): Prehistory. BAR Int. Ser. 244*, pp. 118–151 (eds. C. Malone & S. Stoddart). Oxford: British Archaeological Reports.

Malone, C. 1986 *Exchange Systems and Style in the Central Mediterranean 4500–1700 B.C.* Unpublished PhD Thesis, Trinity Hall, Cambridge.

Miller, D. 1985 *Artefacts as categories.* Cambridge: Cambridge University Press.

Milliken, S., & Skeates, R. 1989 The Alimini Survey: The Mesolithic-Neolithic Transition in the Salento Peninsula (S.E. Italy). *Institute of Archaeology Bulletin* 26:77–98.

Müller-Kosack, G. & Kosack, G. 1988 Reply to David et al. (1988). *Current Anthropology* 29: 384–385.

Murdock G.P. 1968 The Current Status of the World's Hunting and Gathering Peoples. In *Man the Hunter*, pp. 13–20 (eds. R. Lee & I. DeVore). Chicago: Aldine.

Peet, T. 1909 *The Stone and Bronze Ages in Italy and Sicily.* Oxford: Clarendon Press.

Perlés, C. 1990 L'outillage de Pierre Taillee Neolithique en Grece: Approvisionnet et Exploitation des Matieres Premières. *Bulletin de Correspondance Hellenique* 114:1–42.

Perlès, C. 1992 Systems of Exchange and Organization of Production in Neolithic Greece. *Journal of Mediterranean Archaeology* 5(2):115–164.

Peroni, R. 1967 *Archeologia Della Puglia Preistorica.* Roma: De Luca Editore.

Piperno, M. 1978 Scoperta di una Sepoltura Doppia Epigravettiana Nella Grotta Dell'Uzzo (Trapani). *Kokalos* 23:734–760.

Piperno, M., Scali, S., & Tagliacozzo, A. (Piperno *et al.*) 1980a Mesolitico e Neolitico Alla Grotta Dell'Uzzo (Trapani). Primi Dati per Un'interpretazione Paleoeconomica. *Quaternaria* 22:275–300.

Piperno, M., Tusa, S., & Valente, I. (Piperno *et al.*) 1980b Campagne di Scavo 1977 e 1978 Alla Grotta Dell'Uzzo (Trapani). *Sicilia Archeologica* 42:49–64.

Pluciennik, M. 1994 *The mesolithic-neolithic transition in southern Italy.* Unpublished Ph.D. thesis. Department of Archaeology & Prehistory, University of Sheffield. Also available via 'http://www.lampeter.ac.uk/archaeology/'

Pluciennik, M. 1996 Space, time and caves: art in the palaeolithic, mesolithic and neolithic of southern Italy. *Accordia Research Papers* 6: 61–81.

Pluciennik, M. (*in press* a) Deconstructing 'the neolithic' in the mesolithic-neolithic transition.' In *Social life and social change: the Neolithic of North-Western Europe* (eds. M. Edmonds & C. Richards).

Pluciennik, M. (*in press* b) Problems of sex and gender in prehistoric southern Italy. In *Gender and Italian Archaeology* (ed. R. Whitehouse). London: Accordia/Institute of Archaeology.

Quagliati, Q. 1931 L'uomo Neolitico Nella Caverna di Contrada Sant'Angelo ad Ostuni. *Japigia* 2:122–124.

Quagliati, Q. 1934 Caverna Preistorica di Ostuni. *Japigia* 5:3–18.

Rellini, U. 1916 La Caverna di Latronico e il culto delle acque salutari nell'età del bronzo. *Monumenti Antichi* 24: 416–631.

Rellini, U. 1934 *La piu Antica Ceramica Dipinta in Italia.* Roma: Collezione Meridionale Editrice.

Rellini, U. 1935 La Caverna di Ostuni. *Bullettino di Paletnologia Italiana* 55:27–31.

Robb, J. 1994a Burial and social reproduction in the peninsular Italian Neolithic. *Journal of Mediterranean Archaeology* 7: 27–71.

Robb, J. 1994b Gender contradictions, moral coalitions, and inequality in prehistoric Italy. *Journal of European Archaeology* 2: 20–49.

Skeates, R. 1992 Thin-Section Analysis of Italian Neolithic Pottery. In *Papers of the Fourth Conference of Italian Archaeology 3*, pp. 29–34 (eds. E. Herring, R. Whitehouse & J. Wilkins). London: Accordia Research Centre.

Skeates, R. 1993 Neolithic Exchange in Central and Southern Italy. In *Trade and Exchange in Prehistoric Europe*, pp. 109–114 (eds. C. Scarre & F. Healey). Oxford: Oxbow Books.

Sluga Messina, G. 1988 Villasmundo (Siracusa): Tomba Neolitica Presso il Villaggio Preistorico del Petraro. *Sicilia Archeologica* 68:81–85.

Soja, E. 1989 *Postmodern Geographies.* London: Verso.

Stasi, P. 1906 Grotta Funeraria a Badisco. *Archivio per l'Antropologia e la Etnologia* 36: 17–25.

Stevenson, R. 1947 The Neolithic Cultures of South-East Italy. *Proceedings of the Prehistoric Society* 3:85–100.

Tagliacozzo, A. 1993 *Archeozoologia della Grotta dell'Uzzo, Sicilia. (Supplemento al Bullettino di Paletnologia Italiana 84).* Roma: Istituto Poligrafico e Zecca dello Stato.

Testart, A. 1988 Some Major Problems in the Social Anthropology of Hunter-Gatherers. *Current Anthropology* 29(1):1–31.

Thomas, J. 1988 Neolithic Explanations Revisited: The Mesolithic-Neolithic Transition in Britain and Southern Scandinavia. *Proceedings of the Prehistoric Society* 54:59–66.

Thomas, J. 1991 *Rethinking the Neolithic.* Cambridge: Cambridge University Press.

Tiné, S. 1964 La Grotta di S. Angelo III a Cassano Ionio. *Atti e Memorie Della Societa di Magna Grecia* 5:11–55.

Tiné, S. 1970 Lo Stile del Kronio in Sicilia: lo Stile di Ghar Dalam a Malta e la Successione del Neolitico Nelle due Isole. *Atti Della XIII Riunione Scientifica del Istituto Italiano di Preistoria e Protostoria*:75–88.

Tiné, S. 1975 La Civilta Neolitica del Tavoliere. *Atti del Colloquio Internazionale di Preistoria e Protostoria Della Daunia*:99–111.

Tiné, S. 1983 *Passo di Corvo e la Civilta Neolitica del Tavoliere.* Genova: Sagep.

Tiné, S., & Bernabo Brea, M. 1980 Il Villaggio Neolitico del Guadone di S. Severo (Foggia). *Rivista di Scienze Preistoriche* 35:45–74.

Tobert, N. 1984 Ethno-archaeology of pottery firing in Darfur, Sudan: implications for ceramic technology studies. *Oxford Journal of Archaeology* 3: 141–156.

Tusa, S. 1983 *La Sicilia Nella Preistoria.* Palermo: Sellerio Editore.

Tusa, S. 1985 The Beginning of Farming Communities in Sicily: the Evidence of Uzzo Cave. In *Papers in Italian Archaeology IV (ii). BAR Int. Ser. 244.* Malone, C., & Stoddart, S, eds. Pp. 61–82. Oxford: British Archaeological Reports.

Tusa, S. 1992 *La Sicilia Nella Preistoria (Seconda edizione).* Palermo: Sellerio Editore.

Tusa, V. 1977 L'attivita Della Soprintendenza Alle Antichita Della Sicilia Occidentale nel Quadrennio Maggio 1972 – Aprile 1976. *Kokalos* 23:651–679.

Vitelli, K. 1989 Were Pots First Made for Foods? Doubts From Franchthi. *World Archaeology* 21(1):17–29.

Vitelli, K. 1993 Power to the Potters: Comment on Perlès' 'Systems of Exchange and Organization of Production in Neolithic Greece'. *Journal of Mediterranean Archaeology* 6(2):247–257.

Whitehouse, R. 1968a Settlement and Economy in Southern Italy in the Neothermal Period. *Proceedings of the Prehistoric Society* 34:332–367.

Whitehouse, R. 1968b The Early Neolithic of Southern Italy. *Antiquity* 42:188–193.

Whitehouse, R. 1969 The Neolithic Pottery Sequence in Southern Italy. *Proceedings of the Prehistoric Society* 35:267–310.

Whitehouse, R. 1986 Siticulosa Apulia Revisited. *Antiquity* 60:36–44.

Whitehouse, R. 1992 *Underground Religion. Cult and Culture in Prehistoric Italy.* London: Accordia Research Centre.

Williams, J. 1980 Appendice VII: A Petrological Examination of the Prehistoric Pottery From the Excavations in the Castello and Diana Plain of Lipari. In *Meligunis Lipára Vol. IV*, pp. 845–868 (eds. L. Bernabo Brea & M. Cavalier). Palermo: S.F. Flaccovio.

Williams Thorpe, O., Warren, S., & Barfield, L. 1979 The Sources and Distribution of Archaeological Obsidian in Northern Italy. *Preistoria Alpina* 15:73–92.

From ceramic finishes to modes of production: Iron Age finewares from central France

Kevin Andrews

Introduction

Research on the provenancing of prehistoric ceramics has drawn attention away from ceramic surfaces. Problems of surface contamination by percolating ground waters leaching out, or introducing elements (Freestone 1982), has skewed archaeometric analyses towards 'uncontaminated' cores of pottery sherds and away from surfaces whether they were decorated or not. Archaeometric work involving the examination of surface materials of ceramics such as slips and other decorative coatings was almost always avoided, interest being firmly set in analysis of body compositions (Wilson 1978:224). Analyses aimed at questions beyond provenancing have been comparatively rare.

Non-provenancing archaeometric research on coloured surface decoration has been restricted to chemical identification of pigments of well recognised categories of pottery such as the classical wares of the Aegean. Implications of results to the investigation of archaeologically meaningful questions such as those addressing the development of craft specialisation or the organisation of production, are rare. This appears to be a legacy of the emphasis on provenancing research which has, until relatively recently, dominated the scientific analysis of ancient pottery.

Reconstruction of ancient technologies (and the light such research throws onto our model building of the organisation of producing societies) is now healthily supplementing the focus of research into the provenance of an artefact. More archaeometric research is being undertaken which focuses on interpretation rather than technique (see for example, Henderson 1989). The general ability of archaeometrists to apply analyses to archaeologically significant questions, however, continues to be questioned (Jones 1988, Widemann 1982, Dunnell 1993).

Decorative surfaces on special classes of ceramic such as the Attic figure wares have always attracted considerable archaeometric attention. One of the first scientific analyses of decorative surfaces of ancient pottery was undertaken on Attic ware in 1756 (Binns and Fraser 1929:2). Then, as more recently (see Aloupi and Maniatis 1992), the main questions to be answered centred around determination of surface composition and methods of manufacture. With ever more sophisticated techniques, archaeometrists have revealed the enigmatic recipes of ancient decorative surfaces (Noble 1960, 1965; Hoffmann 1962; Noll 1977, 1978, 1979, 1981, 1982; Noll *et al.* 1974, 1972a, 1972b, 1975; 1980, Tite, *et al.* 1982a, 1982b, 1982c; Maniatis and Katsanos 1986; Maniatis and Tite 1978–9, 1981). Information concerning decorative technology gleaned from such analyses is often used for purposes of replication. Theoretical frameworks which use physico-chemical datasets to examine social and economic contexts of pottery manufacture are poorly developed.

This paper describes interpretative model building from results of an integrated archaeometric study of Late Iron Age finewares from the Auvergne region, France. The focus of this paper is on the formulation of models of production based on analytical results, rather than the results themselves. Details of the analyses are available elsewhere (Andrews 1993) and are summarised here (Appendix 1).

The impetus of the original analytical programme for the French material was based on a perceived need for basic information on the chemical composition and microstructure of coatings. What did the decorative coatings consist of? What pigments were present? What archaeometric techniques could provide answers? Such archaeometric information is often sought aimlessly, having been generated by the fashion for 'scientific' addenda which somehow add rigour to research. When scrutinised such applications of material science are often tangential to meaningful archaeological questions. A vital question (and one centred on the theme of this volume) should be: how can details of chemical composition and technological data obtained from ancient pottery help inform our understanding of the past? This information could be used, perhaps, to more accurately model the manufacturing processes involved, and thereby determine the degree of specialisation and labour investment/organisation required for production of slipped wares.

The development of a theory of production is described in the first part of this paper. A series of models is developed which suggest the likely sequence and modes of production involved in the manufacture of a distinctive late Iron Age fineware: slip-decorated (or painted) pottery. The models are based on information derived from physico-chemical analyses of the decorative finishes.

Model building: Formalist economic theory

A major interpretative role of the archaeometric study of decorative coatings is in its ability to illuminate theories concerning the technology of fineware pottery production. Technology has only relatively recently acquired a status in archaeological thinking and practice as a subject area which is of intrinsic interest (cf. Pfaffenberger 1988; Vandiver 1988, Vandiver *et al.* 1990). The first essential step toward a study of prehistoric technology is to unload the ethnocentric pre-understandings with which the word 'technology' is burdened (Pfaffenberger 1988:236). This unloading process includes a consideration of the relationship of 'technology' with the 'economy' within the social framework. Whether we view the 'economy' as a substantive or formal construct will affect our model building.

The principal 'economic' debate within archaeology has concerned the ways in which 'the economy' should be defined and how its role should best be understood in non-capitalist societies. Debate has been undertaken within academic disciplines such as history, anthropology and economics. It has spilled over into archaeology with concepts being borrowed (often with little regard as to whether they are appropriate to our models of prehistoric societies). Although debate has subsided in recent years, it has affected archaeological interpretation, with many archaeologists resting on adopted concepts from very specific anthropological contexts (such as reciprocity and redistribution) which are often (when critically examined) found to be inappropriate to a given prehistoric context.

Formalist (of neo-classical) economic theory rests on the view that all people (despite cultural differences) are essentially 'economic' in that they seek to allocate limited resources to obtain maximum return with respect to a set of ranked goals. Such rationalisation of resources is not, according to formalist theory, necessarily explicit. Rather it is the observer who interprets 'economic' behaviour. The formalist approach was devised to interpret economic behaviour of capitalist societies. Whilst it was realised that the economic organisation of non-capitalist societies was significantly different, the ability of the main elements of the theory (such as rationalisation of the allocation of scarce resources) to cross cultural barriers intact was accepted by the formalists (Schneider 1974:9).

The cultural differences observed in 'primitive' societies in terms of the huge variety in material culture and variety in the complex ritual responses to (for example) birth, marriage and death was seen to mask a straightforward study of simple allocation of materials. Burling (1978:176) considered 'economics' in such societies as the allocation of scarce resources to maintain multiple 'objectives' which moved beyond rationalisation of materials but extended also to more ethereal 'commodities' such as personal relationships and leisure. As Gosden (1983:10) points out, regarding such impalpable elements as 'relationships' and 'leisure time' within the sphere of economic theory threatens to broaden the economic field to include all aspects of human behaviour, and thus devalues any model based on formalist economic theory.

The view that allocative behaviour (for the purposes of maximisation of commodities however defined) is a universal human characteristic is a cornerstone of formalist economic theory (Cumberpatch 1991). Sahlins (1974) and Gregory (1982) have demonstrated that human behaviour is not universally orientated towards the maximisation of goals. The formalist approach copes with such criticism by suggesting that the analyst has not identified the subject of maximisation in behaviour which seemingly has no reference to it. The major criticism of the formalist approach is its failure to explain the variability of human groups and their institutions (Donham 1981).

The ability of formalist economic theory to explain the social fabric of non-capitalist societies is limited. Whilst the study of allocative behaviour is a useful way of analysing the economic behaviour of societies influenced by Western economic logic, to set maximisation behaviour as universal and apply it to those societies operating within logic systems exclusive of capitalist systems imposes ethnocentric values on such societies. The alternative approaches described in the following discussion seek to limit the implication of Western economic thought. It is from the non-formal economic theory that the concept of 'mode of production' has been drawn (see later).

Alternative approaches: substantivism and Marxism

The non-formalist approaches to the economy are united in regarding the economy as being driven by necessities. Such approaches differ from formalism in that such necessities are not based on the principle of maximisation; rather the various forms of economic organisation (past and present) can be explained in historically and culturally specific ways. Space precludes a detailed consideration of the major schools of non-formal economic thought, but a brief consideration of substativism and Marxism and their relationship to archaeological analysis will provide the necessary background to further discussion. A more detailed discussion of the third major non-formal economic school, 'political economy' will show that the non-formal approach holds the highest potential for archaeological interpretation.

Polanyi *et al.* (1971) first used the term 'substantivism' to describe a different outlook to the study of human economic behaviour. He referred to a substantive meaning of economic whereby people interact with their natural and social environment in such a way which results in the satisfaction of a material want (*ibid.*:243). A distinction was made between the formal term economic which can be seen as deriving from 19th and 20th century logical capitalism, and the unconnected substantive meaning. Polyani *et al.*

(1971:244) considered the substantive meaning of economic to have no implications of choice or limited resources. Polyani's explanation of how a non-capitalist economy operates involved reference to the exchange of goods within various social contexts by means of 'forms of integration' which he termed reciprocity, redistribution and exchange. The three types of exchange were economic mechanisms which implied a form of social organisation beyond the realm of production and exchange (Polyani *et al.* 1971: 250). The relationship between the economy and the social structures in which they operated was described by Polyani as being either 'embedded' or 'disembedded'. 'Embedded economies' referred to those in which the economic structures were firmly located within non-economic structures such as familial and kinship groups, and which are governed by such social formations. 'Disembedded economies' referred to those in which the economy is separate from social structure, such as in the capitalist system.

The reciprocal and redistributative categories of Polyani's 'forms of integration' (1971) were investigated in detail by Sahlins (1974). Sahlins' ideas have permeated archaeological interpretation, the connection between reciprocity and redistribution with certain inferred social formations becoming the foundation of many models of prehistoric socio-economic systems (see for example, Brumfiel and Earle 1987).

A serious criticism of the substantivist outlook derives from the school of Marxist anthropology. This school views substantivism as not essentially incorrect but rather too superficial to be of benefit to our understanding of the complexities of the relationship of economic and social organisation (Gosden 1983, Cumberpatch 1991, in prep.).

There is no place here for a detailed discussion of the complex and divided field of marxist anthropological theory. For in depth discussion see Bloch (1983). It will be sufficient here to outline those elements of the Marxist model which are relevant to the present discussion. In the subsequent section on 'political economy' certain Marxist concepts and terms will be re-evaluated and re-defined in an attempt to present a theoretical framework in which the results of the analyses presented here (together with related research) can be most usefully interpreted.

The basis of the Marxist approach to social systems is concerned with an understanding of the ways in which production and organisation of labour influence their structure. The Marxist school considers 'production' as the common basis for all social systems. 'Production' is the means whereby, through labour organised in a variety of ways, the natural world is transformed into products which are necessary or useful to society. The ways in which labour is organised in different societies is central to the Marxist approach. The needs of the social group are seen as being met by the labour of its members, either by production for their own consumption, or for exchange with other groups. The concept of the 'mode of production' is central to the understanding of this process. For now it is sufficient to note that generally the 'mode of production' describes the relationship between the forces of production (work-force, technique and equipment) and the relations of production (the social relationships involved, including such things as rights of access to the forces of production)(Gosden 1983:25). The institutional formations of society are not governed solely by the forces and relations of production, since the mode of production is also governed by rules derived from kinship-based, religious, ideological, legal and political social subsystems. In attempting to model the 'mode of production' for a non-capitalist society, or reconstruct one from archaeological evidence, we are faced with many problems owing to the potential complexity and variability of the interelatedness of the mode of production with such social subsystems.

A basic criticism often levelled at Marxism is that it is a form of economic determinism, and that by placing, as it does, production at the centre of society, its economic organisation is distortedly seen as the origin of cultural, social, political and intellectual activity. The importance attached to the social relations of production by the Marxist school acknowledges the problem of determining the precise role of the economy in society. Far from being mere economic determinism such an approach is a means of attempting to unravel the social role of the economy (Gosden 1983:29).

Only a small proportion of Marx's work concerned non-capitalist societies which were inadequately studied at his time. Marx had nevertheless entered the field of the 'political economy' (Gregory 1982) which assumes that socio-economic formations are historically specific. Contemporary Marxist scholars have therefore found common ground with the substantivist approach in terms of basic frameworks. The emphasis of Marxist theory on the interrelation of economic and social structures offers a more useful approach to archaeological problems than does substantivism.

Political economy

The central idea of the economic theory known as the 'political economy' is that it is impossible to distinguish 'economic' from 'social' activity (Wolf 1982, Cumberpatch 1991, in prep.). All actions are considered as ultimately rooted in the social, or to have social significance. The works of Marx and Adam Smith (and others) formed this school of economic thought, which was effectively eclipsed by the rise of neo-classical economics and sociology (Wolf 1982). Their work has been re-evaluated in the light of anthropological work, especially that of Claude Lévi-Strauss and Marcel Mauss (Gregory 1982). The theoretical framework propounded by Gregory has proven useful for archaeological interpretation (Bradley 1985; Morris 1986; Gosden 1989), and has provided a rewarding approach to the study of the Late Iron Age in central Europe (Cumberpatch, 1989, 1991). Cumberpatch has suggested that the principals of political economy, with their emphasis on the historical specificity of social formations, offers a potentially useful way of describing the organisation of production within a non-capitalist society.

There are several aspects of Gregory's theoretical framework (1982) which have potential in an interpretation of the production of finewares in Iron Age Central Europe. Firstly Gregory's approach to the political economy stresses the need to view the nature of social control over access to the means of production as being historically specific (Gregory 1982:13), any models concerning the control of production through social relations must therefore contain an element of flux and be re-formulated owing to historical specificity. An understanding of the institutionalisation and organisation of control over production is therefore fundamental to any social analysis.

Another definitive aspect of Gregory's approach is the circular model of production and consumption. Marx advocated an economic model in which production, distribution, circulation and consumption were seen holistically, with production as the predominant element. Production and consumption are seen as indivisible since consumption is necessary for production in terms of the labour and materials consumed in the production process. This concept is termed 'productive consumption' (Gregory 1982:30–31). Further to this, consumption is necessary for reproduction. For people to reproduce, consumption of food is necessary (together with the consumption of labour and materials necessary to acquire the food). This concept is termed 'consumptive production' (*ibid.*).

Finally political economy employs a characteristic method of investigation which Gregory calls the 'logical-historical' method. This involves linking a series of general categories with a unifying principle. Gregory uses the relationship of the producer to the means of production as such a principle. Since such a method of enquiry is founded on production, it has enormously wide applicability in archaeological model building (Cumberpatch 1991:118).

Using these principles of political economic theory, Gregory produced a logical-historical categorisation of social formations which stressed a continuum from clan to class based structures. Equal access to land (as a means of production) and the close relationship of the producer with the means of production in clan based societies, gives way in the broad continuum to inequality of access to, and separation from, the means of production in class based societies (Gregory 1982:36–7, Cumberpatch 1991). Within the continuum of social structures were sub-groups defined by methods of transacting labour, lineage control, and exchange mechanisms, which although being seen as useful, have also been criticised as being a rather generalising approach (e.g., see Morris 1986).

Any analysis of a given society and its relationship to Gregory's logical-historical continuum of economic forms requires an *a posteriori* investigation of the organisation of production in the case to be considered. The following sections describe a set of methodological principles based on the political economic theory discussed above. These principles have been formulated to assist in the investigation and description of economic systems and to develop an approach for the interpretation of results of analysis of the Auvergne pottery, of which the archaeometric investigation of the fineware coatings has been an integral part.

The mode of production

Through the discussion of economic theory presented above, it is clear that a meaningful model of the economic behaviour of a given society should recognise the feedback mechanisms of consumptive production and productive consumption through which the social formation operates. Moreover, the model should seek to present the economy as part of the overall social fabric.

The central methodological principle to be considered in the formation of such a model is that of the 'mode of production'. For non-capitalist societies, the 'mode of production' has been defined as: 'an articulated combination of relations and forces of production structured by the dominance of the relations of production' (Hindess and Hurst 1975:10).

Several authors have sought to formulate models of modes of pottery production operating in prehistoric societies. The mode of production models independently developed by Peacock (1982:8–10) and Van der Leeuw (1976:402–3; 1984) differentiate between household (or domestic) production and several modes of specialised production: household industry; individual workshop industry; nucleated workshop industry; and the manufactory. Each mode is defined by a particular configuration of variable factors. These include: the frequency (intensity) and seasonality of pottery production; the number and sex of the workers together with their age and status relationships; the extent of labour division; the degree of investment in specialist equipment such as kilns or wheels; and the variability in the raw materials exploited and in the range of pottery produced. Each mode (as formulated by van der Leeuw 1976:402–3, van der Leeuw and Pritchard 1984 and Peacock 1982:8–10) is described below.

In the household, or domestic, mode of production, each household produces the pottery it requires for its own use. The vessels will be functional and made to traditional (and conservative) cultural recipes with little in the way of experimentation or variability. The production will be sporadic and on an *ad hoc* basis, vessels being produced as they are required (for example to replace a broken vessel). Such production could be in the form of an annual (or longer) cycle (Peacock 1982:8). The limited or sporadic nature of pottery production will preclude investment in elaborate technology such as the wheel, turntable or kiln. Such production is typically seen to be in the hands of women. This mode of production is based on self-sufficiency, with little in the way of intensification or specialisation (Rice 1987:184).

The concept of 'household industry', developed by van de Leeuw (1976), represents a form of craft specialisation. Pottery making is seen to be in the hands of a few skilled artisans. Peacock (1982:8) does not follow van der Leeuw in restricting consumption to group use. This mode has been described as 'potting for profit' (Peacock, *ibid*.). Potting is a part-time activity, perhaps restricted by scheduling conflicts to an activity which is undertaken when there is a lull in the investment required in the major subsistence activity (agriculture). Investment in equipment is likely to be slight. The level of activity may warrant a turntable but not a wheel, and open firings will be the rule, but some form of oven or rudimentary kiln may be employed (Peacock 1982:8). Production in this mode is likely to be in the hands of women (Rice 1987:184) and a feature of areas where agricultural potential is poor and pottery production provides a supplementary income (*ibid*.). It may also be a feature of those areas where control over access to the means of agricultural production is limited by socio-political factors.

In the case of the individual workshop, pottery making is a primary source of subsistence (but perhaps not for the whole year). Since production is aimed at specific markets which demand certain qualities technological investment is likely to include the use of the wheel and a developed kiln (Peacock 1982:9). It has been suggested that the labour force will be increased and may comprise a small team such as a family group. Production is typically in the hands of men who have significant capital investments (kilns, wheels) and who derive their major livelihood from potting. Workshops are usually isolated and distribution may be by 'rudimentary marketing systems' (Rice 1981, 1987:184; Peacock 1982:31).

The 'nucleated' workshop represents an intensification of production. In this mode of production individual workshops are grouped together to form an industrial complex (Peacock 1982:9). Nucleation may be favoured by the availability of raw materials, labour, markets and other socioeconomic and political factors. Pottery production is a major activity, the work-force requiring subsistence support via exchange mechanisms with the rest of society, or being supported by an elite who seek to control access to the products of the workshop. Sometimes climate may preclude year round production, but every effort will be made to expand the season, for example by the use of drying sheds (*ibid*.). An element of competition will help to elevate technique to the highest level and the production will be characterised by a fairly standardised range of high-quality vessels (*ibid*.). Nucleated workshops are typically integrated with urban market economies and rely heavily on the activity of brokers (Rice 1987:184). Also referred to as 'village industry', 'domestic industry', or 'dispersed manufactory' these units may be in urban areas but are especially notable as features of rural regions (*ibid*.).

The manufactory represents an extreme of specialisation whereby a number of artisans are grouped together in a single building or place and co-operate in producing a single, highly specialised product. The production process will be divided into its component steps with the workers specialising to an extreme degree (Peacock 1982:9). Peacock sees scale as the key to the definition of a manufactory and gives an arbitrary figure of twelve or more workers. To avoid ambiguity it may be useful to note that a factory is

defined as a place of manufacture which employs mechanical power other than that of animal or human power, and as such are not generally a feature of prehistoric societies (Peacock 1982:10).

Peacock (1982:8) recognises that in reality the mode of production is infinitely variable, with many examples falling between, rather than within, these modes. There are problems in identifying modes from archaeological remains, few test implications have been developed on the basis of ethnographic data (Rice 1987:204–5; Underhill 1991:12). Rice (1987:222) views the model of mode of production (Table 1) as evolutionary and thus implicitly formalistic. This view has led to the subdivision of the basic model; Underhill (1991:13–14) for example, suggests a subdivision of 'household industry' into 'simple' and 'complex'. This subdivision is unnecessary if the scheme is used as a heuristic, flexible model rather than a formal and definitive one in which the production process in question becomes fossilised within the rigid conceptual framework.

Cumberpatch (1991) has proposed a redefinition of the term 'mode of production' which, whilst retaining the fundamental pivot between forces and relations of production, operates at a methodological (heuristic) level rather than as pure social theory.

The mode of production redefined

Pottery production processes, as discussed above, have been described in terms of various configurations of technical and social variables. The concept of 'mode of production' as outlined by the formulation of such configurations is essentially a technological and behavioural one, with the social aspects remaining implicit (Cumberpatch 1991:129–131). Following the Marxist conception of the mode of production as an aspect of the social formation (whether definitive or not), then the social dimensions of the technologically descriptive configurations become relevant, importantly allowing us access to the social organisation of production through the archaeological record. The mode of production then can be seen as a configuration of relationships which link the social and economic spheres, rather than a simple description of the methods (techniques) of production (Cumberpatch, pers. comm.). Drawing on the work of Balibar (1970) Cumberpatch has developed a scheme defining the elements or 'components' of any mode of production:

Raw material
Labour
Technology
Output

These components are essential to all modes of production, being fundamental to the process in the sense that, in the absence of any one, production could not take place. Each component can also be considered with reference to variables such as the division and intensity of labour involved, or the procurement and processing necessary in

Table 1.

Components and variables	HOUSEHOLD PRODUCTION	HOUSEHOLD INDUSTRY	INDIVIDUAL WORKSHOP	NUCLEATED WORKSHOP	MANUFACTORY
RAW MATERIAL					
Procurement	Haphazard	Increasingly regular	Regular use of known sources with increase in processing	Regular use of known sources with advanced processing such as levigation elutriation, grinding, etc.	Use of known sources with well known properties
Processing	Minimum	Minimum			
LABOUR					
Division/ Organisation	Individual	Individual	Family group	Highly organised	Production processes are specialised so that there are many workers in a force with specialist division of labour. Peacock (1982) gives an arbitrary figure of 12 or more
Intensity (specialisation)	Low	Low specialisation	Individual specialist knowledge	High degree of specialism Several full-time workers with internal hierarchy	
Number of workers	Few	Few	Rising		
Seasonality	High	High	Low	Low seasonality	Non-seasonal
TECHNOLOGY					
Complexity/ investment	Low/Low	Low-rising (e.g. turntable)	Permanent facilities: workshop, wheel, kiln, levigation tanks or similar preparation facilities and increasing number of production steps involved	High investment in permanent facilities such as workshops, drying sheds, kilns etc.	High investment in permanent facilities
Techniques of production	Simple	Low-rising		Complex sequence of production with possible division of labour	Production steps tailored to maximum output
OUTPUT					
Quantity	Low	Low-rising	Rising	High	High
Variability	High	High	Low- standard range	Specific range of products	Very low variability

obtaining raw materials. The components and variables comprising a mode of production are seen in Table 2. Thus the effective redefinition of the mode of production is that it is 'a specific configuration of variables constituting a production process' (Cumberpatch, pers. comm.).

Cumberpatch diverges from Balibar (1970) and other strands of Marxist scholarship in that his conceptualisation of the mode of production allows for coeval modes within the same social formation. Thus society is not dominated or defined by a single mode of production, rather a given social formation can be seen as being composed of a coincidence of modes of production which will vary owing to particular historical circumstances. Cumberpatch (*op. cit.*)

Table 2. Components and variables comprising the mode of production (after Cumberpatch, 1991).

Components	Variables
Raw materials	Procurement (including transport) Processing
Labour	Division/organisation Intensity Number of labourers involved Seasonality
Technology	Complexity/investment Sequence/techniques of production
Output	Quantity Variability

points out that in certain specific historical circumstances, one particular mode may achieve pre-eminence to a degree which allows for the social formation to be defined by that mode, but maintains that in general the concept of the mode of production is not definitive. It can be envisaged that a number of modes of production will increase during periods of transition, or in societies that are especially complex or interactive with others. Thus an additional complexity of the articulation between different modes of production can be seen whilst the social component of each remains integral (Cumberpatch 1991: 131).

In practice the investigation of such articulating modes of production requires the detailed pluralistic examination of the entire pottery assemblage from a series of sites within a given region (as well as examination of other manufactured goods from metals, stone and bone to glass, tile and brick for examples).

Table 1 (based on Cumberpatch 1991: Table 3.2) illustrates five modes of production, derived from those defined by Peacock (1982:6–11) and Van der Leeuw (1976:402–403) which have been discussed above. If the scheme presented in Table 1 is seen as evolutionary, involving a progression from household production to production in the manufactory, then it is implicitly formalist (and as such, as discussed above, of little use in archaeological interpretation). Conversely if it is seen, as it has been formulated here, as a logical-historical categorisation, then it becomes appropriate to the working of a non-capitalist economy (Cumberpatch 1991: chapter 3). It also can be seen as a non-formal, heuristic device, and as such a useful theoretical framework on which to formulate and carry ideas resulting from the archaeometric analyses.

The methodology used to define a mode of pottery production has to be based on detailed examination of the vessels involved from the point of view of production technology. The aim is to reconstruct as fully as possible the components and variables which were involved in the manufacture of the vessels. In this respect the results of the analyses presented here represent an essential contribution, for without a precise knowledge of the nature of the decorative coatings in terms of their composition, preparation, application and the technology involved in their production it is difficult to establish their likely relationship to the mode of production models presented here. We can suggest a mode of production (as re-defined above) for any given artefact based on a detailed knowledge of from what

and how it was made. Once the technological characteristics of an artefact have been defined by detailed physico-chemical analyses, the sequences of its production can be described. The remaining variables constituting the mode of production can then be considered from an ethnographic and inferential viewpoint, (with reference for example to the ethnographically based models described in Table 1) which will serve to suggest definition of those variables which are largely invisible in the archaeological record.

The analysis of Iron Age coated ceramics

The fineware ceramics investigated are from the study area of the Auvergne in central France (Fig.1). They date the Iron Age and early Roman periods (c500BC–50 AD).

The typical excavated assemblage includes a wide range of coated ceramics. This includes the red and white 'painted pottery', black-burnished wares, grey reduced wares, white

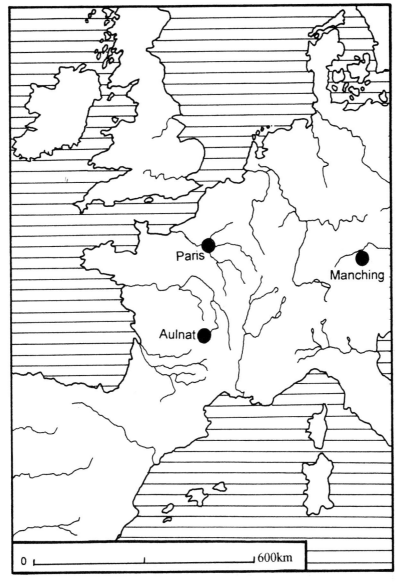

Fig. 1. Map of central Europe showing location of Aulnat.
Aulnat is shown in relation to Paris and the well-known site of Manching in Bavaria. (Source: author).

slipped flagons and a range of less well defined groups such as red-slipped wares and the wares produced by the developing Samian industries in the early Roman period. The later finewares also include samples such as the Campanian wares imported from Italy and imitation Campanian wares which were probably attempts by local potters to reproduce valuable imports using local resources (Morel 1978, 1982), and which represent copies of exotic styles using local materials and technology.

It is increasingly recognised that an integrated approach using several physico-chemical techniques is imperative for the investigation of the technological aspects of ancient ceramics (Rice 1982, Kilikoglou *et al.* 1992:118). Methods used in this present study included: optical microscopy, scanning electron microscopy with associated energy dispersive micro-spectroscopy (SEM/EDAX); x-ray diffraction analysis (XRD); surface examination using fibre optic video-equipment; and refiring experiments. A range of fresh fracture, polished, thin section and as received samples were examined. Three groups of finewares were originally considered; slip decorated (or painted) pottery, black slip-burnished ware, and white slipped flagons (Andrews 1993). For reasons of space only the slip decorated pottery will be dealt with here.

The sequence and mode of production of slip decorated pottery

The fragmentary condition of the assemblage from the sites of Aulnat and Gerzat-Patural (Collis 1975, 1980, 1984, Collis *et. al.* 1983) has limited those observations which could be made concerning the size and shape of the slip decorated

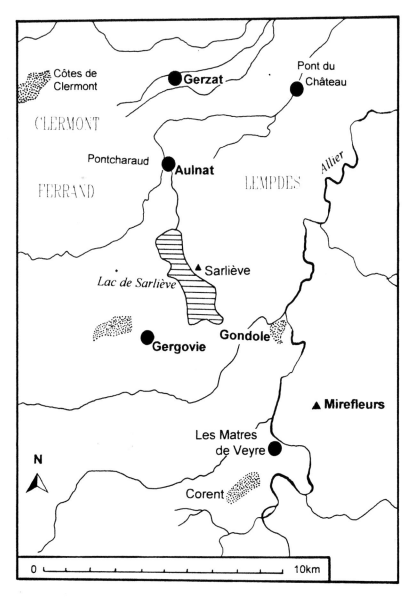

Fig. 1b. Aulnat and Gerzat location map.
The sites of Aulnat and Gerzat are shown in relation to the Auvergne area, in particular the Oppidum site of Gergovie (the 'capital' of the Arverni tribe) and Les Matres de Veyre which became a major pottery production centre following the Roman conquest of Gaul.

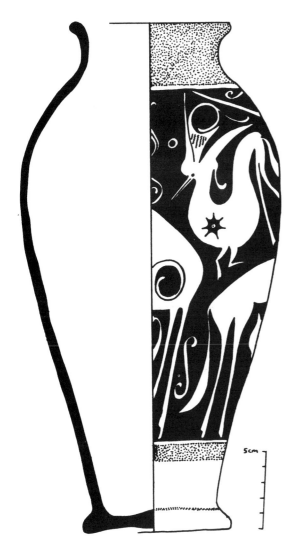

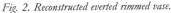

Fig. 2. Reconstructed everted rimmed vase.

Fig. 3. Reconstructed design.

vessels. Complete slip decorated pottery vessels are known in various forms such as dishes, bowls, and bottle-like vessels with amphora shaped bodies. Comparative material from central Europe consists of a variety of forms including deep in-turned rimmed bowls and tall bottle-like forms (e.g. Wirska-Parachoniak 1980, Cumberpatch 1991). Examination of the fragmentary rim, body and bases from the Aulnat assemblage indicates two main vessel forms: everted rimmed, closed vases, and in-turn rimmed open bowls (Watson 1988:50). The thickness of the sherds varied by only 5 mm, all were from fairly thin walled vessels (4–9mm). Figure 2 shows a reconstructed everted rimmed vase whilst figure 3 illustrates the reconstructed design.

Slip decorated pottery was thrown on a fast wheel of a fine, micaceous fabric containing inclusions, most commonly quartz. The distinguishing feature of this distinctive ceramic type is the presence of a coating of coloured slip. Most, if not all, of the external (and rarely some internal) surfaces are coated with slips of one or more colours. The most common colours are reds and whites (red-oranges, dark red/ browns and white/creams, beiges) and more rarely mauve/ greys, which appeared as black on better preserved (for

example water-logged) specimens (Guichard, pers. comm.). Three main colour groups were identified: bright 'paper' white (Münsell: white 5YR 8/2; an "off white", cream colour (Münsell: very pale brown 10YR 7/3; and orange/red (Münsell: red 10R 5/8. A fourth colour, the mauve/grey (Münsell: light brownish gray 10YR 6/2) was often very thin and ephemeral. This colour was used to paint on bold designs, not all of which have survived. Analysis has confirmed the basic divisions of reds, bright whites, creams and the mauve/greys as compositionally distinct (see tables 3– 4) although there were subtle variations in colour within each colour category. It is likely that variations within these colour groups were the result of natural variations caused by largely uncontrollable factors (such as post-depositional colour changes, or variations within the natural materials involved). As will be discussed later, the colour balance was also controlled to a certain degree by the potter through firing techniques, methods of pigment application and surface treatments, although some distortion of colour caused by over-firing may be in evidence.

The slips were painted onto the vessels to form a variety of highly conventionalised decorative motifs. Over 100

Table 3. *Chemical analysis (energy dispersive spectroscopy) of three typical red slips (S), and corresponding body fabric paste analysis (B). Average chemical compositions of normalised % elemental spot analyses (n. 15 for each sample) and standard deviations are shown.*

Na	Mg	Al	Si	S	K	Ca	Mn	Fe	Ti	
0.31	1.20	24.59	48.02	0.22	4.12	2.75	0.04	17.56	1.23	S
0.32	0.27	1.22	3.93	0.14	0.40	1.17	0.05	2.40	0.36	s
0.26	1.95	22.57	51.66	0.17	6.40	3.40	0.03	12.21	1.36	B
0.22	0.52	2.90	2.03	0.09	2.95	1.07	0.05	4.00	0.59	s
0.24	0.98	22.30	53.15	0.24	3.59	2.45	0.03	15.30	1.71	S
0.22	0.35	3.78	3.98	0.08	0.86	0.28	0.03	2.22	0.71	s
0.28	1.37	19.23	54.83	0.21	5.71	3.86	0.18	12.54	1.79	B
0.14	0.82	1.67	3.00	0.15	0.89	1.32	0.18	1.48	0.47	s
0.26	0.93	23.04	48.06	0.24	3.85	2.76	0.09	19.16	1.62	S
0.08	0.48	2.04	3.63	0.12	1.38	0.76	0.06	2.17	0.16	s
0.28	1.28	19.55	54.53	0.30	5.67	4.59	0.20	11.68	1.94	B
0.19	1.06	0.67	3.20	0.16	0.29	1.54	0.24	1.62	0.58	s

Table 4. *Chemical analysis (energy dispersive spectroscopy) of three typical ground slips (S), the overlying bright white slips (shaded) and a body fabric paste analysis (B). Average chemical compositions of normalised % elemental spot analyses (n.15 for each sample) and standard deviations are shown).*

Na	Mg	Al	Si	S	K	Ca	Mn	Fe	Ti	
0.30	1.22	14.20	56.70	1.01	2.89	17.67	0.27	4.50	1.23	S
0.23	0.77	2.19	5.09	0.72	2.05	6.63	0.36	2.54	0.66	σ
0.31	1.18	32.65	55.18	0.66	2.64	3.57	0.16	2.28	1.21	S
0.16	1.06	0.97	2.33	0.53	1.01	1.57	0.09	0.82	0.27	σ
0.33	0.77	13.45	48.01	0.60	3.39	26.40	0.36	5.31	1.39	S
0.18	0.25	0.45	4.44	0.38	0.50	4.56	0.31	0.62	0.54	σ
0.25	1.16	33.03	56.60	0.60	2.07	2.80	0.10	2.27	1.17	S
0.20	1.11	0.94	2.54	0.37	0.24	1.33	0.09	0.83	0.27	σ
0.28	0.81	14.83	47.83	0.64	4.49	22.62	0.22	7.14	1.15	S
0.11	0.17	1.51	3.69	0.73	1.05	4.94	0.09	2.74	0.57	σ
0.21	1.06	32.18	55.18	0.53	2.36	3.06	0.09	2.99	1.34	S
0.20	1.04	0.09	2.71	0.45	0.68	1.34	0.09	1.79	0.44	σ
0.31	0.94	19.78	55.58	0.28	5.86	3.74	0.09	11.64	1.81	B
0.08	0.55	1.87	3.74	0.17	0.81	1.09	0.07	0.87	0.60	s

distinctive designs have been documented (Watson 1988:56). Essentially the motifs can be described as curvilinear, rectilinear, geometric, zoomorphic, complex bands and simple bands. The type is widely held to be characteristic of the late La Tène period and the sherds from early La Tène features at Aulnat (2.6% of the slip decorated pottery) were probably intrusive. The majority of the slip decorated pottery material from Aulnat is fragmentary, one example has been reconstructed (see figure 2) whilst other sherds hint at the elaborate nature of these pots.

Slip decorated pottery is, superficially, uniform across central and western Europe. The only major difference to be detected by art-historical studies is the distribution of zoomorphic patterns which are common in western Atlantic Europe including central France, but are almost completely absent from eastern European contexts (Maier 1970; Guichard 1987, Cumberpatch 1991). Slip decorated pottery normally represents a rare component within Iron Age pottery assemblages, figures below 0.5% of assemblages are normal in central Europe (Cumberpatch 1991). For the site of Aulnat, the slip decorated pottery represent c20% (2,688 sherds) of the overall pottery assemblage, and as such is a large collection.

There has been some interest in the slip decorated pottery as subjects of archaeometric investigation (Wirska-Parchoniak 1980; Cumberpatch and Pawlikowski 1988; Rigby *et al.* 1989; Andrews 1990; 1991). Results of energy dispersive spectroscopy analysis (Andrews 1990, 1991) undertaken on the Aulnat slip decorated pottery material showed a consistent similarity between the elemental suites of the body fabric clay fractions and the decorative coatings. It was therefore concluded that the Aulnat 'painted' pottery are decorated with clay based slips rather than organically based paint. In modelling production processes, the preparation of slips rather than paints has to be considered. This conclusion is supported by other limited analyses of surface painted wares from Iron Age Europe (Wirska-Parchoniak 1980, Cumberpatch and Pawlikowski 1988, Cumberpatch 1991).

Rigby *et al.* (1989) investigated La Tène painted pottery from the Champagne region of France, which is very similar to the Aulnat material, using SEM/XRD (X-ray diffraction). The red and black coatings were examined by XRD. Haematite was shown to be present in the red coatings samples from one vessel, but barely present in another. It is suggested that the haematite rich coatings were produced by burnishing ochre into the leather-hard surface (a conclusion based on the SEM examination of one sample cross section of a coating/body fabric interface which was found to be uneven and showed areas of haematite 'rubbed' into the body fabric). This conclusion was also based on experimental work of rubbing ochre into replica pots which produced similar structures (Rigby et al., 1989:10). The haematite poor coatings may have been achieved by applying iron-rich clay slips to the surface or by simply burnishing the iron rich body fabric as described above. This could be verified by examining the structure of the haematite poor coating since a slip will have an even demarcation at the coating/body fabric interface quite different from simple burnishing or rubbed in powdered application. Rigby *et al.* were not, however, permitted to take sections for SEM study of the haematite poor coatings, and no suggestions are made as to the structural differences between the three main methods of producing a red finish.

Rigby *et al.* (*ibid.*) reported that the black coatings on the Champagne slip decorated pottery did not register on the XRD equipment (illustrating that they were non-crystalline in nature) ruling out graphite (crystalline carbon) or any of various reduced iron oxides such as magnetite and hercynite (see Noll *et al.* 1975a). Whilst the structure of such crystalline pigments are expected to be largely disrupted by the firing process one would expect some residual peaks on the XRD diffractograms had such pigments been major contributors to the colour. Rigby *et al.* therefore conclude that the black coatings probably contain amorphous carbon (1989:10). There is a need to investigate the Aulnat material in a similar way to compare the decorative technologies.

Rigby *et al.* (1989) concluded that the painted pottery from the Champagne region of France was likely fired in open bonfires owing to the fact that the vessels they analysed had black bases. This author disagrees with this conclusion in that the same effect could have been resultant of the pot bases resting on unperforated kiln floors or shelves and might suggest that the pots were not removed immediately from the kiln whilst still hot (which would have resulted in oxidation of the black coloration) but rather left to cool to a sufficient extent so that the black coloration became permanent (perhaps not even a deliberate or desired effect on the part of the potters). Our models concerning the organisation of production and degree of craft specialisation involved in slip decorated pottery production would be markedly different depending on the basic pyrotechnology used.

Table 5 presents a model for the sequence of production for the slip decorated pottery. The analyses have characterised the slips as clay based preparations to which pigments have been added (or in which pigments have been developed by the controlled firing of the slips). Procurement for production therefore involves selection of appro-

Table 5. Model of the sequence of production for slip decorated pottery.

RAW MATERIAL

PROCUREMENT
Clay for body and self-slips
Slip clays (e.g. bright whites)
Procured pigments (calcium carbonates for creams)
  (ocherous materials for reds)
  (carbon paint peparations for greys)
  N.B. unprocured pigments develop during firing, they are not added to slip preparations, therefore procurement of appropriate source clays essential.

Fuel

PROCESSING

BODY FABRIC	SLIP CLAYS
Drying	Levigation and/or elutriation
Grinding	Deflocculation
Sieving/settling	Slip preparation including grinding
Levigation (fine fraction used for self slips)	and addition of procured pigments (?repeat of all or some of the above processes)
Evaporation	N.B. procured pigments may require
Kneading	processing such as calcining of limestone

TECHNOLOGY

Primary forming
Throwing

Secondary forming
Turning/shaping
Surface preparation
Drying to leather hard state

Surface treatment (variable)
Decoration
STAGE 1
Ground or basal slip (self-slip)   Dipping/painting/drying/burnishing
STAGE 2
Red and/or white/cream slip   Dipping/painting/drying/burnishing
STAGE 3
Painting on bands   ?marking out designs/painting/drying/selective burnishing

Additional processes
Selective and pattern burnishing
Incising

Drying/?preheating

First firing
(for some vessels the only firing)
Kiln loading and fuel preparation   Monitoring and control of the firing process

Post-firing decoration
STAGE 4
Zoomorphic, geometric design   Marking/incising (?wax resist) painting
painting with carbon paints

Secondary heating to form   (For some designs there may have been more than one re-heating episode)
amorphous carbon pigments

priate clays for the body fabrics, and for the slips. In the case for the bright white kaolin based coatings, it is probable that a separate source clay was used, whilst analysis has shown that often a basal slip derived from the same source clays as for the body fabrics was also employed. Several techniques for the production of the red coatings have been identified which involve the use of both procured and unprocured pigments. Ocherous particles have been identified by the analysis of some of the red coatings, suggesting that ocherous pigments were selected and processed, whilst for some of the red coatings, the selection of ferruginous clays was essential for the development of pigments during the firing process. Analysis of the cream coatings has shown that calcium carbonates were processed and mixed with the slips to produce the cream colour. The source of the calcium carbonate is unknown at present.

Calcium carbonate ($CaCO_3$) (in the form of prepared chalk, limestones [including marble], bones and other calcium carbonate bearing materials such as mollusc shells) and calcium sulphate (in the form of gypsum ($CaSO_4.2H_2O$), a mineral occurring in some sedimentary rocks and clays) were common ancient white pigments (Hodges 1964; Noll *et al.* 1975; Goffer 1980). For white slips, calcium carbonate added to clay slips (on firing) forms a calcium silicate ($CaO.SiO_2$) which gives a white colour to the slip. Calcium carbonates can be processed by wet or dry grinding to produce a usable pigment. Sedimentary rocks (i.e. limestones and marls) consisting of calcium- and magnesium-carbonates are present in the Auvergne region (Clout 1973:12; Mills 1985:77). Limestone refers to any sedimentary rock consisting essentially of carbonates, the two most important of which are calcite [$CaCO_3$] and dolomite [$CaMg(CO_3)_2$]. Marl is a calcareous mudstone which consists of clay minerals, calcium/magnesium carbonates, and very finely divided quartz and is a marine sedimentary rock. Marl is not plastic when wet, as is clay, but may dissolve when immersed in water and thus yield the necessary constituents for a light coloured slip (Goffer 1980:170).

Suggestions concerning the probable chemical composition of decorative coatings can be made based on a knowledge of the main pigment types used by prehistoric potters. High magnesium content of white slips would indicate use of magnesium based mineral pigment preparation such as talc or huntite (Betancourt 1984: 185). In his analysis of white pigments on Cretan white slipped pottery, Betancourt found high aluminium, silicon, calcium and iron contents indicating a white pigment consisting of a calcium rich argillaceous material such as clay with added calcium or naturally calcium rich clay. A third scenario would be high contents of aluminium and silicon with little iron and calcium which would indicate the use of a purer clay mineral such as kaolin. A slip prepared from a calcium carbonate source would be expected to contain a comparatively high (>5%) amount of calcium (as well as silicon and aluminium from the bulk of the clay binding matrix). Likewise a slip prepared from calcium sulphate sources could be expected to contain relatively high amounts of calcium as well as a

peak (in energy dispersive spectroscopy) for the sulphur component. It is also possible that a highly calcareous, marly clay was used to produce the cream slips (that is the cream colour represents use of an unprocured pigment). The EDS results for the cream coloured slips suggested the use of slip prepared from a calcium carbonate source (see table 4).

Processing of the slip clays likely involved a series of levigation/elutriation episodes, whereby the fine fraction of the clay is ground out of and settled from the source clays by washing the clays in water and leaving the fine fraction to settle. Ethnographic studies have shown that the use of defloculants which act to separate out the finer fractions of the clay to form a suspended colloidal mixture is common. Water in which wood ash has been soaked becomes potassium rich and is a good example of an ethnographically noted defloculant. In some cases, qualitative EDS showed an enrichment of potassium in the coatings, which may reflect this practice. An important aspect of slip preparation obviously was the addition and mixing, where necessary of processed pigments. The self-slip was also produced, probably from the processing steps involved in treating the fabric clays. For finewares such as those represented in this study, the clays would have been processed by drying, sieving and grinding, to achieve the desired consistency. The Limagne area has well-known deposits of excellent quality clays (Mills 1985),although virtually all raw clays require processing before use to remove unwanted detrital material and coarse organics.

Following primary and secondary forming on the wheel, the pots were dried to a leather hard state prior to the application of the prepared slips. Table 5 illustrates the various stages and processes in the sequence of production relating to the application of the slips. The pots were then fired in a kiln. Control of the firing process was essential for the development of pigment and colour balance. Such control may be evident in the examination of the firing cores present on some of the slip decorated pottery samples. It was impossible to examine the complete sample in this way because of its destructiveness, but for sherds prepared for analysis, observation of the cross-sections was undertaken (see Table 6). Of 269 sherds so examined, 57% (153 sherds) were found to exhibit some form of firing core. Of these, 34% (91 sherds) displayed a central diffuse grey core, and 11.5% (31 sherds) displayed a very slight and diffused thinner central grey core. Only 2% (6 sherds) displayed a uniformly grey 'reduced' cross-section, and 7% (18 sherds) displayed very strongly defined dark grey central firing cores. The remainder of the firing cores displayed (7 sherds) were of a complex nature.

In ceramics fired below 1000°C, the appearance of firing cores are caused by the removal of carbon by oxidation or its deposition from a smoky, reducing atmosphere (Rye 1981: 115). Such processes are functions of several variables including the firing atmosphere, duration and temperature of the firing, as well as the composition of the pottery being fired (primarily in the content of organic matter which if incompletely burnt will produce a grey-black

Table 6. Firing core data for slip decorated pottery.

Core type	Red/cream	Red	White	Cream
Slight	6 (2.2)	11 (4.1)	7 (2.6)	7 (2.6)
Reduced	0	0	1 (0.3)	5 (1.8)
Strong	3 (1.1)	4 (1.4)	5 (1.8)	6 (2.2)
Diffuse	14 (5.2)	21 (7.8)	29 (10.8)	27 (10.4)
Complex (banded core)	0	0	4 (1.4)	4 (1.4)
Total core	23	36	46	48
No visible core (oxidised)	26 (9.6)	24 (8.9)	36 (13.3)	30 (11.1)
Total sherds	49	60	82	78 269

The number of sherds of the broad colour group of decorative coating displaying the firing cores indicated are given in the table. The information is based on observation of fresh fractures from 269 samples (whilst preparaing for other analyses). Figures in parentheses are percentages of the total sample observed.

colour). The fact that around 55% of the sample examined displayed a uniform 'chamois' body fabric colour with no firing core, or only very slight, diffuse core bands would suggest that the majority of the slip decorated pottery was fired under fully oxidising conditions and was not heavily tempered with organic materials. The majority of the stronger cores observed were characterised by diffuse margins, typical of terracottas (Rye *ibid.*). Diffuse core margins are characteristic of (but not exclusive to) kiln structures where the cooling rate is slow. Very strong cores with sharply defined margins are more characteristic of firings involving rapid cooling such as bonfires (Rye *ibid.*).

Whilst the firing core evidence cannot be taken on its own to be conclusive proof of the use of developed kiln structures in firing the majority of the slip decorated vessels, it is likely that the completely oxidised wares, together with the core evidence, including the rare complex firing cores illustrated by figure 4, show that control of gaseous firing conditions using a kiln structure typifies the production of the slip decorated pottery. The examination of fresh-

Fig. 4.

fracture cross-sections shows that the pots were fired in a semi-reducing or neutral atmosphere, followed at the end of firing, or during the beginning of the cooling phase, by a strongly oxidising atmosphere. Such conditions would have favoured the maintenance of the colour balance of the cream slips and allowed, at the end of firing, the red haematite pigments to be fully developed. Such control is achievable only with a developed kiln structure, and the hypothesis of bonfire firing can be rejected.

Support for this view came from the results of refiring. These suggested that the slip decorated pottery samples were fired at temperatures ranging between 775°C to 975°C. These firing temperature determinations fall outside the restricted ranges of the open firing technologies based on ethnothermometric data (Gosselain 1993). The open firing conclusion for the Champagne material mentioned earlier, is based more it seems on the fact that there is little evidence for purpose built clay kiln structures in north western Europe (Rigby *et al.* 1989:8). Thus the use of a kiln can not be ruled out for this material.

Evidence for kiln structures in the Auvergne region although not rich, does exist (e.g. Mennessier-Jouannet 1991). To date, as far as the author is aware, there has been little in the way of definitive evidence of slip decorated pottery being found in association with kiln structures in the Auvergne. Elsewhere in Europe, slip decorated pottery has been found in association with Late La Tène D updraft kiln structures, for example at Podleze near Krakow in Poland (Wirska-Parachoniak 1980:156) and several kilns have been uncovered at the site of Sissach-Brül in Switzerland (Okun 1989:45).

In the case of some of the pots, firing was the final element in their production and the red, cream, bright white, and burnished designs would have been fully developed. For those pots displaying ephemeral painted grey designs, however, the final stage of decoration (stage 4 of Table 5) involved the use of carbon paint. In her analysis of the coatings of Late Iron Age slip decorated pottery from Poland, Wirska-Parachoniak (1980) concluded that the grey coatings were carbon based, but that the grey paints were thin clay based slips into which ground carbonaceous material such as soot had been added to give a grey-black pigmentation. According to Wirska-Parachoniak (1980:158) these carbon-black pigments were applied with the red and whites, and fired. The refiring experiments undertaken here have shown that this sequence of production for the grey coatings is impossible. Any carbonaceous material would have been burned out during the oxidation phase of the firing. Without exception, grey designs disappeared during the refiring of sherds, showing conclusively that they are a post-fire application of carbon-black paint.

Given a pigment sample, how can it be unambiguously identified as a carbon pigment? How much can be deduced about how it was made and from what starting materials? The primary division is between crystalline and amorphous forms defined by whether a sharp XRD pattern can be obtained (not an entirely clear distinction since graphite is often partly disordered and defective, therefore not produc-

ing a clear pattern). Also the term 'non-crystalline' does not imply that the material is totally devoid of order) (Whiston 1987:67). The Auvergne black pigments did not produce XRD patterns, confirming their amorphous nature.

It is impossible to determine from what organic precursor materials the carbon black pigment is derived. Black pigments used in prehistory fall into three basic categories: elemental carbon, manganese based blacks involving pyrolusite an abundant, naturally occurring black ore mineral (manganese dioxide (MnO_2)(Winter, 1983) or one of several reduced iron compounds (Gillies and Urch 1983). Presence of iron and manganese based pigments was ruled out for the Auvergne wares via EDS and XRD analyses, but only a few techniques such as Raman and X-ray photoelectron spectroscopy can detect carbon (Hedra 1990; Lambert *et al.* 1990).

Black pigments based on non-crystalline carbon substances were formed by pyrolysis (burning of organic materials to give heavily carbonised products which absorb light and therefore appear black). A wide variety of organics can be used as precursors for the carbon black pigment.

The most obvious optical property of carbons is their strong absorption throughout the visible light region, resulting in the fact that most carbons appear black. This absorption makes it difficult to study pigments microscopically using transmitted light, but is easier using reflected light. In a polished section carbons show a silvery metallic reflection under vertical illumination.

Grey/black colour is also achievable from carbon deposited on the surface in a technique known as 'smudging' (Shepard, 1956). Smudging involves the smoking of a ceramic during a firing under reducing conditions in which carbon is deposited onto the sherd surface turning it black (Winter 1983). This may also be achieved after the firing in specially constructed smoking sheds to produce the same effect (Stout and Hurst 1985). Clays rich in organic matter, or clays into which organic matter such as oils, animal or vegetable charcoals, soot or graphite have been mixed, will produce a black pigment under reducing, smoke laden firing atmospheres.

Cheetham (1985) has experimented with many 'organic liquids' including cabbage water, flour and water, fruit juices and milk to produce carbon-black colours. The paint is applied to the ceramic and re-heated over the smoke-less white ash embers of a bonfire. The organic element of the paint chars in the heating process, and forms the amorphous carbon-black pigment. The presence of thin painted 'guide lines' on the Auvergnian wares would suggest that this process may have involved many reheating episodes, the design being 'roughed out' and the infilling painted on later, once the design had been formulated (figure 5). Cheetham (*ibid.*) has experimented with a wax resist, whereby the areas to remain white are painted with a wax which resists the organic paint which is washed over the entire surface of the design area. The wax resist design is then held over the smokeless heat to char the organic element to carbon-black, whilst the wax resist melts to leave the white slip. There is

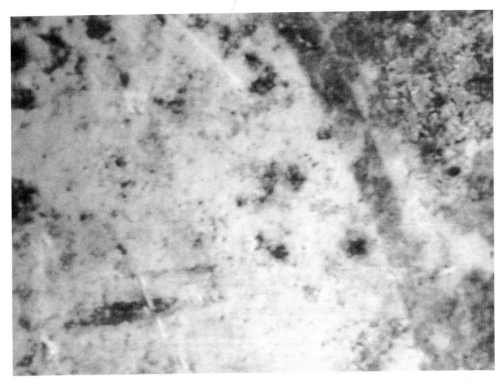

Fig. 5.

some evidence for the use of this technique for the Aulnat pottery in the form of brushmarks which run across the long axes of painted designs, rather than along the axes. This perhaps indicates that the brush was used to wash over the resistant design.

The completion of the grey painted designs represents the end of the production sequence for the slip decorated pottery. On the basis of this reconstruction of the sequence of production, some aspects of the archaeologically invisible variables can be modelled using the components of the production process. A suggested model for the mode of slip decorated pottery production can be seen in Table 7. The production process, from procurement of the raw materials, their processing and formation into the finished vessels (output) are modelled together with the likely labour requirements (in terms of specialist knowledge required) and the technology employed.

The model for the mode of production suggested in Table 7 implies a high level of organisation. It is doubtful that all the necessary source clays and pigments were available in a single location. Some form of organising force is implied. There would also appear to be a high degree of technological investment required for the production of slip decorated pottery. The production of quality slips would require settling tanks or vessels, as well as grinding and sieving equipment, storage facilities to prevent the contamination (for example of the pure white clays used for the bright white coatings) and also in the construction and maintenance of a developed kiln in which the gaseous firing conditions (as well as temperature) could be controlled. A kick wheel is implied, together with other specialist equipment, most obviously brushes for the painting of designs.

The designs imply a wide range of brushes were used, as well as specialist brushes, Guichard, (1987:130) and Cumberpatch (pers. comm) have noted the use of a six pointed brush involved in one design. The production steps imply a range of unskilled, semi-skilled and skilled labour, with the latter most notable in the production of the painted designs. A specialist artist is implied and Guichard has suggested that the designs are based on a coded set of motifs which resemble 'heraldry'. It is doubtful that the painted pots are the result of an individual potter, but rather the result of a team of specialist artisans. The mode of production proposed in Table 7 is nearest to the 'nucleated workshop' model outlined in Table 2.

Discussion

A fuller understanding of pottery production in general will depend on knowledge of the scale of production. Many of the variables of scale, however, are largely invisible in the archaeological record (Rice 1987). For the Auvergne in general, the evidence for kilns is rare, even at well known production sites such as Lezoux where the remains of only one kiln were discovered (Mennessier-Jouannet 1991). Thus, while the presence of pottery in the Auvergne area indicates that pottery production was carried out within the region, modelling the organisation of production has relied on the indirect approach of studying the technology of production as reconstructed by detailed analysis of the decorative coatings, rather than by directly examining the producing units themselves (cf. Rice 1987:205).

The models for the sequence and mode of pottery pro-

Table 7. Suggested mode of production for slip decorated pottery.

RAW MATERIAL	LABOUR	TECHNOLOGY	OUTPUT
PROCUREMENT			
Body fabric source clay Slip source clays Inorganic pigments Deflocculant (?potash) Carbon pigment precursors Water Fuel	Specialist knowledge (for sources of pigments clays and fuel types) Unskilled labour	Transport, local and long distance	Unprocessed materials
PROCESSING			
Drying/crushing Sieving/settling Levigation and/or elutriation of body clays and slip clays Calcining and grinding of calcium carbonate pigment Addition and mixing of prepared pigments e.g. ochres Preparation of amorphous carbon based soot paints	Unskilled labour Semi-skilled labour Specialist knowledge skilled labour and storage	Drying sheds/area Crushing equipment/ area, settling/levigation tanks or vessels Calcining ovens/ fires, grinding and sieving equipment for pigment mixing	Prepared slips (self-slips) Pigmented slips
Drying/crushing Sieving/settling Levigation, evaporation and kneading of body clays	Semi-skilled and unskilled labour	Largely as above	Prepared body clays
FORMING			
Throwing Turning/surface preparation Surface treatments ground (basal) slipping	Skilled labour Skilled labour	Kick wheel Turntable, brushes dipping tanks/vessels	Semi-finished vessels
Drying	Unskilled (storage of prepared vessels) semi-decorated	Drying area (?sheds)	Leather hard
Secondary painting of simple and complex bands Drying General, selective and pattern burnishing	Skilled labour (see above)	Turntable, brushes, marking and burnishing tools	vessels Semi and fully decorated vessels
Firing	Skilled labour	Kiln	Fired vessels (some finished)
Post-firing carbon painting of zoomorphic, curvilinear and geometric designs	Skilled (?peripatetic artists)	Brushes (wax resist?)	Fully decorated vessels
Secondary heating	Skilled	Smokeless fire or oven	Finished vessels

duction presented above are as descriptive as far as the evidence will allow. They stand as postulates against which further evidence can be compared. Such evidence may include analysis of other classes of pottery not considered here (most importantly the black burnished and white slipped wares), or new evidence for the production sites themselves. Such evidence will allow us to test, refute, adapt or confirm the models presented here. We need to put the results into perspective by opening up the range of material analysed with the effective analytical programme and theoretical models which have been developed here. Nevertheless, the application of archaeometric information to theoretical frameworks has strengthened and expanded the scope of archaeological inferences concerning the degree of specialisation and labour investment involved in colour-coated ware production.

Appendix 1
Equipment and operating conditions

SEM (PS500) and the CAMSCAN Mk II scanning electron microscopes with EDS

The Link system used in conjunction with the PS500 SEM was a LINK SYSTEM NOVA 290. The spectroscope used in conjunction with the Camscan Mk II was a Link Systems AN 10000 (resolution at 5.9 KeV = 149 eV). A general purpose standard block from P & H Developments, Glossop was used for the analyses, the block contained a selection of pure elements and standard minerals which could be used to provide calibration and standard spectra against which the unknown spectra could be identified and calibrated. The Ca and Si standards were taken from a wolastonite sample, Mg from periclase, Na from albite, Al from corundum, K from ortoclase, and Mn, Fe and Ti from pure element samples. Noise calibration was achieved by an in sample cobalt standard incorporated into the sample mounting. The stability of the operating conditions of the analyses was checked after every fifth spot analysis.

Optical microscopy

A Nikon Optiphot microscope was used with objectives BD plan 5/0.1 (210/0) magnification ×50 to BD plan 100/0.90 (210/0) magnification x1000. Oblique fibre optic lighting, in conjunction with reflected light filtered through polarisers provided for a range of lighting conditions allowing colour sensitive and phase sensitive micrographs. Transmitted light microscopy was used for the examination of thin sections. A Vickers and the Mettalux II microscope were used for preliminary examination and hardness testing of the ceramics. A Minolta Dark box camera fitted to the Nikon Optiphot was used to take the colour micrographs, together with a 'SCOPEMAN' from Microvision Ltd (model number 5000) which allowed variable magnification from x35–1000 on unmodified samples.

X-ray diffraction

For the XRD analyses a Phillips PW1373 Goniometer with a PW1319 Channel analyser was used together with a Phillips PM8203 single pen recorder. CuKa radiation was used through a Ni filter and operating conditions of 35 Kv and 55mA. Diffracograms were recorded onto calibrated paper for the range 5–65°2θ. Peaks were identified for the whole range for those minerals in the library compiled from JCDPS files

Refiring experiment

Samples of pottery were refired in a P5081 Podmore programmable electric kiln stepwise (in 25–50°C stages) over a range from 400°C – 1050°C. After each firing, sample dimension was measured using a Mitutuyo 0.001mm accuracy micrometer. Colour contrast, surface texture and condition were compared to as received portions. Original firing temperature ranges could be estimated at the resumption of solid state sintering causing shrinkage once original firing temperature had been exceeded. Further details of these experiments are forthcoming.

Acknowledgements

I would like to thank Dr Chris Cumberpatch for initially suggesting this area of research and for commenting on previous drafts of this paper. His help was also invaluable in allowing me access to his ideas concerning the theoretical approach to pottery production. Without Chris Cumberpatch's advice and useful suggestions, this work would not have been possible. I also acknowledge the former Science and Engineering Research Council for supporting initial research and Dr. Barbara Ottaway for her encouragement and helpful advice whilst conducting original research. My thanks also to Vincent Guichard and Professor John Collis for their help in allowing access to material, and to Dr Peter Messer and Dr Anura Gaspe for their technical help with refiring experiments. All errors, of course remain my sole responsibility.

References

Aloupi, E. and Maniatis, Y. 1992 *New Evidence for the Attic Black Gloss.* Abstracts of the 28th International Symposium on Archaeometry. Los Angeles.

Andrews, K. 1990 Slip decorated Iron Age ceramics from central France. In: E. Pernicka (Ed.) *Archaeometry '90.* Proceedings of the 27th International Symposium on Archaeometry. Berkäuser Verlag Basel. 229–236.

Andrews, K. 1991 The Technology of Late La Tène 'Painted Pottery' decoration. In: P. Budd et al (Eds.) *Archaeological Sciences 1989* Oxbow Monograph 9: 1–7.

Andrews, K. 1993 *Slip on something luxurious.* University of Sheffield. Unpublished PhD Thesis.

Balibar, E. 1970 The basic concepts of Historical Materialism. In: L. Althusser and E. Balibar *Reading Capital.* London: N.L.B.: 199–309.

Betancourt, D. P. 1984 Preliminary results from the east Cretan white-on-dark-ware project. In: V.S. Olin and A.D. Franklin (Eds.) *Archaeological Ceramics.* Smithsonian Institution Press. 183–187.

Binns, C.F. and Fraser, A.D. 1929 The Genesis of the Greek Black Glaze. *American Journal of Archaeology* 33: 1–9.

Bloch, M. 1983 *Marxism and Anthropology.* Oxford University Press.

Bradley, R. 1985 Exchange and social distance – the structure of bronze artefact distributions. *Man* 20: 692–704.

Brumfiel, B. and Earle, T. K. 1987 *Specialisation, Exchange and Complex Societies.* Cambridge University Press.

Budd, P., Chapman, B., Jackson, C., Janaway, R. and Ottaway, B. (Eds.) 1991 *Archaeological Sciences 1989 Proceedings of a conference on the application of scientific techniques to archaeology, Bradford, September 1989.* Oxbow Monograph 9.

Burling, R. 1968 Maximisation theories and the study of economic anthropology. In: E.E. Le Claire and H.K. Schnieder (Eds.) *Economic Anthropology: Readings in Theory and Analysis.* New York: Holt, Reinehart and Winston, 168–187.

Cheetham, L. 1985 Pre Columbian negative painted pottery, some notes and observations. *Bulletin of the Experimental Firing Group* 3: 34–42.

Clout, H. 1973 *The Massif Central*. Oxford University Press.

Collis, J. R. 1975 Excavations at Aulnat, Clermont Ferrand a preliminary report with some notes on the earliest towns in France. *The Archaeological Journal* 132: 1–15.

Collis, J. R. 1980 Aulnat and urbanisation in France: a second interim report. *The Archaeological Journal* 137, 1–15.

Collis, J. R. 1984 Aulnat and urbanisation: the theoretical problems. *Etudes Celtiques* 21, 111–117.

Collis, J. R., Duval, A. and Périchon, R. (Eds.) 1983 *Le deuxième âge du Fer en Auvergne et en Forez et ses relation avec les regions voisines.* Sheffield University.

Cumberpatch, C.G. and Pawlikowski, M. 1988 Preliminary results of mineralogical analyses of Late La Tène Painted Pottery from Czechoslovakia. *Archeologické Rozhledy* 40: 184–193.

Cumberpatch, C.G. 1989 The reconstruction of the organisation of prehistoric pottery production: an example from Central France. *Archeologia Polski* 34: 179–191

Cumberpatch, C. G. in prep The concepts of economy and habitus in the study of later medieval ceramic assemblages.

Donham, D. L. 1981 Beyond the domestic mode of production. *Man* 16: 515–541.

Dunnell, R. C. 1993 Why archaeologists don't care about archaeometry. *Archaeomaterials* 7: 161–165.

Freestone, I. C. 1982 Applications and potential of Electron Probe micro-analysis in technological and provenance investigations of ancient ceramics. *Archaeometry* 24(2): 99–116.

Gillies, K.J.S. and Urch, D.S. 1983 Spectroscopic studies of iron and carbon in black surface wares. *Archaeometry* 25(1), 29–44.

Goffer, Z. 1980 *Archaeological Chemistry: A sourcebook on the applications of Chemistry to Archaeology*. John Wiley.

Gosden, C. H. 1983 Iron Age Pottery Trade in Central Europe. Sheffield University: Unpublished PhD Thesis.

Gosden, C. H. 1989 Debt, Production and Prehistory. *Journal of Anthropological Archaeology* 8: 355–387.

Gosselain, O. P. 1993 Bonfire of the enquiries. Pottery firing temperatures in archaeology: what for? *Journal of Archaeological Science* 19: 243–259.

Gregory, C. A. 1982 *Gifts and Commodities*. London and New York: Academic Press.

Guichard, V. 1987 La céramique peinte décor zoomorphe des 2 et 1 s. avant J-C en territoire Ségusiave. *Etudes Celtique*. 24: 103–143.

Hedra, P. 1990 FT Raman Column. *Spectroscopy World* 2(6): 39.

Henderson, J. (Ed.) 1989 *Scientific Analysis in Archaeology*. Oxford University Committee for Archaeology Monograph no 19.

Hindess, B. and Hurst, P. Q. 1975 *Pre-Capitalist Modes of Production*. Routledge and Kegan Paul.

Hodges, H. 1964 *Artefacts: an introduction to early materials and technology*. John Baker.

Hofmann, U. 1962 The chemical basis of ancient Greek Vase painting. *Angewandte Chemie International Edition* 1(7): 341–350.

Hughes, M. J. (Ed.) 1981 *Scientific studies in ancient ceramics*. British Museum Occasional Paper No. 19.

Jones, R. 1988 Introduction. In: A. Slater and J.O. Tate (Eds.) *Science and Archaeology, Glasgow, (1987). Proceedings of a Conference on the application of scientific techniques to Archaeology*. British Archaeology Reports British Series 196(i-ii): 1–8.

Kilikoglou, V., Maniatis, Y. and Vaughan, S. J. 1992 Correlation of chemical, petrographic and microstructural data for the study of Middle Bronze Age pottery from Thera, Greece. *Archaeometry '92 Abstracts*: 118.

Lambert, J. B., Xue, L., Weydert, J. M. and Winter, J. H. 1990 Oxidation states of iron in Bahamian pottery by X-ray photoelectron spectroscopy. *Archaeometry* 32(1): 47–54.

MacReady, S. and Thompson, F. H. (Eds.) 1985 *Archaeological Field Survey in Britain and Abroad*. Society of Antiquiries of London Occasional Paper (new series) 6.

Maier, F. 1970 Die bemalte Spätletène-keramik von Manching. Die Ausgrabungen im Manching. *Germania* 63: 17–55.

Maniatis, Y. and Katsanos, A. 1986 PIXE analysis of ancient ceramic finished surfaces: a preliminary report. PACT 15. *Journal of the European Study Group in Physical, Chemical, Biological and Mathematical Techniques applied to Archaeometry*. First South European Conference in Archaeometry. Delphi, European Cultural Centre: 66.

Maniatis, Y. and Tite, M. S. 1978–9 Examination of Roman and Medieval pottery using the Scanning Electron Microscope. *Acta Praehistorica et Archaeologica* 9/10: 125– 130.

Maniatis, Y. and Tite, M. S. 1981 Technological examination of Neolithic-Bronze Age pottery from central and southeast Europe and from the Near East. *Journal of Archaeological Science* 8, 59–76.

Mennessier-Jouannet, C. 1991 Un four de potier da La Tène D1 à Lezoux (Puy-de-Dome). *Revue Archéologique du Centre de la France* 30: 113–126.

Mills, N. 1985 Iron Age settlement and society in Europe: contributions from field surveys in central France. In: S. MacReady and F.H. Thompson (Eds.) *Archaeological Field Survey in Britain and Abroad*. Society of Antiquaries of London Occasional Paper (new series) 6.

Morel, J. P. 1978 A propos des céramiques campaniennes de France et d'Espagne. *Archéologie en Languedoc* 1. Journées d'études de Montpellier sur la céramiques campanienne: 149–168.

Morel, J. P. 1982 La Céramique à vernis noir de Carthage-Byrsa: nouvelles donées et éléments de comparaison. In: *Actes du colloque sur la céramique antiques*, Carthage CEDAC 43–76.

Morris, I. 1986 Gift and commodity in Archaic Greece. *Man* 21: 1–17.

Noble, J.V. 1960 The technique of Attic Vase Painting. *American Journal of Archaeology* 64: 307–318.

Noble, J.V. 1965 *The Techniques of Painted Attic Pottery*. Faber and Faber.

Noll, W. 1977 Hallstattzeitliche keramik der Heuneburg an der Oberen Donau. *Archaeologie und Naturwissenschaften* 1: 1–19.

Noll, W. 1978 Material and techniques of the Minoan Ceramics of Thera and Crete. *Thera and the Aegean World* I: 493–506.

Noll, W. 1979 Anorganishe pigmente in vorgeschichte und antike. *Fortschritte Mineralisch* 57(2): 203–63.

Noll, W. 1981 Mineralogy and technology of the painted ceramics from ancient Egypt. In: M.J. Hughes (Ed.) *Scientific studies in ancient ceramics*. British Museum Occasional Paper No. 19.

Noll, W. 1982 Mineralogie und technik der Keramiken Altkretas (Mineralogy and Technique of the ceramics of ancient Crete). *Neues Jahbuch für Mineralogie Abhandlungen* 143(2): 150–199.

Noll, W., Born, L. and Holm, R. 1974 Chemie und Technik altretischer vasenmalerei vom Kamares typ., II *Naturwissenschaften* 61: 361–2.

Noll, W., Born, L. and Holm, R. 1975 Keramiken und wandmalereien der Ausgrabungen von Thera. *Naturwissenschaften* 62: 87–94.

Noll, W., Holm, R. and Born, L. 1972a Chemie und phasenbestand der vasenmalerei altischer lekythoi. *Naturwissenschaften* 59: 270–271.

Noll, W., Holm, R. and Born, L. 1972b Manganoxyd-Phasen ab Pigmente antiker vasenmalerei. *Naturwissenschaften* 59: 511–212

Noll, W., Holm, R. and Born, L. 1975 Painting of ancient ceramics. *Angewandte Chemie International Edition* 14: 602–613.

Noll, W., Holm, R., and Born, L. 1980 Mineralogie und technik zinnapplizierter antiker keramik. *Neues Jahbuch für Mineralogie Abhandlungen* 139(1): 26–42.

Okun, M.L. 1989 An example of the process of acculturation in the early Roman Frontier. *Oxford Journal of Archaeology* 8(1): 41–54.

Olin, V. S. and Franklin, A. D. (Eds.) 1982 *Archaeological Ceramics.* Smithsonian Institution Press.

Peacock, D. P. S. 1982 *Pottery in the Roman World.* Longman.

Pernicka, E. (Ed.) 1990 *Archaeometry '90. Proceedings of the 27th International Symposium on Archaeometry.* Berkäuser Verlag Basel.

Pfaffenberger, B. 1988 Fetished objects and humanised nature – towards an anthropology of technology. *Man* 23: 326–252.

Polanyi, K., Arenberg, C. A. and Pearson, H. 1971 *Trade and Markets in Early Empires.* Regnery.

Rice, P. M. 1981 Evolution of specialised pottery production : a trial model. *Current Anthropology* 22(3): 210–240.

Rice, P. M. 1982 Pottery production, pottery classification and the role of physico- chemical analyses. In: V.S. Olin and A.D. Franklin (Eds.) 1982 *Archaeological Ceramics.* Smithsonian Institution Press.: 47–8

Rice, P. M. 1987 *Pottery Analysis.* University of Chicago Press.

Rigby, V., Middleton, A. P. and Freestone, I. C. 1989 The Prunay workshop: technical examination of La Tène bichrome painted pottery from Champagne. *World Archaeology* 21(1): 1–16.

Rye, O. S. 1981 *Pottery Technology Principles and Reconstruction.* Taraxacum Press.

Sahlins, M. 1974 *Stone Age Economics.* Tavistock.

Schneider, H. K. 1974 *Economic Man: The Anthropology of Economics.* The Free Press.

Shepard, A. O. 1956 *Ceramics for the Archaeologist.* Carnegie Institution, Washington Press.

Slater, A. and Tate, J.O. 1988 *Science and Archaeology, Glasgow, (1987). Proceedings of a Conference on the application of scientific techniques to Archaeology* British Archaeology Reports British Series 196(i-ii).

Stout, A. M. and Hurst, A. 1985 X-ray diffraction of Early Iron Age pottery from Western Norway. *Archaeometry* 27(2): 225–230.

Tite, M. S., Bimson, M. and Freestone, I. C. 1982 An examination of the high gloss surface finishes of Greek Attic and Roman Samian wares. *Archaeometry* 24(2): 117–126.

Tite, M. S., Freestone, I. C., Meeks, N. D. and Bimson, M. 1982 The use of scanning microscopy in the technological examination of ancient ceramics. In: V. S.Olin and A.D. Franklin (Eds.) *Archaeological Ceramics* Smithsonian Institution Press.

Tite, M. S. and Maniatis, Y. 1975 Scanning electron microscopy of fired calcareous clays. *Transactions and Journal of the British Ceramic Society* 74: 19–22.

Tite, M. S. and Maniatis, Y. 1975 Examination of ancient pottery using the scanning electron microscope. *Nature* 251: 222–3.

Tite, M. S., Maniatis, Y., Meeks, N. D., Bimson, M., Hughes, M.J. and Leppard, S. C. 1982 Technological studies of ancient ceramics from the Near East, Aegean and South East Europe. In: T.A.Wertime and S.F. Wertime (Eds.) *Early Pyrotechnology.* Smithsonian Institution Press.

Underhill, A. P. 1991 Pottery production in chiefdoms: the Longshan Period in northern China. *World Archaeology* 23(1): 12–27.

Van der Leeuw, S. 1976 *Studies in the Technology of Ancient Pottery.* Private publication Amsterdam.

Van der Leeuw, S. E. and Pritchard, A. C. (Eds.) 1984 *The Many Dimensions of Pottery.* Universiteit van Amsterdam.

Vandiver, P. B. 1988 Reconstructing and interpreting the technologies of ancient ceramics. *Material Research Society Symposium Proceedings* 123: 89–102. Materials Research Society.

Vandiver, P. B., Druzik, J. and Wheeler, G. S. 1990 *Proceedings of the Materials Research Society Symposium.* San Francisco.

Watson, C. 1988 *The painted pottery from Aulnat.* Unpublished B.A. dissertation, La Trobe University.

Wertime, T. A. and Wertime, S. F (Eds.) 1982 *Early Pyrotechnology.* Smithsonian Institution Press.

Whiston, C. 1987 *X-Ray Methods.* John Wiley.

Widemann, F. 1982 Why is archaeometry so boring for archaeologists? In: V.S. Olin, and A.D. Franklin (Eds.) *Archaeological Ceramics* Smithsonian Institution Press. 29–36.

Wilson, A. L. 1978 Elemental analysis of pottery in the study of its provenance: a review. *Journal of Archaeological Science* 5, 219–236.

Winter, J. 1983 The characterisation of pigments based on carbon. *Studies in Conservation* 28(2): 49–66.

Wirska-Parachoniak 1980 Produkcja ceramiczna Celtów na terenach Polski poldniowej. *Materialy Archeologiczne Nowej Huty* 6: 155–158.

Wolf, E. R. 1992 *Europe and the People without History.* University of California Press.

Why do excavation reports have finds' catalogues?

Penelope M. Allison

Introduction

The construction of archaeological inquiry is largely governed by the method of publication of archaeological sites. At present, a common pattern of post-excavation activity is to divide the excavated artefacts into what are now well-established categories. Each category is then assigned to a different "finds specialist" for organisation into a typology which is ultimately published in the excavation report. The categories are largely selected on criteria attributable to the formal or manufacturing characteristics of the artefacts.

However, this publication format is proving to be impracticable for many current research interests. The developing concern for a more sociological and holistic approach to the archaeological record means that the current single-view publication method is becoming outmoded. A large proportion of archaeological excavations are of settlement sites, and the associated artefacts are usually found at their place of consumption, or end-use, rather than their place of manufacture. The present form of publication divides artefacts into categories which does not reflect this, and thus it does not facilitate the accurate reconstruction of the cultural behaviour at the site.

The current standard mode of presentation of artefact reports does not appear to be the most appropriate for producing a tool for teachers, students, cultural resource managers, researchers or anyone else wishing to use material culture to interpret past activity. With information technologies now readily available to facilitate data collection, processing and presentation we should be able to ask, and answer more effectively, more meaningful and complex questions of this data than this standard mode has previously allowed.

This paper is concerned with addressing some of the shortfalls of this traditional mode of presentation and with outlining the development of a methodology which facilitates the application of new and diverse theoretical frameworks to excavated data. It is also an attempt to verbalise some of the thoughts and frustrations which have arisen whilst trying to use the data from standard excavation reports for research purposes.

The paper is written from a personal point of view, *ie* that of an archaeologist who has chosen the remains of Roman material culture in an attempt to gain an understanding of Roman domestic life. This research consists of the analysis of the distribution patterns of Roman material remains, and attempts to explain them. It is not specifically concerned with the isolation of particular categories of artefacts, but rather with a consideration of settlement sites as consumption sites. However, this investigation has been hindered by the current mode of presentation of Roman material culture.

One of the major frustrations has been that the format of, sometimes quite lavish, publications of Roman sites prohibits them from providing useful comparative functional and provenance-related information for a more social analysis of the archaeology of Roman settlement sites. If such reports are written to facilitate access to primary data for more specific research questions, then would it not be more beneficial to the progress of the discipline, more financially expedient and more environmentally friendly if reports which are concerned with the dissemination of information were published in a form which actually does facilitate alternative interpretations of the primary data?

Roman domestic history

Besides material remains, a certain amount of written evidence pertains to the culture and period of the chosen study area, *ie* Roman household behaviour. There was no Roman Mrs Beeton to give an insight into how a Roman matron/patron did or should have ran her/his household in each Roman period, social stratum or part of the Roman world. Nevertheless, Roman historians have extracted information from ancient texts – texts which were often written for quite different purposes (Wallace-Hadrill 1989: 9) – to reconstruct typical Roman domestic life. Such reconstructions have often been made more colourful, and more palatable, by illustrating them with Roman artefacts (e.g. Liversidge 1976: esp. 71ff; McDonald 1966: esp. 13ff). Whilst not wishing to elaborate on this methodology here, it should be pointed out that our current understanding of Roman domestic life is based on fragmentary information which was elicited from a number of sources with widely differing contexts, and has resulted in a belief that we have a greater familiarity with this aspect of the past than is actually the case.

While social historians today are more attuned to the fragmentary nature of their own textual information (e.g. Rawson 1992: 3; Garnsey and Saller 1987: 127), they are still sometimes rather cavalier in their approach to the nature of the information which can be extracted from material culture.

Roman archaeology

Archaeologists, particularly Roman archaeologists, today seem to consider themselves a separate breed from historians. If they are indeed concerned with reconstructing the past, then that concern is often obscured by the treatment and publication of their data. During excavation, including that of settlements, the depositional processes are sometimes documented, but during post-excavation, the excavated "finds" are inevitably divided into a series of pre-determined categories, such as pottery, glass and worked bone. It is often overlooked that this categorisation system is based on that employed by scientists of the 19th century (Knight 1981: 16), and that it has been employed to facilitate the job of the archaeologist in organising his/her data. It is not always evident how or when s/he might use the so-organised material to aid the reconstruction of cultural history (Adams and Adams 1991: 276).

Once divided, excavation data is then assigned to different "specialists" – that is, people who either identify themselves as glass specialists, pottery specialists, lithic specialists etc, or have had these identifications thrust upon them. These specialists tend to form cliques with others of their own kind and develop more and more complex and seemingly scientific methods of analysis for the specific classes of material which has been assigned to them, or which they have taken as their own. Students of archaeology, with short-term funding, are often encouraged to become one of these types of specialists. They produce small, precise theses often consisting of experiments with types of, usually computer-generated, quantitative methods, which might (or might not) be applicable to their chosen class of material.

Sometimes, the excavation is published. For most of this century (Atkinson et al 1904 compare with Stead and Rigby 1986 or Sacket *et al* 1992), this has consisted of a main section phasing the site (usually written by the director), followed by a series of disparate catalogues, each covering one of the artificially-created categories (see Knight 1981: 58ff) of excavated material. In these catalogues, artefacts are arranged into typological sequences which are principally constructed upon variations of fabric type or shape. These are believed to reflect variations in their production techniques. Often, usually in the interests of costs, only one example of each type is catalogued and (sometimes) illustrated, in the published version, although the decision relating to what to publish is usually influenced by how 'interesting' a particular artefact type is seen to be.

Such methods and publication formats undoubtedly allow the development of more specialised knowledge of each of the categories of excavated artefacts. They may even have the potential to eventually tell us more about past actuality, but in the meantime they are having an enormous effect on the construction of archaeological inquiry. It appears that typologies have become ends in themselves, rather than "*conceptual tools*" (Adams and Adams 1991: 8) "*made for a purpose and [which] must be shown to work for that purpose*" (Adams and Adams 1991: 14). Often, historians find this form of presentation of archaeological material incomprehensible, and have difficulty in using it to facilitate their reconstructions of the past. Therefore, they tend to ignore it and concentrate on artefacts as illustrations of written texts, furthering the belief that the aims of historians and archaeologists are unrelated. The problems of the relationship between the activities of historians and archaeologists, and of the relationship between archaeological methodology and reconstructing the past are well documented. To (re)quote Lavell (see Moffett 1991: 25):

> I take it as axiomatic that the whole point of spending millions of pounds yearly on digging and publishing archaeological sites is to improve the sum of human knowledge, that all this information has some future purpose, and is not being collected like stamps or engine numbers.

However, it is not apparent where this acknowledgement is leading us. Are we getting any nearer to doing what we are supposed to do? Does cataloguing actually serve that end or hinder it? I do not intend to try to redress the whole problem here. Rather, it will be examined in the context of some personal experiences of trying to reconstruct Roman domestic life from material remains.

Pompeian house contents

I have been carrying out an examination of house floor assemblages in Pompeii in order to reappraise current interpretations of the depositional processes at that site and of the spatial and functional aspects of Pompeian domestic life. This has involved the assessment of what new information artefact assemblages, independent of traditional, text-based, interpretations of the use of space in Pompeian houses, can bring to our understanding of Pompeian, and Roman, domestic behaviour (Allison 1992a, 1992b).

The primary database consisted of the excavated contents from 30 atrium houses in Pompeii (fig.1), compiled from published reports (e.g. Maiuri 1933; Elia 1934) and site notebooks and inventories. The common pattern for the study of domestic activity in Pompeian households has been the analysis of one house or building in isolation (e.g. Strocka 1984), with interpretations relating to its occupancy consisting of generalisations made from a largely textual perspective, or from expectations based on 19th–20th middle class European "common sense". However, in this study, by dealing with a number of houses and sorting some 10,000 artefacts, I was able to analyse a large body of information and to assess patterns of residential behaviour (Allison 1992b: 40ff; 1993; 1995b 159ff; 1997) and abandonment processes (Allison 1992b: 86ff; 1995a: 167ff) in a more systematic manner than previous studies. Consequently, I was able to argue that the patterns were much more complex than previously believed.

The database was formed from the extant documentation of the excavations, not from a study of the actual artefacts. However, it soon became obvious that I needed a greater familiarity with the objects themselves, in order to understand precisely which artefact was being described in the excavation reports (in Italian) and, where necessary, to be able to assess the validity of the functions ascribed to them.

Catalogue of finds from the Insula del Menandro

The Insula del Menandro was excavated in the 1930s and, with the exception of the Casa del Menando, received cursory publication in the Notizie degli Scavi (Elia 1934). A list of some of the "finds" was provided at the end of the report. The Casa del Menandro was singled for special publication in two volumes (Maiuri 1933), with the first volume concentrating on the aspects of the wall-decoration and those "loose finds" considered the most interesting, specifically the famous silver treasure. The second volume consists of further illustrations of the same material.

The entire Insula is now being reinvestigated in more detail by the Pompeii Research Committee (Ling 1997). Roger Ling is responsible for the reinvestigation of the extant structure and wall-decoration. Kenneth Painter (formerly of the British Museum) has been commissioned as a Roman silver specialist to publish the "silver treasure"; Paul Arthur (University of Lecce) has studied the amphorae left in the houses of this Insula; and Estelle Lazer (University of Sydney) has written a report on the extant skeletal remains from this Insula. The four atrium houses in this Insula were amongst the 30 houses used for my examination of Pompeian house floor assemblages. In 1988 I received permission from Roger Ling to carry out a pilot study of the finds from these atrium houses as part of my Pompeian household assemblages study. The objective of this pilot study was to improve my own knowledge of the actual types of Pompeian, or indeed Roman, household artefacts, to beyond that which I had acquired through the descriptions of the notebooks and inventories. It therefore consisted of a catalogue of all the extant artefacts from the Insula which are housed in the Pompeian collection. It was suggested by Ling that this catalogue could be published as an appendix to the volume dealing with the structure and building history of the Insula. This pilot study was carried out in 1989, but it was found that it was a major task to do even a summary catalogue just of the finds from the ground floor rooms of the Casa del Menandro, let alone the rest of that house, or indeed the rest of the Insula. Nevertheless, the formation of the catalogue was very helpful for the identification of the artefacts described in the records, and for familiarisation with the range and type of objects found in Pompeian houses, and at the same time this study produced a more detailed catalogue for the publication of the British Pompeii Research Committee's project.

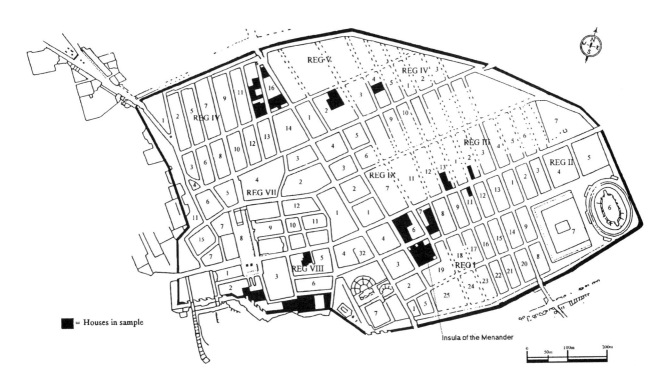

Fig. 1. Plan of Pompeii showing distribution of houses in sample.

Due to the limitations of space, this finds catalogue was not actually included in my Pompeian house floor assemblages study, but, through Roger Ling, the Pompeii Research Committee were convinced that a separate volume on the finds from this Insula, including a full catalogue and distributional analysis, should be included in the project's publications. As a consequence, funded mainly by the British Academy, I spent the first six months of 1993 preparing a catalogue of the all the excavated finds from the Insula, including the smaller dwellings and shops which I had not hitherto researched. The catalogue has been organized according to the house and room in which each artefact was found, and to assemblages within each room. The artefacts within each assemblage are further organised from the most immoveable (e.g. fixtures and furniture) to the most moveable (e.g. coins, jewellery etc.). Thus, the catalogue follows as closely as possible the conditions under which the artefacts where found and, therefore, probably deposited.

In the final publication, I intend that the photographs of the artefacts will be arranged in assemblages according to their findspots, while the drawings of artefact types will be arranged typologically. A tabulated index will also be included, with objects organised, wherever possible, by their designated "class" or "type". My analysis of the distribution will draw on the catalogue to discuss the relationship of the assemblages to the room type and decoration, to other similar assemblages and to assemblages in similar room types in other houses in Pompeii.

Thus, the catalogue has been assembled to present the excavated "finds" from they were found and recorded, and to assess the significance of that distribution. It has a different format from that of most excavation reports because the more usual format is inappropriate the specific purpose of this study. This does not detract from the catalogue's overall usefulness, for, while specialists may have to make more effort to locate all the artefacts from this Insula which belong to their particular specialist class, it will not be impossible for them to do so. On the other hand, the format of this publication might conceivably be a little more comprehensible to students, or indeed other archaeologists, who want to learn more about the context of Roman artefacts and about Roman domestic life in general (e.g. Aisenburg and Harrington 1988: 91f). It might, possibly, even be comprehensible to social historians who are trying to make sense of archaeological documentation. To assist such potential inquiries, a discussion on the function of each particular type of artefact, with references to previous functional studies, is included in each catalogue entry. This discussion is based on specialist catalogues which contain similar types of artefacts and include such functional analysis. The specialists' identification have usually been accepted, unless the context of an artefact or my own specific observations argue against it.

For example, in room 35 of the Casa del Menandro, a small box or chest was found to contain a small set of bronze scales, a bronze statuette of Eros, a bronze base (possibly from a similar statuette), an elaborate double-spouted glazed

Fig.2. Chest contents from room 35, Casa del Menandro (inv nos. 4907,4908,4909B,4909C,4910). Photo: P.M. Allison.

lamp and three bronze pendants (fig.2). The pendants are of a type frequently found in military contexts and reputedly used as decoration for horse harness (Bishop 1988: esp. figs.44–47), but the findspot and associations in the Casa del Menandro do not support this interpretation. Similar pendants led Guenter Ulbert (1969: 21) to conclude that the troops stationed at the early Roman Castel Rheingonheim in Germany were mounted, despite the fact that many of the associated metal finds were buckles and pins from human apparel. In 1897, Louis Jacobi (1897: 500; pls. 68–69) had identified similar enamelled pendants from the Roman military camp of Saalburg as pieces of human adornment. It is conceivable that such pendants could, in fact, have been for both animal and human adornment. This example highlights the potential multifunctional character of many Roman, or any other ancient, artefacts. Too often, when artefacts are farmed out to "specialists", the "specialists" quickly ascribe them with a function pertaining to their own speciality, often on the basis of parallels with other sites, and excluding contextual evidence. In Ulbert's case, he even identified the nature of the site on the basis of such comparative information.

Another example where context can warn specialists of the possibly multipurpose nature of artefacts is a Roman tomb in Germany which reputedly contained painting equip-

Fig.3. Scoop probe from House I 10,3 (inv no.5083). Photo: J. Agee.

ment (Neuburger 1927: 203 figs. 254–255). Included in the assemblage is a bronze instrument with a leaf-shaped scoop at one end and an olivary at the other, similar to one from the House I 10,3 in the Insula del Menandro in Pompeii (fig.3). Such instruments, called scoop probes, are more commonly identified as toilet or medical instruments (Jackson 1986: 158).

But, aside from this potential multifunctionality, one of the main problems encountered in the identification of artefact use is that recent catalogues which contain comparanda often lack comprehensible functional analyses, or references to such. Many have short (often one line) entries, with no references to the terminology used, or to other published examples which might aid their understanding. For example, in one recent catalogue (Stead and Rigby 1986: fig. 59 no. 371), a metal object is illustrated which provided a parallel for one from the Pompeii Collection (invno. 5093, House I 10,1). It was catalogued under a section titled "Other Bronze Objects" (i.e. other than brooches and coins), under a sub-section "Miscellaneous Objects". The catalogue entry reads "Slide key, perhaps for casket, A418, fourth century". Its discovery in a quarry with material dating from mid 1st–4th century AD (Stead and Rigby 1986: 423) presumably meant that it warranted no further discussion or interest beyond this labelling. This was of little help in comprehending the comparable object from Pompeii. Being neither a locksmith nor a Roman key specialist, a lot of time and effort was expended in finding other publications, such as a catalogue of iron implements from the British Museum (Manning 1985) or Albert Neuburger's *Technik des Altertums* (1927) to find out what the term "slide key" meant. Despite referring to theses sources, I was unable to obtain a full understanding of the workings of slide keys, lift keys and tumbler locks, nor, more specifically, was it possible to relate fragmentary remains to a particular lock or key type. Consultation of the catalogue of the finds from Sardis (Waldbaum 1983: esp. 69ff and pl.23) created only further confusion, so eventually, I consulted Professor Manning personally.

Given that I do not believe that I am more stupid or ill-informed than the average archaeologist, the amount of energy expended in discovering the function of every arte-

fact type begs the question: *Why are these specialist catalogues written?* If an archaeologist specialising in domestic life finds such catalogues of limited use, then who are the specialists publishing them for? If they are only intended for other specialists in the same artefact type, then why are they published at all?

I am not advocating that every excavation is published in the format of the re-publication of the finds from the Insula del Menandro. I am merely demonstrating that there is more than one way of discussing, for example, a bronze pendant or a bronze key. Many archaeological artefacts are of mixed fabric character or are potentially multipurpose. The single view site report, which is supposed to have the potential to be valuable to someone some day, is mainly of use to scholars writing similar reports (Hodder 1989: 273), and should thus be done away with, and the paper saved for more useful purposes.

Excavation Publishing

The Frere Report of 1975 (Moffett 1991: 22) stated that there were four levels of archaeological data:

Level I: The site and its excavated finds

Level II: The site notebooks, recording forms, drawings, photographs and negatives

Level III: Full illustration and description of all the structural and stratigraphical relationships, as well as classified finds lists and specialist report

Level IV: a synthesised description with supporting data, selected finds and specialist reports

Thus, the extant material from Level I–III, usually excluding the site itself (although not always) is considered to belong to the excavators or the authority under which they carried out the excavation. Only the Level IV, selected at the discretion of the project director, possibly in consultation with the excavation team, reaches the public domain, usually in the form of an excavation or site report. In the past, the archiving of Level II–III information was largely due to the format in which it was produced – that is, hand-written day books and context sheets with hand-drawn maps and a single set of negatives. This often fragile material has had to be carefully guarded by its owners for fear of irreparable damage and loss to information which could not be regathered.

Nowadays, many excavators have computerized their datasets, usually at both Level II and Level III. There appears no reason why artefact specialists cannot do the same. This system in itself is publication of the data. It can be easily distributed in its entirety, perhaps on CDRom or the Internet, at little cost and without risk of loss or damage to the original dataset. Therefore, one could argue that the publication of the single-view Level IV data need only be in the form of a preliminary report where the excavators present their specific insights on the material with which, at that stage, they have a greater familiarity than other scholars. Once the database management system and the quick-release report have been produced, and the original dataset is safely archived, the main task of the excavators is complete. Other scholars do not, as at present, need to wait up to twenty years for the excavators' interpretation of what they often consider to be their own material. It has already been published. Subsequently, the excavators, or anyone else preferably in consultation with the excavators and specialists, would be free to interpret whichever part of the excavation data they wished. In other words, other archaeologists, such as myself or bronze key specialists, can gain access to this information for whatever investigation we might currently be involved in. In such an ideal situation, I, for one, would not have to wait patiently for an excavation report to be produced, and then discover that the published version is in a format which is not useful to me. Under the current conditions, it is nearly always necessary to consult the primary archive to collect the data necessary for a inquiry in an area which was of little interest to the original excavators.

The concept of database management systems is by no means new. It has been the one of the main areas of discussion at most computer-aided archaeology conferences and workshops since the mid-1960's (Moffett 1991: 97). But, in nearly every paper on the subject, the ideal state where everyone can access everybody else's data systems is dismissed because a) archaeologists are not that generous with what they conceive of as **their** information and b) how could they read datasets produced by other people on other systems (Allison 1994)? These are not unsurmountable problems.

1) In the first instance, there is the belief of some excavators that the material s/he has excavated is her/his personal property. This would seem to be a "hang-up" which can be traced back to the 18th century origins of archaeology when the archaeologist normally funded his (it was usually a "his") own project and considered that he therefore owned anything that was excavated, and that he had sole rights to discuss its intellectual or artistic value. This ownership was still acceptable at the beginning of the 20th century (Evans

1899–1900: 4f). However, even in 18th century excavations, for example those of Herculaneum, there was considerable reaction amongst intellectuals against this proprietorial approach to information about the past (Trevelyan 1976: 44). Today, in theory, the excavator works to produce archaeological information for the profession and for the public, and we have come to terms with the fact that the artefacts themselves no longer belong to the excavator. In fact, the concept of archaeologists building up their own private collections is quite abhorrent. However, we still appear to accept that excavators own the information they have excavated. It will be another small step in the education of some archaeologists when they learn to give due credit to colleagues who have carried out an excavation and who have willingly released the material for whatever interpretation it might inspire. The excavator is then free to critically appraise the interpretations of others.

2) The second problem is that of reading the data systems of other excavators. Again this appears to be a problem of education rather than inability. When database management systems were first introduced into the documentation of field archaeology, computer-literate archaeologists felt that commercial databases were inappropriate for the needs of archaeologists and therefore they needed to design their own software. Many years on, with many more computer-literate archaeologists in practice, these specially-designed packages have become outmoded. Also, the spread of computer knowledge among everyday archaeologists has meant that we have been able to adapt commercially available software for our own needs without the aid of archaeological computing experts (Moffett 1991: esp. 20). This means that the archaeological data can remain stored on easily available software which is regularly updated and adapted to suit the needs of the commercial world. If one can cope with the frustrations of reading manuals designed for the creation of company mailing lists and stock-taking requirements, and conceive of how this could adapted to fit one's own needs, then anyone can make their own database management system.

But that still does not mean that anyone can read anyone else's system. Therefore, there has been much discussion and many ideas put forward, with the Danes appearing to lead the field (Masden 1994), concerning the creation of a uniform worldwide database management system which we would all learn to use and read (Moffett 1991: 31). This appears to have about as much chance of eventuating as Esperanto. Instead, it would seem that we should think more laterally. Rather than designing a system to suit all needs, we must, again, educate future archaeologists to be able to read the various and diverse systems of their colleagues. If archaeologists use commercially available software and students are trained, not to familiarise themselves with one system, but to be able to adapt to dealing with a variety of systems (Moffet 1991: 97f), then the problem is reduced to one of being able to cope with the manner in which the data is presented – that is, the terminology and classification systems used in the input. Going by the discussion on the Archaeological Institute of America electronic bulletin board in 1993–4, the Archaeological Data Archive Project which is being set up at Bryn Mawr appears mainly concerned with the establishment of "data dictionaries" and accompanying explanations of data structure and terms.

Conclusions

If we can say that we can and have learnt to master the art of reading and understanding other archaeologists' excavation reports in their present form, then why can future archaeologists not learn to read and understand other archaeologists' database management systems? Or is it, indeed, nearer the truth to admit that we have not actually achieved sufficient an understanding of others' excavation reports to be able to fully utilise them in our own writings about the past. Has this lack of comprehension contributed to the current self-reflexive view of the discipline and the debate about how the practice of archaeology can be brought in touch with the theory, or vice versa?

It might be argued that a similar gap is evident between the concept of computer database management systems for excavations and their use by investigators other than those who were instrumental in setting them up. The phrase *"computer applications in archaeology"* bandied about in many circles has tended to mean *"how do we get the data in?"*. We should also be concerning ourselves with getting the data out and using it to improve our knowledge of the past. Excavation data should to be presented in the most flexible mode possible, so that scholars with research questions which might differ from those of the excavator can have access to the material in as simple a form as possible, as soon as possible. As Sebastian Rahtz has pointed out (1986: 3), most excavation reports are concerned with dissemination of information, not opinions. If we archaeologists who work with excavated data did not have to spend all our time manually extracting the excavation information or reworking other peoples' data, we might have enough time to actually use material culture to write about the past – whatever that means.

Acknowledgements

I am very grateful to Paul Blinkhorn and Christopher Cumberpatch for including a version of this paper in their session "New approaches to Artefact Analysis" at the fifteenth annual conference of the Theoretical Archaeology Group, University of Durham, December 1993. I would also like to thank Roger Ling and the Pompeii Research Committee for inviting me to study the finds from the Insula del Menandro in Pompeii, and the Soprintendenza archeologica di Pompei for permitting me to work in the archives and storerooms. In addition I am grateful to Roland Fletcher, Estelle Lazer and Stephanie Moser for reading versions of this paper and for their comments.

Bibliography

Adams, W.Y. and Adams, E.W. 1991. *Archaeological typology and practical reality* (Cambridge).

Aisenburg, N. and Harrington, M. 1987. *Women of Academe* (Massachusetts).

Allison, P.M. 1992a. 'Artefact assemblages: not "the Pompeii Premise"', in R. Whitehouse et al, eds., *Papers of the Fourth Conference of Italian Archaeology* 3 part 1 (London) 49–56.

Allison, P.M. 1992b. *The distribution of Pompeian house contents and it significance* (PhD, University of Sydney, UMI Ann Arbor 1994).

Allison, P.M. 1993. 'How do we identify the use of space in Roman housing?', in: E. Moormann, ed., *Proceedings of the Fifth International Congress on Ancient Wall-painting*, BABESCH Suppl.3, 4–11.

Allison, P.M. 1994. 'Issues of data exchange and accessibility: Pompeii' in: I. Johnson, ed. *Methods in the Mountains: Proceedings of the UISPP Commission IV Meeting* (Sydney) 35–42.

Allison, P.M 1995a. 'On-going seismic activity and its effect on living conditions in Pompeii in the last decades', in: T. Fröhlich and L. Jacobelli, eds., *Archeologie & Seismology. La regione vesuviana dal 62 al 79 d.C. problemi archeologici e sismologici* (Rome).

Allison, P.M. 1995b. 'Pompeian House Contents: Data Collection and Interpretative Procedures for a reappraisal of Roman Domestic life and site formation processes' *Journal of European Archaeol* 3.1, 145–176.

Allison P.M. 1997. 'Artefact Distribution and Spatial Function in Pompeian Houses' in B. Rawson and P. Weaver, eds., *The Roman Family in Italy: Status Sentiment and Space* (Oxford University Press).

Atkinson et al. 1904. Excavations at Phylakopi in Melos (London).

Bishop, M.C. 1988. 'Cavalry equipment of the Roman army in the first century AD' in: J. C. Coulston, ed., *Military equipment and the identity of Roman soldiers, Proceedings of the Fourth Roman Military Conference* (Oxford) 67–195.

Evans, A.J. 1899–1900. 'Knossos I, the palace' *Annual of the British School at Athens* 6, 3–70.

Elia, O. 1934. 'Pompei – Relazione sullo scavo dell'Insula X della Regio I' *Notizie degli Scavi* XII, 264–344.

Finley, M.I. 1985. *Ancient History: evidence and models* (London).

Garnsey, P. and Saller, R. 1987. *The Roman Empire: economy, society and culture* (London).

Hodder, I. 1989. 'Writing archaeology: site reports in context' *Antiquity* 63, 268–74.

Jackson, R. 1986. 'A set of Roman medical instruments from Roman Italy' *Britannia* 17, 119–167.

Jacobi, L. 1897. *Das Romerkastell Saalburg bei Homburg* (Homburg).

Knight, D. 1981. *Ordering the World: a history of classifying man* (London).

Ling, R. 1997. The Insula of the Menander at Pompeii, vol I: The Structures (Oxford).

Liversidge, J. 1976. *Everyday Life in the Roman Empire* (London and New York).

McDonald, A.H. 1966. *Republican Rome* (London).

Maiuri, A. 1933. *La Casa del Menandro e il suo tesoro di argenteria* (Roma).

Manning W.H. 1985. *Catalogue of Romano-British iron tools, fittings and weapons in the British Museum* (London).

Masden, T. 1994. 'Integrating methods and data: reflections on archaeological research in an IT environment' in: I. Johnson, ed., *Methods in the Mountains: Proceedings of the UISPP Commission IV Meeting* (Sydney), 27–34.

Moffett, J. 1991. 'Computers in Archaeology: approaches and applications past and present' in: S. Ross, J. Moffet and J. Henderson, eds., 13–39.

Neuburger, A. 1927. *Technik des Altertums* (Leipzig).

Rawson, B. 1992. *The Family in Ancient Rome* (2nd edition, London).

Rahtz, S.P.Q. 1986. 'Possible directions in electronic publishing' in: S. Laflin, ed., *Computer Applications in Archaeology*, 3–13.

Ross, S., Moffet, J. and Henderson, J., eds., 1991. *Computing for Archaeologists* (Oxford).

Sackett L.H. *et al.* 1992. *Knossos from Greek City to Roman Colony: Excavations at the Unexplored Mansion II* (Oxford).

Stead, I.M. and Rigby, Valerie. 1986. *Baldock, the excavation of a Roman and pre-Roman settlement, 1968–72* (London).

Strocka, V.M. 1984. *Casa del Principe di Napoli*, Häuser in Pompeji 1 (Tübingen).

Trevelyan, R. 1976. *The Shadow of Vesuvius. Pompeii AD79* (London).

Ulbert, G. 1969. *Das frührömische Kastell Rheingenheim* (Berlin).

Vorrips. A. 1982. 'Mabrino's helmet: a framework for structuring archaeological data' in: Robert Whallon and James A. Brown, eds., *Essays on Archaeological Typology*, 93–126 (Evanston).

Waldbaum, J.C. 1983. *Metalwork from Sardis: The finds through 1974* (Harvard).

Wallace-Hadrill, A., ed., 1989. *Patronage in Ancient Society* (London).

Family, Household and Production:
The Potters of the Saintonge, France, 1500 to 1800

Elizabeth Musgrave

From the thirteenth to the seventeenth centuries one of the primary production centres for the supply of exotic pottery to Britain and northern Europe was the Saintonge region of western France (Hurst, Neal & Beuningen, 1986: 76). The principal pottery manufacturing sites lay on a wooded, limestone plateau bordered by the river Charente, to the east and north east of Saintes, some 50 kilometres downstream from the maritime port of La Rochelle. Using a series of riverine ports such as Port-Berteau and Taillebourg, and a network of Roman roads running north-south along the plateau and east-west from Saintes to Cognac, ceramic vessels produced in rural workshops were distributed in Aunis and Saintonge, around the North Sea and, from the seventeenth century, throughout the Atlantic world, in a trade that spanned five hundred years.

The chronology and evolution of both the pottery industries and their products are known from archaeological fieldwork in the Saintonge and from site finds throughout northern Europe and North America (see Chapelot n.d.; Renimel 1978). Interpretation of the material evidence suggests that workshops producing Saintonge wares were first founded in the early thirteenth century, in the present-day commune of La Chapelle-des-Pots. For approximately one and a half centuries the workshops produced fine plain, glazed and decorated wares which have been found on local châteaux and abbey sites and which were exported to the North Sea region. This coincided with the English possession of Gascony and was part of a trade in commodities between the two regions which included wine. Ceramic production and distribution was disrupted by the wars of the late fourteenth and fifteenth centuries which devastated the Saintonge, for it lay at the heart of the Anglo-French conflict. The numbers of kiln sites in the area around La Chapelle fell and production was much reduced in scale.

From the mid fifteenth to the seventeenth centuries, pottery production increased, although on fewer sites, and both high quality, polychrome ornamental wares and plain, household vessels were exported. After the mid seventeenth century there was an important product change, to a relatively coarse household ware, perhaps because high status

stoneware and porcelaine, then faïence, began to replace decorated earthenwares and as colonial trade increased demand for household goods. Workshop sites increased in number, production seems to have grown in volume and products were both distributed regionally and exported. The early modern centuries also saw the rise of other forms of ceramic production, notably the manufacture of roofing tile in the modern-day communes of Ecoyeux, Vénérand, Brizambourg and Saint-Bris, and the manufacture of *bujour*, large, coil-made vessels used for the salting of meat, perhaps for the provisioning of ships for the growing maritime trade. By the early nineteenth century in the eight communes to the north-east of Saintes there were 36 kilns for the production of pottery and 120 tile kilns. The industry continued at roughly this level until just before the first world war (Renimel 1978: 237).

The production methods of Saintonge pottery manufacture have been reconstructed using both archaeological and documentary evidence. The excavation of a half dozen medieval kiln sites has allowed for the technical processes of the manufacture and firing of vessels to be reconstituted (Barton 1963, Dunning 1968). Using records from the *seigneurie* of Ecoyeux, Chapelot has examined the resources used by ceramicists and their conditions of exploitation, which has also allowed for comment on the production methods of potters (Chapelot 1983). Discoveries at Port-Berteau on the river Charente have facilitated the reconstruction of some aspects of the marketing and transportation of finished products during both the thirteenth and seventeenth centuries (Chapelot 1972).

The social processes of manufacture have, as with other pottery industries, received less attention. Household and community relationships are difficult to reconstruct from artefacts or production sites and there is no surviving corpus of documents from either the middle ages or the early modern period which can be used to study the industry in depth (*c.f.* Le Patourel 1968: 101). The potters of La Chapelle and neighbouring Ecoyeux are not absent from all documentary records, although surviving evidence is scattered through a wide variety of sources and over time. From the sixteenth century there are notarial and seigneurial archives for the communes around La Chapelle in which land transactions and other property transfers are found. The baptisms, marriages and burials of potters and their household members are recorded in the registers of the Catholic church from the mid seventeenth century, sometimes with comments about household structure and relationships. Occasional dispute material involving potters can be found in the, admittedly thin, records of the local seigneurial courts.

Using this diverse documentary evidence, the aim of this chapter is to reconstruct the social means of production of the pottery industries of La Chapelle and Ecoyeux in the early modern period, from the mid sixteenth century to the revolution of 1789. The methods of pottery production will be examined; who made pots and how the means of production of pottery were owned, used and transmitted from one generation to the next. Secondly, mechanisms of trade and distribution will be discussed and the impact of market relations on individuals and communities will be assessed. Finally, the significance of the pottery industries to the families and communities of the La Chapelle region will be evaluated; did the householders engaged in pottery production identify themselves as potters or was manufacture simply another means of subsistence in a domestic economy of varied strategies and multiple livelihoods? This paper offers a tentative exploration of these issues.

From at least the late fifteenth century, the primary unit of production of earthenware pottery in the Saintonge region was the household workshop, with its combination of domestic unit and industrial site. The pottery industries combined Van der Leeuw's categories of 'household industry' and 'workshop industry' (Sinopoli 1991: 99–100). In some households pottery was produced and sold by family members on a part-time basis whereas other family enterprises comprised full-time production specialists. The household was the social and economic unit which gave access to raw materials, labour and capital equipment such as kilns. The availability of these commodities to individual households, together with other resources such as arable and woodland, determined whether family members would be full or part-time artisans or specialists in other economic activities. Families could move from one strategy to the other, as resources and need arose. The household mode of organisation was most suited to an industry where the participants were poor in capital and where the main utilisable resource was labour, which could be provided by the family. Taxation records showing relative wealth do not survive for early modern Saintonge but the small dowries and small-scale property ownership of potters indicated in the notarial records reveal that they were part of the poor to middling peasantry rather than of the rural elite.[1]

The production of roofing tile differed in several respects from that of domestic pottery. As with ceramic vessels, much tile production was carried out by household enterprises. Between 1552 and 1557, the seigneur of Ecoyeux issued eight *baillettes* (leases) to small-scale manufacturers; that granted to Mathurin for 'his house, outbuildings, tile kiln and other appurtenances consisting of meadow, wood, waste and arable' show a clear association of household and enterprise (Chapelot 1983:158). But tile manufacturers and domestic potters were distinct, with different families specialising in one or other and they lived in different locations; in La Chapelle parish in the seventeenth and eighteenth centuries the tilers resided in hamlets on the northern edge of the parish while the majority of potters were resident in the *bourg*. Tile production required greater amounts of raw materials, clay, wood and limestone than pottery production and to reduce costs, workshops were sited as close as possible to exploitable resources. Secondly, tile manufacture sometimes necessitated large sites, away from the household. In 1672 the prior of Saint Vaize rented a meadow to Jean Herouard, merchant tiler, on which to build a workshop, a kiln and drying sheds to produce roofing tile. Herouard was also permitted to extract clay and limestone from nearby land belonging to the prior over a six year period, for which he paid 80 *livres* per year.[2] The tile was to be produced in some quantity and exported out of the region using the nearby river Charente.

The household workshop or enterprise of potters and tilers was based on the labour skills and pooled resources of the nuclear family of a married couple and their children, sometimes together with other family members and employees, the latter often on a temporary or short-term basis. Marriage contracts of the seventeenth and eighteenth centuries show that pottery producing enterprises in the Saintonge were initially created upon or following the marriage of a craftsman and his wife, when present or future family property was transferred to a new social unit. The combined capital of bride and groom would equip their residence and provide them with a means of subsistence, which included the skill to produce and sell pottery, and marriage conferred adult status as head of a household on a male artisan. In 1734, Pierre Tenot of La Chapelle married Michelle Nadaud of Saint-Eutrophe, Saintes. His parents endowed him with the equipment necessary to set up a pottery workshop, a potter's wheel, two spatulas of elm wood and a rod for beating earth, to be conveyed to him on the day of the marriage ceremony. Tenot also brought a small area of coppiced woodland and a few rows of newly-planted vine, along with some linen, to provide for the needs of the new household. Nadaud brought household equipment, linen and a walnut chest to furnish the new home.[3] François Noureau who married Marie Rambaud in 1735, likewise brought a potter's wheel, a spatula, a set of tables and the future inheritance of his parents' goods, while his bride, the widow of a potter, brought 'all of her possessions' to the match.[4] Parish registers and marriage contracts, where the occupations of grooms are listed, show a difference in labour status between unmarried men, who were likely to be workers in family or other workshops or casual labourers employing a variety of skills, and their occupations once married. Pierre Tenot was described as 'potier journalier, fils de Guillaume Tenot, potier' in 1734 and his own son François was a 'journalier' when he married in 1779.[5]

Marriage and independent economic status did not always immediately coincide, however. When a couple married before family property could be transferred to them, an extended household unit might be created, usually temporarily, for this was not a common permanent social unit in the west of France in this period. When Jean Gautret, potter, married Elizabeth Forestier in 1687, they went to live with or adjacent to Gautret's parents who ran a pottery workshop. Gautret was promised one quarter of his parents' goods on their death while Forestier brought her paternal inheritance of a small area of arable land and a small garden, abutting the Gautrets' house and kiln. The Gautrets probably worked an extended family enterprise until the death of the parents allowed Jean to create an independent workshop.[6] Other households were formed on the basis of very small or no landed property or capital equipment, the industrial and agrarian skills of the couple being the only means of their future subsistence. When Jean Turpeaud, 'earthenware potter', married Jeanne Pilier in 1729 he brought a house and garden and she brought linen, a walnut chest, a cauldron, a small area of woodland and a small piece of meadow, to the marriage.[7] Their combined property and skills as a potter and spinner or pastoralist were the basis of their future prosperity; such small pottery workshop enterprises, based on little capital but craft skill, were typical of this period.

The combined economic and social importance of marriage in the formation of households has led historians to examine 'strategies' of union amongst different social groups. Trade endogamy has been observed in many early modern towns; in sixteenth-century Lyons 25 per cent of the daughters of artisans married men in the same occupation as their fathers, which rises to 33 per cent if closely allied trades are included (Davies 1981: 144). Less attention has been paid to rural artisans but Rowlands' study of the West Midlands in the eighteenth century shows that over 43 per cent of the known daughters of artisans married artisans, in many cases men in the same crafts as their fathers (Rowlands 1989: 146). It is difficult to quantify clear marriage strategies amongst the potters of La Chapelle but there is a relatively high coincidence of unions between daughters of potters and men who would become potters at some time after their wedding. Reconstruction of the family and descendants of Guillaume Tenot and Suzanne Deminié, who married in the 1680s, shows that of their four daughters, two married potters. Of their five granddaughters born to Pierre Tenot and his wife Michelle Nadaud, three married potters.

Trade endogamy is clearest in the marriage patterns of widows. Widows had a legal right to continue the trade of their husbands after his death and to act as the legal head of a household of minor children. Few such women continued to work as artisans: debts to be paid, preoccupation with children and lack of formal craft training meant that women were dependent upon male artisanal labour, the costs of which could outweigh the profits of a small enterprise (see Musgrave 1993). To continue potting or tile making, widows needed the assistance of relatives or journeymen, or a new husband, although the chances of any widow remarrying in this period were low (Dupâcquier 1979: 25). Widows with property or potting contacts did remarry in La Chapelle, often with potters; in 1735 Marie Rambaud, widow of Jean Tenot, potter, married François Noureau, 'potier journalier' and in 1780, Catherine Renaud, widow and daughter of a potter, married Pierre Loiseau, 'journalier', who was a potter by 1787.[8] What was important in all marriages was partly the occupational skills of the bride and her familiarity with and tolerance for the work practices of a particular craft, but also the combined resources of the couple and the social and economic contacts that alliance with the bride's family would provide for workshop units based on household and kin labour. For couples entering into a second marriage, the re-establishment of a disrupted household, an extension of kin contacts and consolidation of an existing social position were important.

The household was the legal unit through which land and other resources necessary for pottery production were owned and exploited. Land transferred to a household upon marriage or after, as inheritance, provided industrial and domestic resources. Coppiced woodland provided fuel for house and kiln; pasture was used for livestock or exploited for clay; the household also had important rights in common and waste lands, both for pasturage and for mineral resources. The rights of householders to exploit waste and to collect brushwood on the seigneurial domaine were established or re-established in the later fifteenth century, when the region around La Chapelle was resettled and tenancies reconstituted after the Anglo-French wars. All land in this area was held in lordship, independent of ownership; seigneurs had the right to levy taxes in kind on peasant exploitation of waste and other 'communal' resources, which, in turn, were only a 'right' where an agreement had been negotiated between lord and tenant. In the late fifteenth century certain residents of the parish of Ecoyeux were granted permission to build kilns and to extract clay and stone from domaine property to make roofing tiles and lime, in return for the production of tile for the reconstruction of houses and settlements within the *seigneurie* and on payment of one *pipe* of lime per year to the seigneur (Chapelot, 1983: 130–1). Although there were periodic disputes between lord and peasants over the terms of land exploitation the rights of householders to exploit domainial and waste lands in return for fixed dues, in and around La Chapelle, were extant until the Revolution (Chapelot, 1983: 123).

Householders without property or lacking adequate rights in waste and domainial land, or who simply required greater amounts of raw materials than they could supply from their own holdings, could rent or purchase exploitable resources, with the male head of household acting as legal representative of the domestic and industrial unit. The notarial records for La Chapelle contain frequent, scattered references to purchases and leases of small areas of woodland to exploit for fuel: for example, in 1734 Jean Tenot, potter of La Chapelle, purchased 'three small pieces of woodland' at different locations in the parish and in 1749 Jean Bouen, potter of Ecoyeux, purchased a 'tiny piece of woodland' one *journal* in extent, for 18 *livres*.[9] More commonly, rents were paid to exploit woodland, as when Jacques Romballay, tiler, of Brizambourg parish contracted to cut wood from an area of the domainial forest and paid 26 *livres* 10 *sous* per *journal* of woodland exploited.[10] But more simply and commonly, Pierre Portier of Saint Césaire paid a farmer 37 *livres* for sale and delivery of faggots in 1747.[11]

The household was the main source of labour for the manufacture of ceramics in the Saintonge region between at least the fifteenth and the nineteenth centuries. The basic work unit was the nuclear family of husband, wife and children. The transmission rate of potters' skills from father to son is striking: the two sons of Guillaume Tenot, Jean and Pierre, both became potters and Pierre's two sons were also employed in the craft; training in craft skill was acquired within the household through informal assistance and the direct teaching of children. Households might also include extended family members and servants, both male and female, were frequently resident even in modest households. In the 1580s the tiler Denis Jouhan worked with his wife, his children, his brother-in-law and a servant (Chapelot 1983: 122). The godfather of Anne, daughter of potter Pierre Boutinet, baptised in 1728, was a servant in their household and in 1729, Jean Rouleau, potter of La Chapelle, was sued for compensation for fathering an illegitimate child by a maid servant who had worked for three to four years in his household.[12] In addition, workshops would take on temporary or daily workers, usually young, single men, who would be paid by 'contract', a pre-arranged sum to cover a specified term of employment, by the task or by the day. Pierre Tenot in 1734 and, a generation later, his son François, were both 'journalier' or day workers when they married. probably combining work for established pottery workshops with a range of agricultural and other casual, manual work. Formal apprenticeship also occurred. In 1730, Jean Baron, potter of La Chapelle, took on Pierre, son of Mathurin Baron, aged 15–16, as apprentice. Pierre would reside in Baron's household for two years, was to be fed and furnished with tools, trained as a potter and to receive 10 *sous* for each kiln load of pottery which he stacked and unloaded during his apprenticeship, the agreed cost of which was settled at 30 *livres*.[13]

The involvement of family and household members in pottery production was dependent upon gender, age and the location of the production site. Le Patourel suggests that in late Medieval England labour was male and female; in Toynton a woman who sued a potter for arrears of wages in 1308 had been employed at clay pits and at piece work, although the nature of the tasks is not clear (Le Patourel 1968: 116). But in much of early modern Europe there was a clear and often strict gendered division of labour within household enterprises which affected the roles men and women played in craft work. Craft production was, in many trades, male work: in woodworking, leather, metal and building for example, men took part in skilled manufacture and

production work, hired and supervised male employees, sought new contracts for work and performed all other legal and public functions associated with the enterprise. Artisanal families with limited resources invested in craft training for sons while daughters would be taught domestic skills, hence their predominance in the textile, food preparation and petty retailing trades. In household workshops, a woman's tasks were to prepare raw materials, financial organisation and help with the marketing of finished goods (Musgrave, forthcoming). A wife was a husband's assistant, providing services for the better completion of his skilled work. If a husband died and his widow continued his trade she could hire workers, furnish raw materials and act in a public capacity but she often lacked the skill to fashion materials or perform craft work, because in the majority of trades formal training was a male monopoly.

The division of labour in the Saintonge ceramics industries seems to have followed this model. Men and women brought different resources to a new household; husbands might contribute land, portable craft equipment such as a wheel and other tools and the craft skill to throw and fire vessels and to oversee the pottery production process. Wives would contribute land, domestic equipment, craft skills learned while assisting their fathers and mothers and during their employment as domestic servants. Female household members, wives, daughters and servants, might thus assist with the collection and preparation of clay for throwing, aid the potter, help to decorate and stack vessels, as the need for labour arose and as their other domestic duties related to household management, small holding and child care permitted. The division of labour between males and females was culturally and economically determined but the complementary contributions of each to the household was vital for its survival.

The participation of household members in ceramics production was conditioned by the physical relationship between the workshop and the household residence. Women, the elderly and small children participated more in crafts where household and workshop coincided. Contemporary attitudes to the different roles of men and women, public versus private, had important effects on the social and physical spaces occupied by each gender. Women were most economically and socially active in the household and local community, using skills and techniques traditionally practised as part of the domestic economy. Men had a public and a legal role, moved frequently away from their homes and even their communities to work and to socialise. Hanusse has shown that in the pottery industries of eighteenth-century Sadirac, the domestic and artisanal functions of buildings were completely intermingled and that each dwelling was also a potential workshop (Hanusse 1987: 104). This is also true of the buildings of La Chapelle. The preparation of clay, throwing of pots and drying of products could have taken place in almost any household, using outbuildings, gardens and lean-to sheds that were associated with dwellings. Structural requirements for pottery production were few (see Baker 1991: 8–9). The parish registers show that the majority of potters in La Chapelle parish resided in the *bourg* and so the production of ceramic vessels may have taken place next to their houses. Jean Tenot, potter, rented a house with outhouses, lean-tos, gardens, as well as arable, vines and woodland, for 35 *livres* per year in 1727, and vessel production could have taken place in the outbuildings.[14] Thus women and children were likely to contribute their labour to the pottery industry.

While the household provided the basic unit for pottery production, co-operation between household and transactions between enterprises were frequent and important: the individual workshop did not work in isolation from its neighbours. Le Patourel's model of late medieval English pottery production, where artisans seldom co-operated, either in the digging of clay or in the manufacture of vessels, is not true of the late middle ages and the early modern period in the Saintonge (see Vince 1981: 319). Family associations for all or part of pottery production were widespread. Of eight *baillettes* issued by the seigneur of Ecoyeux between 1552 and 1557 for kiln building and resource exploitation, two were to family groups of fathers and sons or brothers, and three to associations of artisans, perhaps neighbours or brothers-in-law (Chapelot 1983: 128). When Jean Tenot, potter of La Chapelle, married Marie, daughter of Pierre Loiseau, potter, in 1728, as part of the marriage settlement Pierre promised to help extract a certain quantity of earth for making pottery from an area of woodland belonging to Jean's father Guillaume, also a potter.[15] The Tenot family exploited resources in common, despite the establishment of separate households after the marriage of adult children, while marriage itself extended the range of work associations of an artisan.

Co-operation was particularly important in kiln use. Hanusse's study of kiln use at Sadirac (Gironde), showed that individual production and firing was not realised before the nineteenth century; from the sixteenth century, when the industry was established, co-operation and association were normal (Hanusse 1987: 105). A household could own or rent a whole kiln or part of a kiln, anything between one sixth and three quarters of a single structure. In the latter cases, negotiation and co-operation in the use of the kiln was essential (Hanusse 1987: 104). In 1770, Jeanne Portier, widow of a tiler, paid 500 *livres* for buildings and land, including 'including one half portion and a quarter of the second half portion of a pottery kiln' in Les Moines, Ecoyeux, in which Jean Geraud and François Merlet jointly owned the remaining portion.[16] In 1731, Jean Mourin, potter, purchased one sixth of a share in a kiln together with one sixth of the surrounding structures and work spaces at Les Portiers, Vénérand.[17] The firing of kilns may have taken place on a rotational basis, between associated owners, but given the cost of fuel in early modern France, negotiated, collective firing seems more likely.

As at Sadirac, kilns were collectively owned in the Saintonge. What is clear about these pottery industries is that the production of vessels, based within the household, was a separate social and economic process to the firing of pots in kilns. Kiln ownership did not necessarily coincide with the manufacture of vessels. While kiln owners could and did make pots, often in an adjacent household workshop, much vessel manufacture took place at different locations, by potters who negotiated access to firing or who sold their unfired products to artisans with kilns. Kiln ownership may have distinguished one group of potters from their peers, for in some of the Saintonge *seigneuries* it alone conveyed rights of resource exploitation in the lord's domainial lands. In sixteenth-century Ecoyeux the construction of kilns required seigneurial consent; the payment of dues, annually before 1560 and thereafter per kiln firing, conferred both the right to build and use a kiln and to exploit the lord's domaine for clay and fuel. In the 1580s, Denis Jouhan took over the use of a kiln and workshop after its builder, his neighbour, had died. Use and ownership were distinct in the lord's eye, for the former and not the latter conferred rights to exploit domaine resources (Chapelot 1983: 138). A lawsuit of 1703 with the seigneur of Brizambourg shows that potters who owned a kiln in this *seigneurie* were obliged to pay a yearly rent of 12 *livres*, which included rights to extract clay from the lord's domaine (Chapelot 1983: 146). The implication here is that potters who did not own kilns and who did not pay dues, lacked these rights.

Many potters who produced ceramic vessels did not have regular access to kilns and thus had to negotiate temporary or occasional use with kiln owners. At the end of the seventeenth century a potter from Les Moines, Ecoyeux, rented the use of a kiln to fire his products in return for a 'rent' of 50 per cent of his fired vessels. Whether this was as an individual or as part of a collective firing enterprise is unknown (Chapelot 1983: 134). In 1715, Texier, potter of Ecoyeux, fired pots in his neighbours' kilns (Chapelot 1983: 145). Many potters seem to have produced unfired pots as their primary occupation, being commissioned or subcontracted or simply selling the product to artisans who owned or had regular access to kilns. Chapelot cites a law suit of 1735 between two potters of Archingeay who regularly worked together, one with a kiln and one without. In this instance, 150 pots and seven dozen 'buies' were 'sold' to the kiln owner (Chapelot 1983: 134). Subcontracting was widespread in all artisanal industries in the eighteenth century, from the textile to the metal-working trades. Where craft labour rather than fixed capital was the main resource, it was the main way in which an increase in demand for manufactured goods could be satisfied. In the Saintonge as in nineteenth-century Beauce many artisans were in effect little more than journeymen or salaried employees, wholly dependent upon the client-employer, 'a plebeian artisan group merging into the day labourer class' (Farcy 1984: 232). Part-time or seasonal work producing air-dried pots was a useful supplement to household income. This might account for the strong presence of potters in the *bourg* of La Chapelle revealed by documentary sources but the detection of kiln sites in the surrounding hamlets and countryside, by archaeological survey.

The period after 1750 witnessed some important changes in the organisation of production in the Saintonge industries. Firstly, new products were introduced into the parish, notably faïence – tin glazed and painted earthenware – used as a table ware and as household ornament. The two faïenciers for whom there is evidence in the eighteenth century were both migrants from other regions of France and had close links with merchants in Saintes. In the 1750s and 1760s, Jean Laurant, from Toulouse, traded his faïence with Saintais merchants, from amongst whom came his wife and godparents for several of his children. In 1789, Daniel Bodin of Cognac worked in La Chapelle while his sister was married to a porcelaine dealer in Saintes. Through these individuals new production and marketing techniques may have been introduced to the Saintonge earthenware potters; Bodin at least had close links with the La Chapelle potters for his second wife, Madeleine, was a native of the parish and the godmother of their first child was her relative, the wife of the potter Pierre Boutinet.[18]

Secondly, the archaeological record shows that the late seventeenth and eighteenth centuries were a period of expansion in pottery production, with evidence for a proliferation of kiln sites in La Chapelle, although they need not all be strictly contemporary. An expansion in pottery production coincided with growth in all industrial and manufactured products in France in this period, a result of expansion in overseas, particularly colonial, trade, a growth in population, especially in towns, and what Cissie Fairchilds has called a 'consumer revolution' whose main characteristic was a desire of all sections of society for dress, personal and domestic ornamentation, particularly cheap, popular copies of elite items (Fairchilds 1993: 228–9). The increased demand for earthenware pottery seems to have been met in two ways. Firstly, there was some increase in the numbers of permanent workshops producing pottery, but this was temporary and limited in scope. In the absence of surviving taxation records from the Saintonge an attempt has been made to estimate the numbers of households headed by potters in La Chapelle using entries of ecclesiastical events in the parish records. While this is not an accurate reflection of all workshops, it does provide an illustrative index of change over time.

Table 1. Decadal Total of Potters as Heads of Household, from the Parish Registers of La Chapelle

1721–30	=	20
1731–40	=	31
1741–50	=	21
1751–60	=	20
1761–70	=	20
1771–80	=	23
1781–90	=	22

With the exception of the 1730s, when the number rose by 50 per cent, there was remarkable stability in the numbers of 'visible' professed potters. In the 1730s, certain households may have been temporarily attracted to change their primary economic focus to pottery production or even to move into the parish to work. When production and market conditions declined in the following decade, the normal level of participation of around 20 'visible' households resumed.

Table 2: Estimated Longevity of Potters' Household/Workshops as Indicated by Entries in the Parish Registers of La Chapelle

Decade	Total households appearing for first time	Longevity of enterprise					
		<3 years	3–5 years	6–9 years	10–14 years	15+ years	Mean years
1710–19	9	2	1	2	2	2	9
1720–9	15	0	0	4	5	6	13
1730–9	18	1	5	5	0	7	9.3
1740–9	5	2	1	0	1	1	7.1
1750–9	10	0	2	2	2	4	11.2
1760–9	5	0	0	1	2	2	12.5
1770–9	10	3	1	1	3	2	8.5

The period of the greatest rate of establishment of 'visible' potters' establishments likewise occurred in the 1720s and 1730s, when 50 to 75 per cent more enterprises were founded than in the decade after 1710. Work on rural households in other regions of France suggests that this period was one of relative affluence, when employment was buoyant and the lower classes relatively prosperous, indicated in Baulant's study of the Meaux region by increased material possessions of peasant households, in both quantity and value, as recorded in post-mortem inventories (Baulant, 1975). The decades of the 1740s and 1760s, conversely, saw an 'appearance' rate of only five households each, 50 per cent less than during a 'normal' decade. Both of these decades were periods of warfare, of the Austrian Succession and the Seven Years War respectively, which much reduced overseas trade and depressed internal markets within France. Also, after 1750, real wage levels dropped throughout France by about a third, a depression in real income which persisted into the 1790s, again reducing domestic market demand for ceramics.

The relative stability in the numbers of households whose head was primarily identified as a potter and the longevity of many potting households, once founded, suggests either that real expansion in the industry by an increase in the number of permanent workshops was limited in time to the 1720s and 1730s and that growth was achieved elsewhere by other means, above all by the increased fragmentation of production processes and increased subcontraction of vessel production to potters involved in only part of the manufacturing process (Rowlands 1989: 109). Sonenscher has shown the importance of fragmentation and growth in product specialisation in urban trades such as hatting and furniture making in this period (Sonenscher 1989: 22–7, 31–4, 131–51). Artisans or labourers with mixed economic interests and relevant craft skill took on some aspects of pottery as subcontractors of other workshops, producing the vessels in their own households with their own materials and tools.

Thirdly, there was some small growth of larger enterprises. By 1811–12, in La Chapelle commune, 15 pottery workshops employed 60 workers, a mean of four workers per shop. In Saint Césaire, six workshops employed 24 artisans, again a mean of 4 per shop and in Vénérand, three workshops employed 14 workers or 4.5 per shop (Renimel 1978: 323). The median and the modal size of workshops are unknown, but some enterprises were clearly employing more than male family labour. A core of large and a mass of small scale producers has been shown for many urban trades; in Nantes, for example, in 1738 2.6 per cent of locksmiths employed more than four journeymen whereas 81.5 per cent employed one or none at all.[19] Yet over time the work practices and the trade organisations of the larger workshops influenced the smaller ones. The move away from the household to the larger workshop had important implications for the domestic economy and especially for the participation of women in craft work, reducing the opportunity for family members to participate in the enterprise, and forcing them to take up alternative occupations. There was an increased need for formal craft training, which was open only to males. But the rate of change was slow in the Saintonge pottery industries before 1800, where the average size of workshop remained small, based on and adjacent to the household.

The wide distribution of Saintonge pottery vessels throughout the North Sea and Atlantic worlds after 1500 raises questions about the marketing methods employed in the industry. Archaeological evidence suggests that during the middle ages pottery distribution was concentrated towards high status settlements, châteaux and abbeys, and overseas, through the maritime port of La Rochelle. The latter was the concern of merchants who traded in a range of regional commodities, above all wine.

From the fifteenth century, a range of clients, local and regional, popular and elite, European and colonial, were customers of the Saintonge industries. Primary distribution at the local and the regional level was effected largely by the artisans themselves, selling directly to clients or working to contract. Primary customers might be local residents or merchants who would then be responsible for secondary distribution to a wider clientele, through urban markets. Tilers and potters themselves might work as both producers and distributors, of their own and other artisans' products. What is certain is that the ceramics industries were never subject to 'putting out' in any form, the provision of raw materials or capital assets such as kilns by urban merchants, nor were they dependent on urban merchants for the distribution of their products. A wide variety of marketing methods are observed in the documentary sources.

The local trade in ceramic products was based on the small scale exchange of goods, often for domestic or private consumption, frequently as part of a barter transaction. The majority of tile production and a good quantity of earthenware pottery was consumed locally. Landowners serviced the repairs of their properties by including tile as part of their rents; in 1667, François Nadaud, tiler, rented a piece of wasteland in Brizambourg parish on condition that he render the land cultivable and that he provide the seigneur of Brizambourg, the landlord, with a kiln-load of tile, delivered to the latter's farms and barns.[20] Transactions between peasants also included similar provisions. Vivien Joubert of Ecoyeux purchased one *journal* of land from Vinet, cattle farmer, in 1727; the value of the land, worth 30 *livres,* was redeemed by Joubert's supply of one year's labour planting and tending vine on one *journal* of Vinet's land and with 1,000 tile from Joubert's kiln.[21] Michel Turpeaud, potter, redeemed two pieces of waste land in Ecoyeux parish worth 45 *livres* with six *livres* of cash and 28 dozens of 'pottery' of unspecified type in 1729.[22] In the local trade of ceramic goods, there was no clear demarcation between producers and distributors; ceramics formed part of a wide currency of goods and services perhaps indicating the partially monetarised nature of the rural economy before 1800.

Regional trade with nearby towns such as Saintes was more organised and formalised: the role of the merchant was important here, although the socio-economic origins and functions of merchants were wide. Many were local to the Saintonge and had themselves worked as potters or tilers. Repairs to the roof of the château of Brizambourg in 1683, requiring a large quantity of tile, were supplied by a merchant who purchased from 12 separate tilers and transported the products to the building site.[23] In 1652, Toussaint Bertelot of Saint Jean d'Angelys purchased tile from a producer in Ecoyeux and had it transported by a local farmer to the town, for wider distribution.[24] Transactions between merchants or middle men and potters or tilers could either be by commission, which seems to have been the most common way of assuring an adequate and timely supply, or by direct purchase of existing stock. In 1633, Jehan Tonnelier, merchant of Brizambourg, agreed a one-year supply contract with Nadaud, tiler of the same parish, where Tonnelier supplied fuel for the kiln, Nadaud the tile and lime to be fired and they divided the profits of the sale between themselves.[25] Michel Renaud, potter of La Chapelle, sold finished pottery to Jacques Mau, merchant of the same village, in 1733.[26]

The overseas trade in pottery appears to have been organised by merchants based in La Rochelle. Allen's work on the port books of sixteenth and seventeenth-century England shows that the trade in ceramic vessels was part of mixed consignments of regional products which included salt, vinegar and prunes, shipped out of La Rochelle (Allen 1983: 42). The merchants who organised such cargoes were secondary distributors. They did not control the pottery industries but rather purchased or commissioned pots from producers. In 1545, Liet de la Mothe, potter of La Chapelle, sold his products to Rochelais merchants, possibly after seeking out these customers himself (David and Gabet 1988: 5). In 1633, Louis and Rapsart Gelineau, acting for themselves and 'others', drew up a contract with four Rochelais merchants for an immediate supply of decorated and undecorated pottery, including plates, jugs and 'chauferettes', paid by the gross for larger vessels and by the hundred for smaller ones. In addition, the artisans' production was to be reserved exclusively for the same merchants for a further six years, at agreed piece rates according to vessel type, for finished and delivered products.[27] Direct commissions for special vessels are also in evidence. In 1553, Jean Morichon contacted to make ceramic vessels for refining sugar, again for a Rochelais client (David and Gabet 1988: 5). The potters of the Saintonge engaged in a variety of marketing and distribution networks and were themselves dependent upon merchants for some of their own supplies: in 1468 a potter of La Chapelle received 350 pounds of lead from a merchant of La Roche-sur-Yonne, shipped via La Rochelle, for glazing pots; other colour minerals such as manganese, copper and iron must also have been acquired in this way (Chapelot 1987: 173).

As domestic consumption of household goods increased during the eighteenth century, in towns and in the French North American colonies, the role of the merchant may have also grown. Certainly the new product of faïence, made in La Chapelle from the mid eighteenth century, seems to have been marketed by specialist distributors. Both Laurant and Bodin, faïenciers, were allied by marriage to porcelaine dealers in Saintes. The consumption of faïence by wealthier customers and its largely urban distribution may have caused a greater division of production and supply than with earthenware goods. But in the later eighteenth century in La Chapelle there was some specialisation in earthenware distribution. Pierre Chauvin, son of a potter, was acting as a merchant potter by the 1780s; his son Jean was a 'scholar', possibly training for the priesthood, and Pierre became a municipal officer in the new commune of La Chapelle after 1791, indicating the family's relative wealth and status in the local community. As with changes in household workshops, distribution mechanisms were slow to alter before 1790. The household enterprise, alone and in association with other units, was the basis of both production and distribution at the primary level, although the more distant the trade, the more reliant was the producer on associations of local potter-merchants, some of whom at least had expertise in legal and contract negotiations, and on merchants based in towns.

The significance of ceramic production to the local and regional economy of the Saintonge is difficult to assess in quantitative terms. In a *Mémoire* of 1698 on the resources and industries of Aunis and Saintonge, the intendant of the *généralité* of La Rochelle made no mention of commerce in pottery (David and Gabet 1988: 5). During the eighteenth century, faïence manufactures such as those of La Rochelle, Marans and Saintes, were described by contemporaries, because of the art of their products, their role in the luxury goods and colonial trades and because these industries were granted royal privileges to manufacture. Earthenware pottery and tile did not merit such attention because of the low value of the products and their mundane use.

At the level of the household and local economy of the region around La Chapelle, ceramic production was an important source of income for both individuals and for communities. Yet the pottery and tile industries did not dominate either local or family economies. The land and agriculture remained the leading sector, and the possession of landed resources determined the extent to which a family was dependent upon agrarian or industrial sources of income. Mixed arable farming remained the primary source of employment for the inhabitants of the Saintonge. Most potters and tilers and their families owned or rented some land, however small, and worked seasonally as agricultural labourers. On their marriage in 1729, Jean Turpeaud, potter of La Chapelle, and Jeanne Pilier had a house and garden, 10 *sillons* of meadow, one piece of woodland and four ewes, to provide them with vegetables, fuel, wool and milk products, for consumption and sale, as necessity determined.[28] In 1731, Jean Mourin, potter, purchased seven small plots of arable land, one plot of meadow, six of woodland and two strips of vine, sufficient again to contribute to the subsistence needs of the household in bread, fuel and wine, and possibly to support a small number of livestock such as sheep.[29] The artisan as small-holding peasant is true of much of rural France, down to the late nineteenth century. Of a sample of 153 artisans who married between 1811–20 in the canton of Chartres-sud in the Beauce region of northern France who also left post-mortem declarations of their estates, landed property represented 74.8 per cent of their total wealth (Farcy 1984: 232). Likewise in England, in eighteenth-century Staffordshire, Baker claims that the proportion of potters' assets tied up in agriculture was far greater than in their manufacturing businesses (Baker 1991: 7).

The potters and tilers of the Saintonge were not large-scale farmers; their holdings contributed towards rather than sustained their households' subsistence needs. These artisans had to resort to the market for bread and sought alternative means of gaining cash to pay land rents, feudal dues and royal taxes, all of which increased during the seventeenth and eighteenth centuries. Gullickson has shown that at Auffay in the *pays* de Caux, the seasonal nature of agricultural work for small holders and day labourers meant chronic underemployment; the result was widespread employment for men and women in rural domestic industry, spinning and weaving, for merchants based in Rouen (Gullickson 1986: 52–3). In the Saintonge region around La Chapelle, households engaged in ceramics production to the same ends. The availability of clay and wood, water transport to a sea port and merchant penetration into the region for other goods such as wine and salt, favoured the adoption of pottery production – and a local market favoured that of tile – as part of a widely-conceived family subsistence strategy.

In pre-industrial societies there was no absolute distinction between industrial and agricultural sectors in the economy, however, either in terms of the perceptions or the strategies of the household (Musgrave 1992: 163). The domestic economies of poor, middling and even wealthier peasants were based on diversity; survival could not depend on the vagaries of a single source of production. Economic sectors overlapped in the Saintonge. Agricultural products were eaten but also processed and sold, both primary products such as grain and wood and secondary products such as wine, dried fruit and spun wool. In La Chapelle women and men were involved in the preparation of hemp, if not in weaving canvas; in 1734, Pierre Baron, potter of La Chapelle, rented a house and appurtenances, including a 'motte' for preparing hemp, a feature listed in numerous property rentals of the early eighteenth century.[30] But a combination of clay and limestone with wood, transport and under-employed small-holders in the Saintonge favoured pottery and tile production as the major rural industries. Ceramics production provided an exchange commodity for local products, cash for purchases of food and the payment of rents, dues and taxes. For some households, it was the primary source of income.

Pottery manufacture was thus one of many sources of income for peasant families of the Saintonge, its local importance shown in the identification of heads of household as 'potters' or 'tilers' and their numeric frequency in the parish registers of the seventeenth and eighteenth centuries. Rural households were multi-purpose, with agricultural, industrial and other concerns, the skills, age and gender of each member determining the individual's contribution to the group's survival. This was an 'economy of makeshifts' where the work of all family members, at a variety of cash and kind producing ventures, was important.

Notes

1. In 1776 the five children and heirs of Pierre Renaud, potter of La Chapelle, repudiated their personal inheritance because of the poverty of their succession. Archives Départamentales de la Charente Maritime (hereafter A.D.C.M.) B 2842. Seigneurie de La Chapelle-des-Pots.
2. A.D.C.M. E 133. Notaire Dussault à Taillebourg 1669–77.
3. A.D.C.M. 3E LVIII/194. Notaire Corbineau 1733–7.
4. *Ibid.*
5. État Civil Series E. La Chapelle-des-Pots, 1734, 1779.
6. A.D.C.M. E 969. Notaire Maray à Ecoyeux 1653–91.
7. A.D.C.M. 3E XXXVIII/30 Notaire Pipaud à Brizambourg, 1729.
8. A.D.C.M. 3E LVIII/194. *Idem*; État Civil Series E. La Chapelle-des-Pots 1780.
9. A.D.C.M. 3E LVIII/194 *Idem*; 3E XXXVIII/31 Notaire Pipaud à Brizambourg 1749.
10. A.D.C.M. E 878 Notaire Brault à Taillebourg et Brizambourg 1660–88.
11. A.D.C.M. 3E XXXVIII/31. *Idem.*
12. État Civil Series E La Chapelle-des-Pots 1728; A.D.C.M. 3E LVIII/193 Notaire Corbineau 1728–32.
13. A.D.C.M. 3E LVIII/193 *Ibid.*
14. A.D.C.M. 3E XXXVIII/29 Notaire Pipaud à Brizambourg 1727.
15. A.D.C.M. 3E LVIII/193, *Idem.*
16. A.D.C.M. 3E LVIII/157. Notaire Godet à Ecoyeux 1770.
17. A.D.C.M. 3E LVIII/193 *Idem.*
18. État Civil Series E La Chapelle-des-Pots 1789, 1790.

19. Archives Municipales de Nantes. HH 165 Serruriers: contraventions 1738–90.
20. A.D.C.M. 4 J 828. Baillette d'un lopin de terre, Brizambourg, 1667.
21. A.D.C.M. 3E XXXVIII/29. *Idem.*
22. A.D.C.M. 3E XXXVIII/30. *Idem.*
23. A.D.C.M. E 877. *Idem.*
24. A.D.C.M. B 2967. Seigneurie d'Ecoyeux 1657–1787.
25. A.D.C.M. E 783. Notaire Huteau à Taillebourg et Brizambourg 1632–5.
26. A.D.C.M. 3E LVIII/194. *Idem.*
27. Bibliothèque Municipale de La Rochelle. 1824 Notaire Moreau, 30 May 1633.
28. A.D.C.M. 3E XXXVIII/30. *Idem.*
29. A.D.C.M. 3E LVIII/193. *Idem.*
30. A.D.C.M. 3E LVIII/194. *Idem.*

Bibliography

Allen, J., 1983. 'Some post-medieval documentary evidence for the trade in ceramics', in P. Davey and R. Hodges (eds.), *Ceramics and Trade*, (Sheffield), pp. 37–48.

Baker, D., 1991. *Potworks,* (London.).

Barton, K.J., 1964. 'The medieval pottery of the Saintonge', *Archaeological Journal*, 120, pp. 201–14.

Baulant, M., 1975. 'Niveaux de vies paysans autour de Meaux en 1700 et 1750', *Annales Economie, Société, Civilisation*, 30, pp. 505–18.

Chapelot, J., n.d. Artisans potiers en Saintonge du moyen age au XIXème siècle – techniques et production (typed manuscript, Archives Départementales de la Charente-Maritime).

Chapelot, J., 1972. *L'Artisanat céramique en Saintonge (XIIIème – XIXème siècles). Rapport préliminaire,* (Paris).

Chapelot, J., 1983. 'Le droit d'accès à l'argile et à la pierre des tuiliers-chauniers d'Ecoyeux (Charente-Maritime) aux XVème – XVIème siècles: l'apport des sources judiciaires', in P. Benoit and P. Braunstein, *Mines, carrières et metallurgie dans la France médiévale*, Actes du colloque de Paris 19–21 juin 1980 (Paris), pp. 117–68.

Chapelot, J., 1987. 'Discussion' in J. Chapelot, H. Galinié & J. Pilet-Lemière eds., *La céramique (Vème – XIXème siècles). Fabrication, commercialisation, utilisation,* (Caen), pp. 168–78.

David, P. & Gabet, C., 1988. *La céramique saintongeaise du XIIème au XVIIIème siècle,* (Rochefort).

Davies, N.Z., 1981. 'Women in the *arts mécaniques* in sixteenth-century Lyon', in *Lyon et l'Europe: hommes et sociétés: mélanges offerts à Richard Gascon*, vol I., (Lyons), pp. 139–67.

Dunning, G.C., 1968. *The Trade in Mediaeval Pottery Around the North Sea*, Rotterdam Papers I (Rotterdam).

Dupâcquier, J., 1979. *La population française aux XVIIème et XVIIIème siècles,* (Paris).

Fairchild, C., 1993. 'The production and marketing of "populuxe" goods in eighteenth-century Paris', in J. Brewer & R. Porter eds., *Consumption and the World of Goods*, (London), pp. 228–48.

Farcy, J.-C., 1984. 'Rural artisans in the Beauce during the nineteenth century', in G. Crossick & H.G. Haupt eds., *Shopkeepers and Master Artisans in Nineteenth-Century Europe*, (London), pp. 219–38.

Gullickson, G.L., 1986. *Spinners and Weavers of Auffay,* (Cambridge).

Hanusse, C., 1987. 'La rélation four-atelier d'après les sources écrits: l'exemple de Sadirac (Gironde) du XVIème au XVIIIème siècle', in J. Chapelot, H. Galinié & J. Pilet-Lemière eds., *La céramique (Vème – XIXème siècles). Fabrication, commercialisation, utilisation,* (Caen), pp. 101–5.

Hurst, J.G., Neal, D.S., & Van Beuningen, H.J.E., 1986. *Pottery Produced and Traded in North West Europe 1350–1650,* Rotterdam Papers VI, (Rotterdam).

Le Patourel, H.E.J., 1968. 'Documentary evidence and the medieval pottery industry', *Medieval Archaeology,* XII, pp. 101–126.

McCarthy, M.R., & Brookes, C. 1988. *Medieval Pottery in Britain A.D. 900–1600,* (Leicester).

Musgrave, E.C., 1993. 'Women in the male world of work: the building industries of eighteenth-century Brittany', *French History,* 7, pp. 30–52.

Musgrave, E.C., Forthcoming. 'Women and the craft guilds in eighteenth-century Nantes', in G. Crossick ed., *The Artisan and the European Town in the Eighteenth Century,* (Aldershot).

Musgrave, P., 1992. *Land and Economy in Baroque Italy: The Valpolicella 1630–1797,* (Leicester).

Renimel, S., 1978. L'artisanat céramique de Saintonge du XIIIème siècle à nos jours – essai de reconnaissance documentaire et archéologique d'un éspace rurale, (Thèse du 3ème cycle, Université de Paris).

Rowlands, M.B., 1989. 'Continuity and change in an industrialising society: the case of the West Midlands industries', in P. Hudson ed., *Regions and Industries,* (Cambridge), pp. 103–31.

Sinopoli, C.M., 1991. *Approaches to Archaeological Ceramics,* (London).

Sonenscher, M., 1989. *Work and Wages. Natural Law, Politics and the Eighteenth-Century Trades in France,* (Cambridge).

Streeten, A.D.F., 1981. 'Craft and industry: medieval and later potters in S.E. England', in H. Howard & E. Morris eds., *Production and Distribution: a ceramic viewpoint,* B.A.R. International Series 120, (Oxford), pp. 323–46.

Vince, A.G., 1981. 'The medieval pottery industry in Southern England: tenth to thirteenth centuries', in H. Howard & E. Morris eds., *Production and Distribution: a ceramic viewpoint,* B.A.R. International Series 120, (Oxford), pp. 309–22.

The Social Significance of Imported Medieval Pottery

Duncan H. Brown

Three questions are typically asked of medieval pottery. These lead to interpretations based partly in practical necessity and partly in accepted meanings. The first, and most common, of these enquiries is *'what date is this?'*. The answer, if there is one, will facilitate the establishment of a stratigraphic sequence, and is rarely explored any further. The second question, *'where was this made?'* is supposed to lead to an understanding of mechanisms of trade and exchange through the further query *'how did this get here?'*. In addition, the identification of foreign pottery, especially international imports, will often excite comments on social standing. Types of fine pottery such as Saintonge Polychrome jugs, or Valencian lustreware bowls are commonly regarded by British analysts as luxury products and thus signifiers of high status living. The third basic question, *'how was this made?'* is rarely of interest to field archaeologists, but is often the easiest to answer. Techniques of manufacture can be deduced from most pottery fragments, and will often help to answer the other two questions. Beyond that however, although it is intrinsically interesting, this line of enquiry will rarely lead to any profound revelations concerning the consumer.

It is notable that of those three questions, two are directed towards an understanding of the site and one is related to the substance itself. Function and the culture of pottery use are rarely considered and have often been viewed as irrelevant to the real business of excavation. In the late 1990's ceramic assemblages are usually too small to allow much more than the characterisation of a site and its deposits and sometimes even that is not attempted. Archaeology is apparently the study of evidence of human activity in the past, but unfortunately that human aspect is all too often forgotten. Pottery, as the most ubiquitous artefact recovered by excavation, has great value for understanding medieval life (Brown 1988), but the right questions have to be asked and they must go beyond those three introduced above.

This paper brings together evidence from a variety of excavations, of various sizes, and which have been conducted over many years to different standards of recovery and recording. The intent is to take the principal elements of

archaeological enquiry, those of dating and provenance, and use our understanding of them to examine the functional role of pottery throughout the medieval period. This will hopefully return attention to the people who used and discarded pots, to what they needed, what they had and what they desired. After all, it is unlikely that many consumers were especially interested in those issues which archaeologists find so fascinating. Did it really matter to medieval folk at what date, where or how a pot was made? They might consider whether it appealed to their tastes but it also seems likely that they would want to establish whether it would do its job and how much they would have to pay for it, and what could be more pragmatic than that?

This analysis is based on pottery excavated in the port of Southampton, Hampshire. Three different medieval settlements have been identified, as shown in figure 1, and each seems to have been among the most significant ports on the south coast of England. Archaeologically, this is reflected in the large quantities of Continental imported pottery found on excavations in the town. The middle Saxon, or seventh-to ninth-century, town, now known as *Hamwic,* lay on the east side of the Southampton peninsula and the west bank of the river Itchen. The late Saxon *burh* town may have been sited on the east bank of the river Test, where intensive settlement evidence of the tenth and eleventh centuries has been excavated. This area was subsequently developed into the Norman and later medieval walled town of Southampton. Each of these three settlements has it own distinct ceramic character. Much of the archaeological evidence from each of them, including analyses of the pottery, has been, or is about to be published. This discussion draws together all that evidence in order to tell the story of the consumption of pottery in medieval Southampton. The ceramic character of each period has been defined and quantified by place of origin and vessel type. Here, particular attention is paid to the relationship between imported and locally-produced pottery. The spatial distribution of imported wares within each settlement is also examined. The discussion of vessel types is based on the quantities shown in Table 1 which are summarised for each period in a series of pie charts. Tables are also presented

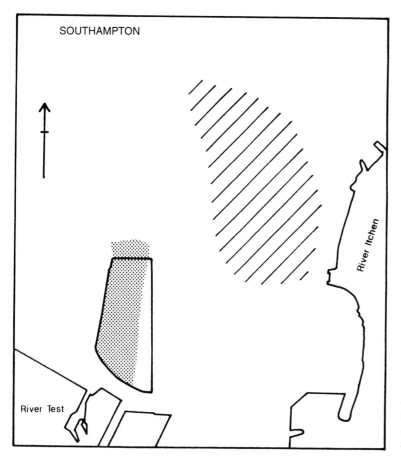

SOUTHAMPTON

River Itchen

River Test

Fig. 1. Location map showing the medieval walled town (outline), the known extent of the late Saxon settlement (stippled) and the known extent of the middle Saxon town (hatched).

to give accurate quantities of imported and local wares for each period. This information has been plotted onto plans which locate each site and compare their assemblages. In every table both weights, in grammes, and sherd numbers are given. The pie charts and distribution plots are based on weight.

This is the first time that all this evidence has been drawn together in a single study and the exercise has, as ever, produced as many questions as answers. The limitations of the evidence have also been exposed. The varying nature of different excavations including their size, the range of features excavated, and the percentage of their fills that have been excavated are all influencing factors. Site-by-site comparisons can be misleading but remain our most useful approach. Once it is accepted that the existing data represents a resource which can continually be enhanced, the potential of this kind of study is revealed.

This chronological study progresses backwards through time, starting in the late medieval period and finishing in the middle Saxon. This may seem a wilfully idiosyncratic approach but there are two reasons for it. Most importantly, the first section, on the late medieval town, establishes a pattern, a standard perhaps, for the importance of imported pottery, which is sought for in the data from earlier periods. Secondly, going backwards in time is what archaeologists do when they excavate. By beginning with the latest medieval evidence and finishing with the earliest, I am emulating the process of recovery in the hope that this might lead the reader to consider how that process might affect

archaeological interpretation. Furthermore, one aim of this paper is to challenge the notion that pottery has most value as a chronological indicator, and abandoning the traditional framework for archaeological story-telling is a way of making that point, albeit perhaps rather crudely.

References are made throughout to types of pottery with which the reader may not be familiar. A number of published works illustrate these types and are listed here in order to avoid littering the discussion with bibliographic references: the middle Saxon assemblage may be found in Timby (1988); the late Saxon in Brown (1995); the material from medieval Southampton in Platt and Coleman-Smith (1975) and in Brown (forthcoming). Many of the imported wares mentioned in the discussion of the late medieval period are shown in Hurst *et al* (1986).

The Medieval Town

The medieval walled town of Southampton may be broadly divided into four quarters, each of which has its own social character (Platt 1973). Figure 3 locates the excavations and street names referred to here. Much of the north-western corner was occupied by Southampton castle, a royal foundation of the 11th century. It continued to be owned and maintained by the Kings of England as a warehouse for imported goods, especially wine. Evidence for the commercial importance of the castle is shown by the two large vaulted cellars that survive to-day. There have been major

Table 1. *Vessel Type quantities. Quantities of each class of vessel represented for the late medieval, high medieval, Anglo-Norman and late Saxon periods. Weights, in grammes, are shown in normal type; the number of sherds in italics.*

	BOWL	CPOT	DISH	J/F	JUG	MUG	PCHR	OTHER
LMED LOCAL	17128	13029		822			22264	1589
	342	*327*		*12*			*480*	*31*
LMED IMPORT	7733	17143	3910	26240	6453	22169	6193	8674
	272	*503*	*97*	*1273*	*219*	*231*	*114*	*202*
HMED LOCAL	2070	73494		29	69549			7896
	108	*5158*		*4*	*3750*			*216*
HMED IMPORT	24	48			28117			5874
	1	*2*			*1984*			*41*
A-N LOCAL	379	70975			9252			158
	13	*3697*			*333*			*9*
A-N IMPORT		296			5601			305
		10			*346*			*11*
LSAX LOCAL	461	13121					878	
	10	*342*					*10*	
LSAX IMPORT				2412			2898	
				127			*56*	

sections through the motte ditch at two sites (site codes SOU 123, SOU 124) and one major trench was opened in the area of the castle bailey (SOU 29). Excavations at SOU 123 also extended inside the bailey wall and revealed a stone-built latrine pit that contained a large and important group of 13th century pottery. The ceramic assemblages from each of those excavations have been published (Brown 1986) and are included in this analysis.

The north-eastern quarter, east of High Street and centred around East Street, was probably the poorest part of the intra-mural town. Here were the homes of the artisans, carters, porters and other workers who serviced the town and laboured on the quays. Little excavation has been carried out in this part of the town, with the exception of a series of trenches at York Buildings (SOU 175), the finds from which are discussed here. At present, the pottery from that site has been quantified by weight only, and it is not possible to present sherd numbers for this assemblage.

The Franciscan Friary was sited in the south-eastern quarter. Several excavations have been conducted on the site of the Friary, but no quantified ceramic evidence from any of them is available for discussion here. The pottery from one trench in this quarter, situated north of the Friary on the site of a domestic dwelling (SOU 105), has been analysed and is included.

The south-western quarter, south of the castle and west of High Street, was the home of most of Southampton's wealthiest townsfolk. This was the part of town closest to the quays that lay along the western shorelines, so attracting the merchants and burgesses who represented the town's governing class. This area is still studded with a number of vaulted stone cellars, testament to Southampton's importance as a medieval trade centre. Most archaeological activity in the walled town has been concentrated here, where excavations have consistently produced large ceramic assemblages of high quality. The evidence from seven such

sites is considered here (SOUs 25, 110, 122, 123, 124, 125, 128). As described above, two of these excavations extended into the castle ditch, and one of them (SOU 123) also exposed areas within the castle wall. The pottery from all these sites is due to be published as part of the Southampton Museums Monograph Series (Brown forthcoming).

This social pattern is a simple interpretation of the evidence, and the reality was doubtless more complex. The 1454 Terrier, for example, shows many small cottage plots among the grand high-status tenements in the south-west quarter (Burgess 1976). However, for the purposes of this discussion, the broad picture is sufficient. One other important aspect of the medieval town was the suburbs. A number of excavations to the north and east of the walled settlement have been carried out, but their ceramic assemblages have not been analysed to the same level and so the suburban population cannot, unfortunately, be considered in this discussion. This is certainly an area for future research.

The pottery from the medieval walled town has been divided into three ceramic periods as follows: the Anglo-Norman period ranges from *c.*1070 to *c.*1250; the high medieval period *c.*1250 to *c.*1350; the late medieval period *c.*1350 to *c.*1520. The character of each of these three periods is discussed in turn, beginning with the late medieval.

The Late Medieval period

The last half of the fourteenth century brought plague and war to England and much of northern Europe. The ensuing recession affected Southampton badly, and this is evidenced archaeologically by the relative paucity of deposits and finds from this period (Brown forthcoming). The fifteenth century brought recovery as Italian merchant families established a base in Southampton and revitalised the economy of the port. This period is characterised by the redevelopment of previously abandoned house-plots and

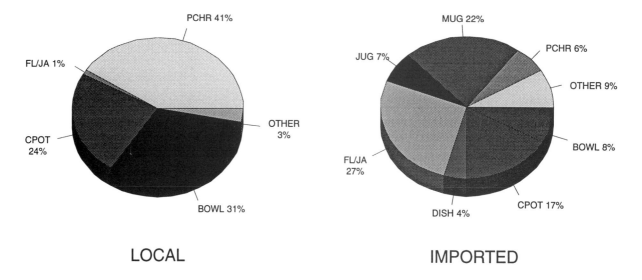

Fig. 2. *Pie charts comparing the relative quantities by weight of local and imported vessel types in the late medieval period.*
Key: CPOT = cooking pot; FL / JA = flask / jar; PCHR = pitcher.

the alteration of existing structures. In the merchant's quarter of the town prosperity is indicated by several large deposits that have produced huge quantities of finds, including fine pottery and glass.

The Pottery

A more comprehensive version of this discussion has already been published (Brown 1993). Pottery imported during this period originated from a variety of sources, including France, the Low Countries, the Rhineland, the Iberian peninsula and Italy. Among the French types are utilitarian earthenwares and stonewares from Normandy, fine glazed products and plain flasks from Picardy, and Saintonge earthenwares from the south-west. Pottery from the Low Countries comprises mainly earthenware cooking pots and highly decorated tin-glazed wares. Stonewares were the most common type of pottery brought from the Rhineland. Iberian wares include coarsewares from Seville and Alentjo. Fine Iberian pottery is represented by Sevillian tin-glazed wares and Valencian lustreware. Beautifully-painted maiolicas, mainly from around Florence and Faenza, typify the Italian products found in Southampton.

In contrast with the fine tablewares that figure among the imports, the local pottery of this period is dull. It comprises plain, partially glazed, sandy earthenwares with technical merit but little character. Non-local English pottery, although representing only 1% by weight of the total assemblage for this period, is noteworthy because it is much finer and thus closer in spirit to some of the Continental imported pottery. This is the fine Tudor Green ware, produced at a number of kilns around the Surrey/Hampshire border, which has a characteristic vibrant green glaze, quite different to the local pottery.

The pottery of this period may be divided into two classes of vessel, utilitarian and decorative. Utilitarian types are those which were used either in storage or food preparation and

consequently must have remained in the background. This category includes all the local products, as shown in figure 2; bowls, cooking pots, jars, pitchers and 'others' such as dripping pans and watering pots. Imported wares of utilitarian character include cooking pots from the Low Countries, flasks, jars and pitchers from France, and Iberian storage jars. Decorative pottery is more likely to have been used in display, especially at table during mealtimes. Vessel types which may be classified as decorative include dishes, jugs and mugs. These are all represented by non-local or Continental imported types including Tudor Green ware, Beauvais (Picardy) earthenwares, Rhenish stonewares, and Low Countries, Iberian and Italian tin-glazed wares. Bowls and flasks made in any of these wares are also classed as decorative. Amongst the 'other' imported vessel types are utilitarian dripping and frying pans and decorative chafing dishes.

The contrast between the local and imported pottery can be demonstrated by a comparison of the quantities of different vessel types as shown in table 1 and figure 2. These figures do not adequately reveal those profound differences in form and style but they do show some of the shortcomings of the local production. It is clear that imported products represent a far greater range of vessel types, including all the decorative products. This suggests that in the late medieval period fine tablewares were brought into the town to satisfy a demand that local producers could not meet.

Distribution

Table 2 shows that imported wares represent 42% by weight of the total sample presented here. This unusually high figure must reflect the high level of trade in decorative tablewares. Figure 3 is a plot of the distribution of imported wares within Southampton. It is intended to show levels of consumption of these products in different parts of the town. The size of each circle represents the relative size, by weight,

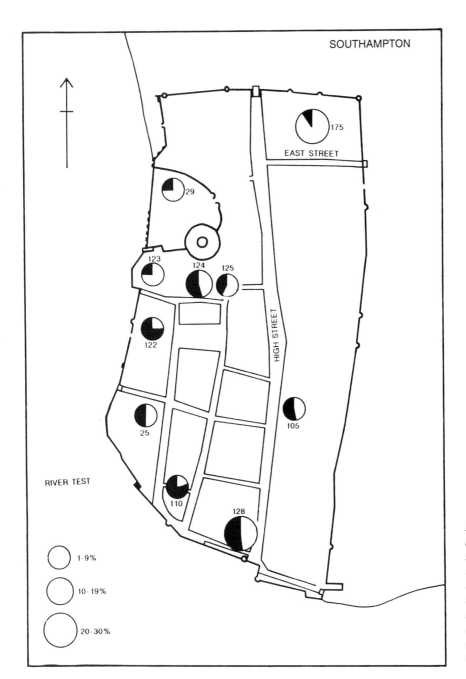

Fig. 3. Pottery distribution for the late medieval period. Plan of the medieval walled town, locating each site represented in table 2. The size of each circle represents the percentage each site assemblage represents of the total late medieval pottery weight. The black segment indicates the percentage of each site assemblage that is represented by imported pottery.

of each late medieval assemblage, while the pie-chart slices show the percentages of local and imported wares present. This information is given in greater detail in table 2.

It is clear that imported wares represent over 50%, by weight, of nearly all the assemblages in the prosperous south-western quarter of the town. The area around the castle, and the assemblage from the north-eastern quarter produced imported pottery in much smaller quantities. This might be seen as evidence that the wealthiest householders bought the finest pottery. However, fine pottery is present in the assemblage from SOU 175 and a figure of 16% for imported wares is high in comparison with earlier periods (see below). There is therefore no reason to suggest that fine imported products were not available to the inhabitants of every quarter of the town. The castle site, SOU 29,

is of some further interest. The late medieval deposits there represent a build-up of rubbish in the abandoned bailey yard. It is likely that this was dumped by the townsfolk rather than the occupants of the castle itself (Oxley 1986, 67, 112, 117), and this material may therefore have more in common with assemblages from sites outside the bailey wall.

Characterising the social condition of the sites represented here cannot be based solely on the presence of certain ceramics. Their quantity is more significant. It seems likely that wealthy people would have used fine tablewares most frequently, and thus consumed them at a greater rate. This is indicated in the pattern of distribution shown in figure 3 and supported by the fact that in the south-western quarter the most productive deposits are the fills of stone-built cellars or garderobes. Some of these groups are enormous,

Table 2. Late Medieval Sites. Quantities and proportions, by weight in grammes, and number of sherds, of imported wares occurring on each site in the late medieval period. The percentage, by weight, each site assemblage represents of the late medieval total is also shown.

| SITE CODE | IMPORTED WARES % | | IMPORTED | | TOTAL | TOTAL | % OVERALL |
	WEIGHT	SHERDS	WEIGHT	SHERDS	WEIGHT	SHERDS	WEIGHT
25	1731	133	51	48	3380	277	1
29	5197	186	24	25	21646	749	7
105	8028	565	55	49	14575	1159	5
110	5360	452	82	87	6520	521	2
122	16520	391	76	63	21633	620	7
123	2473	127	27	27	9070	465	3
124	18630	479	55	56	33993	850	12
125	3694	148	37	37	9983	400	3
128	48465	2481	55	59	87904	4206	30
175	13593	u/k	16	u/k	83496	u/k	28
TOTAL	123691	4962	42	Jh	292200	9247	

Table 3. High Medieval Sites. Quantities and proportions, by weight in grammes, and number of sherds, of imported wares occurring on each site in the high medieval period. The percentage, by weight, each site assemblage represents of the high medieval total is also shown.

| SITE CODE | IMPORTED WARES % | | IMPORTED | | TOTAL | TOTAL | % OVERALL |
	WEIGHT	SHERDS	WEIGHT	SHERDS	WEIGHT	SHERDS	WEIGHT
25	17236	651	31	26	55512	2542	19
29	166	18	1	1	17009	1274	6
105	3622	830	7	14	48427	6119	17
110	2546	375	38	48	6627	776	2
122	8521	394	24	20	35261	1983	12
123	1085	120	4	7	27672	1772	9
124	1316	140	10	13	13530	1080	5
125	3207	211	10	12	30456	1699	10
175	2421	u/k	4		57789	u/k	20
	40120	2739	14		292283	17245	

for example all the material shown here from SOU 128, the largest of these assemblages, represents the fill of a single cellar. This may serve to indicate the scale of ceramic consumption at some of these dwellings.

Discussion

The evidence shown above should allow an interpretation of the relative importance of different types of pottery to late medieval society. It appears that pots were used principally in storage, food preparation and for display at table. The wide variety of vessel types suggests that very specific activities might be represented within those broad functional categories. The earthenware cooking pots imported from the Low Countries, for instance, were globular vessels with three feet and two opposed handles (eg. Hurst 1986, Figure 59) and are quite different from the locally-made flat-based jar-type forms (eg. Platt and Coleman-Smith 1975, no. 676). Other local products used in the kitchen include single-handled saucepans or pipkins (eg. *ibid.* no. 644). The diversity of vessel form suggests that a range of cooking methods was being practised. This may be carried over into an interpretation of the various types of tableware used. It is possible that the various forms of bowl, dish, jug, cup and mug reflect not only differences in origin, but more importantly the variety of foods and liquids being brought to the table. For example, documentary sources refer to Rhenish stoneware imports as 'beer-mugs' (eg. Quinn 1938, 164) and it may be that such vessels were used principally for ale or beer. It is also important to remember that vessels of more valuable materials, namely metal and glass, would have been prominent in most high-status dining-halls. Highly decorated pottery might therefore have been preferred because it did not altogether lose its appeal in comparison.

Pottery imported for its decorative qualities is found in quantities that represent a regular trade in such products. Because no corresponding local types were being produced at this time it is possible that the origin of this fine pottery was irrelevant to the consumer. What was important to the people of Southampton was that they were able to acquire ware for the table. Quantitative analysis has revealed no particular preference for any of the French, Low Countries, Spanish and Italian products represented (Brown forthcoming), either overall or for individual dwellings. It is therefore not possible to relate groups of pottery with consumers of different ethnic origins. The house at SOU 110, for example, known as West Hall, has been established as the residence of Italian merchants (Platt 1973) but the assemblage does not contain higher quantities of Italian pottery. Table 2 does show that the percentage of imported wares is higher at SOU 110 than at any other site. If this is significant at all it may simply reflect the business concerns of the occupants rather than their cultural origins, for as merchants they might have found it easier to acquire imported ceramics.

Southampton's status as a port meant that Continental pottery was freely available. Furthermore, documentary records show that it was not given a high monetary value, especially in comparison with vessels of glass and metal (Brown 1993 and forthcoming). If 'fine' ceramic products were for sale in Southampton they were presumably available for anyone to buy, and this is shown by the occurrence of such pottery all over the town. Nevertheless, twice as much imported pottery was consumed in the high-status households of the south-western quarter than in poorer parts of the town. This is evidence of wealth manifested in visible consumption on a grand scale, not in the mere presence of fine ceramics.

The High Medieval Period

Southampton enjoyed a period of prosperous stability in the late 13th and early 14th centuries which was underpinned by the vital trade of English wool for Gascon wine. That trade is reflected archaeologically by the quantities of pottery imported from the Saintonge region, situated just to the north of the port of Bordeaux. During this period, over 90% of the imported pottery was made in the Saintonge (Brown forthcoming). Southampton was densely occupied at this time, with houses packed together and back-yards riddled with cess and rubbish pits. It is those features that have yielded the most finds in assemblages of this date.

The Pottery

Saintonge pottery at this period is commonly a fine white ware, richly glazed and often highly decorated; the polychrome jugs are perhaps the best known type (see Platt and Coleman-Smith 1975, figure 186). Jugs are the most common Saintonge form but there are also three-handled pitchers (*pégaux*) and mortars (Brown forthcoming). The few other types of imported pottery represented at this time include jugs from the Seine valley, Paris and the Low Countries, which together comprise less than 10% of the total quantities of Continental imports (*ibid.*).

The locally-made pottery has been classified into two types, coarsewares and sandy wares. Coarsewares usually take the form of plain, unglazed, jar-type cooking pots in a red-brown, sandy fabric with flint and chalk inclusions. A few bowls, often with an internal glaze, and other vessels such as curfews and dripping pans, were also produced. The sandy wares occur principally as glazed jugs or pitchers in finer fabrics that appear red, pink or white. At this period local potters were at their most productive and imaginative and jugs were often decorated with incised and applied motifs which include anthropomorphic and zoomorphic designs. Among the other forms produced were bowls, dripping pans, costrels and money-boxes. The pie-charts in figure 4 show that at this period local cooking pots and jugs occur in roughly equal proportions, and dominate the assemblage.

There is little point in distinguishing jugs from pitchers at this period. Some jugs may appear more suitable for tableware than others, but most of these vessels could have been used for a variety of purposes. These include storage and carrying as well as serving. There is therefore little functional difference between the bulk of the imported vessels and their locally-made counterparts. This contrasts significantly with the late medieval period. It is clear that in the high medieval period pottery was not imported in response to a demand for types that were not otherwise available, because local producers were making both utilitarian and finer wares.

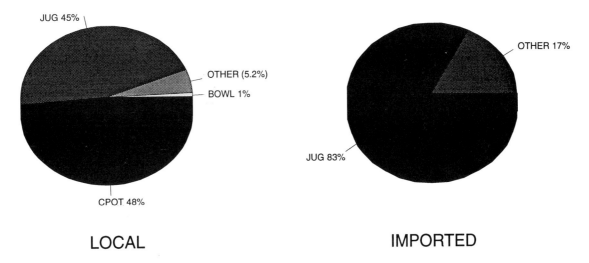

LOCAL   IMPORTED

Fig. 4. Pie charts comparing the relative quantities of local and imported vessel types in the high medieval period. Key: CPOT = cooking pot.

Distribution

The distribution of imported pottery, shown in figure 5, clearly differs from that shown for the late medieval period. It is apparent that imported pottery comprises a much smaller proportion of site assemblages (14% by weight overall). However, a similar social pattern may be observed. The most productive sites for imported pottery are situated in the south-western quarter, on merchant tenements. The excavations within the castle bailey have produced very little imported material. As this was a period when the castle was at its peak as a Royal warehouse, the relative lack of imported material may seem surprising. However, at this active period the bailey yard would have been kept reasonably free of rubbish and excavation has not revealed any features deliberately dug as rubbish pits. There is thus little evidence for the types of pottery the inhabitants of the castle would have used at this time. However, as the building functioned primarily as a warehouse it is possible that its occupants had neither the need nor the resources to consume pottery on the same grand scale indicated for merchant houses such as those sited at SOU 25 and SOU 110. This is probably also true for the inhabitants of the north-eastern quarter, where finds of imported medieval pottery are at a similarly low level. Continental wares are also poorly-represented at SOU 105, on the east side of High Street. A pottery kiln was established in this vicinity for a brief time and this might indicate that the occupants of adjacent plots were not of the highest position, as it may seem unlikely

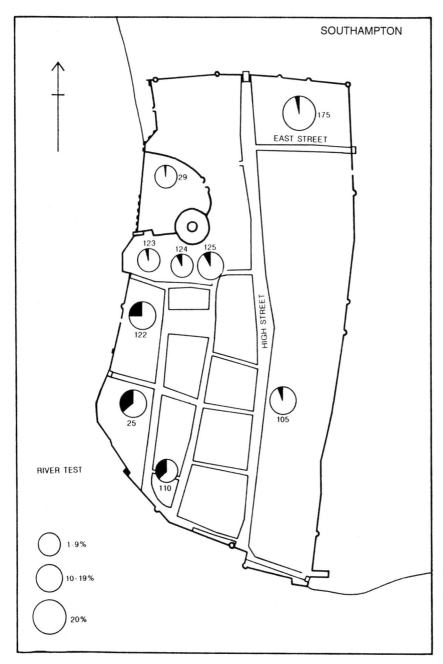

Fig. 5. Pottery distribution for the high medieval period. Plan of the medieval walled town, locating each site represented in table 3. The size of each circle represents the percentage each site assemblage represents of the total high medieval pottery weight. The black segment indicates the percentage of each site assemblage that is represented by imported pottery.

that a high-status dwelling would have been sited so close to such a pollutant. Saintonge jugs were found on all these sites and no firm characterisation of the householders of this area can be made. However, the pattern of distribution suggests that pottery was not imported for the exclusive use of Southampton's wealthy burgesses.

This is reinforced by a comparison of this evidence with a ceramic assemblage from Winchester, one of the most important towns in Southampton's hinterland. A tenement excavated at the Brooks and occupied by one of Winchester's most influential citizens yielded a medieval assemblage of over 21,000 sherds, and 189 kilos. Imported pottery represents only 1% of that weight, and 0.4% of the total sherd count (Thomson and Brown forthcoming). Such figures are typical for 13th century assemblages from the hinterland towns, and suggest that the pottery brought into Southampton was mainly consumed there and not intended for major re-distribution.

Discussion

The evidence from a comparison of high medieval vessel types and patterns of distribution suggests that imported pottery was less important at this time than it was in the 15th century. Archaeologists often view Saintonge pottery as a high status, luxury product because it is very fine, technically excellent and often exotically decorated, but these attributes seem to have meant little to the inhabitants of Southampton. Saintonge pottery is found all over Britain. It may indeed have been carried so widely because it was different, but most of it never travelled further than the ports where it was unloaded. In high medieval Southampton imported wares may therefore be viewed simply as another local product, especially as, in terms of function, Saintonge pottery is no different from the more plentiful local products. Traffic between this port and those in Gascony was so regular that the supply of Saintonge pots would not have been difficult. However, neither the scale of demand, nor the level of commercial gain, seems to have been high enough to encourage trade on a very large scale. Imported material should therefore be regarded as one more among the range of ceramic products available to the inhabitants of Southampton at this period, and seems to have little value as an indicator of high social status.

The Anglo-Norman period

Southampton developed rapidly after the Norman conquest. The social topography of the medieval town, including perhaps the street pattern, was established at this time around the castle and the quays. The prosperity of the port is reflected in the 12th-century construction of the stone cellars and great houses that characterise the south-western quarter. This was a period of increased activity and intensive occupation. Unfortunately, archaeological deposits survive intermittently amidst the intrusions of later periods and the ceramic record is relatively poor.

The Pottery

The pottery of this period spans a transitional phase between the pre-Conquest ceramic traditions and the beginnings of those that blossomed in the later 13th century. The range of vessel types is small and the quantities of imported wares are low, as is the overall size of the assemblage in comparison with later medieval periods. Imported pottery represents on average just 7% of any site assemblage. As with the high medieval period, most of this comes from a single source area, although here it is Normandy rather than the Saintonge. There are two principal types. Normandy Gritty ware was an unglazed, wheelthrown product that took the form of small cooking pots and large pitchers (eg Platt and Coleman-Smith 1975, nos 871, 875). Normandy glazed wares occur solely as brightly coloured jugs, often decorated with pellets, applied strips and roulettes (eg. *ibid.* nos. 943, 971). Other imports include amber-glazed Andenne-type wares from the Moselle region (Brown forthcoming).

Local pottery appears technically inferior to these products and may be divided into coarse and glazed wares. The coarsewares, with a range of large inclusions, especially flint, are handbuilt and low-fired. Cooking pots, often thick-walled and poorly finished, comprise over 90% of the coarseware vessel types, the only other form being bowls. The glazed wares, in handbuilt coarse sandy fabrics with ill-fitting glazes, usually took the form of three-footed jugs known as tripod pitchers.

Figure 6 shows the limited range of vessel types used at this period. Cooking pots were the most common while jugs were the principal imported form. This might be interpreted as evidence that imported pottery was filling a gap in the market. However, as these wares represent such a small proportion of any assemblage, it would seem that the quantity of imported types is less than half that of the local jugs. It appears that at this period pottery was not required for a very wide range of functions. The cooking pot type vessels may be regarded as multi-purpose, equally suitable for storage as well as cooking, but there is nothing like the variety of forms shown in later periods. A limited output implies a limited demand, and the evidence suggests that pottery vessels were not very important in domestic activities.

Distribution

Table 4 and figure 7 show above-average quantities of imported pottery concentrated in the southern half of the town, at four sites in particular (SOUs 25, 105, 110 and 122). As this was a period of cultural change, when new tastes were being introduced to Southampton, a pattern related to social status might be expected and is suggested. Furthermore, it is tempting to consider a pattern related to ethnicity but unfortunately, although the Domesday survey indicates a high proportion of new residents of French origin in the early Norman town (Platt 1973, 6), the origins of the people who lived on these particular sites have not been established. One would expect the occupants of the castle to be Norman, but the ceramic evidence does not obviously re-

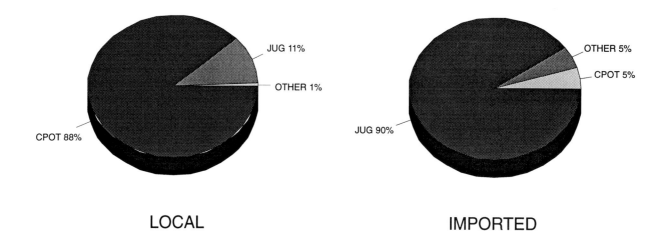

LOCAL   IMPORTED

Fig. 6. Pie charts comparing the relative quantities of local and imported vessel types in the Anglo-Norman period. Key: CPOT = cooking pot.

flect that. The largest castle group, at over 21kg, came from a garderobe built inside the bailey wall at SOU 123. Imported wares represent just 5% by weight of that group. They are more frequent within pottery recovered from the castle bailey (Table 4, SOU 29), but the overall quantity of Anglo-Norman material is very small and this evidence is not enough to demonstrate a high rate of consumption of Normandy pottery in the castle. No firm conclusions concerning either the ethnic origins or social standing of the inhabitants can therefore be drawn. The adjacent sites of SOU 124 and SOU 125 produced small amounts of imported material in comparison with those located further to the south. It is possible that the area closest to the castle was not, at this early period, developed by merchants. In the north-eastern quarter of the town imported wares are present in quantities comparable with those from the sites around the castle. It may be that this part of the town was occupied mainly by English people, but the higher frequency of Normandy pottery in the western half does not necessarily identify Norman inhabitants. There are many reasons, not least that of the surviving architecture, to identify a

Norman or Anglo-Norman enclave in the south-western part of the town, but the ceramic evidence is not one of them.

Discussion

This was a period of change. Assemblages with a high proportion of imported Normandy wares might reflect cultural status, but the ceramic evidence alone cannot support such an interpretation. The castle sites are those where one would expect to find imported pottery well represented, but the evidence is not conclusive. Overall, the range of products consumed shows little variety. The demand for tablewares shown in the high and late medieval periods is not in evidence here. Normandy glazed jugs may be interpreted as tablewares, and tripod pitchers should be regarded as the local equivalent, produced to satisfy a growing market. However, a low level of demand is shown by the small quantities of imported pottery overall. This surely does not indicate limitations in cross-channel trade, for there has been continuous contact between Southampton and Normandy

Table 4. Anglo-Norman Sites. Quantities and proportions, by weight in grammes, and number of sherds, of imported wares occurring on each site in the Anglo-Norman period. The percentage, by weight, each site assemblage represents of the Anglo-Norman total is also shown.

SITE CODE	IMPORTED WARES % WEIGHT	SHERDS	IMPORTED WEIGHT	SHERDS	TOTAL WEIGHT	TOTAL SHERDS	% OVERALL WEIGHT
25	1623	112	14	13	11621	859	7
29	655	54	11	11	5746	493	4
105	654	103	8	14	8413	715	5
110	1719	141	12	13	14813	1055	9
122	762	27	22	20	3435	136	2
123	1406	94	5	10	25784	966	16
124	634	61	4	7	15072	923	9
125	843	78	3	4	31982	2097	20
175	2370	u/k	5		44180	u/k	27
	10666	670	7		161046	7244	

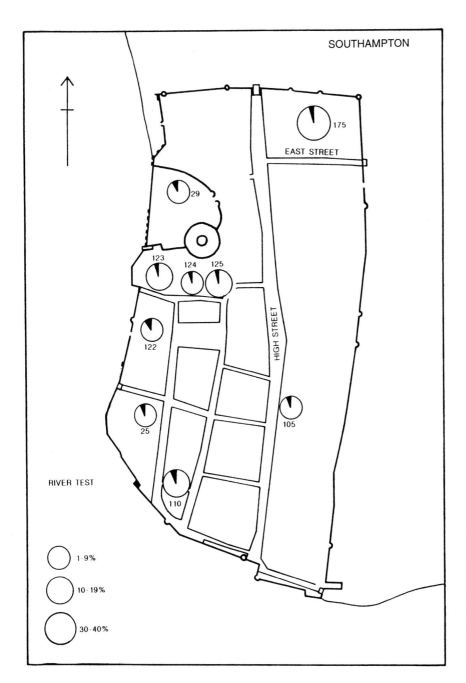

SOUTHAMPTON

EAST STREET

HIGH STREET

RIVER TEST

1-9%

10-19%

30-40%

Fig. 7. Pottery distribution for the Anglo-Norman period. Plan of the medieval walled town, locating each site represented in table 4. The size of each circle represents the percentage each site assemblage represents of the total Anglo-Norman pottery weight. The black segment indicates the percentage of each site assemblage that is represented by imported pottery.

and indeed that was a factor in the increasing importance of the Anglo-Norman port (Platt 1973). It therefore seems that the early medieval period was one in which pottery was not yet viewed as a significant domestic material. It certainly seems apparent that it was not required to perform a very extensive range of functions.

The Late Saxon Town

Evidence for late Saxon settlement activity on the western side of the Southampton peninsula has been recovered from twelve excavations. Those finds extend over an area larger than that of the walled town and may indicate a more open, less densely populated settlement. The area to the south-

west has been the most productive, with roadways, pits and a well among the features revealed. This, however may simply reflect the relative intensity of excavation in that area of Southampton because the largest ceramic assemblage came from a site further north, outside the walled area. Here, at SOU 142 a single pit produced over 12 kilos of pottery. The true extent and nature of the late Saxon settlement thus remains to be established, particularly since a few finds in the area of the middle Saxon town, although not sufficiently well analysed to be included in this discussion, hint at continuing activity further east.

It is no easier to determine the social structure of the settlement. There is no evidence to suggest any concentrations of high or low status dwellings and a less rigidly stratified society may be suggested.

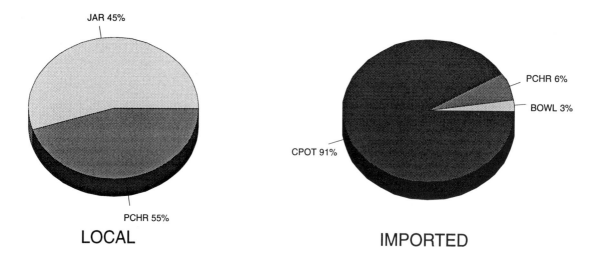

JAR 45%

PCHR 55%

LOCAL

CPOT 91%

PCHR 6%

BOWL 3%

IMPORTED

Fig. 8. Pie charts comparing the relative quantities of local and imported vessel types in the late Saxon period. Key: CPOT = cooking pot; PCHR = pitcher.

The Pottery

The ceramic evidence for late Saxon Southampton has been described and interpreted in some detail (Brown 1995). Imported pottery represents 16% of the total assemblage. This came almost entirely from northern France, principally the Seine valley and Beauvais. North French white and black wares take the form of wheelthrown, flat-based, high-shouldered jars. These developed out of a tradition with Gallo-Roman origins and represent the equivalent of the local cooking pot. Most of the Southampton examples have sooted bases, showing that here they were commonly used in cooking. Pitchers of Beauvais-type ware, usually decorated with painted red lines, represent the other principal type of north French imported pottery.

Over 90% of the local pottery is comprised of handbuilt, flint-tempered coarsewares. These, together with the less common handbuilt sandy wares, were probably produced

very close to the settlement. Globular cooking pots comprise over 90% of the local pottery; bowls were also made. Two non-local English products, Chalk-tempered ware and the wheelthrown Michelmersh ware, represent a small proportion of the late Saxon assemblage. Chalk-tempered ware occurs as large, stamp-decorated pitchers with tubular spouts that belong within a tradition seen over most of Wessex at this time. Michelmersh ware is a finer product that took the from of plain cooking pots and tubular-spouted pitchers with rouletted decoration. This product may have been made mainly for the market at the capital of Wessex, Winchester, where Michelmersh types occur more frequently.

Figure 8 illustrates the relative proportions of different vessel types in the late Saxon period. It appears that pitchers are a significant imported product, but this picture, based on weight, is misleading. In terms of vessel numbers there are twice as many jars as pitchers represented among the

Table 5. Late Saxon Sites. Quantities and proportions, by weight in grammes, and number of sherds, of imported wares occurring on each site in the late Saxon town. The percentage, by weight, each site assemblage represents of the late Saxon total is also shown.

SITE CODE	IMPORTED WARES %		IMPORTED		TOTAL WEIGHT	TOTAL SHERDS	% OVERALL WEIGHT
	WEIGHT	SHERDS	WEIGHT	SHERDS			
25	762	64	9	11	8441	569	18
29	25	2	2	4	977	49	2
105	64	2	5	9	1154	23	2
106	0	0			1138	175	2
110	23	1	1	1	2237	168	5
111	1050	40	33	16	3172	245	7
124	19	3	6	13	339	23	1
125	258	30	33	33	772	90	2
129	0	0			900	90	2
142	4047	128	33	24	12291	537	27
149	109	11	9	15	1163	74	2
161	10	1	2	3	924	32	2
164	169	7	47	33	362	21	1
175	996	u/k	5		12252	u/k	27
TOTALS	7532	289	16		46122		

Continental pottery (*ibid.* 139). It is therefore apparent that the majority of the imported pottery was used in the same way as the local products and pitchers represent a very small proportion of the overall assemblage. This suggests that pottery was used for a limited range of purposes and mainly in cooking.

Distribution

No obvious pattern emerges from the distribution shown in figure 9 and described in table 5. The largest assemblages are not concentrated in any one area, nor are those with a high proportion of imported wares. This indicates a dispersed settlement, or certainly one that was less controlled than the later walled town. It is likely that whatever settlement was sited here functioned as a port. The range of imported types may not be very great, but together they form a significant proportion of the whole late Saxon assemblage, especially in comparison with the Anglo-Norman period. As has been suggested for later periods, imported pottery may often be viewed as a common by-product of a

trade in more significant goods and there is no reason to interpret this material differently. There is certainly no reason to suggest that pottery was imported to satisfy a demand that local producers could not meet, or that it was being consumed more consistently in dwellings of specific social or cultural character.

Discussion

Imported wares are a consistent and relatively frequent presence in late Saxon site assemblages. They are also very different to the bulk of the local pottery, which might be one reason why they were not apparently redistributed into the hinterland. Excavations at Winchester, the most important town in Wessex at this time, have produced very little imported ceramics apart from fine, glazed pottery of a type which is extremely rare in Southampton. Michelmersh and chalk-tempered types occur in both places but these would have been supplied directly from the centres of production. This suggests very little movement of pottery between the two towns. The Continental imports which remained in

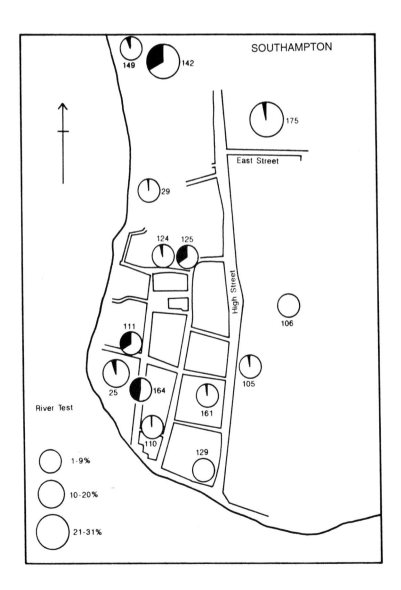

Fig. 9. Pottery distribution for the late Saxon settlement. Plan of the known extent of the late Saxon settlement, locating each site represented in table 5. The size of each circle represents the percentage each site assemblage represents of the total late Saxon pottery weight. The black segment indicates the percentage of each site assemblage that is represented by imported pottery.

Southampton may therefore be viewed as a supplement to the goods made locally, and need have no special social or symbolic significance attached to them. It is likely that local and Continental pots were used for the same, limited, purposes. Cooking pots are the overwhelmingly dominant form. Pitchers might be interpreted as tablewares, but the culture of pottery use seems to preclude the need for such products and it is more likely that these forms were used for storage rather than serving. It is suggested that some types of pottery, such as the glazed wares found at Winchester, were not widely consumed in Southampton because they were not required. This might indicate a low social status for the population of the port but it may be worth considering that there were cultural distinctions between the people of Southampton and the inhabitants of Winchester which were reflected in the ways pottery was used. There are certainly differences between the patterns of late Saxon ceramic consumption and those revealed in later periods.

The Middle Saxon Town

Hamwic was sited on the east side of the Southampton peninsula, on an area of low-lying land alongside the River Itchen. Excavations here have revealed a sprawling settlement that covered a much greater area than that suggested for the late Saxon or post-Conquest towns. The nature and function of this settlement has been discussed in print at some length (Morton 1992). Current opinion identifies Hamwic as a major commercial port, planned, organised, and perhaps controlled, by a political power.

The pottery discussed here has all been published and represents 36 excavations located over the known extent of Hamwic. The finds from 35 sites were examined in a single work (Timby 1988) while the assemblage from an additional excavation, SOU 254, (Pieksma 1994) is also considered here. One problem that besets any analysis of the Hamwic evidence is the lack of any well-defined chronological sequence for the development of the settlement. As a result the pottery is often portrayed as representing a single period, when in fact certain ceramic types may only have been current for short periods. This discussion of pottery use within Hamwic is based on the evidence of form rather than fabric, and there is little development in terms of vessel type throughout the middle Saxon period. Nevertheless, the difficulty of establishing a firm chronology for Hamwic must be acknowledged and the problem requires further research.

The Pottery

A wider variety of ceramic sources than those suggested for the late Saxon period is indicated for this period. Most of the imported pottery was made in northern France or the Low Countries, although some wares are difficult to provenance with certainty. Among the well-known types are Tating ware, Mayen ware and North French white and black wares. Imported pottery comprises 18% of the total assemblage by weight. The local products are handbuilt coarse and sandy wares.

Two major analyses of the pottery from Hamwic have been published (Hodges 1981; Timby 1988). Neither of them, nor the later site report (Pieksma 1994), quantifies the range of vessel types present. The two works from which the substance of this discussion is drawn present quantifications, by weight and sherd number, of fabric types but not forms. Middle Saxon pottery is therefore not shown in table 1 and it is not possible to present pie-charts comparing the range of locally-made and imported vessel types. In discussion Timby shows that bag-shaped cooking pots, a few bowls and even fewer lamps, represent the extent of the local repertoire. These were produced in a variety of sandy and gritty fabrics. Imported vessels were mainly jars and spouted pitchers along with a few flared bowls which have been identified as mortars. Both the jars and the mortars are forms descended from Gallo-Roman potting traditions, demonstrating continuity for ceramic production on the Continent.

At Hamwic imported pottery accounts for 18% of the total assemblage weight and the figure is 16% for the late Saxon. This gives some inkling of the frequency of different vessel types in the middle Saxon settlement. The cooking pot form probably represents over 90% of the local pottery by weight and thus close to 80% of the whole assemblage. If jars and pitchers are present in roughly equal proportions among the imported wares, then they each represent less than 9% of the total assemblage. Mortars are apparently rare and comprise a very small proportion of the imported pottery. Cooking pot vessels, of the same round-based form, dominate the local output, as is the case with the late Saxon assemblage, and once again it is probable that many of the imported jars were used for cooking. Pitchers appear to be more common among the middle Saxon imported vessels than they were later on, but nevertheless represent a small proportion of the whole assemblage. This fact, together with the absence of any locally-made equivalent, suggests that pitchers were not in frequent use, and thus not in great demand.

Distribution

Figure 10 shows how the middle Saxon assemblage is distributed over the area of Hamwic. It combines evidence from Timby's multi-site assemblage with the material from SOU 254. The larger group consists of pottery from 35 different sites. Timby grouped these into nine general areas (1988, 78) and this grouping has been followed in figure 10, with one exception. Her 'western periphery' general area comprises two sites, SOUs 36 and 99, which are sufficiently far apart to be represented individually here. Pie charts that represent pottery from area groups are positioned as far as possible at the mid-point between the relevant sites. Each general area is denoted by a letter which accords with those given in table 6. Timby presented a similar distribution plot (*ibid.* 119, fig. 24) which shows the proportion rep-

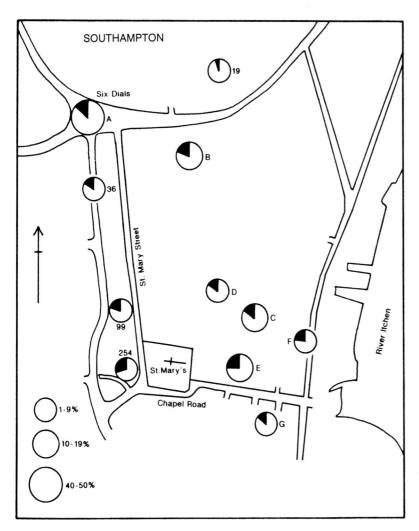

Fig.10. Pottery distribution for the middle Saxon town. Plan of the known extent of the middle Saxon town, locating each site represented in table 6. Letters correspond to the general areas identified in table 6. The size of each circle represents the percentage each site assemblage represents of the total middle Saxon pottery weight. The black segment indicates the percentage of each site assemblage that is represented by imported pottery.

Table 6. Middle Saxon Sites. Quantities and proportions, by weight in grammes, and number of sherds, of imported wares for each site or general area in the middle Saxon town. The percentage, by weight, each site assemblage represents of the middle Saxon total is also shown.

SITE CODE	AREA GROUP	IMPORTED WARES		% IMPORTED		TOTAL WEIGHT	TOTAL SHERDS	% OVERALL WEIGHT
		WEIGHT	SHERDS	WEIGHT	SHERDS			
A	SIX DIALS	40836	2504	15	13	269651	19567	43
B	CLIFFORD ST.	17976	1276	20	17	91768	7543	15
C	MELBOURNE ST.	10940	740	18	18	59708	4203	10
D	CENTRE	5269	481	18	17	29172	2823	5
E	N. OF CHAPEL RD.	19239	1054	25	21	76076	5025	12
F	MARINE PARADE	318	32	23	23	1377	136	1
G	SOUTHERN PERIPHERY	4951	350	14	14	34592	2524	5
SOU 19		24	4	5	11	459	36	1
36		6495	257	19	11	33961	2417	5
99		3868	204	22	20	17395	1016	3
254		2538	250	26	26	9700	966	1
TOTALS		112454	7152	18	15	623859	46256	

resented by imports in 25 site assemblages. This indicates high concentrations of imported wares around the centre of the settlement and although such a pattern is not exactly matched in figure 10, nor is it utterly refuted. Unfortunately, Timby did not compare the relative size of each assemblage, and doing so serves to unbalance her argument. Almost half of the middle Saxon assemblage was recovered from the sites at Six Dials, in the northern area of Hamwic. There, imported wares comprise 15% of the assemblage by weight. This is only just below the overall figure of 18%, but considerably lower than the 25% recorded for the excavations north of Chapel Road and 23% for those at Marine Parade. However, the Marine Parade sites produced only 1% of all the pottery in this assemblage; 32 sherds in all. A single imported vessel could be represented in the percentage figure for that general area. The same could be said of the assemblage from SOU 254, also close to the centre. Furthermore, at SOU 99, which Timby characterises as 'peripheral', pottery comprises three percent of the total assemblage, 22% of which is imported. The group of sites north of Chapel Road produced a much larger quantity of pottery but the significance of the 25% figure for imported wares from this group must be weakened by the fact that a larger assemblage still, from the more northerly sites at Clifford Street, produced imports at 20%. It appears from this re-examination that no specific concentrations of imported pottery can be clearly defined within Hamwic and a more even pattern of distribution is now indicated. Nevertheless, the proposition that the central and riverside areas of the settlement are those where imported pottery occurs with greatest frequency is certainly attractive, and is not entirely contradicted by this evidence. A future study might seek to determine how different types of Continental ware are distributed between these sites.

Timby suggests three possible explanations for her pattern of distribution (*ibid.* 119). The first is that pottery brought in by sea is likely to be lost or discarded close to the waterfront. This is undermined by the significant presence of Continental material some way from the projected waterfront area. Her second explanation, that foreign traders occupied the area adjacent to the river, seems more reasonable and is paralleled in later periods in Southampton. Thirdly, Timby suggests that imported pottery is more frequent in earlier deposits and that this distribution relates to the original core of the settlement. This must be set against evidence from excavations at Six Dials where, as Timby herself reveals, early buildings have been identified (*ibid.* 116). It is tempting to characterise the central and riverside areas of Hamwic as an area favoured by traders, but such an interpretation cannot be based solely on the ceramic evidence. There were, after all, other imported goods, such as glass and stone, and these need to be studied in comparison.

Discussion

The vessel type evidence from Hamwic indicates that some pottery was imported in part to increase the range of pots

available. Pitchers are a type not produced locally, although the imported jar form may be regarded simply as a foreign equivalent of the local cooking-pot. Previous commentators have drawn out different points from the vessel type evidence. Timby suggests that

> 'It may have been the case the average Hamwic household did not perceive the imported wares as better or more desirable commodities than their traditional types...' (ibid. 110).

This is given as a possible explanation for the absence of local products that imitate imported pots. However, the point is also made that there was no high demand for imported pottery. As in the late Saxon period, it seems that ceramic vessels were not used for a very wide range of activities within the household. The fact that imported pitchers were not reproduced locally suggests a low demand and thus that they did not play an important part in domestic activities. The low numbers represented may therefore have been sufficient to supply what little demand there was. Pottery was not usually made for export at this period and it is possible that if these types had not been introduced to the town, nobody would have noticed. The means of their introduction therefore requires some explanation.

Hodges suggests that

> 'The traders were evidently bringing their own cooking-pots and wine-pitchers so that their cuisine could be effectively made without using the crude, native, Middle Saxon wares.' (Hodges 1982, 57–8).

An entire domestic assemblage, from one dwelling, representing a single occupancy, would have to be recovered in order to prove such an argument. No foreign trader's homes have been identified and the generally consistent distribution of imported pottery over a number of sites defies the cultural characterisation of particular parts of Hamwic. The evidence of later periods shows the highest concentrations of Continental wares in the merchant's quarter of the walled town. There is, however, nothing in the ceramic evidence to denote the ethnic origins of any of the people represented by those assemblages. Hodges' point is further undermined by the fact that on every site, and in every feature, local wares occur in considerably greater proportions than imported types. This may also be observed in the later medieval town, even in the Anglo-Norman period, when foreign settlement is well attested. A more detailed study of vessel form is required before any further conclusions can be drawn for the use of pottery in Hamwic but it is at present very difficult to argue that pottery was imported for the exclusive use of a distinct class of resident.

Morton, in his elegant discussion of the nature of Hamwic, has considered the comments of both Timby and Hodges in his section on trade (1992, 67–68). He accepts that

> 'Continental pottery was brought into Hamwic for its intrinsic worth'

and that

'..it is difficult to escape the conclusion that Continental pottery was imported to serve the needs of a small group'.

before eventually concluding

'..that small group was made up of traders – perhaps foreign traders, lodging in English houses'.

It is difficult to find agreement with his first point, as this study has sought to show that imported pottery had little functional significance. It cannot have had any great commercial value either, so any intrinsic worth it may have had remains unclear. Other evidence might influence Morton's search for a small group for whom pottery was imported. Hinton, in his analysis of the non-ferrous metal objects from Hamwic, acknowledges the possible existence of a wealthy group early in the development of the settlement (Hinton 1996, 102). This is based on the presence of glass palm cups in graves. The implication that glass vessels might have been regarded as a luxury is paralleled in the later medieval periods, but there, as at Hamwic, there is little to suggest that imported pottery was accorded a similar status. The evidence from late medieval Southampton is that such groups are identified not solely by a higher consumption of imported wares, but also by a higher rate of consumption of pottery in general. As Morton recognises, this has not been shown for Hamwic (Morton 1992, 68). All that is left, therefore, is pottery as an indicator of cultural distinctions, hence Morton's 'small group'. It seems, however, that imported wares were used all over Hamwic, which argues against importation to supply a separate cultural enclave. Hinton also addresses the matter of a culturally distinct social group, and concludes that the homogeneity of the copper-alloy objects cannot support such a suggestion (Hinton 1996, 102–104). It is revealing that imported copper-alloy objects represent a small percentage of an assemblage that is principally local in origin, for the same is true of the pottery. There is no dispute that foreigners probably resided in Hamwic but it must be concluded that they were not the sole consumers of imported pottery, and no cultural or economic emphasis can yet be properly established through a study of ceramic distribution.

Conclusion

The evidence from the late medieval period provides a model for the importation of pottery on a commercial scale. Here, Continental wares average over 50% by weight of all the pottery of this period. It also occurs in a range of forms not reproduced locally. This was clearly a period when ceramics were used in a wide variety of ways and consumed at a high rate, as reflected in the range of different vessel types present. Such a pattern cannot be observed in any of the earlier medieval periods. Imported pottery of the high medieval period may be regarded as a supplement to existing local forms rather than increasing the range of vessels available. The intensity of ceramic consumption was relatively high at this period and a fairly wide variety of vessel types was in use, but most of those were locally-produced. Overall, two basic forms are dominant, cooking pots and jugs and the latter were easily the most common imported type. Cooking pots were the dominant form in the Anglo-Norman, late Saxon and middle Saxon assemblages. In each case a low level of ceramic use is indicated. Imported pottery is at its lowest levels in the Anglo-Norman period, which suggests a low level of demand for the jug forms in which it typically occurs. In the late Saxon town, cooking pots were the most common imported, as well as local, product. This suggests that pottery at this period did not serve a very wide range of domestic activities. The middle Saxon assemblage is of a similar character, although here all pitchers were imported. This has prompted attempts to define a specific group of people for whom imported pottery was more important than local products but the evidence cannot support such a claim.

This chronological comparison of vessel forms shows that at the outset of the medieval period in Southampton, ceramics did not play a major role in the household. One reason for this may be technological. Nearly all local pottery of the middle and late Saxon and Anglo-Norman periods was handbuilt and low-fired. This might have reduced the reliability of these products and may explain the reluctance of local potters to produce an elaborate range of forms. One result of that might be that the expectations of the consumer remained at a low level. The circular conclusion must be that the production of a narrow range of forms was led by the limited range of uses to which they were put, which in turn was due to the range of forms available. When local potters adopted the throwing wheel and more efficient kilns, the variety of vessels increases dramatically. So too does the rate of ceramic consumption. Throughout all these periods, imported wares were nearly always technically superior but this apparently did not render them more desirable. Before the 15th century, these products were not brought into Southampton, or either of the Saxon settlements, in sufficient quantities to compete with the local output. This must relate to the culture of ceramic use as much as to the trading function of those settlements.

The study of distribution patterns allows the comparison of rates of ceramic consumption within a settlement and between periods. This has led to some discussion of social status, especially for the walled town. The south-western quarter contained the most prestigious houses and attracted the wealthiest residents. It is here that the highest concentrations of imported ceramics occur. Nevertheless, Continental pottery is found in every part of the town. Clearly, relative quantities must be understood when judging the status of any household. On this basis, the evidence for the late Saxon town is inconclusive. No obvious pattern can be observed and no social interpretations can be made. In previously published analyses of the Hamwic pottery a supposed concentration of imported pottery around the centre of the settlement has been interpreted as evidence for a mercantile enclave. The evidence from Hamwic is considerably more slight than it is for a similar phenomenon in the walled town and there are more obvious parallels with the late Saxon period. However one reads the evidence, it is important to understand that these distribution plots do not indicate the reasons for importing pottery.

The settlement-wide patterns of ceramic use presented here are insufficient to reach any understanding of individual requirements. This might be achieved by examining the range of vessel types used, and their distribution within a single dwelling. This is rarely possible because excavations usually extend over parts of tenements rather than a single, complete house plot. The excavations in Southampton castle have revealed something of the ceramic culture of that establishment and a composite picture of other dwellings can be built from the results of more than one excavation. Most pottery is recovered from rubbish deposits, usually in pits or back-filled garderobes and cellars, because occupation layers were kept clean (Brown forthcoming). As a result all vessel types tend to occur together. Documentary research, using will inventories for example, may help to show where in the house pottery was kept and used. Nevertheless, this study has shown the importance of pottery to the people of medieval and Saxon Southampton. There is no doubt that the quantities of Continental wares present here are related to the significance of the Southampton area as a port and it is also probable that the presence of foreign traders stimulated the importation of different types of ceramics. However, it has been shown that at different times pottery was brought in for different reasons. It would seem that in any period people got what they wanted, whether it was produced locally or imported. One advantage of living in a port seems to have been that a wider choice of wares was on offer.

Acknowledgements

I am very grateful, as ever, to Bob Thomson for reading this paper and to Mort, who commented most helpfully and in great detail. Thanks to Paul Blinkhorn, who edited my original text and to Simon Griffin for producing drawings.

Bibliography

Brown, D.H. 1988 Pottery and Archaeology *Medieval Ceramics* 12, 15–21.

Brown, D.H. 1993 The Imported Pottery of Late Medieval Southampton *Medieval Ceramics* 17, 77–81.

Brown, D.H. 1994 Pottery and Late Saxon Southampton *Proceedings of the Hampshire Field Club and Archaeological Society*, 50, 127–52.

Brown, D.H. forthcoming *Pottery in Medieval Southampton c.1070–1530*.

Hinton, D.A. 1996 *The Gold, Silver and Other Non-ferrous Alloy Objects from Hamwic* Southampton Finds Volume 2.

Hodges, R. 1981 *The Hamwih Pottery: the local and imported wares from 30 years' excavations at Middle Saxon Southampton and their European context* Council for British Archaeology Research Report 37.

Hodges, R. 1982 *Dark Age Economics: the origins of towns and trade, AD 600–1000* Duckworth.

Hurst, J.G., Neal, D.S. and van Beuningen, H.J.E. 1986 *Pottery Produced and Traded in North-West Europe 1350–1650* Rotterdam Papers VI.

Morton, A.D. (ed.) 1992 *Excavations at Hamwic: Volume 1*. Council for British Archaeology Research Report 84.

Oxley, J. 1986 *Excavations at Southampton Castle* Southampton Archaeology Monographs 3.

Pieksma, E. 1994 'Pottery' In: M. Garner Middle Saxon Evidence at Cook Street, Southampton. *Proceedings Hampshire Field Club and Archaeological Society* 49, 77–127.

Platt, C. 1973 *Medieval Southampton: The Port and Trading Community, AD 1000–1600*. Routledge and Kegan Paul.

Platt, C. and Coleman-Smith, R. 1975 *Excavations in Medieval Southampton, 1953–1969*. (2 volumes) Leicester.

Thomson, R.G. and Brown D.H. forthcoming *Post-Roman Pottery from the Brooks, Winchester*.

Timby, J. 1988 The Pottery In P. Andrews (ed.) *Southampton Finds, Volume 1: the coins and pottery from Hamwic* 73–124.

Habitus, social identity and Anglo-Saxon pottery

Paul Blinkhorn

'The answer to the great question, of life, the universe and everything ... '

'Yes!'

'Is ...'

'Yes!!'

'Forty-two!'

'Forty-two? Is that all you've got to show for seven and a half million years work?'

'I think the problem is that you've never actually known what the question is'

(Douglas Adams: *The Hitchhiker's Guide to the Galaxy*)

Introduction

The study of Anglo-Saxon pottery, when compared with that of the ceramics of other periods such as Roman and post-Medieval, is a relatively recent phenomenon (see Richards 1987 for a full history of the discipline). It will be argued here that the influence of the study of the industri-ally-produced ceramics of those periods has resulted in deeply embedded methodological flaws in the analysis of the handmade, generally domestically produced, pottery of the period AD450–650.

Our present state of knowledge of the material is built mainly on academic foundations laid in the period 1950–1977, particularly J. N. L. Myres' *Anglo-Saxon Pottery and the Settlement of England* (1969) and *A Corpus of Anglo-Saxon Pottery of the Pagan Period* (1977). There is no doubt that Myres' work was of immense value in identifying the continental parallels for the earliest decorated English pottery of the period, but it is unfortunate that his analytical methodology was deeply flawed. The art-historical approach of his time was simply not appropriate to the character of the material. Consequently, analyses of Anglo-Saxon pottery generally start from the assumption that the undecorated pottery was functional, and thus, as with the industrially-produced 'coarsewares' of other periods, it should be possible to identify chronological development. However, re-peated attempts by Myres and others to do just that have met with failure. Such failures are, however, usually blamed on the pottery rather than the analytical methodology. For example, Myres saw one of the main bars to successful chronotypological analyses being due to the potters having

differ(ed) widely in technical skill, from the highly sophisti-cated products of professional craftsmen capable of conceiv-ing complex designs and executing them with precision and sensitivity, to the crude efforts of amateur housewives with little idea of relating half remembered patterns to the available space on the pot (Myres 1977:12)

Since Myres' time the development of a wealth of scientific and statistical analyses, ethnography, regional studies and theoretical perspectives means that ceramicists now have many different analytical methodologies at their disposal. Despite this, the material is still basically an enigma; some significant progress in understanding the decorated funerary wares of the period has been made, but as the vast majority of the material from settlement sites is undecorated, it is quite obvious that there is still a long way to go before we can claim to understand early Anglo-Saxon pottery. Unfor-tunately, with a few notable exceptions, most of the reports dealing with Anglo-Saxon pottery from excavations can be summarised as having the following contents:

1. A list of the fabrics types.
2. A list of the main form types and 'variants'
3. A list of the decoration types
4. An absolute chronology for the excavated features based mainly on 3.
5. Drawings which illustrate 1, 2, 3 & 4

which can be seen to be the traditional analytical method-ology of the pottery of the Roman and post-medieval pe-riods. In this paper it will be argued that the necessities of chronology and the formalities of archaeological publica-tion notwithstanding, such a methodology is entirely inap-propriate for Anglo-Saxon domestic pottery and produces data which offers no understanding of the majority of the material under scrutiny. It will be suggested that rather than being of casual and slapdash manufacture, the wares are in fact imbued with significance, with conscious decisions having been made at every stage of production from the selection of the fabric temper to the final shape of the pot.

Factors which may have influenced these decisions will be discussed. An attempt will be made to identify the reasons why the study of early Saxon pottery is all but moribund, and, using some extremely basic theory, to offer some possible explanations.

The answer is 'early Saxon domestic pottery'; however, we do not appear to know what the question is. This paper will suggest some possibilities.

Pottery Analysis in the Real World

> The assignment of meaning to material culture is a necessary stage of analysis (Hodder 1991: 45).

Practice

One of the major constraints to the meaningful analysis of early and middle Anglo-Saxon pottery may be the nature of the discipline. The present structure of field archaeology means that most ceramic analysts tend to work in isolation, from the site, from each other and, often, from the archaeologists involved with the excavation and publication. In addition it is necessary to count, weigh and identify every sherd of pottery from an excavation before any meaningful analytical work can be carried out. In the case of early/ middle Saxon domestic pottery, virtually every sherd has to be examined with a microscope before the fabric can be placed within a prescribed group. Having personally spent four years single-handedly processing three-quarters of a million sherds of Saxon and Medieval pottery from the excavations at Ipswich in Suffolk, I can state with confidence that it is not a task which is guaranteed to stimulate the imagination, and often becomes a war of attrition between the analyst and the dataset.

> To most archaeologists, pottery is a mountain, vast and unassailable: a challenge to be conquered … it has to be conquered 'because it is there'. The vast literature on pottery reflects this with … vast masses of data … presented in an ill-digested and ill-conceived form, simply because the material exists. Once presented, the material is all too often of little use to other scholars (Millett 1979: v)

Academia also appears rather baffled by the material. Analyses of Anglo-Saxon pottery are sometimes carried out as undergraduate theses, many of which consist, inevitably, of an exercise in thin-section petrological analysis, despite the fact that it is by now glaringly obvious that the material does not respond to such treatment, except in the broadest manner. Similarly, few theoreticians have turned their attention to the Anglo-Saxon era, despite the fact that in the early period, the quality of the archaeological evidence can be seen to be on a par with that of the late Iron Age, but with the bonus that there is historical evidence at the analysts disposal.

Another the problem is the fact that in recent years, very few large settlement sites of the period have been excavated, and some of those that have were done in a manner which has proved to be a major handicap to their understanding.

For example, the whole of the early/middle Anglo-Saxon settlement at West Stow, Suffolk was covered in a thick occupation deposit containing large quantities of pottery and bone, the result of the site having been buried in wind-blown sand during the medieval period. Such deposits are extremely rare on sites of the period, usually due to the ravages of later agriculture or natural erosion. Despite this, at West Stow, most of the occupation horizon was deliberately machined-off by the excavators, with the remainder shovelled-off in spits (West 1985). The position of the finds in the remnants of this layer were largely unrecorded, due to the fact that the excavator could not discern any features within the layer. The potential information which could have been gained by the spatial analysis of the finds from the horizon does not bear thinking about, but the episode demonstrates the tendency for some field archaeologists to think of very little apart from settlement dynamics and chronology (Blinkhorn and Cumberpatch: in press), and shows that, in some cases, such an approach does more harm than good.

If these methodological problems alone were not enough to stifle the discipline, then the policy-makers are certainly contributing to the moribundity of Anglo-Saxon ceramic analysis. Contract archaeology renders any analysis beyond fabric, chronology and form (or, in some cases, merely dating features from the pottery) an expensive luxury which may result in the loss of the tender to a rival who utilises such a methodology. The situation has arisen purely and simply from the present legislation concerning field archaeology, and whilst it is better than the haphazard situation which preceded it, this is akin to saying that a bread and water diet is better than starvation. Archaeology claims the status of an academic discipline, not that of a branch of the building trade, yet at this time, it is the developer who decides which 'contractor' is to excavate the site. As few developers have a grounding in the theory and practice of field archaeology, and tend to care very little about the validity of the analytical methodologies employed by their archaeological sub-contractor, it is the cheapest tender which generally wins the contract. The inevitable result is that only the minimum allowable amount of work is carried out. Personal experience has also shown that this system has resulted in a climate where it is impossible for those who owe their livelihoods to contractors to make any criticism of developers for fear that they will take future business elsewhere. There is thus a real danger that, under the present system, few archaeological sites will ever be excavated in a way which will allow meaningful analysis of the results, as the size of most datasets retrieved under the present conditions are rarely useful for anything other than the assignation of broad chronology to features (Blinkhorn and Cumberpatch in press).

Theory

Perhaps the two most significant recently-excavated Anglo-Saxon settlement sites, in terms of the pottery, have been those at West Stow (West 1985) and Mucking, Essex (Hamerow 1993). Both sites were excavated over many seasons in the 1950's, 60's and 70's, often in extremely adverse conditions (Hamerow 1993: 1–2). This paper will concentrate mainly on the evidence from these excavations. As well as West Stow and Mucking, many references will be made to Julian Richards' *The Significance of Form and Decoration of Anglo-Saxon Cremation Urns* (1987). This is, arguably, one of the most important analyses of the ceramics of the period yet carried out, and demonstrates that there is far more to such pottery than the two F's of Form and Fabric. Despite this, the impact of Richards' work on the post-Roman ceramic community appears negligible, and there have been few attempts to build on his foundations. At the 1994 TAG conference, for example, only three papers were concerned with the post-Roman period. In spite of this neglect, there seems good reason to believe that the Anglo-Saxon period is as ripe for examination by theoreticians as any period of prehistory. Furthermore it appears possible to explain the nature of Anglo-Saxon pottery using a blend of archaeology, history and theory. The basic theoretical tenet used here, *habitus*, developed by Pierre Bourdieu (1977, 1992) is not a new one, and has been discussed at length by a number of archaeologists, including Hodder (1991). *Habitus* consists of a series of

> Principles which generate and organise practices ... objectively 'regulated' and 'regular' without being in any way the product of obedience to rules, they can be collectively orchestrated without being the product of the organising action of a conductor' (Bourdieu 1992: 53).

Numerous ethnographic and anthropological studies have shown the existence of such conductorless orchestration of practice in many modern unindustrialised societies (eg Hodder 1979), whether recognised by the analysts at the time or not. By identifying the nature of the prevailing *habitus*, the archaeologist can perhaps gain insights into the nature of a society which the trowel could never reveal.

> 'The habitus – embodied history, internalised as second nature and so forgotten as history – is the active presence of the whole past of which it is the product' (Bourdieu 1992: 56).

The manufacture of many artefact types, including pottery, can be seen to have been structured by *habitus*, and it will be argued below that we should recognise its presence in objects as humble as the simple Anglo-Saxon 'cooking pot'.

The second main theoretical thread of this paper, obliquely connected to the notion of *habitus*, is the concept of an apparently functional object being an essential part of the social and cultural identity of its user, one of the media through which that identity could be broadcast. Again, numerous ethnographic and anthropological studies have produced evidence of this. For example, in Hodder's (1979) study of the pottery of the various tribal groups in the Lake Baringo area of Kenya, each of the tribes in the area used pottery water jars, which, when seen through typologists' eyes, could be regarded as purely functional. They were of a coarse fabric, undecorated, of baggy shape, possessed a

narrow neck to lessen the effects of evaporation and had two small pierced lugs on the shoulder for transportation. However, each tribe had its own individual version of the basic shape, and would not use jars of a shape which were seen to identify membership of another tribe. The differences were quite subtle, being related to neck and body width, but the users were willing to travel to relatively distant markets to obtain pots of the desired type, even when sources of the other types were closer to hand. Similarly, a case-study of pottery use in modern Guatemala, cited by Rice (1987), showed that four neighbouring groups in the highland region used water jars which, although very similar, were each of a different form. The vessels were undecorated, and, like the Kenyan vessels, had attributes which confirmed their function. However, each individual group used a different form to the other, and, because of the different handle positions on the vessels, had a different method of carrying them. From a purely functional point of view, the vessels each had modes of carriage which could be seen to be more efficient than that of the others in certain situations. One left both hands free, allowing the carrier to perform other tasks, whereas another enabled two jars to be carried at once, and thus facilitated the transportation of a greater quantity of water at any one time. Possession of the full range of such vessels would have allowed a greater flexibility of response to a given situation, but the individual groups each used only a single traditional form. This not only shows that habitual practice, or *habitus*, may override functional efficiency, but that the way in which the jars are carried makes a public statement concerning the cultural identity of the user.

There seems some evidence to suspect that the pottery of the early/middle Saxon period was a similarly vital part of the social identity of the people who used them. John Hurst noted this in 1976, although the theoretical equipment to provide the explanation he sought was not available at the time.

> The Anglo-Saxon settlers used handmade pottery because this was the pottery which was made and used in their homelands ... It is not so clear why they did not take over the Roman pottery industry, especially now we know that there was at least a two-generation overlap in the early fifth century. (Hurst 1976: 294)

Many ceramicists appear intimidated by Theory. The problem was highlighted by McCarthy and Brooks in the introduction to their *Medieval Pottery in Britain AD 900–1600* (1988):

> We are still a long way from using pottery in a way that prehistorians or anthropologists use their data in reconstructing patterns of social or economic behaviour. Indeed, it is a matter for concern that students of Saxon and Medieval pottery in Britain are not exploiting the very fertile grounds for ideas present in the vast ethnographic literature on ceramics (1988: 2).

This admirable call to ceramicists to break away from trainspotting was, however, somewhat undermined on the same page of their volume by the assertion that:

It is one of the archaeological tragedies of the last twenty years or so that so much useful work has been written on both sides of the Atlantic in incomprehensible jargon; this has delayed the adoption by many archaeologists, including those specialising in Roman or medieval Britain, of alternative ways of thinking about their subjects (1988: 2).

There is no doubt that many archaeologists (including this one) find some of the obscurities of high-level theory baffling, but all branches of archaeology have their own arcane jargon. It is doubtful that many individuals outside the walls of the early Anglo-Saxon ceramic ghetto either know the difference between a *Schalenurne* and a *Standfussschale*, or are aware of their significance.

Most analysts, when dealing with early/middle Saxon domestic pottery dismiss it, explicitly or implicitly, as functional, despite Julian Richards (1987) having demonstrated that just about every single aspect of the decorated funerary wares was symbolic in one way or another. The commonest sentiments appear to be those expressed by Myres:

> Throughout the (early Saxon) period the continuing need for undecorated cookpots and other domestic utensils suited to unchanging household requirements checked the evolution of new fashions and so makes a typological series hard to establish over much of this material (1977: 8)

This interpretative standpoint is demonstrated by the view of two techniques of surface finishing which were employed by potters of the early Saxon period: combing and rustication (the pinching or stabbing of the surface of the still-damp pot with the fingers, figure 1). The techniques have their origins in the Germanic regions of Europe during the late Iron Age (Hamerow 1993: 31) and, despite the fact that Iron Age analysts have accepted that combed prehistoric pottery (Scored Ware) is of cultural significance (Elsdon 1992), both techniques are generally considered by Anglo-Saxon ceramicists to be functional. Various authorities see them as having been no more than a method of roughening the surface of a pot to make it easier to grip (eg. Hamerow 1993). If this is so, why do some pots have combing, others rustication and others no treatment at all? If the techniques improved the functional efficiency of domestic pottery by making it easier to grip, then why were not all such 'functional' pots so treated? Similarly, it was surely far quicker to comb a pot than to rusticate it, so why were some vessels rusticated?

Rusticated vessels are rare but universal finds on Anglo-Saxon settlement sites. At West Stow, 618 sherds of such vessels occurred in assemblage of over 53,000 sherds (West 1985: 135), which implies that vessels of the type were almost as scarce as stamped and incised wares (463 sherds). Also, in the cases where it was possible to identify the vessel type, the technique was only used on bowl forms. At Mucking, the picture appears similar, although a count of sherds of the type is not given. Rustication is restricted largely to wide-mouthed forms, a pattern which Hamerow notes as being the same as in the pre-Roman Iron Age in Germany (Hamerow 1993: 54). Wide-mouthed Anglo-Saxon cremation containers are strongly linked to females (see below), which has further implications for the significance of rustication. Three rusticated 'plates' also occurred at Mucking, although no contemporary parallels are known and there seems to have been a strong link between rustication and chaff-tempered fabrics at the site. At both West Stow and Mucking, the technique is mainly limited to the lower part of such vessels and usually an unimpressed area was left below the rim. At the site of Roksem in Belgium both combing and rustication occured but, significantly, the former was found only on chaff tempered pottery and the latter on sherds in a sandy fabric (Hamerow *et al* 1994:11).

The evidence suggests therefore, that far from being purely functional, rusticated vessels were marked out as special, whether in terms of function or social symbolism. The evidence from West Stow, Mucking, and, for that matter, the pre-Roman German Iron Age, shows that there were restrictions relating to the form and fabric of such vessels, and that, in a domestic context, they are almost as rare as the heavily-symbolic stamp-decorated wares. Such correlations are strongly reminiscent of the findings of Richards' analysis of cremation urns. What the symbolism may relate to is another matter, but a programme of organic residue analysis comparing rusticated and plain vessels, such as that being carried out by Richard Evershed as part of the Ipswich Ware Project (Blinkhorn, forthcoming), may yield significant results.

Certainly, it is time to confront some of the assumptions made about the nature of Anglo-Saxon domestic pottery.

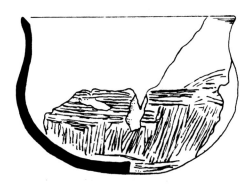

Fig 1. 1) Rusticated vessel from West Stow, Suffolk (Scale 1:4. After Myres 1977: Fig. 112, no 2063). 2) Scored vessel from Mucking, Essex (Scale 1:3. After Hamerow 1993: Fig.127 no 6)

Tackling the Two F's

Fabric

The detailed definition of fabric types during the analysis of early/middle Saxon pottery appears to be a totally automatic action, usually resulting in a long list of descriptions of variations on basic themes. Despite this, nobody has yet seen fit to ask the most basic of questions of the practice, with perhaps one of the most obvious being '*What does this mean?*'. The identification of fabric, as with form (see below), is subjective. It is true that petrological analysis can sometimes link the fabric to a general geological source, such as Alan Vince's work examining the distribution of Early/Middle Saxon pottery tempered with granite from the Charnwood Forest area of Leicestershire (pers. comm.), but most analysts continue to subdivide fabrics with a similar geological content, creating sub-groups based on the size, shape and frequency of the major inclusions, and, in some cases, of the presence of small quantities of other minerals.

Myres, in his *Corpus of Anglo-Saxon Pottery of the Pagan Period* (1977) describes undecorated early Saxon pottery as

> so uninformative and unrewarding … that excavators … sometimes have difficulty in illustrating it at all. In view of the extremely casual and slapdash methods used by Anglo-Saxon craftsmen in preparation of their raw material and in the shaping of their home-made products, not to mention their customary reliance on the caprices of a garden bonfire to bake them, it is open to question whether conclusions of much significance can be expected from such technical analyses (1977: 1).

This is a reasonable summary of the picture of the material which is gained through using traditional methods of analysis. Despite this, using a different set of 'technical analyses' does not seem to be on the agenda.

Since undecorated pottery usually constitutes *c* 95% of settlement assemblages, the traditional analytical approach results in the majority of pottery from non-funerary contexts being archaeologically worthless, other than as a provider of a broad period date for the features from which it came. However, the application of some basic archaeological theory can explain why Early Saxon domestic pottery does not produce the sort of fabric-related data which keeps the traditionalists happy.

At the time of writing, English Heritage are funding a major research project into middle Saxon Ipswich Ware pottery (Blinkhorn forthcoming), including the petrological and chemical analyses of around 180 sherds of the ware. Amongst the analysed sherds are four from different vessels which had all been stamped with the same die. In thin-section, two of these sherds were quite obviously the 'same' fabric, but the other two differed from both these and each other. When, as part of the same project, the sherds were subject to chemical analysis using inductively coupled plasma – atomic emission spectrometry (ICP-AES), three were found to be chemically 'the same', but the fourth was of a noticeably different chemical composition, although within the range of the known products of the industry. By con-

ventional wisdom, vessels stamped with the same die are the products of one potter. In this case, the potter was producing vessels which were different in terms of mineralogical and chemical composition, but the broadly the same in terms of form, manufacture and decoration . The vessels are therefore, according to traditional analytical practice, different. It seems highly likely that, to the potter and the user, they were the same. Who is right? Had the potter failed to make the correct pot? What understanding of the material do we gain by regarding them as different? Clay is a notoriously variable material, especially the glacial drifts which covers a large part of the area occupied by the Anglo-Saxons (Hamerow 1993: 28). Were the potters aware of this whilst digging their clay? The average Saxon potter was not able to examine his/her clay through a microscope, nor send samples to a university to allow a breakdown of the chemical composition in parts per million. If the clay came from the traditional source, looked and felt right, and behaved in a satisfactory manner when worked, would the potter have declined to use it because the quartz inclusions were 0.5mm in diameter and rounded, rather than generally around 0.2mm and angular?

The ethnographic record has many instances of potters who have traditional 'recipes' for clay/temper mixes, with one of the most widely-cited being the Shipibo-Conibo of eastern Peru (cf Rice 1987: 121). The people in question generally use three different clays and tempers to manufacture pots, with the mixes depending upon the type of vessel to be manufactured. In some cases, different mixes are used for the same parts of different vessels. However, these rules are not always adhered to, and the potters sometimes deliberately use the 'wrong' mix for the type of vessel that they are making. What would traditional archaeological fabric analyses make of such practice?

In pre-industrial societies, using the most basic of technology, clay preparation and mixing appears instinctive, although constant methodologies of preparation and manufacture are inevitably used to reach the end result. Modern fabric analysis utilises technology which looks for (literally) microscopic variations from vessel to vessel, yet in the end, the decision to pronounce two sherds as having the same fabric is made in a subjective, and often purely instinctive manner, rather perhaps in the same manner in which an ancient potter mixed his/her clay. Once such decisions are made, interpretation of the meaning of the data is rarely, if ever, carried out, other than to produce a list of the number of sherds per fabric type. Such lists are of questionable use, and it could be said that they have no meaning.

Mucking and West Stow are very good examples of the apparent futility of the microscopic fabric analysis of the early/middle Saxon handmade pottery. The West Stow assemblage comprised 53,370 sherds which were divided into 7 fabric groups (West 1985: 129) based, as usual, on the size, type and frequency of occurrence of the inclusions. These groups were further subdivided, resulting in the definition of 29 fabrics, despite their validity being questioned by their creator:

Many of the subdivisions may merge into each other, on the basis of the frequency of the inclusions. The distinctions of 'much', 'some' and 'rare' must remain subjective until detailed statistical studies can be done (West 1985: 129).

A series of sherds in the various fabric types were submitted for thin-section analysis and 'detailed statistical studies' (Russel 1985). The fifty-nine samples were analysed using the standard techniques of textural analysis, with the data processed using a Clustan package. A presence-absence table of inclusions was drawn up

> which did not show any great difference between the groups, except for the macroscopic inclusions, and even then the groups were not exclusive (Russel 1985: 130)

The textural analysis of the fabrics containing quartz showed that there were similarities between members of the same main fabric groups in terms of the size and shape of the quartz inclusions, but the usefulness such information is entirely questionable:

> Any conclusions must remain tentative until more is known about the local geology, and sources for all the clays used on the site have been tracked down, a task that is difficult in an area of mixed glacial deposits, and may well prove impossible if riverine deposits, long since eroded, were sources for clays or temper (Russel 1985)

To again quote West,

> (Russel) confirmed that the difficulty encountered by simple visual techniques produced a distorted view of the pottery fabrics (1985: 130)

The West Stow pottery report occupies ten pages of the site report, of which one page deals with the actual fabrics and their significance and the rest consists of data tables, the identification of decoration types and a brief summary of the middle Saxon Ipswich Ware. When reading the petrological analysis, one can sense an air of despair as the authors try to find something meaningful to say about such the massive dataset, despite having used a veritable battery of the 'correct' analytical techniques. As usual, the ultimate use of the pottery at West Stow was to date the various excavated features, but even this most basic of operations relied upon the decorated pottery. Only 2% of the West Stow pottery was decorated, which means that 98% of a dataset of over 50,000 sherds yielded no useful information. This would suggest that the standard techniques of analysis are unsuitable to the material, and one wonders why so much time and effort are spent repeatedly proving this.

At Mucking, similar problems were encountered.

> The thin-sectioning programme was hampered ... by inconsistencies in classification resulting from an undistinctive mineralogical composition ... found in nearly all fabrics. Indeed, these inconsistencies were such that a number of sherds which were assigned to different fabric groups were subsequently

found to cross-join ... fabric groupings had to be based primarily upon qualitative differences in matrix and inclusions which were readily identifiable under 10x magnification and could be readily confirmed by thin-section. Such grouping is inevitably to a degree subjective ... (Hamerow 1993: 27)

Hamerow then goes on to define 8 different fabric groups based on thin-section and macroscopic analyses, but with the warning that

> It must be remembered that a certain degree of overlap between the fabric groups remains (1993: 28)

Both the West Stow and Mucking reports (and they are by no means the only examples) indicate that the definition of tight fabric groups is an almost Pavlovian response by ceramic analysts to an early Saxon dataset. Obviously, some form of fabric description is necessary, but Hamerow herself highlighted, perhaps unintentionally, the way forward in dealing with such material when she says that due to problems in locating missing sherds of pottery from Mucking

> (some) fabrics could be classed simply as either sandy or grass-tempered (and) much of the overall fabric classification has had to be restricted to this distinction (1993: 27).

Despite Hamerow's somewhat apologetic tone for such methodological heresy, when the fabrics are defined in this way, analysis of the distribution yields useful information. Hamerow showed that the distribution of chaff-tempered pottery around the settlement demonstrated distinct clustering, with the greatest amounts in the northern area of the site, and the least in the south. Similarly, fabric 7, a chalk/limestone tempered ware occured mainly in southern area of the site, in direct contrast to the chaff-tempered vessels. The mica- and haematite-tempered vessels show a similar distribution to the chalk-tempered wares, as do the sand-tempered wares (Hamerow 1993: figs. 13 and 16–19). If these fabrics are taken as being parts of a broad class rather than distinctive fabrics, then mineral-tempered wares occur mainly in the southern end of the site, and chaff-tempered examples in the northern and more central areas. The use of this simplified approach to fabric analysis can explain why the traditional methodologies do not work and also sets the scene for the establishment of an alternative agenda for new avenues of investigation.

The fifth century Germanic settlers in England made and used decorated pottery in similar styles to the vessels found in their continental homelands, and although the decoration developed along a divergent path over the next hundred years or so, the pottery remains within the Germanic tradition, presumably indicating a strong retention of cultural identity. The undecorated wares too can be seen to demonstrate traits which reflect the *habitus* of these settlers and their descendants and their need to express their identity. For example, in the south-east Midlands of England, nearly all the locally-made 'coarse' pottery from the Bronze Age to the Late Medieval period was tempered with local Jurassic shelly limestones, despite the fact that large deposits of glacial sand and gravel are common in the area. The exception, apart from a few Roman fineware industries, is Early Saxon pottery, which is tempered with either minerals or chaff ('grass-temper'). This would indicate, as noted by Hurst (1976: 294), that the domestic wares were subject to constraints which demanded that they should be made in a manner which ignored the long-established British potting methods, and continued the Germanic tradition in a new location. The fact that settlers made pots in the manner which they were used to, and (presumably) taught their successors the same methods, is hardly startling, yet appears to be the key to understanding the material.

The analysis of a group of over 7,000 sherds of undecorated early/middle Saxon pottery from excavations in the 1980's at the town of Raunds in Northamptonshire (Blinkhorn in print a) resulted in the definition of 10 fabric types, which were based, as usual, on the size, shape and type of inclusions present. As with the Mucking and West Stow pottery, the mixed geology resulted in the fabric groups being very broad, and the placing of a sherd into a particular group rather subjective. It was noted, however, that the ten main fabrics could be grouped into three fabric classes, based on the physical treatment of the temper added to the clay before manufacture, rather than the actual minerals used. These were

a) Sand from local deposits, characterised by rounded grains of varied geological types and shaped by natural erosion processes,

b) grit, a narrow suite of relatively larger, more angular mineral fragments,

c) organic temper, a mixture of chaff and other chopped organic material.

Unlike at Mucking, organic temper formed a very small proportion of the assemblage, but a plot of the distribution of the mineral tempered wares at North Raunds showed that the sandy and gritty wares, whilst occurring on all parts of the site, were grouped as the major ware in different areas, with the split roughly running down the north-south axis of the excavated area. This was originally interpreted as having chronological significance, as the sandy wares were commoner in an area of the site which saw the focus of the middle Saxon activity. The reasons for the change in temper preparation were seen as functional: at the foundation of the Raunds settlement, two main traditional methods of pottery manufacture were in use. One group tempered their clay with natural sand, the other utilised the more time-consuming method of crushing rock. Over time, it became obvious to the potters in the settlement that using sand was a far quicker and therefore more efficient way of making pots, and so they gradually utilised that method, with the presence of the grit-tempered sherds in the later features being due to residuality. Another triumph for functionality. However, when this model was applied to pottery from an

early and middle Saxon settlement at Pennyland, Milton Keynes (Blinkhorn 1993), some 30 kilometres from Raunds, it was found to be flawed. Unsurprisingly, due to the reasonably close proximity of the two sites, geological constraints resulted in the range of fabrics and temper types of the Pennyland pottery being very similar to those from Raunds, and once again, sand, crushed rock and organic temper were all used. However, when the chronology of the Pennyland material was considered in the same manner as that from Raunds, a rather different picture emerged. During the earliest part of the settlement, the majority of the plain pottery was again grit-tempered, making up some 51% of the assemblage, but by the latest phase of occupation, some 72% of the pottery was grit-tempered, in direct opposition to the trend at Raunds. The less functionally-efficient technique of temper preparation had become the more common with time. It could have been that there was simply a large degree of redeposition on the site, but the fact that early Saxon decorated pottery was not redeposited in any of the middle Saxon features would seem to suggest otherwise. *Habitus* provides the explanation. It is accepted that the earliest decorated Anglo-Saxon pottery is directly relatable to contemporary continental types (Myres 1977). The fact that, in England, pottery of different culturally-specific Germanic types occurs within the same settlements (such as Mucking or West Stow) indicates that the inhabitants were of various cultural origins. If these groups, as well as having differing traditional form types, also had differing traditional methods of pottery manufacture, forces of *habitus* would have resulted in them making their pots in culturally 'correct' fashion, despite there being more functionally efficient possibilities available, which may have included those of their neighbours. The continuation of their traditional practices through time and across generations would cause fluctuations in the proportions of the different temper classes, reflecting the rise and fall of the populations of the various cultural groups within the settlement. There is also the fact that chaff-tempered pottery varies enormously in its occurrence in different areas of England. At sites such as Raunds and Pennyland, it forms less than 10% of the assemblage, whereas at Mucking, in the latest features, it represents over 90% of the pottery. This fact could also be explained by the settlements having different mixes of the various Germanic cultural groups.

Hamerow demonstrated that the distribution of the various types of decorated pottery showed that the focus of the Mucking settlement shifted from the south to the north of the site between the fifth to the eighth centuries (1993: fig. 3). As discussed above, the chaff-tempered pottery is commonest in the northern area of the site, whereas the mineral-tempered fabrics were more abundant at the southern end. Thus, Mucking shows a similar pattern to North Raunds, and the same interpretation can be advanced: Mucking was occupied by people of different cultural origins who continued to use their traditional and differing methods of pottery manufacture, despite other, and arguably, more efficient, possibilities being available to them.

The increase in the proportion of chaff-tempered fabric over time was due to the increase in the proportion of the population who utilised that particular method of manufacture. The distribution of the ethnically-relatable decorated pottery at the settlement provides some support for this idea. Faceted carinated bowls, *Schalenurnen*, a pottery type closely associated with people of Saxon origin (Myres 1986: 66–8) occur in greater quantities in the southern area of the site, whereas bossed vessels, which Myres demonstrated as being the products of the Anglian/Jutish *kulturkreis* (1986: 64) occur in both the northern and southern areas. Only one faceted carinated bowl had a chaff-tempered fabric (Hamerow 1993: 56), whereas the bossed pottery shows a fairly even split between the two fabric groups. The fact that, at Mucking *Schalenurnen*, which were rarely made in chaff-tempered fabrics, occurred mainly in the southern area would suggest that chaff-tempering was utilised by a different social group to that which used *Schalenurnen*, and that both the fabric as well as the form of the pottery of the period had social significance. This supports the idea that, despite appearances to the contrary, in Anglo-Saxon England, the method of manufacture of 'crude domestic utensils' was part of the social identity of the people of the period, and that its manufacture was subject to strict internally consistent regulation, part of the *habitus* of the groups in question. On the continent chaff tempered pottery appears restricted to a relatively small area of Belgium, and dates to between the 5th and 8th centuries after which vegetable tempers are replaced by shell and sand. Chronologically this

corresponds to the period when the area came under the hegemony of Carolingia. Petrological analyses of the chaff tempered material from Belgium have shown that they are very similar to samples of chaff tempered pottery from Mucking, but are significantly different to wares from Gloucestershire and Warwickshire (Hamerow *et al* 1994: 9–12). Whilst it is possible that this may be due to the similar geology of the lower Thames valley and coastal Flanders, it may be that this is a demonstration of the arrival of settlers from north-west Europe who continued with their traditional methods of pottery manufacture.

The situation is by no means clear-cut, but there are social factors to take into account. If, for example, a potter from one ethnic group 'married' into another (which was highly likely in a settlement with a population of differing ethnic origins), did they continue to use their traditional forms and methods of manufacture, or did they change to that of the cultural group into which they had married? Alternately, did they use a combination of their own traditional techniques and those of the newly acquired kin group, symbolic of their union? Obviously, the answers to such questions will be, to a degree, speculative, but they indicate that there are very good grounds for further investigation. Furthermore, they suggest that the potential exists for far more sophisticated explanations for the nature of early Anglo-Saxon pottery than the traditionalist's view that the people of the period were not very good at making pottery.

Form

> Many of these crude domestic utensils … look a great deal more neat and tidy when presented as archaeological drawings than they do as objects in a museum show-case … Each of these main (form) groups merges imperceptibly into others, and a number of the urns … could be placed in a different group from that in which they are…shown (Myres 1977: 1–2).

As with fabric, ceramicists appear somewhat baffled when confronted with the forms of early/middle Anglo-Saxon pottery. As stated above the material is seen as purely functional; they are the shape they are because they fulfilled their intended purpose and that is the end of it. No-one has felt any need to pursue the matter further, other than to repeatedly confirm Myres' findings that typology does not work.

Anglo-Saxon pottery does show change and variation, but not in the regulated, precise manner of the ceramics of the classical or post-medieval world. Attempts at typologising the pottery of the Saxon period have shown that whilst there are identifiable form-types, at the same time there are other vessels in 'grey areas' which do not fit neatly into perceived categories, and do not follow each other in neat chronotypological procession.

It is not just early Saxon pottery which demonstrates this. Strong conservatism is evident in the manufacture of some of the pottery of the middle Saxon period. For example, at the middle Saxon settlement of Hamwic (Timby 1988) the

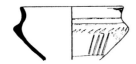

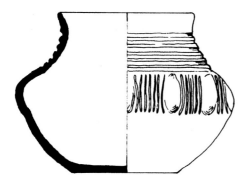

Fig. 2. 1) Faceted Carinated Bowl from Mucking, Essex (1:4 Scale. After Myres 1977: Fig 201, no. 3410. 2) Bossed vessel from Caistor-by-Norwich, Norfolk (1:4 Scale. After Myres 1977: Fig. 220, no 1590.

locally-made pottery, is, in many aspects of its form, fabric and manufacture, similar to some early Saxon wares, but was used alongside high-quality, wheel-thrown and kiln-fired imported Frankish wares. The imports were far from rare, comprising 11% of the excavated assemblage but, despite the apparent functional and aesthetic superiority of the Frankish wares, there appears to have been little, if any, attempt by the indigenous Hamwic potters to copy the form, fabric or manufacturing techniques of the continental wares. The locally-made pottery, despite being produced in a range of fabrics, has a very strong consistency of form. The vast majority of vessels were jars, most of which have elongated globular bodies, high, flaring, everted rims, and flat bases (Timby 1988: figs. 2–8). Bowls were also made, but pitchers are extremely rare, despite imported vessels of that functional type being relatively common. Decoration is extremely rare, and usually consists of stamping in geometric incised lozenges, spirals, or incised lattices, none of which can be paralleled in the decorative styles of the imported pottery.

This implies that generally, the makers (and users) of the Hamwic middle Saxon pottery resisted change, again supporting the idea that hand-made 'domestic' pottery was an important part of Anglo-Saxon cultural identity, and that the use of it affirmed that identity. The ceramics of the middle Saxon urban centres of London and York show a similar resistance to outside influences. In London, local hand-made wares account for between 50–60% of the sherds from Jubilee Hall and Maiden Lane, with the rest of the assemblage comprising continental imports and Ipswich Ware (Blackmore 1988: table 1). The chaff-tempered wares generally have very rounded, globular bodies, perfunctory upright or everted rims and flat bases, and are very obviously different to the non-local types (Blackmore 1988: figs. 20, 24–5). Vessels appear largely confined to jars, with no pitchers, although there are relatively large numbers of imported pitchers, whether from Ipswich or the continent. Despite such vessels showing that there was a market for pitchers, the local potters appear to have made no attempt to copy them. As ethnography has repeatedly demonstrated, *habitus* overrides economic rationality.

Middle Saxon Ipswich Ware, the only English pottery of the period which is wheel-turned and kiln-fired (cf Hurst 1976), was first made in the eponymous Suffolk town in the late seventh or early eighth centuries (Blinkhorn forthcoming). However, the locally-made pottery in the earliest middle Saxon areas of the town are of a similar tradition to those of the other major middle Saxon settlements. The reason for change in Ipswich could be explained if there had been, as seems possible a large Frisian presence in the town in the late seventh or early eighth century, which resulted in pottery being manufactured to meet their requirements of culturally-acceptable pottery (Blinkhorn forthcoming). Despite there being some differences in the form and fabric of Ipswich Ware and Frisian pottery, the features of a pot which defined it as 'Frisian' in the eighth century are not necessarily those that a modern archaeologist would define (such as, for instance, the fabric inclusions). In the case of Ipswich Ware, the basic shape of the body, upright rim, peaked lugs, stamp-decoration and range of functional types, all of which can be paralleled on contemporary Frisian pottery, may have been enough to make the pots culturally 'correct'. Rice's discussion of the Guatemalan water jars shows that the cultural differentiation in ceramics can be related by simple variations in neck width, body shape and handle position. Cultural 'correctness' may have operated in a similar manner in middle Saxon England.

The fact that most early Saxon domestic pottery is undecorated cannot be used as a pretext for dismissing it as merely 'functional'. Examples of apparently functional items having symbolic significance occur widely in ethnoarchaeological studies, and whilst ethnographic evidence cannot be used to prove an archaeological theory, it is a useful device for blowing large holes in comfortably-held assumptions. The lack of decorative embellishment is not necessarily an indicator of a low status of either an object or its user. Rice (1987) cites an ethnographic study by Braithwaite of the Azande people of southern Sudan which noted that the only person who used undecorated eating utensils was the tribal chief. This, is, as Rice phrases it

an unsettling observation in view of archaeologists frequent assumptions concerning decoration and social status (Rice 1987: 268)

On a similar theme, Ian Hodder's work in the Lake Baringo district of Western Kenya noted that the three main tribes in the area all possessed simple wooden stools, an apparently functional item if ever there was one. However, such stools played a vital part in the marriage and circumcision rituals of the one of the groups, and, consequently, they were willing to pay a far higher purchase price for them than the people of the other groups (1979). Nor should we overlook the fact that the notion of an object being 'purely functional' is one which owes a great deal to our own utilitarian ethic and is an ideological construct in its own right.

Nevertheless, the undecorated domestic pottery of early Saxon England is still generally regarded as functional, and attempts are still made to impose tight, art-historical form series upon the material. Generally, when placing the form of an Anglo-Saxon pot into a conveniently labelled category, two methodologies tend to be used. The first is the purely subjective 'that-looks-close-enough-let's-call-it-a-wide-mouthed-biconical' approach, whilst the second involves a multitude of measurements of such parameters as carination angle, rim angle, the ratio of maximum diameter to total height and so on. This results in mathematical formulae which can be used to define vessel types. For example, Hamerow (1993: 37–40) defines a carinated vessel as one which has an internal angle at the waist which is less than 120 degrees, whilst a vessel which is greater than 120 degrees is regarded as biconical. The definition is based on the fact that range of waist angles of such vessels at Mucking appears to have a bimodal distribution around a critical value of 120 degrees. However, Hamerow admits that statistical analysis of the data does not support her claim. The null hypothesis that the spread of the carination angles of the Mucking vessels is unimodal, and that there is no difference between the two perceived categories, gives a significance level which suggests that there is a valid reason to suspect just that. Despite this, she goes on to classify vessels as falling into one or other of the categories, with the implication that it is the dataset and not the theory which is at fault.

Hamerow is not the only person who has used such an approach, and all have produced the similar results. Vessels are forced into perceived groupings, although with many references to 'broad categories' and 'wide ranges of variants'. The implication often appears to be that there was a failure on the part of the potter to produce a vessel which corresponded to the analyst's typological classifications, rather than a failure on the part of the ceramicist to understand the potters intentions. The idea that the shape of a vessel may have been symbolic does not appear to be an issue, despite the fact that Richards (1987: 148–54) has shown this to have been the case with funerary pottery. He defined a series of form variables which appear to have been the crucial factors in the potter's mind when shaping a cremation vessel, with the width and height of various parts of the pot being of importance. He went on to demonstrate that certain grave-goods are associated with particular vessel shapes, with that the age and sex of the contained individual also being a factor. Generally, males are linked with narrow pots and females with wide ones (1987: 150), and cremations without grave-goods are linked to wide-mouthed vessels, whereas those with are linked to narrow-necked examples. He suggested that the fact that poorer cremations were placed in vessels which can be seen (in form terms) as cooking pots shows that the functional form perhaps reflected the individual's social status. Additionally, the vessel height is related to the age and status of the deceased (1987: 135–6). Infants were buried in the shortest vessels, adults in the tallest. Cremations without grave-goods are found in shorter vessels, those with are found in larger, suggesting that status, signified by the presence of grave-goods, was gained with age. Vessel width also appears related to age, as is the height of the maximum diameter of the pot, and the rim diameter appears to be linked to gender, with wider-mouthed vessels being strongly female-linked (1987: 139). Richards also notes that there are differences between vessels in Anglian and Saxon cemeteries, with, for example, Saxon urns generally having a lower average height than Anglian examples (1987: 194), suggesting that the different cultural groupings may each have had their own dialects of the symbolic language. It would seem therefore, that in the as far as decorated early Anglo-Saxon cremation urns were concerned, the shape of the pot made basic statement about age, gender and rank, with the decoration adding further detail which was linked to social identity.

Either the cremation pottery was consciously produced in the different forms considered appropriate for each individual, or,

if existing pottery was selected, then it was chosen as being appropriate for the individual. Either way, the Anglo-Saxons conceived of shape according to these criteria, and used them to signify social identity (Richards 1987: 148)

Richards analysed only cremation vessels, as domestic pottery cannot be directly linked to individuals, but there seems no reason why the variations in the size and shape of domestic pottery did not broadcast information about the user that was related to their age, gender and social station. If certain sizes and shapes of pottery were appropriate in death, why not so too in life? Certainly, other objects were 'decorated' with the same symbolic language as was used on cremation containers. Some annular brooches were incised with geometric patterns which renders them near-identical to corresponding cremation containers when viewed from above (Richards 1992) suggesting that brooches were as much badges of social identity as clothes fasteners, and transmitting the same information as the pottery. Viewing a decorated pot from above is the only way in which all the decoration can be seen at the same time, as it is mainly limited to the upper parts of vessels, above the carination or shoulder. Generally, the only time a pot would have been viewed in this manner was when it was placed in the grave-hole (Richards 1992). This would indicate that in life the Anglo-Saxons were transmitting the same information about themselves as did the decoration on cremation containers, but through the medium of their personal material culture, such as brooches. Doubtless, perishable items such as clothing also played a part. Because of this, it would not have been necessary for domestic pottery to transmit the same data, and thus there was no need for such ceramics to be decorated. As mentioned, Richards showed that the descriptive symbols on the pots were strongly linked to the type of grave-goods, which further suggests that, in life, such artefacts transmitted information which was related to the social identity of the wearer and that merely observing an individual would have been sufficient to assess their station. When the person had been reduced to cremated bone and the fragments placed in a pot the information normally broadcast by personal objects would not have been readily forthcoming. Thus, the message conveyed by the objects would have had to have been broadcast in some other way. The marking of the pot, with symbols which corresponded with the personal material culture of the deceased, was in this case the chosen method.

Thus, it would seem that undecorated early Anglo-Saxon pots were somewhat personal items. There is general agreement that undecorated wares were generally produced at a household/domestic level, and therefore it seems highly likely that the potter and the consumer were, in most cases, well-known to each other, or even the same person. Thus, the production of pottery of a morphological type which was appropriate for their social status, age and sex of the user would not have been difficult.

Other aspects of the form of early/middle Saxon domestic pottery would appear to be equally clearly in need of a rethink. A small proportion of early Saxon vessels are equipped with applied lugs and are rare but almost universal finds on settlement sites both in England and on the continent (Myres 1977: 10). They appear to have been predominantly used as cooking vessels, with the lugs allowing the suspension of the vessel over a fire. Lugs were attached to the body or the rim of the vessel, but never both, and are never found on decorated vessels (Figure 3). From a purely functional point of view, both methods of lug positioning appear to have been equally efficient for the task of suspending a vessel, but the potters obviously had to make a decision when selecting their location. Examination of the North Raunds and Pennylands material produced no obvious correlation between the lug arrangement, temper type or vessel form, but the Myres Corpus indicates that a high proportion of English lugged vessels have footring bases (Myres 1977: 10), an attribute which is an otherwise rare feature on early Saxon ceramics. Footrings are found on pottery in many places within the Germanic homelands (1977: 347), but, in England, are exceptionally unusual on domestic vessels without lugs. Despite this, when they occur on such pots they are generally regarded as being a functional attribute, with Myres stating that they were

presumably for convenience in standing by the hearth when not embedded in it or suspended over it (1977: 10)

If this was the case, why were some lugged vessels not equipped with footrings? At the same time, why equip 'functional' cooking pottery with a footring? Round bases, without footrings, are far less prone to thermal shock fracture (Rice 1987), and therefore more functionally efficient for everyday cookery. To have used a vessel when others of a functionally superior design were in common use would suggest that the attributes in question had some sort of social or cultural significance. Certainly, on the continent, lugged vessels with feet are extremely rare in the Jutish region (Myres 1977: 10).

The position of the lugs on a pot does not seem to make any difference to the functional efficiency of the vessels, but if both lugs and footrings were, as part of the *habitus* of the society, conveying social information about their users in a similar manner to the basic shape of the vessel, then a suspended cooking pot would have been an ideal medium of transmission. The living areas of early Anglo-Saxon 'halls' generally consisted of a large room with a central hearth, and thus it can be argued that the fire would have been the visual focus of the living area. A pot suspended over the hearth would have been extremely visible, with the position of the lugs and the shape of the base obvious to any viewer. Placing a vessel which transmitted social information at the visual focus of a room would have meant that its message could not have been missed by anyone present.

Conclusions

The crux of this paper is that, despite appearances to the contrary, there are grounds for suspecting that early Anglo-Saxon domestic pottery was a vital part of the cultural equipment of the people of the period, a result of the application of unwritten (and even unthought) rules and social mores which cannot be identified by art-historical or chronotypological compartmentalisation.

As implied in the introduction, the author does not claim to have all, or perhaps even any, of the answers, but is concerned more to search for the correct questions to ask. The suggestion that the undecorated domestic pottery in Anglo-Saxon England was governed by the social standing and cultural origins of the user seems a valid one to start with. It would explain why undecorated pottery does not respond to attempts by analysts to force vessels into morphological groups; each human being, although of the same species, is physically different to the next. When social factors are taken into account, the differences become multiplied still further. Thus, rather than looking for the 'correct' rigid form and fabric categories to place the vessels into, we should be attempting to identify the meaning of their shape in terms of the social standing and cultural origins of their users. Until this is achieved, we cannot hope to gain the understanding which the traditional methods of analysis are so clearly failing to provide. Hamerow (1993) has stated that there is no hope

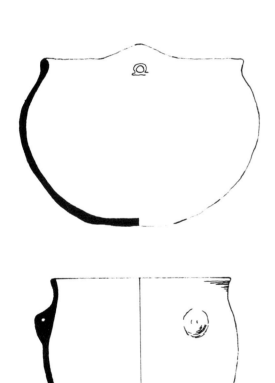

Fig. 3. 1) Lugged vessel, West Stow, Suffolk (1:4 Scale. After Myres 1977: Fig. 74, no 3994). 2) Lugged vessel, Caistor-by-Norwich (1:4 Scale. After Myres 1977: Fig. 76, no 1805).

of identifying cultural traits in undecorated domestic pottery from excavation assemblages due to their fragmented state. This may to an extent be true, but should not mean that we do not try. Otherwise we shall merely continue to confirm that the answer is, indeed, forty-two.

Altogether, it would seem that early Saxon domestic pottery was far more than functional, to the extent that it was deliberately used to make statements with regard to the social and cultural identity of its users even though, in some cases, this lessened its functional efficiency, with the force for the origins of the symbols (in terms of form and manufacture) being that of habitus.

The Anglo-Saxons, at that time, were a collection of people from disparate backgrounds, living in small, culturally-mixed groups in a foreign land without any real identity other than that which they had brought with them. In such circumstances, it is not hard to believe that they clung onto that identity with determination, to the extent that even something as simple as a cooking pot made a statement about who they were. The resistance to the influence of imported pottery in the middle Saxon period would appear to underline the idea. Generalisations are dangerous where human behaviour is concerned, but the need to belong to a social group and the attendant pressures to conform to that group's identity appears virtually universal. It is therefore suggested that many of the supposedly functional attributes of early Saxon domestic pottery are in fact the material manifestation of such pressures.

Bibliography

Blackmore, L. 1988 The Pottery. In: R. Cowie and R.L. Whitehead *Two Middle Saxon Occupation Sites: Excavations at Jubilee Hall and 21–22 Maiden Lane* Transactions of the London and Middlesex Archaeological Society 39.

Blinkhorn, P. W. 1993 Early and Middle Saxon Pottery from Pennyland and Hartigans. In: R.J. Williams *Pennyland and Hartigans. Two Iron Age and Saxon sites in Milton Keynes* Buckinghamshire Archaeology Society Monograph Series 4.

Blinkhorn, P.W. in print a) The Saxon and Medieval Pottery. In: M. Audouy *Excavations at North Raunds, Northamptonshire* English Heritage Monograph Series.

Blinkhorn, P. W. forthcoming *The Ipswich Ware Project. Society, Ceramics and Trade in Middle Saxon England* Medieval Pottery Research Group Monograph.

Bourdieu, P. 1977 *Outline of a theory of practice* Cambridge University Press.

Bourdieu, P. 1992 *The Logic of Practice* Polity Press.

Elsdon, S. 1992 East Midlands Scored Ware. *Transactions of the Leicestershire Archaeological and Historical Society* 66:83–91.

Hamerow, H. 1993 *Excavations at Mucking. Volume 2: The Anglo-Saxon Settlement* English Heritage Archaeological Report 21.

Hamerow, H., Hollevoet, Y. and Vince A. 1994 Migration period settlements and 'Anglo-Saxon' pottery from Flanders. *Medieval Archaeology* 38:1–18.

Hodder, I. 1979 Pottery Distributions: Service and Tribal Areas. In: M. Millett (Ed.) *Pottery and the Archaeologist* Institute of Archaeology Occasional Publication 4.

Hurst, J. G. 1976 The Pottery. In: D.M. Wilson (Ed.) *The Archaeology of Anglo-Saxon England.* Cambridge University Press.

McCarthy, M.R. and Brooks, C.M. 1988 *Medieval Pottery in Britain AD900–1600* Leicester University Press.

Myres, J. N. L. 1969 *Anglo-Saxon Pottery and the Settlement of England* Cambridge University Press.

Myres, J. N. L. 1977 *A Corpus of Anglo-Saxon Pottery of the Pagan Period* 2 volumes. Cambridge University Press.

Myres, J. N. L. 1986 *The English Settlements* Oxford History of England. Clarendon Press.

Rice, P. 1987 *Pottery Analysis. A Sourcebook.* University of Chicago Press.

Richards, J. D. 1987 *The Significance of Form and Decoration of Anglo-Saxon Cremation Urns* British Archaeological Reports British Series 166.

Richards, J. D. 1992 Anglo-Saxon Symbolism. In: M. Carver (Ed.) *The Age of Sutton Hoo* The Boydell Press 131–48.

Russel, A. D. 1985 Petrological Report on the West Stow Saxon Pottery. In: S.E. West *West Stow: The Anglo Saxon Village* (2 volumes) East Anglian Archaeology 24.

Timby, J. R. 1988 The Middle Saxon Pottery. In: P. Andrews *The Coins and Pottery from Hamwic* Southampton Finds 1. Southampton City Museums 73–123.

West, S. E. 1985 *West Stow: The Anglo Saxon Village* East Anglian Archaeology 24.

Towards a phenomenological approach to the study of medieval pottery

C. G. Cumberpatch

Introduction

> Phenomenology involves the understanding and description of things as they are experienced by a subject. It is about the relationship between Being and Being-in-the-world. Being-in-the-world resides in a process of objectification in which people objectify the world by setting themselves apart from it. This results in a gap, a distance in space. To be human is both to create this distance between the self and that which is beyond and to attempt to bridge this distance through a variety of means – through perception ... bodily actions and movements, and intentionality, emotion and awareness residing in systems of belief and decision making, remembrance and evaluation. (Tilley 1994:12)

In this article I shall consider medieval pottery from a broadly phenomenological perspective. As the quote from Chris Tilley's recent book 'A Phenomenology of Landscape' above makes clear, at least one strand of phenomenological thought can be considered as being concerned with the relationship between people and the variety of objects which constitute the world which they inhabit. A phenomenological perspective applied to material culture might be considered to stress the experience of things, as perceived by the human subject. Thus a pottery vessel has an existence, and is experienced, as part of a wider context, one of the many elements which makes up the human subject's world.

Archaeological (as opposed to art historical or aesthetic) studies of artefacts, and particularly pottery, have traditionally been dominated by two perspectives, both of which can be termed *objectivist*. These are, firstly, functional interpretation and, secondly, a kind of etic objectivism which has seen pottery as a means of calibrating archaeological stratigraphy and of reconstructing patterns of trade and exchange or as a source of information about ancient pyrotechnology (to take but three examples). Both approaches have the intention of deriving information from the data about aspects of the society deemed important from the perspective of the analyst. Both have their place, and have been instrumental in contributing to considerable advances in our understanding of past societies in many parts of the world and at many different times. It is not my intention in this discussion to denigrate these approaches but rather to suggest that a consideration of pottery from a phenomenological perspective will contribute to our understanding of the societies which we choose to study by adding a further dimension to our appreciation of their complexity. Taken together with the more traditional 'socio-economic' approaches which have dominated ceramic analysis over the last 15 or 20 years, an appreciation of ceramic vessels and artefacts as situated within a social context of everyday action and negotiable meaning gives us access to a wider range of aspects of society than has hitherto been envisaged.

On this theme Pierre Bourdieu has commented

> Social science ... has to take account of ... two kinds of properties that are objectively attached to [objects]: on the one hand material properties, starting with the body, that can be counted and measured like any other thing of the physical world; and on the other symbolic properties which are nothing other than material properties when perceived and appreciated in their mutual relationships, that is, as distinctive properties.
>
> An intrinsically twofold reality of this kind requires one to move beyond the false choice in which social science generally allows itself to be trapped, that between social physics and social phenomenology. Social physics, which often appears in the form of an objectivist economism, seeks to grasp an 'objective reality' quite inaccessible to ordinary experience by analysing the statistical relationships among distributions of material properties, quantitative expressions of the distribution of capital (in its different kinds) among the individuals competing to appropriate it. Social phenomenology, which records and deciphers the meanings that agents produce as such by a differential perception of these same properties which are thus constituted as distinctive signs, tends towards a kind of social marginalism (Bourdieu 1992:135)

Bourdieu's resolution of these 'spurious alternatives' (1992:140) is achieved through the employment of his concept of *habitus* (cf. Cumberpatch in prep. 1) and the grasping of

> the principle of the dialectical relationship that is established between the regularities of the material world of properties and

the classificatory schemes of the *habitus*, that product of the regularities of the social world for which and through which there *is* a social world (1992:140).

By virtue of its ubiquity and primarily utilitarian nature in the period which I have chosen to describe, pottery offers an excellent avenue down which we may be able to approach some of these aspects of society. I want to draw attention to, and offer some tentative explanations for, certain regularities within assemblages of later medieval (broadly defined as between the Norman Conquest and c1450) pottery in South and West Yorkshire and Humberside which, I feel, have either been overlooked or not given the attention which they seem to deserve. In tackling this theme I shall develop the perspectives which I have outlined elsewhere (Cumberpatch unpublished 1 and in prep. 1). The extent to which the points made are relevant to the rest of Britain is an important one but must, for the moment, remain for others to judge. In the course of the paper I shall try and link the established local typologies of medieval pottery with other areas of research, notably the history of food and medieval symbolism.

The perception of pottery

From the perspective of its makers and users, medieval and post-medieval pottery can be said to have had three directly perceptible characteristics which formed the basis upon which it was conceptualised and classified. These are texture, colour and shape. All three are aspects which could have been, and, it is my contention, were, manipulated by the potters to produce a vessel or object which would be acceptable to the consumer; which would, in other words, have fitted within a given, understood and workable category, part of the *habitus* of the society (Bourdieu 1992). In the following sections I shall take each of these categories and demonstrate how stability and change within each might be related to other categories of material culture and wider aspects of society.

Colour

A number of sources can be used to suggest that colour and texture were of considerable significance in medieval (and early post-medieval) society. In a general consideration of medieval aesthetics Umberto Eco has commented that

> The medieval love of colour was reflected both in metaphysical metaphors and in everyday life (1986:49)

and, although he goes on to consider the subject chiefly from the point of view of metaphysics, it can be argued from other sources that the appreciation of colour was every bit as important in day-to-day medieval life as it was in the metaphysical speculations of Robert Grosseteste and St. Bonaventure.

In Britain militant changes in modes of devotion and representation have deprived us of the bulk of medieval church painting; the natural stone of the contemporary English parish church or cathedral would almost certainly be alien to a medieval worshipper who would perhaps have been more susceptible to instruction through the medium of the painted friezes than through the liturgy (cf. Johnson 1996:198). As Graves has noted

> The walls and windows of a cathedral, or a parish church, would be covered with scenes and figures from the lives of the saints and scriptures. Iconography is a powerful cognitive map and the Church expressed a cosmology through its textual references. (Graves 1989:309, cf. Phillips 1973:Chapter 1, Pearsall 1982).

Examples of brightly coloured paintings and frescoes in medieval churches in France and Italy may be some guide to the original appearance of English parish churches. Discussing medieval aesthetics, Eco has noted that at various times the luxurious decoration of churches was condemned by those, chiefly mystics and ascetics, who thought it inappropriate. He stresses that such decoration was not attacked for irrelevancy but rather that it distracted the worshipper from the contemplation of God and has argued that the stress placed upon the problems caused by excessive decoration is an indication of its significance (1986:6–7).

The analysis of samples of pigments preserved in corners of the ornate carvings on the West Front of Exeter Cathedral prompted the analyst to comment that

> there are no words to describe the excitement and visual impact of seeing a paint sample ... reveal itself ... to be a glowing azurite blue, a rare arsenic yellow, or a brilliant copper-green. A sample of vermilion (the most magnificent red, which glows even when seen with the naked eye) is seen through the microscope to be comprised of both fine and unusually large crystals and was obviously carefully prepared to create the most stunning visual impact (Sinclair 1985:19)

The enthusiasm of Sinclair's account is perhaps an unconscious echo of that of William of Malmesbury who, when visiting Canterbury Cathedral in the early 12th century, wrote of

> 'the brilliance of its glass windows, the beauty of its marble pavement, [and] the many coloured pictures which led wondering eyes to the very summit of the ceiling' (quoted by Kidson 1979:58)

Somewhat later, in first half of the 13th century, the architects of Salisbury Cathedral employed light and coloured glass to dramatic effect

> The stress on windows suggests that they were ... interested ... in lighting effects ... Today light comes flooding in through the lancets, and Salisbury is perhaps the lightest church of its period. But it must be remembered that originally these windows would be filled with stained glass, and in the first half of

the thirteenth century stained glass tended to be dark toned and brilliant in the intensity of its colour. Salisbury would have been particularly well suited for the presentation of a display of such glass; and the chromatic effects still evident in the alternating horizontal bands of dark and light material in the nave seem to imply that colour was the primary consideration, as it had been at Canterbury (Kidson 1979:90)

A similar concern with colour is also found in Westminster Abbey (Kidson 1979:98) and the recent restoration of the 12th century frieze on the west front of Lincoln Cathedral has revealed traces of paint similar to that found at Exeter.

While it was the images themselves which probably made the greatest impact on the congregations, it is interesting to note that the principal colours employed by religious artists had specific symbolic associations (Ferguson 1954) and also that the colours of priest's vestments, which changed with the seasons, did so according to established rules (Woolf pers. comm.). The extent to which such symbolic associations were reflected in the low status, largely secular, world of ceramics is unclear, but it does seem that colours were more than simply naturalistic and were deployed with deliberate symbolic intent.

An example drawn from an exclusively elite context is that discussed by Baxandall (1988) in the context of 15th century Italian painting. While there does not have appear to have been a single accepted symbolic code employed by renaissance painters, it is clear from the examples cited by Baxandall that there was a considerable interest in, and concern with, the formulation of series of symbolically important colours. As he notes

Assembling symbolic series of colours was a late medieval game still played in the Renaissance (Baxandall 1988:81)

Examples of the use of colour in everyday contexts are harder to find, but one good example is their use in the popular theatre.

Medieval people were very fond of bright colours ... and there is little doubt that colour had symbolic associations ... although these were not by any means systematised. White and black were perhaps the most clearly defined. White was a good colour associated with purity ... black by contrast usually implied the presence of evil, envy, death or misfortune. Violet and purple were always colours of nobility ... and yellow and gold usually implied the presence of wealth. Blue was the colour of good reputation and of heaven ... Green was widely used to signify 'what exists' like truth, or nature, or sensual delight – indeed it was the colour of Venus, and green sleeves were worn by women of pleasure who wanted to encourage sexual advances. Red was a very ambivalent colour, on its good side it was associated with energy, both mental and physical, strength, power and militant righteousness, but on its bad side it could also represent pride, ambition, blood and violence ... The catalogue is almost endless. (Harris 1992:146–7)

In medieval medicine colour had an intimate association with the human body via the four humours and these supplied metaphors for the character traits of individuals.

McCarthy and Brooks have noted that

red is associated with blood or the male principle, white with anaemia, yellow with the liver and green with fertility or the female principle (1988:134).

Red and green here may find counterparts in the example of theatrical costumes outlined above. Other, less systematic, examples are not uncommon. To her irate father Shakespeare's Juliet is but a 'green sickness carrion'; a girl unfit to make her own decisions. In remoter parts of Britain it seems that the epithets applied to individuals (Aid the Black, 'a very bloody man' in Adomnan's life of St. Columba, for example), might relate as much to the individual's character as to his or her physical colouring (Woolf pers. comm.).

Sumptuary laws, reiterated at various times during the medieval period and into the early years of the 17th century, regulated the types and colours of materials which could be worn by the different 'degrees' within society. While the accounts of the laws of 1363 and 1463 given by Keen (1990) and that of 1510 by Youings (1984) stress the role of furs, notably imported furs, in marking out the upper levels of society, it is clear that they represent a general principle of drawing attention to distinction, in this case in social rank, through the use of different colours and textures of material (Johnson 1996:191). In a more detailed discussion of the relationship between sumptuary laws and governance, Hunt (1996) has drawn attention to both specific instances (the requirement for prostitutes to wear yellow for example) and to the more general point that such laws were 'a form of symbolic politics' (1996:414).

Such restrictions did not however prevent the ordinary people obtaining a wide variety of dyed cloth, as the evidence from excavations in Beverley, York, London and other towns has demonstrated (Evans and Tomlinson 1992, Walton 1989, Crowfoot, Pritchard and Staniland 1992). On the basis of chemical analyses of cloth Walton has concluded that

the dyes in the textiles show a predominance of reds. Purples and blues are present in small numbers and also yellows and browns and possibly black ... The work has ... demonstrated that the rich warm tones of madder were amongst the most popular colours worn in medieval London. (Walton 1992:201).

The use of colour as a classificatory principle might be seen to run through heraldry with its strict controls on the combinations of colours permitted on armourial blazons. A practical example of the importance of heraldry in communicating to the illiterate has been given by Graves (1989:312).

The colour of pottery

Given the evident importance of colour to medieval people, I would argue that the colours chosen by the potters for the vessels which they produced were dictated neither by chance elements in the production process nor, primarily, by technological constraints. The regularity seen within a typical assemblage from the study area argues rather that the potters were knowledgeable agents participating, through production, in the reproduction of conventionally acceptable categories of material culture. The production of socially acceptable goods is simultaneously the production of useable utilitarian artefacts and the production of goods which conform to the norms and values which constitute the *habitus* of that society. In producing goods the artisan reacts to the prevailing *habitus*, not necessarily in conformity with it, but certainly with respect to it. At one level it might seem that the low value and status of pottery would make it an unlikely medium for the enacting of major conflicts but, as ethnography has repeatedly demonstrated, it is in the sphere of the domestic and utilitarian that the structuring principles of a society are most firmly founded (eg. Gregory 1982:78–9, Parker Pearson and Richards 1994).

Vessel shape

At one level vessel shape or form can be considered to be dictated by function. Two strands of archaeological thought have ascribed a privileged position to the functional over other considerations. The first of these, the naive positivism represented by the New Archaeology, has now been discredited and virtually abandoned, at least in Britain (Gibbon 1989, Moreland 1991, Pluciennik 1994), but the second, a kind of common sense, ethnocentric, folk wisdom persists, remaining strong perhaps because of its appeal to the self-styled 'anti-theoretical' bias so proudly and loudly claimed by many 'field' archaeologists, particularly at the managerial level (Blinkhorn and Cumberpatch, in press). Such a view sees form as following function, decoration and colour as 'fashion' and quality dictated by price. While the majority of ceramicists avoid such self-centred value judgements, there appears to be an underlying resistance (a semi-self-conscious anti-intellectualism) to the analytical deconstruction of such commonsense categories, which may explain why the main thrust of ceramic studies in Britain lags behind the study of colonial assemblages from the eastern USA (eg. Yentsch 1991a, 1991b).

In his recent exploration of a phenomenological approach to landscape Chris Tilley has commented

> 'People do not … deliberately occupy inhospitable habitats or those with few resources by virtue of some slavish accommodation to a symbolic scheme; but the places that they do occupy take on, through time, particular sets of meanings and connotations' (Tilley 1994:2).

In a similar way I would argue that people do not perversely use functionally inefficient vessels, but rather that there is a continual reflexive relationship between the suitability of a particular vessel type for a certain purpose and the perception of the attributes appropriate for the type of vessel and the functions for which it is intended (cf. Sterner 1989). This implies that while function and form are inevitably linked, the link is not a simple one. Rather the connection is mediated through cultural and historical factors which act recursively and reflexively to influence the shape (and texture and colour) which the potter makes. There can, for example, be no Platonic ideal of a cooking pot which does not take into account the specific cultural and historical aspects of the concepts of 'food', 'cooking' and 'eating'. The cooking, serving and consumption of food are primary arenas of social discourse, in which the spaces involved, the utensils and the specific practices are heavily laden with meanings, to be understood and manipulated by the participants. I shall discuss some specific aspects of medieval food and cooking elsewhere, but for the present purpose it will be sufficient to note that the extensive literature on the ethnography of cooking and the consumption of food (Gregory 1982, Goody 1982, *contra* Braudel 1981:190) does not support the existence of simple functional relationships between food preparation and the form of the utensils. Thus we cannot understand the repertoire of domestic utensils without considering them as part of more extensive networks of signification and discourse, part of an important and broad 'field of discourse' (Barrett 1989, 1994) which may be subsumed within the term 'domestic'.

Texture and touch

The texture of the clay pastes used to make different types of pottery are a key element in the categorisation of archaeological ceramics. A basic division into 'coarse' and 'fine' wares may be regarded as seriously over-simplified, but a consideration of the size, frequency and density of rock, sand, grog and other fragments within the clay matrix remains an important criterion in the categorisation of a sherd (quite apart from the question of the type of inclusions and their potential for determining the origin of the clay from which the vessel was made). In an interesting discussion of the nature of cooking pots Ann Woods (1986) has noted that coarse sandy and gritty inclusions in ceramic pastes fulfil three important roles in relation to the functionality of the vessels. Two of these relate to the manufacturing process. Such materials open the clay body during drying to speed up and even out the process. They also open the clay body during the early stages of firing to facilitate the removal of remnant water and to prevent spalling and shattering during the water smoking phase. During the use-life of the vessel they also appear to act to reduce problems of thermal shock by limiting the spread of cracks within the body (Woods 1986:170). Clearly, to deny the fact that the nature of the clay from which a vessel was made had some relevance to functional and technical requirements would be absurd. There is however increasing evidence, prehistoric (Cleal 1995), early medieval (Blinkhorn 1993) and ethnographic (Sillar, this volume), that variations in temper and paste texture have been, and are, used to differentiate between the products of different potters and to emphasise cultural boundaries. Other studies have shown that deliberate variations in other parts of the manufacturing process can be employed for similar purposes (eg. Hosler 1996).

As I shall demonstrate below, there are regularities within

later medieval ceramic assemblages which imply that variations in texture had a significance which went beyond the purely technical and which would have certainly affected the perceptions of the vessel by the user and might thus have had implications for its classification.

The character of later medieval pottery assemblages

Conventionally the report on a pottery assemblage recovered from a British excavation consists of a number of standard elements. These include a type series, in which the wares present on the site are described and referenced, their places of origin discussed and selected examples illustrated. The narrative which follows typically consists of two strands. The first concerns the information derived from the pottery regarding the stratigraphic sequence recorded by the excavators, and particularly its chronological calibration, while the second consists of information regarding the connections of the site with others within Britain and in Europe. The contemporary socio-political imperatives which direct and legitimise these narratives and the intra-disciplinary discourses of which they form part are of considerable interest in their own right, but are beyond the scope of this article. In the following discussion I shall use some of the less commonly employed data which are contained within these traditional narratives.

Type series and chronologies

The primary tool of the pottery analyst is the type series. Currently, and for good reason, the tendency within British medieval ceramic studies is to attempt to define types according to their mineralogical characteristics and to link these characteristics to specific places of origin. The definition of a type is thus tied closely to the identification of production sites and potteries. This is not, of course, the only method of defining ceramic types and the decision as to which characteristics should be used to define a type is a strategic one, closely tied to the broader understanding of what constitutes a significant difference within the artefact class as a whole. In what follows I shall try to show that other types, related to traditions of manufacture (Cumberpatch unpublished 1, 2, in prep. 1, 1996a), can be defined without contradicting the established type series for the area under consideration.

It is my contention that the colour, texture, decoration and shape of ceramic vessels were of greater importance to the medieval (and also post-medieval) user of pottery than was its precise origin. I shall try to demonstrate that there is a logic to the use of particular textures of clay, glaze and body colours and decorative motifs which may relate to the local classificatory and symbolic schemes which formed part of the *habitus* of medieval society.

In table 1 the principal types of later medieval pottery found in the area under discussion have been split into three broad categories; sandy textured wares, Shell Tempered wares and Gritty textured wares. These may be regarded as forming traditions of manufacture in the sense which I have discussed elsewhere (Cumberpatch 1996a, in prep. 1). Bibliographic details can be found in appendix 1.

As an aside it might also be noted that the table also summarises the variable state of our knowledge regarding the location of production of a number of ware types. The range of names, drawn from individual streets (Hallgate), towns (Beverley), regions (Humberware, Southwest Midlands Gritty ware), the physical characteristics of ware types (Shell Tempered ware, Gritty ware) or antiquarian misunderstandings (Cistercian ware) reflects the slow growth and change of orientation within ceramic studies and the highly variable nature of our knowledge of medieval ceramics. As the earlier discussion of colour and texture has indicated, I wish to concentrate on aspects of the consumption and use of pottery, and for this purpose will attempt to highlight some of those characteristics of the pottery, which, though normally acknowledged and described in reports, have rarely formed the keystone of attempts at interpretation.

Considered chronologically it is clear that hard and fast inception and termination dates cannot, as yet, be ascribed to most individual types. What is clear is that the potters changed the characteristics of their pottery over time (most notably towards the end of the medieval period, a subject to be considered in detail elsewhere), presumably as part of wider changes in social practice and the domestic *habitus* as well as producing a variety of types in conformity with the prevailing perceptions of what constituted an acceptable vessel. Beyond this little else regarding the processes of change are understood. What aspects of social practice underlie the change from late Saxon to early Medieval forms for example? The later phases of Stamford ware production (c1150) show a change from yellow glazed ware to green glazed ware (Kilmurry 1980:134) but the reasons for this, for the demise of the production of Late Saxon wares and for the rise of medieval wares remain to be fully established (cf. McCarthy and Brooks 1988: 68–70).

The end of medieval potting traditions and the emergence of the rather different post-medieval traditions are equally poorly understood in terms of practice and habituation, although Johnson (1996) has recently related it to the commodification of material culture. The reasons for such changes must be sought at a broader scale than simply that of the potter and his/her products. There are clearly complex, reflexive, relationships between craft traditions, ideology and social structure which must be investigated contextually; this paper is an attempt to outline some of these with respect to pottery; further work is needed to consider other types of material culture. A future paper will consider the nature of the transition between the medieval and post-medieval ceramic traditions.

I would suggest that between the latter part of the 11th or early 12th century and the mid to late 15th century, two principal ceramic traditions existed in Yorkshire and Humberside (and possibly also more widely), Gritty wares and Sandy wares, defined by the texture of the clay paste and further distinguished by decoration, glaze and body colour

(Hayfield 1992). These appear to be related to the contexts in which different types of vessels were used. In the following sections I shall attempt to define the distinctive characteristics of these traditions more closely. The enduring appeal of Shell Tempered ware in a wide variety of societies (from the later Bronze age to the 15th century AD) remains to be tackled elsewhere.

The scheme presented here may have only limited applicability outside the study area (although Duncan Brown's paper elsewhere in this volume contains some interesting data which suggest a parallel situation may have existed in medieval Southampton). Regional variability in tradition, perception and practice might lead to different arrangements elsewhere. Rules of practice (and fields of discourse) may

Table 1. Traditions and types discussed in the text (Sources: see appendix 1).

Tradition	Constituent types	Notes
Gritty wares	Gritty ware	As defined by Brooks (1987)
	York type G ware	
	Pimply ware	
	Hillam ware	
	Northern Gritty ware	
	Orange Gritty ware	
	Other Gritty wares (1)	Sandal Castle types 3c,8c,9c, 24c,26c,31c
	Other Gritty wares (2)	See Pontefract report (Cumberpatch unpublished 2)
	Splash Glazed Gritty wares	
	Green Glazed Gritty wares	
	Late Medieval Gritty ware	
	Purple Glazed Gritty ware	
	Coarse Sandy ware	
	Staxton-Potter Brompton ware	
	Hallgate type C ware	
	Hedon Coarse ware CH1	
	Hedon Coarse ware CH2	
	Hedon Coarse ware CH3	
	Hedon Coarse ware CH4	
	Beverley 1 ware Fabric A	Cooking pots contain larger quartz grain inclusions
	Humberware 2	
	Coal Measures White ware	AKA South Yorkshire Gritty ware group B
Shell Tempered ware	Types defined by chronology and source	
Sandy wares	Hedon Fine wares FH1	
	Hedon Fine wares FH2	
	Hedon Fine wares FH3	
	Hedon Fine wares FH4	
	Hedon Fine wares FH5	
	Nottingham Sandy ware	
	Nottingham Splash Glazed ware	
	North Lincolnshire Sandy ware	
	Lincoln Medieval Sandy ware	
	Toynton All Saints ware	
	Brandsby ware	
	Beverley 1 ware fabric A	Discussed in text
	Beverley 2 ware fabric B and C	
	Orangeware	= Beverley ware 2 (Watkins and Didsbury 1992)
	Hallgate A ware	
	Hallgate type	
	Hallgate A1	
	Hallgate D	
	Hallgate E	
	Hallgate F	
	Hallgate B ware	Discussed in the text
	Humberware 1	
	Humberware 3	
	York White ware	

vary in space as well as time, although the fact that people operate according to practical logics does not.

Paste texture and vessel form

In order to investigate the connections between texture and vessel form within the space constraints of this article a number of specific examples have been selected which appear to be representative of a broader general principle. The sites have been selected on the basis of having been fully and accessibly published and of having produced useful ceramic assemblages. For the sake of simplicity continental wares have been omitted from the tables and from the discussion. A number of common categories of vessel are notable by their absence. These include skillets, frying pans and urinals. No clear explanation can be advanced for these absences. Minor types (lamps, candlesticks etc) have been grouped under the category of 'other'.

The first case study is of three burgage tenements excavated in Hull during the mid-1970's (Armstrong and Ayers 1987). In Tables 2, 3 and 4 the ceramic assemblages from the medieval phases have been amalgamated to give a broad picture of the pattern of pottery use on the sites during the medieval period. Two observations can be made. Jugs, pipkins, dripping pans, and bowls appear regularly in the sandy ware category. Pancheons and cooking pots are found more commonly in the gritty fabrics. Clearly the terms applied should be interpreted somewhat loosely; cooking pots might be better described as 'multi-functional wide mouthed vessels' and, in some of the following cases, the term 'jar' has been preferred by the analysts. However this may be, the dichotomy still appears to be a real one.

Table 5 summarises the data from Middle Lane, Hedon (Hayfield and Slater 1984), a site occupied by two houses (early 12th century to late 13th/early 14th century) and, subsequently, by a single larger building which was abandoned by the later 14th century after which the site reverted to pasture. Five local fabrics (FH 1 – 5) dominated the sandy ware group and here again jugs, pipkins, basting dishes (equivalent to dripping pans) were the commonest types. Four types of local gritty wares (CH 1 – 4) dominated the coarser component, with cooking pots the commonest types. It should be noted that the apparent presence of pancheons in the sandy ware category is an artefact of the terminology; Hayfield has distinguished between glazed bowls (which he has termed pancheons) and unglazed bowls (U/G Bowl).

Table 6 summarises data from twelve groups of pottery excavated in Eastgate, Beverley (Didsbury and Watkins 1992). Once again a broad split between jugs and pipkins on the one hand and cooking pots on the other is visible, although here there are some further aspects which need to be considered in greater detail, notably the question of the different sub-types of the Beverley wares.

The distinction between Beverley 1 and 2 is a primarily chronological one; Beverley 1 predating Beverley 2 (formerly known as Orangeware). Didsbury and Watkins (1992:108) have added the suffixes A, B, C and X to each type to in-dicate variations in the character of the fabric and it is these which are of particular significance here. Fabric A

> is defined as containing abundant fine sand tempering; large quartz grains are frequently present, particularly where the vessel is of cooking pot form (Didsbury and Watkins 1992:108)

In an earlier discussion of Beverley 1 ware Watkins noted that

> Jug surfaces have a fine sandy texture ... . Cooking pots, however, were manufactured in a much more heavily tempered fabric containing larger quartz particles and frequent flecks of chalk (1991:80).

The explanation for the presence of both principal vessel types in the same fabric thus appears to be a result of the potters adding more grit to the mixture while making cooking pots, apparently creating a coarser textured sub-type specifically for one purpose. In contrast the other Beverley types, although manufactured in a range of forms, are clearly dominated by the 'sandy ware forms', the twelve cooking pots in fabric 2B forming only 7.8% of the recognisable forms in that fabric.

In addition to the Beverley A evidence there are indications in assemblages from pottery workshops that the potters were deliberately creating a distinction between paste textures. Recent excavations in Hallgate, Doncaster (Atkinson, in prep.) have revealed a kiln, dating to the late 11th or early 12th century, close to the site of a later kiln excavated in 1965 and published by Buckland *et al* (1979). Unlike the original Hallgate kiln, the recent discovery (known as Hallgate 95) yielded an assemblage consisting of five major fabric types which were apparently manufactured simultaneously. Of these, one, Hallgate C1 (and its subdivisions, C2, C3 and C type) was heavily tempered with red ferrous grit, while the remainder (A1, D, E and F, with subdivisions) were sandy in texture (Cumberpatch 1996b). Table 7 summarises the relationship between the fabric type and the vessel form. Although the numbers of identifiable vessel forms were relatively low, there still appears to be a relationship between the finer, sandy, fabrics and jugs, pitchers and related forms. The more neutral terms 'jar' and 'everted rim jar' (ERJ) have been preferred to 'cooking pot' and in these categories the gritty fabrics are commoner. The assemblage from the later Hallgate kiln provides only limited support for the relationship between form and fabric (Buckland *et al* 1979:Table 1, reproduced as table 8). C type fabrics were only present in small quantities within this assemblage which was dominated by jugs and pipkins with a relatively small number of cooking pots. The explanation for this would appear to be that gritty ware production ended in Doncaster sometime during the 12th century and continued in the lower Don valley. The early Coal Measures wares (CMW or South Yorkshire Gritty ware group B) are characterised by a coarse gritty fabric containing abundant quartz, ferrous and other inclusions (Hayfield and Buckland 1989). Figures derived from field walking at Firsby (table

Table 2. Pottery from the Wytelard property phases 1 to 7 inclusive. Key on page 133. (Source Watkins 1987)

Phase 1–7 (Mid 13th to 15th centuries)

	Sandy												Gritty				Other	
	Orange 1	Orange 2	Humber 1	Humber 3	NYorks 1	NYorks 2	Scarb 1	Scarb 2	Scarb 3	Tynt 1	Tynt 2	York W	CSW	StaxPB	Humber 2	SYG	Other	Humber 5
Jug	190	6	270	4	43	26	17	6	6	14	8	9				2	3	
D/Jug			24															
Pipkin	11			1			1											
Jar			1															
Pancheon	2												14	1	9			
Cook pot			5										111	6				
D/Pan													1		1			
Cup	1						2											1
Bowl	2																	1
S/Bowl	1																	
Curfew			7										3					
M/Jar																		
M/Jug																		
Cistern			2		1											1		
Other	3		4		1								4		3			6

Table 3. Pottery from the Ousefleet property, phases 1 to 3e inclusive. Key on page 133. (Source Watkins 1987)

Phase 1–3e (late 13th century to mid 14th century)

	Sandy											Gritty			
	Orange 1	Orange 2	Humber 1	NYorks 1	NYorks 2	Scarb 1	Scarb 2	Scarb 3	Tynt 1	Tynt 2	York W	CSW	StaxPB	SYG	Shell
Jug	200	2	44	49	13	4	4	3	13	43	4			1	
D/Jug	16														
Pipkin							2								
Jar	3		1												
Pancheon	1											6			
Cook pot												46	2		1
D/Pan	23														
Cup															
Bowl	4											1			
Small Bowl															
Curfew															
M/Jar															
M/Jug															
Cistern	1														
Other	6			2		2		1				17		1	

Table 4. Pottery from the Hotham / Celererman property. Phase 1 to 3Wb inclusive. (Source Watkins 1987).

| Phase 1 to 3Wb Late 13th century to mid/late 14th century | | | | | | | | | | | | | | |
| Sandy | | | | | | | | | | | Gritty | | | Other |
Orange 1	Orange 2	Humber 1	Humber 3	NYorks 1	NYorks 2	Scarb 1	Scarb 2	Tynt 1	Tynt 2	York W	CSW	StaxPB	Humber 2	Other
Jug — 226	11	143	3	26	10	13	3	15	27	1			2	1
D/Jug		1												
Pipkin — 11														
Jar — 1														
Pancheon — 1											3		2	
Cook pot											38	2		
D/Pan — 2													2	
Cup — 1														
Bowl — 3														
S/Bowl — 10											1			
Curfew — 1											2			
M/Jar														
M/Jug — 1														
Cistern				1										
Other — 18		2									18		3	

Key to tables 2, 3 and 4

Orange 1	Orangeware 1	Scarb 2	Scarborough ware 2	Shell	Shell Tempered ware
Orange 2	Orangeware 2	Tynt 1	Toynton AllSaints ware	Humber 2	Humberware 2
Humber 1	Humberware 1	Tynt 2	Toynton - Calcareous		
Humber 3	Humberware 3	YorkW	York White ware	D/Jug	Drinking jug
NYorks 1	Brandsby ware	CSW	Coarse Sandy ware	D/Pan	Dripping pan
NYorks 2	Reduced North Yorkshire ware	StaxPB	Staxton-Potter Brompton ware	S/Bowl	Small bowl
Scarb 1	Scarborough ware 1	SYG	South Yorkshire Gritty ware	M/Jar	Minature jar
				M/Jug	Minature jug

Table 5. Pottery from all phases at Middle Lane, Hedon. (Source: Hayfield and Slater 1984)

Middle Lane, Hedon.											
All contexts (mid 12th century to 14th century)											
	Sandy								**Gritty**		
	FH1–5	Stam	DStam	Scarb (WS)	Bev? (WB)	Orange (OB, OH)	HaB (WD)	Humber	CH1–4	Shell	Other
C/Pot	3			1		1			3141	5	9
U/G Bowl	1								121		
Curfew									7		
U/G Other									13		
Jug	3218	3	14	17	12	522	35	422	5	3	47
Pipkin	117					15	1				1
B/Dish	14					1		1			
Panch	21							4			
D/Mug	1							2			
Gl Other	15			1		3		2			1
Dec. vessel	2		1			3					

Key

FH 1 - 5	Hedon Fine wares 1 to 5	CH 1 - 4	Hedon Coarseware 1 to 4
Stam	Stamford ware	Shell	Shell Tempered ware
DStam	Developed Stamford ware		
Scarb (WS)	Scarborough ware	U/G Bowl	Unglazed bowl
Bev ? (WB)	Beverley ware (?)	U/G Other	Unglazed other vessel
Orange (OB, OH)	Orangeware	B/Dish	Basting dish
HaB (WD)	Hallgate type B	D/Mug	Drinking mug
Humber	Humberware	Gl. Other	Other glazed vessel

9) suggest that jugs were significantly rarer than cooking pots and pancheons.

There are considerable problems with the Firsby material, notably the fact that the figures are based upon data from one seasons field walking but the general pattern is one which supports the case being made here.

Doncaster Hallgate type B ware occupies a somewhat ambiguous position, possibly analogous to that of the Beverley A ware described above. Although the characteristics of the type clearly include green glaze, decorative motifs and the manufacture of jugs and pipkins, the type also includes cooking pots and pancheons (table 8). Further investigation is needed to determine whether there was any variation within the fabric type according to vessel form.

Unquantified, but qualitatively suggestive, information supporting the association of vessel forms with specific fabrics can be found in Manby's report on the assemblage from the pottery workshop at Upper Heaton in West Yorkshire (1964).

The site dates to the early 14th century and forms part of the long-lived local gritty ware tradition. Discussing the pottery Manby noted that

> Some 90 per cent of the pottery from Upper Heaton is in a hard, compact fabric, liberally mixed with a moderately coarse grit which protrudes through the surface to give a distinctive pimply appearance …

The second fabric is represented by only some 2 per cent of the pottery, all jugs except for a single cooking pot. This is similar to the first common fabric but lacks the coarse grit content, fine sand being used instead. (Manby 1964:80). Jugs certainly occurred in the gritty fabric but totalled only 110 examples (including those in the fine fabric) compared with 2600 cooking pots and 200 pancheons. In his discussion of parallels for the assemblage Manby refers to the largely unpublished assemblage from Staxton (Brewster 1958).

> No jugs or glazed ware were produced … About 15 per cent of the Staxton ware vessels are pancheons …, 25 percent large cooking pots or storage jars…, 40 per cent shallow broad-based cooking pots …, 15 percent medium cooking pots …, and 5 percent small cooking pots (Manby 1964:105).

Although there are clearly exceptions to the general case (small numbers of gritty ware jugs and sandy ware jars/cooking pots do occur) there appears to be a good correlation between vessel form and the texture of the fabric. Further questions concerns the extent to which this is paralleled by variations in the use of glaze, of body colour and decoration.

Vessel colour and glaze

Colour, whether of glaze or the fired body, is somewhat more difficult to discuss than the texture of the fabric. Colour variations are rarely quantified, largely because of the difficulty of accurately describing colour ranges on vessels which vary greatly across their glazed and unglazed surfaces. The presence or absence of glaze is somewhat more

Table 6. Summary of pottery groups A to L from Eastgate, Beverley (Source Didsbury and Watkins 1992)

Type	Tork	Stam	Bev1A	Bev1B	Bev1C	Bev1X	Bev2A	Bev2B	Bev2C	Hum1	Hum3	U/Spl	YkWh	NYk1	NYk2	Scarb1	Scarb2	PBuff	YorkG	Pimply	RChalky	CSW	StaxPB	U/G	Pchalk	Other	Shell
Jug			86		2	7	1	104	14	11	5	6	26	4	1	2	3	7								13	
D/Jug																											
Pipkin							1	10	1	2																	
Dish								2																			
Jar									1																	3	
Panch																											
C/Pot	24	3	35	1		2	3	12				2							4	14	71	9	54	22	5	24	2
D/Pan								2																			
Cup																											
Bowl	1																				3						
S/Bowl																											
Curfew								1																			
M/Jar							1		1																		
M/Jug																											
Cistern								21	8	1		18	3					2	4	16	19		7	36		65	9
Other	9	5	37			2	1	1	1																		
Lid																											

Key

Tork	Torksey ware		
Stam	Stamford ware		
Bev1A	Beverley 1A		
Bev1B	Beverely 1B		
Bev1C	Beverley 1C		
Bev1X	Beverley 1X		
Bev2A	Beverley 2A		
Bev2B	Beverley 2B		
Bev2C	Beverley 2C		
Hum1	Humber ware 1	YorkG	York Glazed ware
Hum3	Humberware 3	Pimply	Pimply ware
U/Spl	Unclassified splash glazed	RChalky	Reduced Chalky ware
YkWh	York White ware	CSW	Coarse Sandy ware
NYk1	Brandsby ware	StaxPB	Staxton Potter Brompton ware
NYk2	Reduced North Yorkshire ware	U/G	Unglazed ware
Scarb1	Scarborough phase I ware	Pchalk	Pitted Chalky ware
Scarb2	Scarborough phase II ware	Oth	Other
PBuff	Pinky Buff ware	Shell	Shell Tempered ware

135

Table 7. Hallgate 95 Fabric type and vessel form (local kiln types only)

Fabric	Data	Jar	ERJ	Jar/Jug	Jug	Jug(?)	Jug/Pitcher	Bowl	Pen/Bowl	Pancheon	ERB	ERVs	C Pot	U/ID	Total
A	Sum of sherd No.	0	0	1	1	0	1	0	0	0	0	0	0	45	48
	Sum of sherd Wt.	0	0	75	15	0	20	0	0	0	0	0	0	525	635
A type	Sum of sherd no.	0	0	0	0	0	0	0	0	0	0	0	0	11	11
	Sum of sherd Wt.	0	0	0	0	0	0	0	0	0	0	0	0	90	90
A/A1 type	Sum of sherd No.	0	0	0	0	0	0	0	0	0	0	0	0	2	2
	Sum of sherd Wt.	0	0	0	0	0	0	0	0	0	0	0	0	55	55
A1	Sum of sherd No.	2	2	0	64	2	17	0	0	0	0	0	0	491	578
	Sum of sherd Wt.	50	110	0	3110	100	1200	0	0	0	0	0	0	10985	15555
A1 R	Sum of sherd No.	0	0	0	9	0	1	0	0	0	0	0	0	34	44
	Sum of sherd Wt.	0	0	0	650	0	50	0	0	0	0	0	0	1350	2050
A1 type	Sum of sherd No.	0	2	0	7	0	1	0	0	0	0	0	0	48	58
	Sum of sherd Wt.	0	10	0	265	0	25	0	0	0	0	0	0	1225	1525
B type	Sum of sherd No.	0	0	0	0	0	0	0	0	0	0	0	0	5	5
	Sum of sherd Wt.	0	0	0	0	0	0	0	0	0	0	0	0	25	25
C type	Sum of sherd No.	0	0	0	0	0	0	0	0	0	0	0	0	34	34
	Sum of sherd Wt.	0	0	0	0	0	0	0	0	0	0	0	0	75	75
C1	Sum of sherd No.	11	58	0	0	0	1	2	2	5	1	1	0	782	863
	Sum of sherd Wt.	380	1410	0	0	0	5	35	320	285	15	15	0	9685	12150
C1 type	Sum of sherd No.	0	0	0	1	0	1	0	0	0	0	0	0	37	39
	Sum of sherd Wt.	0	0	0	15	0	60	0	0	0	0	0	0	190	265
C2	Sum of sherd No.	0	1	0	0	0	0	0	0	0	0	0	0	2	3
	Sum of sherd Wt.	0	135	0	0	0	0	0	0	0	0	0	0	25	160
C3	Sum of sherd No.	0	0	0	4	0	2	0	0	1	0	0	0	160	167
	Sum of sherd Wt.	0	0	0	200	0	65	0	0	10	0	0	0	1150	1425
C3 type	Sum of sherd No.	0	0	0	0	0	0	0	0	0	0	0	0	5	5
	Sum of sherd Wt.	0	0	0	0	0	0	0	0	0	0	0	0	70	70
D	Sum of sherd No.	0	0	0	13	0	6	0	0	0	0	0	0	121	140
	Sum of sherd Wt.	0	0	0	830	0	205	0	0	0	0	0	0	3450	4485
D type	Sum of sherd No.	0	0	0	0	0	1	0	0	0	0	0	0	0	1
	Sum of sherd Wt.	0	0	0	0	0	55	0	0	0	0	0	0	0	55
E	Sum of sherd No.	0	8	0	39	0	22	0	0	8	0	0	0	476	553
	Sum of sherd Wt.	0	95	0	2430	0	1505	0	0	155	0	0	0	7180	11365
ER	Sum of sherd No.	0	0	0	0	0	0	0	0	0	0	0	0	1	1
	Sum of sherd Wt.	0	0	0	0	0	0	0	0	0	0	0	0	25	25
E type	Sum of sherd No.	0	0	0	2	0	0	0	0	1	0	0	0	48	51
	Sum of sherd Wt.	0	0	0	130	0	0	0	0	10	0	0	0	820	960
F	Sum of sherd No.	0	0	0	4	0	2	0	0	0	0	0	0	6	12
	Sum of sherd Wt.	0	0	0	195	0	20	0	0	0	0	0	0	55	270
F type	Sum of sherd No.	0	0	0	2	0	0	0	0	0	0	0	0	0	2
	Sum of sherd Wt.	0	0	0	365	0	0	0	0	0	0	0	0	0	365
Total sum of sherd No.		13	71	1	146	2	55	2	2	14	1	1	0	2308	2616
Total sum of sherd Wt.		430	1760	75	8205	100	3210	35	320	450	15	15	0	36980	51595

Key

ERJ	Everted rim jar
Pcn/Bowl	Pancheon / bowl
ERB	Everted rim bowl
ERVs	Everted rim vessels
C Pot	Cooking pot
U/ID	Unidentified

Table 8. Hallgate: Vessel type subdivided by fabric type (numbers of sherds) (Source Buckland et al 1979)

Context 1	Bases	C/Pot	Cauldron	Cistern	Curfew	Jug	Face Jug	Pipkin	Pancheon	Lamp	Urinal	Total
A	3806	59	16	1	1	3300	16	1862	65	1	1	9128
B	232	68	0	0	0	163	0	49	52	0	0	564
C	2	9	0	0	0	1	0	0	0	0	0	12
												9704
Context 2												
A	0	0	0	0	0	0	0	0	0	0	0	0
B	1908	459	2	0	1	1530	0	74	140	0	0	4114
C	0	15	0	0	0	1	0	0	8	0	0	24
												4138
Context 3												
A	59	5	0	0	0	84	0	10	11	0	0	169
B	155	32	1	0	0	76	0	15	19	0	0	298
C	0	0	0	0	0	0	0	0	0	0	0	0
												467
Context 4												
A	0	0	0	0	0	1	0	0	0	0	0	1
B	611	95	1	1	0	551	0	61	41	0	0	1361
C	0	0	0	0	0	0	0	0	0	0	0	0
												1362
Total	6773	742	20	2	2	5544	179	2071	336	1	1	15671

Table 9. Pottery from Firsby. (Source Buckland and Hayfield 1989:Table 1)

	Cooking Pot	Jug	Cistern	Pancheon	Drinking Mug	Lid	Dish	Total
Area A								
No. Sherds	20	8	0	8	0	0	1	37
Percentage	54.05	21.62	0	21.62	0	0	2.7	99.99
Area B								
No. Sherds	9	3	1	18	3	3	0	37
Percentage	24.32	8.11	2.7	48.64	8.11	8.11	0	99.99

straightforward and the rather imprecise colour definitions used by many ceramicists may actually give a reasonably good impression of the range and variability of the colours, in spite of their limited value in terms of absolute definitions.

Table 10 links the fabric traditions and their constituent types with the presence and approximate colour of the glaze.

Although the information in table 10 is unquantified there is a clear indication that glazing is commoner on sandy ware vessels than on gritty ware vessels and that shades of green are the overwhelmingly dominant colour. The principal exceptions are the gritty ware types identified and defined by Moorhouse at Sandal Castle and Kirkstall Abbey (notably Splash Glazed, Green Glazed, Late Medieval and Purple Glazed gritty wares). These types (and the latter site) show a number of divergences from the apparent norm and will be discussed further below.

The distinction between glazed sandy and unglazed gritty wares is supported by the evidence from Middle Lane, Hedon (table 5). Glazed bowls (Hayfield's 'pancheons'), were

manufactured in sandy fabrics while the unglazed bowls were, with one exception, of local gritty fabrics. Furthermore, unidentified types also split along glaze/texture lines with unglazed gritty vessels and glazed sandy vessels.

In the case of Upper Heaton Manby has noted that

> Glaze is found on all vessels produced at Upper Heaton, except for small jars; on the cooking pots and pancheons the glaze is confined to spots and trickles or a transparent sheen, all indicating that the glaze was not intentional but acquired from other vessels during firing. The jugs and minor items were deliberately glazed on the exterior and a dish on the interior (Manby 1964:80).

The presence of accidental spots and splashes of glaze has been noted on other sites including Hedon (Hayfield and Slater 1984:26), Epworth (Hayfield 1984:43), Firsby (Hayfield and Buckland 1989:14), and Lurk Lane, Beverley (Watkins 1991:80). Such spots were particularly clear in the assemblage from the Hallgate 95 kiln. The information from the latter site is summarised in table 11. The gritty fabrics

Table 10. Presence and colour of glazing on medieval pottery (Sources: see appendix 1)

Tradition / type	Glaze	Colours
Gritty wares		
Gritty ware	Rarely glazed	Shades of green where present
York type G ware	Unglazed (rare splash glaze)	
Pimply ware	Unglazed	
Hillam ware	Unglazed	
Northern Gritty ware	Rare (noted on jugs only)	Green or brown
Orange Gritty ware	Jugs only glazed	Green or brown on upper surface
Other Gritty wares (1)	3c - unglazed	
	8c - unglazed	
	9c - unglazed	
	24c - some glazed	Purple, occasionally light brown
	26c - usually unglazed,	Purple (when glazed)
	31c- some glazed	Green
Other Gritty wares (2)	Mainly unglazed	
Splash Glazed Gritty wares	Glazed	Green, more rarely yellow brown
Green Glazed Gritty wares	Glazed	Green
Late Medieval Gritty ware	Glazed	Purple (rdc) or brownish-green (ox)
Purple Glazed Gritty ware	Glazed	Purple
Coarse Sandy ware	Very rare glaze	Accidental splashes
Staxton-Potter Brompton ware	Very rare glaze	Accidental splashes
Hallgate type C ware	Sparse glaze	Yellow-green or pale green
Hallgate C1 and types	Rare glaze	Green, clear (often accidental)
Hedon Coarse ware CH1	Unglazed	
Hedon Coarse ware CH2	Unglazed	
Hedon Coarse ware CH3	Unglazed	
Hedon Coarse ware CH4	Unglazed	
Beverley 1 ware Fabric A	Spots and splashes of glaze	Accidental splashes
Humberware 2	Internal, partial glaze	Olive green
Coal Measures White ware	Glazed	Yellow-green or green
Shell Tempered ware	Unglazed or incidentally glazed	
Sandy wares		
Hedon Fine ware FH 1	Splash glazed	Olive-green, occasionally orange/yellow
Hedon Fine ware FH 2	Glazed	Olive-green, occasionally orange-brown
Hedon Fine ware FH 3	Glazed	Olive-green
Hedon Fine ware FH 4	Splash glazed	As FH1
Hedon Fine ware FH 5	Glazed	As FH2
Nottingham Sandy ware	Glazed	Green
Nottingham Splash Glazed ware	Splash glazed	When present, mottled orange and green
North Lincolnshire Sandy ware	Glazed	Green
Lincoln Medieval Sandy ware	Glazed	Deep green
Toynton All Saints ware	Glazed	Olive-green
Brandsby ware	Glazed	Apple or dark green,
Beverley 1 ware fabric A	Jugs glazed	Green
Beverley 2 ware fabrics B and C	Glazed	Green, some jugs with iron-rich strips
Orangeware (= Beverley 2 ware)	Glazed	Green, olive green
Hallgate A ware	Glazed	Green, varying shades
Hallgate A1	Glazed	
Hallgate D	Glazed	Dark green
Hallgate E	Glazed	
Hallgate F	Glazed	
Hallgate B ware	Glazed	Olive green to yellow
Humberware 1	Glazed	Green
Humberware 3	Glazed	Deep (copper) green
York White ware (=York Glazed)	Glazed	Rich copper green

Table 11. Summary of occurrence of glaze in the assemblage from the kiln in Hallgate, Doncaster (Source: Cumberpatch in 1996b)

Fabric	Glazed	Unglazed	Total	Accidentally glazed	Underside of base glazed	Deliberately glazed
A and A type	39	20	59	0	0	39
A1 + A1 types	612	74	686	21	47	544
C1 + Ci type	269	633	902	128	71	70
C type	6	32	38	0	0	6
C2	1	2	3	1	0	0
C3 + C3 type	143	29	172	32	0	111
D + D type	138	3	141	16	15	107
E + E types	435	171	606	26	34	375
F + F type	14	0	14	0	0	14
Total	1657	964	2621	224	167	1266
A and A type	66.10%	33.89%	99.99%	0	0	66.10%
A1 + A1 types	89.21%	10.78%	99.99%	0.8%	1.79%	79.30%
c! + C1 type	29.82%	70.17%	99.99%	4.88%	2.70%	7.76%
C type	15.78%	84.21%	99.99%	0	0	15.78%
C2	33.33%	66.66%	99.99%	0.03%	0	0
C3 + C3 type	83.13%	16.86%	99.99%	1.22%	0	64.53%
D + D type	97.87%	2.12%	99.99%	0.61%	0.57%	75.88%
E + E types	71.78%	28.21%	99.99%	0.99%	1.29%	61.88%
F + F type	100%	0	100%	0	0	100%
Total	63.22%	36.77%	99.99%	8.54%	6.37%	48.30%

(C1, C2, C3 and their sub-types) were apparently glazed on a much less regular basis than were the sandy wares, although the presence of accidental spots of glaze and glaze on the underside of the bases indicates that they were fired in the same kilns. A fuller discussion of this can be found in the report on the assemblage (Cumberpatch 1996b).

On the basis of this data it would seem possible to extend the correlation between jars/cooking pots, pancheons (or unglazed bowls) and gritty fabrics to include an absence of glaze and, conversely, jugs/pitchers, pipkins and dripping pans, sandy fabrics and green glaze.

Body colour

Unglazed body colour poses many of the same problems as the glaze, with the additional consideration that the rougher surfaces of unglazed fabrics are likely to be more seriously affected by use-related deposits (particularly soot and smoke blackening) than the smoother, glazed, surfaces. Indeed, the persistence of sooty deposits is being increasingly used as an indicator of vessel function and the recording of such deposits is now common (eg. Moorhouse and Slowikowski 1987). Table 12 summarises the available information on unglazed body colour.

While Gritty wares occur in a wide variety of colours, the sandy wares are more homogeneous with orange to red (usually the result of oxidation) being the commonest colour.

Decoration and fabric type

As with the occurrence of glaze, decoration is rarely quantified with respect to the fabric types or the proportion of decorated vessels within an assemblage. In part this may be due to the difficulty of deciding what aspects of the decoration to quantify and how to deal with partially preserved motifs (cf. Cumberpatch 1991). More particularly there has been a marked reluctance to engage with the problem of the significance of medieval decorated pottery. Decoration is frequently treated as idiosyncratic, aesthetic or functional and in this respect approaches to medieval pottery differ considerably from those common in prehistoric and ethnographic pottery studies.

Table 13 summarises the qualitative data available for the study area. With some exceptions there is again a split between the Gritty and Sandy wares, with decoration commoner on the latter than on the former. That this relates more to vessel form rather than specifically to fabric type is suggested by the examples of Northern Gritty ware and Orange Gritty ware where forms more commonly found in sandy fabrics are decorated while other forms are undecorated. It has been suggested that the lack of decoration on the earlier Hedon fine wares (Hayfield and Slater 1984:27) is a function of chronology, although the extent to which decoration increased through the later medieval period is perhaps open to question.

Quantification appears to bear out some of these observations. In table 14 the occurrence of decorated sherds in the Hallgate 95 kiln assemblage has been quantified (by sherd number). 357 sherds of pottery from the kiln were decorated, (12.7% of the assemblage). 316 of these (88.5% of the decorated sherds) bore combed or stabbed motifs; continuous or broken wavy lines, short, interrupted combed lines or stabbed comb impressions. Fifteen (4.2%) had thumb impressions on the rims or outer edges of the handles and twenty

Table 12. Medieval pottery: unglazed external body colour (Sources: see appendix 1)

Tradition / type Gritty wares	Body colour
Gritty ware	White, pink, light red
York type G ware	Red to pink
Pimply ware	White - buff
Hillam ware	Buff-pink
Northern Gritty ware	Orange-brown (ox) light to dark grey (rdc)
Orange Gritty ware	Orange
Other Gritty wares (1)	3c-brown,
	8c-dull purple (rdc)
	9c-light brown surface, blue-grey core
	24c-light brown surface
	26c-light brown
	31c-white slip, green glaze
Other Gritty wares (2)	
Splash Glazed Gritty wares	Oxidised
Green Glazed Gritty wares	Oxidised
Late Medieval Gritty ware	Highly variable, oxidised to reduced
Purple Glazed Gritty ware	Reduced
Coarse Sandy ware	Orange to dull orange but with much variation
Staxton-Potter Brompton ware	Buff
Hallgate type C wares	Red with prominent red grit
Hedon Coarse ware CH1	Variable - off white/buff, orange, red, brown
Hedon Coarse ware CH2	Red-brown buff,
Hedon Coarse ware CH3	Buff, orange, brown (ox), Grey-black (rdc)
Hedon Coarse ware CH4	Pale buff/brown, orange (ox)
Beverley 1 ware Fabric A	Brick red to bright orange (Cooking pots only)
Humberware 2	Orange to brick red
Coal Measures White ware	Buff to white
Shell Tempered ware	Grey-brown to brown
Sandy wares	
Hedon Fine ware FH 1	Orange red (ox), grey (rdc)
Hedon Fine ware FH 2	Orange red/pink (ox), blue grey (rdc)
Hedon Fine ware FH 3	Orange red (ox), blue grey (rdc)
Hedon Fine ware FH 4	Orange red (ox), grey (rdc)
Hedon Fine ware FH 5	Orange red (ox), grey (rdc)
Nottingham Sandy ware	Orange
Nottingham Splash Glazed ware	Orange
North Lincolnshire Sandy ware	Orange (See Hayfield 1983)
Lincoln Medieval Sandy ware	Oxidised
Toynton All Saints ware	Orange to buff (ox), Dark to light grey (rdc)
Brandsby ware	Buff
Beverley 1 ware fabric A	Orange
Beverley 2 ware fabric B and C	Orange
Orangeware (= Beverley wares)	Orange
Hallgate A ware	Red
Hallgate A1	Orange to red, grey when reduced (A1 R)
Hallgate D	Buff to grey
Hallgate E	Buff to pale pink
Hallgate F	Pale grey
Doncaster Hallgate B	Pale brown, sometimes grey
Humberware 1	Orange to brick red
Humberware 3	Orange to brick red
York White ware	Buff to white

ox = oxidised

rdc = reduced

Table 13. Medieval pottery: Decorative treatments and motifs (Sources: See appendix 1)

Tradition / type	Decoration
Gritty wares	
Gritty ware	Undecorated
York type G ware	Undecorated
Pimply ware	Rare, vertical thumbed strips
Hillam ware	Undecorated
Northern Gritty ware	Absent on jars, rare on bowls, commoner on jugs - applied strips, combed lines
Orange Gritty ware	Jugs only. Applied and impressed white clay, horizontal incised lines
Other Gritty wares (1)	
3C	Undecorated
8C	Undecorated
9C	Undecorated
24C	Undecorated
26C	Horizontal grooves
31C	Rare, horizontal or wavy lines on jugs, one with rosette stamp
Other Gritty wares (2)	
Splash Glazed Gritty wares	Rare
Green Glazed Gritty wares	Rare
Late Medieval Gritty ware	Undecorated
Purple Glazed Gritty ware	Rare
Coarse Sandy ware	Very rare applied strips and impressed rims
Staxton-Potter Brompton ware	Rare wavy incised lines
Hallgate type C wares	Rare - thumb impressed rims, incised wavy lines. See table 14
Hedon Coarse ware CH1	Rare - occasional thumbing on rim edge
Hedon Coarse ware CH2	Rare - occasional thumbing on rim edge
Hedon Coarse ware CH3	Rare - occasional thumbing on rim edge, applied strips on large cooking pots
Hedon Coarse ware CH4	Rare
Beverley 1 ware Fabric A	Cooking pots undecorated, jugs/pitchers - combed lines
Humberware 2	Undecorated
Coal Measures White ware	Rare
Shell Tempered ware	Undecorated
Sandy wares	
Hedon Fine ware FH 1	Undecorated
Hedon Fine ware FH 2	Common from 13th century, applied and incised motifs
Hedon Fine ware FH 3	Applied and incised motifs
Hedon Fine ware FH 4	Undecorated
Hedon Fine ware FH 5	Undecorated
Nottingham Sandy ware	Rare
Nottingham Splash Glazed ware	Incised and combed on bodies and thumb impressed handles
Lincoln Medieval Sandy ware	Unknown
Toynton All Saints ware	Applied strips with iron pigment, stamped (Toynton 2)
Brandsby ware	Combed wavy lines, rilling, rouletting, applied scales
Beverley 1 ware fabric A	Combed lines (jugs/pitchers only)
Beverley 2 ware fabric B	Highly decorated; applied scales, applied iron rich strips, face jugs
Beverley 2 ware fabric C	Highly decorated; applied strips, applied pellets, moulded motifs
Hallgate A ware	Knight and face jugs, applied strips, combed lines, impressed comb marks
Hallgate A1	See table 14
Hallgate D	See table 14
Hallgate E	See table 14
Hallgate F	See table 14
Doncaster Hallgate B	Varied - combed, applied, rouletted
Humberware 1	Applied strips and pads, rilling, shoulder rouletting. Stamps are rare
Humberware 3	Unknown
York White ware	Iron pellets, combed lines, seal jugs, rare anthropomorphic jugs, aquamaniles

Table 14. Decorative motifs and fabric types from Hallgate 95 (Source Cumberpatch 1996b)

	A	A type	A/A1 type	A1	A1R	A1 type	C type	C1	C1 type	C2	C3	C3 type	D	D type	ER	E	E type	F	F type	Ha type	Total
Undecorated	48	11	2	493	40	57	34	832	38	3	147	0	99	1	1	405	35	7	2	26	2281
Combed wavy lines (body)	0	0	0	49	4	1	0	17	1	0	19	0	39	0	0	97	13	4	0	0	244
Horizontal lines (body)	0	0	0	18	0	0	0	1	0	0	0	0	0	0	0	13	0	1	0	0	33
Thumb decorated handle	0	0	0	2	0	0	0	0	0	0	0	0	0	0	0	2	0	0	0	0	4
Vertical combed wavy lines	0	0	0	0	0	0	0	0	0	0	0	0	0	0	0	2	3	0	0	0	5
Thumb decorated rim	0	0	0	0	0	0	0	9	0	0	0	0	0	0	0	2	0	0	0	0	11
Other	0	0	0	11	0	0	0	4	0	0	1	0	0	0	0	10	0	0	0	0	26
Incised wavy lines	0	0	0	1	0	0	0	0	0	0	0	0	1	0	0	1	0	0	0	0	3
Stabbed comb decoration (body)	0	0	0	1	0	0	0	0	0	0	0	0	0	0	0	3	0	0	0	0	4
Short combed lines (body)	0	0	0	3	0	0	0	0	0	0	0	5	1	0	0	18	0	0	0	0	27
Total decorated	0	0	0	85	4	1	0	31	1	0	20	5	41	0	0	148	16	5	0	0	357
Total	48	11	2	578	44	58	34	863	39	3	167	5	140	1	1	553	51	12	2	26	2638

six (7.2%) various other motifs, predominantly grooves and ridges created during the turning and finishing of the vessels. There were none of the elaborate face jugs or knight jugs of the types found in the later Hallgate assemblage. With the exception of a single, ambiguous, sherd, applied decoration was absent.

The most notable aspect of table 14 is the low percentage of decorated sherds in fabric C1 and related types. Whereas decorated sherds in fabrics A1, C3, D, E and F varied between 13% and 36% of those groups, only 3.5 % of the C1 sherds were decorated. Added to the relatively low incidence of glazing, this suggests that vessels in the C1 fabric were plain and unelaborate. The relatively high percentage of decorated sherds in fabric C3 (14.5% of the group) reflects the presence of six jugs/pitchers within this rather small group of sherds and possibly distorts the true picture.

None of the A type sherds from Hallgate 95 were decorated, although 138 sherds (0.8% of the total assemblage and 1.48% of the type A sherds) from the later Hallgate assemblage were decorated, a figure which includes a knight jug and sixteen face jugs (Buckland et al 1979).

Numbers of recognisable vessel types from Hallgate 95 which were also decorated were low (2.86% of the total assemblage). The figures are summarised in table 15. Jugs and pitchers were the most frequently decorated type of vessel, combed lines of various kinds being the commonest motif. Thumb decorated rims, absent from the jug/pitcher category, formed half the decorative motifs on jars. Only one jar was decorated with combed lines. A similar distinction applied to bowls and pancheons which also had thumbed rims but no combed or incised lines.

Although he never states exactly how many of the jugs from Upper Heaton were decorated, it is clear from Manby's description that combed wavy lines, impressed comb marks, applied strips, bosses and medallions were not uncommon. In contrast decoration on cooking pots was found on 'less than ten vessels' (Manby 1964:90) and was equally rare on pancheons.

Decorated vessels, rare at Hedon (table 5), were not found amongst the gritty ware types.

Discussion

Before attempting to interpret this data two points should be noted. The first concerns the functional aspects of ceramic pastes. A number of practical advantages of gritty fabrics were noted in the initial discussion of paste texture, above. These undoubtedly had some influence on the manufacture of what were, primarily, utilitarian vessels. It is notable however that the two of the three supposed technical advantages possessed by the Gritty wares (those relating to the performance of the material during firing) should be equally applicable to the sandy wares, yet the fact remains that the commonest of vessel types were manufactured in sandy fabrics. Indeed it may be that the 'sandy' fabrics are in fact coarse enough to benefit from the advantages conferred by the presence of temper. The terms Gritty and Sandy are relative

Table 15. Decorative motifs and vessel type from Hallgate 95 (Source: Cumberpatch 1996)

	Bowl	C Pot	ERB	ERJ	ERV	Jar	Jar/ jug	Jug	Jug(?)	Jug/ pitcher	Panc.	Pcn/ bowl	U/ ID	Total
Undecorated	2	2	1	61	1	9	1	104	2	42	7	1	2202	2435
Combed wavy lines (body)	0	0	0	0	0	0	0	22	0	3	0	0	219	244
Horizontal lines (body)	0	0	0	1	0	0	0	6	0	3	0	0	23	33
Short combed lines (body)	0	0	0	0	0	0	0	4	0	2	0	0	21	27
Thumb decorated handles	0	0	0	0	0	0	0	4	0	0	0	0	0	4
Verical wavy lines	0	0	0	0	0	0	0	0	0	2	0	0	3	5
Thumb decorated rims	0	0	0	6	0	1	0	0	0	0	3	1	0	11
Other	0	0	0	3	0	3	0	7	0	1	5	0	7	26
Interrupted wavy lines (handle)	0	0	0	0	0	0	0	1	0	2	0	0	0	3
Stabbed combed decoration (body)	0	0	0	0	0	0	0	0	0	0	0	0	4	4
Total decorated	*0*	*0*	*0*	*10*	*0*	*4*	*0*	*44*	*0*	*13*	*8*	*1*	*277*	*357*
Total	2	2	1	71	1	13	1	148	2	55	15	2	2479	2792

Key

C Pot	Cooking pot	ERJ	Everted rim jar	Panc.	Pancheon	U/ID	Unidentified
ERB	Everted rim bowl	ERV	Everted rim vessel	Pcn/bowl	Pancheon / Bowl		

ones; in other contexts the sandy fabrics themselves might be considered to be rather coarse. Only a study of the mechanical characteristics of the two types would resolve the question of their properties. In phenomenological terms the distinction between them remains real.

One piece of evidence must be cited which appears to contradict the situation so far described. With the exception of Sandal Castle, Upper Heaton and Staxton, the sites which have been described in greatest detail, and upon which this discussion is based, are located in the Humber basin, although most of the ceramic types have distributions which extend beyond this geographical area. The assemblage from Kirkstall Abbey near Leeds (Moorhouse and Slowikowski 1987) includes a number of these as well as other, more local, types. The assemblage, summarised in table 16, has a rather different overall character to those from the Humber basin. While jars (which are equivalent here to cooking pots elsewhere) and bowls are found almost exclusively in gritty fabrics, jugs are found in both the local gritty fabrics and in the more usual sandy fabrics. This raises a number of questions, notably that of the nature of the patterns described above. Is the situation in the Humber basin a purely local one, and are there other, different, patterns to be found elsewhere? If so, to what do these relate and does such regionalism occur in other categories of medieval material culture? McCarthy and Brooks have noted regional variations in vessel forms (1988:122–126), but have not considered the characters of the clay pastes. An alternative suggestion, given the situation at Upper Heaton, is that the assemblage from Kirkstall Abbey may reflect a peculiarity of monastic assemblages, related perhaps to an ascetic lifestyle, although such a distinction has not been commented

on in the cases of other ecclesiastical assemblages. Unfortunately the largest and most significant assemblages from West Yorkshire (Sandal Castle, Pontefract Castle and Tanners Row, Pontefract) are either unpublished (in the latter two cases) or presented in such a way as to be unquantifiable in the kind of analysis presented here (Sandal Castle). The evidence from Upper Heaton tends to support the divisions seen amongst the Humber basin assemblages, but the qualitative information in the Sandal Castle report (Moorhouse 1983, summarised in tables 1, 10, 12 and 13) tends to suggest that the situation is more complex. While jugs and dripping pans appear in Northern and Orange Gritty ware fabrics, other attributes of these vessels reflect the situation in the Humber basin; glaze is found on jugs, but rarely on other forms (table 10), jugs and pitchers are decorated while bowls and jars are plain (table 13). The extent to which the surface colour follows this trend is impossible to determine from the published data. Clearly this is a situation which requires further empirical investigation. Most importantly it requires the full publication of assemblages from West Yorkshire and from later medieval phases of sites in York.

While the significance of colour and decorative elaboration appear to have been widely shared, the evidence of the West Yorkshire sites suggests that texture may have been of more local importance, although once again further detailed studies are required to assess this suggestion.

Distinctions

The distinctions between the two principal components of the ceramic assemblages from the Humber basin can be summed up as a series of oppositions and contrasts;

Table 16. Pottery from Kirkstall Abbey (Source: Moorhouse and Slowikowski 1987)

Kirkstall Abbey (all phases)	Sandy												Gritty								
	DStam	TriPit	U/IDNL	FSand	PFine	OxHumb	RdcHumb	SkOSw	YorkWh	TudGr	WhSHumb	Baildon	Pimply	YorkTp	Hillam	SWMC	NorGrit	OrnGrit	StepJg	RawM	LMedGr
Jar	1				1	1				1			36	1	1	4	18	5			1
Jug	1		18	6	1	14		17	20	1		1	11		1		150	20	1	2	
Bowl									1				2				23	14			
TriPitch		3																			
Curfew																	1				
D/Pan																	3				
Strainer																	1				
Lid									1								2				
Cistern									1											8	
Cups											1										
Other																	1				
U/ID							2		8				57				149	25		15	

Key

DStam	Developed Stamford ware	OxHumb	Oxidised Humberware
TriPit	Tripod Pitchers	RdcHumb	Reduced Humberware
U/IDNL	Unidentified non-local	SkOSw	Skipton-on-Swale
FSand	Fine Sandy ware	YorkWh	York White ware
PFine	Pink Fine ware	TudGr	Tudor Green
		WhSHumb	White Slipped Humberware

Baildon	Baildon ware	OrnGrit	Orange Gritty ware
Pimply	Pimply ware	StepJg	Stepped Jug ware
York Tp	York type ware	RawM	Rawmarsh type
Hillam	Hillam ware	LMedGr	Late Medieval Gritty ware
SWMC	Southwest Midlands Coarseware	TriPitch	Tripod Pitcher
NorGrit	Northern Gritty ware	D/Pan	Dripping Pan

Sandy fabrics	Gritty fabrics
Commonly glazed	Less commonly glazed
Green and orange/red	Buff, grey, red, brown (discoloured to grey and black)
Commonly decorated	Rarely decorated
Comb decorated	Rare thumb impressions
Jugs/pitchers	
Pipkins	
Dripping pans	
	Jars/Cooking pots
	Bowls
	Pancheons

It does not seem unreasonable, on the basis of the evidence for the importance of the phenomenological variables discussed in the first part of this paper, to suggest that these regularities and distinctions were of a significance beyond the purely functional or technological. Sets of binary oppositions, Public : Private, Male : Female, Inside : Outside, the mainstay of much High Structuralist thought are relatively easy to draw up, but, in the final analysis, require grounding in the specific historical context, often a somewhat more difficult task. In the absence of corroborative data (such as detailed studies of the use of space in medieval town houses) and in the light of the ambiguities concerning the loci and extent of gendered labour, the postulation of such simple oppositions in the present context is fraught with problems; the realities are likely to be more complex with material culture being manipulated to both support and subvert established and oppositional views of society. In what follows an attempt will be made to relate pottery to the wider context of medieval life and in particular to the relationship between pottery vessels and food and drink.

Function and symbol in medieval ceramic assemblages

Questions concerning the uses of pottery vessels are difficult to answer convincingly (McCarthy and Brooks 1988, Moorhouse 1978). Analyses of fat and other organic residues remain rare (although of considerable potential, e.g. Blinkhorn, in prep.) and the recording of carbon residues on the outside of pots has been carried out on a haphazard basis (although it is now increasingly common). Evidence from documentary sources is both scarce and subject to a range of biases sometimes overlooked by the non-specialist (Moorhouse 1978:4, Woolf pers. comm.). In spite of these problems evidence does exist which is useable, if difficult to interpret.

Table 17 summarises the range of uses ascribed to the vessel types most common in the area and period under discussion. These are based upon the documentary sources summarised by Moorhouse (1978) and McCarthy and Brooks (1988) and upon inference from archaeological data. There is some blurring of distinctions between different functions. Discussing the commonly used descriptive category of cooking pots for example, Moorhouse has noted that

> Many vessels of this basic shape were used for cooking, for they are fire-blackened externally on or near the base, although a large number show no signs of having been near a fire. It is therefore likely that the traditional medieval 'cooking pot' or open mouthed pot, was an extremely versatile vessel (Moorhouse 1978:7).

In spite of this, the uses of vessels can be seen to exhibit some structure which coincides with their characteristics and two general assertions can be made and assessed against more detailed analyses:

Table 17. Medieval pottery: Vessel types and ascribed functions (Sources: McCarthy and Brooks 1988, Moorhouse 1978)

Vessel form	Uses
Sandy wares	
Jug / Pitcher	Serving of liquid (ale, wine, milk, water)
Pipkin	Cooking (boiling, simmering)
Dripping tray	Cooking (roasting)
Basting dish	Cooking (roasting)
Drinking jug	Drinking, serving food
Gritty wares	
Cooking pot	Cooking (boiling/stewing, steaming), storage,
Jar	Cooking (boiling/stewing), storage,
Pancheon	Cooking (boiling/stewing), storage, mixing and preparing food (cf. bowls)
Bowl	Dairying, mixing and preparing food
Dish	Dairying,
Cistern	Storing and serving ale and beer
Curfew	Covering fire
Small bowls	Drinking

– Green glazed, decorated and brightly coloured vessels, usually in a sandy fabric, are associated with the more public aspects of cooking, with the serving of food and drink and with the roasting of meat, a higher status form of cooking than stewing or boiling. The use of pipkins for cooking is relatively well attested from documentary sources, and they may have been used for the preparation of sauces which, by their very nature, might be expected to accompany roast meat rather than the more ubiquitous and lower status stews and pottages (McCarthy and Brooks 1988:107).

– Unglazed, undecorated and often discoloured vessels, normally in gritty fabrics, appear associated with the more mundane boiling and stewing of food, with the preparation of food, notably dairy products, the brewing of ale and the storing of food.

These distinctions are not exclusive; the use of small drinking jugs as urinals, gritty ware bowls for drinking, bowls for catching blood during bleeding and jugs for filling baths (McCarthy and Brooks 1988:Fig. 52) are evidence of both a lack of clarity in the data and, possibly, of regional and chronological variations in practice.

In addition to these distinctions within the ceramic assemblages there is also the issue of 'invisible' material culture. Wood, metal and glass vessels were all of significance in medieval households, although they tend to be under-represented in archaeological assemblages. There is some evidence that metal cooking vessels became commoner during the medieval period, and may have displaced ceramic cooking vessels during the later 14th century. Glass was probably restricted to richer households, but wooden vessels appear to have been even cheaper than pottery. The scarcity of wood and wood products on archaeological sites and the low status of wooden vessels should not be allowed to obscure the importance of wood as a raw material. Wooden vessels are rare and the low numbers makes the task of drawing conclusions hazardous. Examples are known from a number of sites within the study area however (including Hull, Beverley and York) and the vessel types represented are open bowls, platters, shallow dishes and beakers (MacGregor 1982, Watkin 1987, 1993, Foreman 1991, Morris and Evans 1992). It is notable that this is precisely the range of vessels which is under-represented in the ceramic repertoire. As MacGregor has commented (albeit with reference to the Anglo-Scandinavian period);

> It is interesting to note that the bowls preponderate in the lower levels of the excavation, where open forms are strikingly infrequent amongst the pottery … . In no instance can comparisons be made between forms in the two media (MacGregor 1982:147)

It might be possible to suggest that wooden vessels constitute a distinct classificatory group, distinguished from ceramics by their material (or perhaps by the attributes and associations of that material) as well as by their form and range of functions. This distinction must be seen as adding a further level of complexity to the phenomenological world inhabited by medieval people.

The distinctions within the ceramic assemblages can be related to idealised sets of oppositions (analogous perhaps to the kind of High Structuralist binary oppositions advocated by Levi-Strauss) which must be assessed and verified empirically.

Public	Private
Male	Female
Higher status	Lower status
Food/drink presentation	Food/drink storage
Consumption of beverages	
	Food/drink preparation

Thus the glazed, brightly coloured, sandy textured vessels may have been associated with activities in the left hand column, the more public and prestigious activities, while the unglazed, duller, gritty wares might be more readily associated with the right hand column, the less public, lower status, and possibly female, domain of action. In this sense we might be dealing with gendered, status related components of practical actions acting to structure the constitution of ceramic assemblages, with the perception of the character of activities reflected in the nature of the ceramic vessels which were involved in them.

The issue of gender finds a counterpart in Yentsch's analysis of the 16th and 17th century colonial American situation (1991a, 1991b), particularly in the suggestion of a gendering of pottery through its context of use, marked by physical, or phenomenological, distinctions which would have been readily perceptible to the participants, if unarticulated by them. An extreme example of this in the present context might be that of face jugs and knight jugs, a regular, if not an abundant, component of the later medieval ceramic repertoire within the study area. Such sandy textured, green glazed and often highly decorated vessels are overwhelmingly male, with bearded heads being the commonest form (Le Patourel 1966). Phallic figures are known from other parts of England, while female examples, although extant, are rare (Blinkhorn pers. comm.).

How do the colours of the vessels relate to the apparent symbolic associations of colour described in the first part of this article? How far are the associations with gender confused by the practical blurring of idealised male and female roles? Are the associations of the pots reflected in the use of space within medieval houses and domestic spaces? The key to some of these questions appears to be food.

In spite of Braudel's gallocentric comments (1981:190) it is clear that food and drink was of immense symbolic, as well as practical, importance in medieval life. Religious rules, legal requirements and constraints and the unarticulated practices constituting the *habitus* surrounded, prescribed and proscribed what was eaten and drunk, when it was eaten and drunk and the structure of its production, processing and marketing (Goody 1982:133–153, Dyer 1983, 1989, Mennell 1985, Hammond 1993, Johnson 1996).

There is extensive evidence of the importance of ale as a drink in medieval society. Dyer has cited figures of a gallon of ale per person per day in aristocratic households (1983:193) and lower, variable, but still substantial, amounts in the less well documented peasant households (1983:202–3, 209, see also Hammond 1993). After bread, ale was one of the largest components of household expenditure in upper class households (Dyer 1989:56). Ale was purchased from brewers and much was also made in the home and it appears that many brewers were women (Clark 1983, Hanawalt 1986:132, Rigby 1995: chapter 7, Johnson 1996:174), an association which may predate the later medieval period (Dickinson 1993). While medieval ale was somewhat weaker than modern beer, the tendency to view it from a functional perspective, contributing calories and vitamins to the diet, overlooks the widespread, indeed almost universal, association between drug use and social activity (Blinkhorn, pers. comm.). Vencl (1994) and Woolf and 'Eldridge' (1994) have pointed out the importance of drinking to the maintenance of social relationships and the recognition of status, and, although they have not considered the later medieval English case directly, the examples cited in both articles find powerful resonances in the present context. Ale can be seen as a beverage in which a variety of powerful elements came together; male and female labour in the harvest, female labour in the brewing and distribution, obligations on the part of landowners to provide ale to harvest and other workers, intoxication and social interaction. All of these were habitual, and powerful, elements in medieval life. The associations between sexual activity and alcohol in our own society are so powerful as to urge caution in imposing them on the past, but one is strongly tempted to recall Shakespeare's porter (Macbeth: Act 2, scene 3) who was in no doubt of the association between drink and lechery, quite apart from the early medieval examples cited by Woolf and 'Eldridge' (1994:337). Later writers drew attention to alehouses as places of potential disorder and antisocial activity (Clark 1983) particularly with respect to their use by women (Johnson 1996:186) although it is also clear that they played an important role in the community.

Ale might be seen as a counterpart and partial opposite to the other staple of medieval life, bread, which, surrounded with an aura of sanctity and devoid of the sensual licence associated with alcohol, held a distinct, but equally powerful place in medieval society. Unlike ale, bread has left fewer material traces and, in the form of trenchers, actually took the place of durable material culture at the table. It is consequently far harder to trace the networks of symbolism (other than the formally religious) which may have surrounded it.

The question of symbolic associations which might connect ceramic jugs and ale is one which, initially, invites a cautious approach. In both the cases where the colour green has specific associations (theatrical costumes and medicine) they are with women, and particularly with fertility and sexuality. Red (and, by association, orange), the equally dominant colour of the sandy wares, was a more ambiguous colour in the theatrical context, but it certainly had powerful associations, including blood and a variety of masculine attributes notably strength, power and violence. If we can transfer these symbolic associations to the field of food and drink, the combination of the two colours on vessels used in the serving of ale might imply the existence of complex associations and meanings, constituted by, and derived from, the symbolism of its production, distribution and consumption.

The distinctions between the vessels used for the preparation of food are equally explicable in symbolic terms, although the connections with known referents are even more obscure. The consumption of meat varied greatly between and within the social classes. In spite of the difficulties of determining the details of the composition of the medieval diet and the variations in supply and patterns of consumption over time, the main outlines are clear. Vegetable, cereal and pulse-based stews and pottages were the staple diet of the mass of the population, supplemented by dairy products and with meat and fish relatively rare elements. In contrast the consumption of meat by the aristocracy and, later, wealthy town-dwellers, was an important aspect of their status. As Dyer has noted

> The distinguishing characteristics of upper-class diet lay in the ample amounts of meat and fish, which were eaten in almost equal quantities because of the generally strict observance of fish days ... A third to a half of expenditure on food, depending on the wealth of the lord went on meat and fish so that the average per capita consumption in magnate households was in the region of two or three pounds per day (Dyer 1983:193)

The symbolic importance of such food is underlined by the use of exotic ingredients, notably spices and imported wine. These appear to have provided a link with the perceived sophistication of the Mediterranean world (Dyer 1983:194) and a statement of the wealth and power of the individual who could offer such things to guests. As Sass has commented

> In the strictly defined social hierarchy of the medieval world, a man's rank was to a large extent defined by the food he could set on his table. Certain ingredients and methods of preparation were reserved for the very rich .... These foods and dishes took on a symbolic value and came to stand for the very wealth and power the king and his barons wished to display (1981:256).

Under these circumstances the roasting and serving of large portions of an animal would have formed part of a powerful statement by and about the host and his attitudes to his position and to his guests. The use of glazed, sandy textured dripping trays and basting dishes would thus have been associated with the preparation (and perhaps the serving) of the highest status type of food, roast meat. For the household where meat was a luxury, the possession of pottery vessels connected with meat may have been a partial, symbolic, substitute.

Aristocratic (and wealthy urban) households also consumed significant quantities of imported spices. These were presumably prepared in sauces using relatively small vessels and served together with the roast meat. Although direct evidence is lacking it does not seem unreasonable to suggest that pipkins would have been used for this purpose, their small size restricting the quantities used and their handles permitting swift removal from the heat to avoid burning or overcooking. The tripod legs, handles and small spouts made them suitable for use as tablewares.

Dripping pans, basting dishes and pipkins all shared the characteristics seen in the case of the jugs and pitchers and which have been related to the complexity of the symbolism surrounding the consumption of ale. This might imply that the significance of the colours and textures has more to do with the public context of consumption than is has to do with the specifics of the preparation of the food and drink, a suggestion which suggests that the symbolic associations of red and green were linked with licensed excess and indulgence in general rather than with gender-specific sexuality and passionate emotions in particular.

The rarity of individual ceramic drinking vessels serves to highlight the unusual character of the 'Skipton-on-Swale' drinking jugs. The precise purpose of these vessels remains unknown and name applied to them appears to be based largely on intuition and tradition. As Sarah Jennings has recently pointed out (1994:82) they probably had a variety of uses and cannot be classed as 'fine table wares'. The fact that they were unglazed but were made in a sandy fabric makes them somewhat anomalous in the present context. Their relatively late date in relation to other types discussed here (later 14th and 15th century) may suggest that they are an early part of the changes in practice which, somewhat later, marked the end of the medieval ceramic tradition.

In contrast to the decorated, sandy textured wares, the plain gritty wares were most probably used primarily in less public, lower status contexts. Pottages and stews cooked in the wide mouthed jars and cooking pots probably remained close to the fire with the undifferentiated food ladled into wooden bowls for serving. As Moorhouse and Slowikowski have shown (1987:Figure 57) a number of methods of cooking are indicated by the patterns of sooting on individual vessels, and it seems clear that one of the chief functions of the 'cooking pot' style of vessel was indeed for cooking over or adjacent to an open fire. As pottage or stew pots the gritty ware vessels were associated with the mass of the population whose diet was largely boiled or stewed vegetables (Mennell 1985:42, with references).

Other gritty ware vessels (including cooking pots used for storage) were employed in categories of activity which would have remained outside the public areas of larger houses, in the service areas spatially and/or physically separated from the hall and other public spaces (cf. Johnson 1993, 1996:81). Pancheons, dishes and bowls were used for the processing of dairy products and, probably, the preserving of food, as well as the making of bread. While such tasks were dependant upon female labour, the pots themselves make no clear reference to the more overt attributes of femaleness noted above. As with the sandy wares the symbolism appears to be a generalised one of production/ preparation : consumption/display, rather than with a direct male : female dichotomy.

Conclusion

The interpretation of material culture as a meaning bearing medium, centrally implicated in the maintenance of the practices which constitute human society remains a controversial one. An ideological commitment to a view of material culture as primarily functional with symbolism as an added element is strongly rooted in the curious and complex sociology of British Archaeology. That this position should be so strongly maintained is particularly unusual in view of the fact that archaeologists themselves habitually employ a variety of objects (including clothing, tools, motor vehicles as well as their own bodies), not only as a means of demarcating themselves as a distinctive group, rejecting or scorning commodities which are seen as symbolising other groups, defined as constituting the 'non-archaeological', but also as committing themselves to certain political positions within the profession itself.

In this paper I have tried to demonstrate, albeit in a preliminary manner, that certain attributes of medieval ceramics can be interpreted from other perspectives than the exclusively etic. Ceramic assemblages possess structured characteristics (notably colour, decoration and texture) which appear to share symbolic attributes with other categories of material culture, even if the details of the symbolism are of considerably greater complexity than is easily comprehensible through the medium of archaeological data. The subject clearly requires further research and hitherto disparate pieces of research need to be brought together. The question of the use of space in medieval town houses, somewhat more complex in terms of their spatial divisions than those studied by Johnson (1993), might have a considerable amount to contribute to our understanding of the structure of artefact assemblages. The suggestions presented here, that the colour and texture of pottery is related to the status and symbolic associations of the food and drink with which it was associated, are relatively simple ones. The question of the relationship to gender has, to some extent, been sidestepped, in part because of the concentration in medieval gender studies on the more overt manifestations of gender difference, notably religion, which appears to have distracted attention from questions of the significance of gender in the organisation of the production, circulation and consumption of food and material culture. When these subjects have been tackled it will be possible to see material culture not merely as a reflection of medieval social practices, but as one of their more important constituents.

Acknowledgements

Acknowledgements are due to the following for discussions and information which have contributed to the final form and content of this paper; Alex Woolf, Louise Barnes, Paul Blinkhorn, Tim Cooper, Emily La Trobe-Bateman, Colin

Appendix 1
Bibliographic references

Tradition / type	Bibliography
Gritty wares	
Gritty ware	Manby 1964, Brooks 1987, Mainman 1990, Cumberpatch u/p 2
York type G ware	Holdsworth 1978, Watkins 1991
Pimply ware	Moorhouse 1983, Moorhouse and Slowikowski 1987
Hillam ware	Moorhouse and Slowikowski 1987, Slowikowski unpublished
Northern Gritty ware	Moorhouse 1983, Moorhouse and Slowikowski 1987
Orange Gritty ware	Moorhouse and Slowikowski 1987
Other Gritty wares (1)	
3c	Moorhouse 1983
8c	Moorhouse 1983
9c	Moorhouse 1983
24c	Moorhouse 1983
26c	Moorhouse 1983
31c	Moorhouse 1983
Other Gritty wares (2)	Defined in Cumberpatch unpublished 2
Splash Glazed Gritty wares	Cumberpatch unpublished 2, Slowikowski unpublished
Green Glazed Gritty wares	Cumberpatch unpublished 2
Late Medieval Gritty ware	Moorhouse and Slowikowski 1987
Purple Glazed Gritty ware	Cumberpatch unpublished 2
Coarse Sandy ware	Watkins 1987
Staxton-Potter Brompton ware	Manby 1964, Watkins 1987, Didsbury and Watkins 1992
Hedon Coarse ware CH1	Hayfield 1984
Hedon Coarse ware CH2	Hayfield 1984
Hedon Coarse ware CH3	Hayfield 1984
Hedon Coarse ware CH4	Hayfield 1984
Beverley 1 ware Fabric A	Didsbury and Watkins 1992
Humberware 2	Watkins 1987
Coal Measures White ware	Hayfield and Buckland 1989
Doncaster Hallgate C	Buckland et al 1979
Doncaster Hallgate C1 ware	Cumberpatch, in prep.
Shell Tempered ware	Adams Gilmour 1988, pers. obs.
Sandy wares	
Hedon Fine ware FH 1	Hayfield 1984
Hedon Fine ware FH 2	Hayfield 1984
Hedon Fine ware FH 3	Hayfield 1984
Hedon Fine ware FH 4	Hayfield 1984
Hedon Fine ware FH 5	Hayfield 1984
Nottingham Sandy ware	Woodland 1993
Nottingham Splash Glazed ware	Woodland 1993
North Lincolnshire Sandy ware	
Lincoln Medieval Sandy ware	Adams Gilmour 1988
Toynton All Saints ware	Watkins 1987
Brandsby ware	Brooks 1987, Watkins 1987
Beverley 1 ware fabric A	Didsbury and Watkins 1992
Beverley 2 ware fabrics B and C	Watkins 1987, Didsbury and Watkins 1992
Orangeware (= Beverley 2 ware)	Watkins 1987, 1993
Hallgate A ware	Buckland et al 1979
Hallgate A1	Cumberpatch, in prep.
Hallgate D	Cumberpatch, in prep
Hallgate E	Cumberpatch, in prep
Hallgate F	Cumberpatch, in prep
Hallgate B	Buckland et al 1979
Humberware 1	Watkins 1987
Humberware 3	Watkins 1987
York White ware	Watkins 1987, Brooks 1987 (=York Glazed ware, Mainman 1993)

Merrony, John Moreland, Anna Moss, Mike Parker Pearson, Mark Pluciennik, John Roberts, Graham Robbins, Alan Vince, Gareth Watkins, Jane Young. None of them are responsible for the opinions or the interpretations contained in the paper, final responsibility for which rests with the author. The analysis of the assemblage from Hallgate, Doncaster was funded by The Tetley Pub Company Limited. The excavation was undertaken by the South Yorkshire Archaeology Field and Research Unit under the direction of Simon Atkinson. Initial processing of the material was undertaken by members of excavation team and by the Doncaster branch of the Yorkshire Archaeological Society whose careful work under difficult conditions is gratefully acknowledged.

Bibliography

Armstrong, P. and Ayers, B. 1987 *Excavations in High Street and Blackfriargate*. Hull Old Town Report Series No. 5. East Riding Archaeologist 8, 208–216.

Atkinson, S. in prep. Excavations in Hallgate and Wood Street, Doncaster, South Yorkshire.

Barrett, J. 1989 Fields of Discourse. Reconstituting a social archaeology. *Critique of Anthropology* 7, 5–16.

Barrett, J. 1994 *Fragments from Antiquity*. Blackwell.

Baxandall, M. 1988 *Painting and experience in fifteenth century Italy.* (second ed.) Oxford University Press.

Blinkhorn, P.W. in prep. The Ipswich ware project. English Heritage

Blinkhorn, P.W. 1993 Cultural identity markers in early Anglo-Saxon domestic pottery. Paper delivered at the 1993 T.A.G. conference, University of Durham.

Blinkhorn, P.W. and Cumberpatch, C.G. in press The interpretation of artefacts and the tyranny of the field archaeologist. In: H.Dalwood (Ed.) *Proceedings of the sixth Interpreting Stratigraphy conference.*

Bourdieu, P. 1992 *The Logic of Practice*. Polity Press.

Braudel, F. 1981 *Civilization and Capitalism 15th – 18th century volume 1: The Structures of Everyday Life.* Fontana.

Brewster, T. 1958 Staxton ware – an interim report. *Yorkshire Archaeological Journal* 39, 445–446.

Brooks, C.M. 1987 *Medieval and Later Pottery from Aldwark and Other Sites.* The Archaeology of York: The Pottery 16/3. C.B.A.

Buckland, P.C., Dolby, M.J., Hayfield, C. and Magilton, J.R. 1979 *The Medieval Pottery Industry at Hallgate, Doncaster.* The Archaeology of Doncaster: The Medieval Town 2/1. Doncaster Museums and Arts Service.

Clark, P. 1983 *The English alehouse: a social history 1200–1830.* Longman.

Cleal, R. 1995 British prehistoric ceramics – a long view. Paper delivered at the 1995 T.A.G. conference, Reading University.

Crowfoot, E. Pritchard, F. and Staniland, K. 1992 *Textiles and Clothing c1150 – 1450.* Museum of London / HMSO.

Cumberpatch, C. G. Unpublished 1 *The concepts of economy and habitus in the study of medieval pottery assemblages.* Paper presented at the 14th T.A.G. conference Durham University December 1994.

Cumberpatch, C.G. Unpublished 2 *Medieval pottery from six sites in Pontefract, West Yorkshire. Archive Report.* West Yorkshire Archaeology Service.

Cumberpatch, C.G. in prep. 1 The concepts of economy and habitus in the study of later medieval ceramic assemblages. Paper submitted to *Archaeological Review from Cambridge* 1996.

Cumberpatch, C.G. 1991 *The production and circulation of Late Iron Age slip decorated pottery in Central Europe.* Unpublished PhD thesis. Sheffield University.

Cumberpatch, C.G. 1996a The Pottery. In: J. Dunkley and C. Cumberpatch (Eds.) *Excavations at 16 – 20 Church Street, Bawtry.* South Yorkshire County Archaeology Monograph No. 3. British Archaeological Reports. British Series 248.

Cumberpatch, C.G. 1996b *Medieval pottery from Hallgate, Doncaster, South Yorkshire.* Archive Report. South Yorkshire Archaeology Field and Research Unit.

Dickinson, T.M. 1993 An Anglo-Saxon 'cunning woman' from Bidford-on-Avon. In: M. Carver (Ed.) *In search of cult; archaeological investigations in honour of Philip Rahtz.* University of York / The Boydell Press.

Didsbury, P. and Watkins, J.G. 1992 The Pottery. In: D.H. Evans and D.G. Tomlinson *Excavations at 33 – 35 Eastgate, Beverley.* Sheffield Excavation Reports 3, 81–121.

Dyer, C. 1983 English diet in the later Middle Ages. In: T. Aston, P. Cross, C. Dyer and J. Thirsk (Eds.) *Social relations and ideas.* Cambridge University Press.

Dyer, C. 1989 *Standards of living in the later Middle Ages.* Cambridge University Press.

Earnshaw, J. and Watkins, J.G. 1984 *An Excavation at Kirkgate Bridlington.* Humberside Leisure Services.

Eco, U. 1986 *Art and Beauty in the Middle Ages.* Yale University Press

Evans, D.H. and Tomlinson, D.G. 1992 *Excavations at 33 – 35 Eastgate, Beverley.* Sheffield Excavation Reports 3, 81–121.

Ferguson, G. 1954 *Signs and Symbols in Christian Art.* Oxford University Press.

Foreman, M. 1991 The wood. In: P. Armstrong, D. Tomlinson and D.H. Evans (Eds.) *Excavations at Lurk Lane, Beverley 1979–82.* Sheffield Excavation Report 1, Department of Archaeology and Prehistory, University of Sheffield, 174–182.

Gibbon, G. 1989 *Explanation in Archaeology.* Blackwell.

Goody, J. 1982 *Cooking, Cuisine and Class.* Cambridge University Press.

Graves, C. P. 1989 Social space in the English medieval parish church. *Economy and Society* 18:3, 297–322.

Gregory, C.A. 1982 *Gifts and Commodities.* Academic Press.

Hammond, P.W. 1993 *Food and Feast in Medieval England.* Alan Sutton Publishing Ltd.

Hanawalt, B. 1986 *The Ties that Bound.* Oxford University Press.

Harris, J.W. 1992 *Medieval Theatre in Context.* Routledge.

Hayfield, C. and Buckland, P.C. 1989 Late Medieval Pottery Wasters from Firsby, South Yorkshire. *Transactions of the Hunter Archaeological Society* 15 8–24.

Hayfield, C and Slater, T. 1984 *The Medieval town of Hedon.* Humberside Leisure Services.

Hayfield, C. 1984 Excavations on the Site of the Mowbray Manor House at the Vinegarth, Epworth, Lincolnshire, 1975–1976. *Lincolnshire History and Archaeology* 9: 5–28.

Hayfield, C. 1985 *Humberside Medieval Pottery.* BAR British Series 140.

Hayfield, C. 1992 Humberware: the development of a late-medieval pottery tradition. In: D. Gaimster and M. Redknap (Eds.) *Everyday and exotic pottery from Europe.* Oxbow Books.

Holdsworth, J. 1978 *Selected pottery groups AD 650 – 1780.* The Archaeology of York: The Pottery 16/1. CBA / York Archaeological Trust.

Hosler, D. 1996 Technical choices, social categories and meaning among the Andean potters of Las Animas. *Journal of Material Culture* 1:1, 63–92.

Hunt, A. 1996 The governance of consumption: sumptuary laws and shifting forms of regulation. *Economy and Society* 25:3, 410–427.

Jennings, S. 1994 Coin hoard pots, Humber ware drinking jugs and the problems of nomenclature. *Medieval Ceramics* 18:82–3.

Johnson, M. 1993 *Housing Culture. Traditional architecture in an English Landscape*. UCL Press.

Johnson, M. 1996 *An Archaeology of Capitalism*. Blackwell.

Keen, M. 1990 *English Society in the Later Middle Ages 1348–1500*. Penguin Books.

Kidson, P. 1979 Part 1 In: P. Kidson, P. Murray and P. Thompson *A History of English Architecture*. Pelican.

Kilmurry, K. 1980 *The Pottery Industry of Stamford, Lincolnshire*. B.A.R. British Series 84.

Le Patourel, H.E.J 1966 Hallgate, Doncaster and the incidence of face-jugs with beards. *Medieval Archaeology* 10:160–164.

MacGregor, A. 1982 *Anglo-Scandinavian finds from Lloyds Bank, Pavement and other sites*. The Archaeology of York 17/3 The York Archaeological Trust/Council for British Archaeology Manby, T. 1964 Medieval pottery kilns at Upper Heaton, West Yorkshire. *Archaeological Journal* 121, 70–110.

Manby, T. 1964 Medieval Pottery kilns at Upper Heaton, West Yorkshire *Archaeological Journal* 121, 70–110.

McCarthy, M. and Brooks, C. 1988 *Medieval Pottery in Britain*. Leicester University Press.

Mennell, S. 1985 *All Manner of Food* Blackwell.

Miller, D. 1995 Consumption as the vanguard of history. In: D. Miller (Ed.) *Acknowledging Consumption*. Routledge.

Moorhouse, S. 1978 Documentary evidence for the uses of medieval pottery. An interim statement. *Medieval Ceramics* 2: 3 – 19.

Moorhouse, S. 1983 The Pottery In: P. Mayes and L. Butler (Eds.) *Sandal Castle Excavations 1964–1973*. Wakefield Historical Publications, Wakefield. 83–198.

Moorhouse S. and Slowikowski, A. 1987 The Pottery. In: *Kirkstall Abbey. The 1950–64 excavations: a reassessment*. Yorkshire Archaeology 1. West Yorkshire Archaeology Service.

Moreland, J. 1991 Method and Theory in Medieval Archaeology in the 1990's. *Archeologia Medievale* 18: 7–42.

Morris, C. A. and Evans, D.H. 1992 The wood. In: D.H. Evans and D.G. Tomlinson *Excavations at 33–35 Eastgate, Beverley*. Sheffield Excavation Reports 3, 189–209.

Ormerod, P. 1994 *The Death of Economics*. Faber and Faber.

Parker Pearson, M. and Richards, C. 1994 *Architecture and Order; approaches to social space*. Routledge.

Pearsall, D 1982 The visual world of the Middle Ages. In: B. Ford (Ed.) *Medieval Literature. Part 1 Chaucer and the Alliterative Tradition*. Pelican.

Phillips, J. 1973 *The Reformation of Images: destruction of art in England 1535–1660*. Berkeley.

Pluciennik, M.Z. 1994 *The Mesolithic – Neolithic Transition in Southern Italy*. Unpub. PhD thesis. Sheffield University.

Polanyi, K., Arensburg, C. and Pearson, H. 1957 *Trade and market in the early empires*. Free Press.

Rigby, S.H. 1995 *English society in the later Middle Ages*. Macmillan.

Sass, L.J. 1981 The preference for sweets, spices and almond milk in late Medieval English cuisine. In: A. Fenton and T.M. Owen (Eds.) *Food in perspective*. John Donald Ltd.

Sinclair, E. 1985 Medieval polychromy on Exeter West Front. *Friends of Exeter Cathedral 55th Annual Report*.

Slowikowski, A. unpublished. Medieval pottery from Tanners Row, Pontefract. Archive Report, West Yorkshire Archaeology Service.

Sterner, J. 1989 Who is signalling whom? Ceramic style, ethnicity and taphonomy amongst the Sirak Bulahay. *Antiquity* 63, 451–9.

Tilley, C. 1994 *A Phenomenology of Landscape*. Berg.

Vencl, S. 1994 The archaeology of thirst. *Journal of European Archaeology* 2.2, 299–326.

Walton, P. 1992 The dyes. In: E. Crowfoot, F. Pritchard and K. Staniland. *Textiles and Clothing c1150 – 1450*. Museum of London/HMSO.

Walton, P. 1989 *Textiles, cordage and raw fibre from 16 – 22 Coppergate*. The Archaeology of York 17 / 5. The York Archaeological Trust/ Council for British Archaeology.

Watkin, J. 1987 Objects of wood. In: P. Armstrong and B. Ayers (Eds.) *Excavations in High Street and Blackfriargate*, Hull Old Town Report Series No. 5. East Riding Archaeologist 8, 208–216.

Watkin, J. 1993 Objects of wood. In: In: D.H. Evans (Ed.) *Excavations in Hull 1975–76*. Hull Old Town Report Series No. 2. East Riding Archaeologist 4, 169–173.

Watkins, J. G. 1987 The Pottery In: P. Armstrong and B. Ayers (Eds.) *Excavations in High Street and Blackfriargate*, Hull Old Town Report Series No. 5. East Riding Archaeologist 8, 53–181.

Watkins, J. G. 1991 The Pottery In: P. Armstrong, D. Tomlinson and D.H. Evans (Eds.) *Excavations at Lurk Lane, Beverley 1979–82*. Sheffield Excavation Report 1, Department of Archaeology and Prehistory, University of Sheffield. 61–103.

Woodland, R. 1993 Ceramics. In: A.G. Kinsley (Ed.) *Excavations on the Saxo-Norman Defences at Slaughterhouse Lane, Newark-on-Trent, Nottinghamshire*. Transactions of the Thoroton Society volume 97, 33–47.

Woods, A. 1986 Form, Fabric and Function: Some Observations on the Cooking Pot in Antiquity. In: W.D. Kingery (ed.) *Ceramics and Civilisation Vol. 2: Technology and Style*. The American Ceramics Society: 157–172.

Woolf, A. and 'Eldridge, R.' 1994 Sharing a drink with Marcel Mauss. *Journal of European Archaeology* 2.2: 327–340

Yentsch, A. 1991a Chesapeake artefacts and their cultural context: pottery and the food domain. *Post-Medieval Archaeology* 25. 25–72.

Yentsch, A. 1991b The symbolic divisions of pottery: Sex related attributes of English and Anglo-American Household Pots. In: R.H. McGuire and R. Paynter (Eds.) *The Archaeology of Inequality*. Blackwell. 192–231.

Youings, J. 1984 *Sixteenth-century England*. Pelican.

Size is important:
Iron Age vessel capacities in central and southern England

Ann Woodward and Paul Blinkhorn

Introduction

Since serious studies began, the backbone of research in the later prehistoric period has been formed by the analysis of pottery. Early attempts at classification and interpretation concentrated almost exclusively on aspects of vessel form, or shape, and decorative schemes. The pottery was divided into cultural groups and then arranged in chronological sequences, with it being intuitively felt that the variations in shape and decoration reflected temporal and spatial changes most accurately. Thus, details of vessel shape and style have been illustrated, described, and categorised in the minutest detail. As a result, detailed classifications of many ceramic types have been erected, and an overall chronological framework is in place. Now, the time has come to explore new avenues of pottery analysis.

Scant attention has ever been paid to variations in vessel size, yet it is surely this parameter that should most directly relate to the use of any vessel as a container. Furthermore, variations in standardisation of size groupings have the potential to provide powerful indications of the scale of organised production at the household, site or regional levels. Such variations may denote the specific production of tight or looser size groups designed for particular functions, either in the domestic, ritual or sepulchral context, or signifying the unique identity of a group of people. This signification could occur at the site level: indicating the existence of age and sex grades, types of household, or the presence of ritual or other specialists, while at the regional or supra-regional level it might aid the definition of ethnic groupings of varying size and/or cohesion. For example, Julian Richards (1987) has demonstrated that, in the case of pagan Anglo-Saxon cremation urns, the size of the vessel is related to the age of the contained individual.

Possible uses for ceramic containers are myriad: the most common include the storage of food, water or other substances at the communal or household level, the preparation and cooking of food and drink, provision for individual eating or communal feasting, the accurate measurement of commodities, ritual display in secular or funerary contexts, the presentation of libations or offerings, the preparation and presentation of specialist substances such as medicines or hallucinogens, or , finally, the safe storage, in perpetuity, of human remains. To the multiplicity of this list must be added a few complicating factors. In particular, it should be noted that the uses of any one ceramic form in a single chronological period might be multiple, or singularly successive: a single pot, during its lifetime, may have functioned simultaneously as water container, a serving bowl, a cooking vessel and an heirloom on display, whilst another might have been used as a storage container and then a cremation urn. In spite of these provisos, the analysis of size in relation to primary function does appear to be a potentially powerful tool in the study of ceramic assemblages, and this point has been well demonstrated by some research programmes which have attempted to characterise present-day potting traditions (e.g. Miller 1985).

The few studies of vessel size that have been undertaken in Britain relate to the earlier periods of prehistory, the Neolithic and Bronze Age periods. For the major Early Neolithic assemblage from Windmill Hill, Howard was able to demonstrate the range of vessel sizes present by plotting rim diameter against vessel height (Howard 1981, Figs 1.3 and 1.4). Despite the size categories being cross-cut by the observed fabric types and the degree of decoration present, Howard was able to define a complex listing of functional ascriptions. However, close inspection of her graph depicting the relationship between rim diameter and height for the measurable vessels (Fig 1.3) shows that although smaller vessels were more common than larger ones, there were no clear clusters of points that indicated tightly-defined size categories. A similar impression is provided by the Early Neolithic vessel volume data presented by Thomas (1991, Fig. 5.8). Whilst bowls of the Peterborough tradition at present seem to have similar generalised ranges of vessel size, by the Late Neolithic and Early Bronze Age periods there are classes of pottery which do appear to have been manufactured according to more limiting size rules. In the case of Grooved Ware, Cleal has noted that vessels in the Woodlands and Clacton styles tend to be small (in Barrett, Bradley and Hall 1991, 146), whilst pots in the Durrington

Walls style are remarkably large. A plot of the rim diameter data from the type site (Woodward 1995, Fig. 17.3) showed that the large vessels grouped into three distinct size ranges. Despite Grooved Ware being generally regarded as having ritual connotations, it is sometimes found on domestic sites. The size categories may be connected to varying function at the domestic or cult level, and may reflect closely controlled rules or embedded strict modes of production which involved the manufacture of pots of specific sizes to suit specific social or ritual scenarios. Viewed at the national scale, detailed plotting of the size parameters of Collared Urns suggested that the vessels conformed to a continuous size range (Longworth 1984, Figs. 27,33 and 36). However, closer plotting of one regional group, the Collared Urns from Dorset and Hampshire, did suggest that a bimodal pattern may have been present (Woodward 1995, Fig. 17.3).

From the Middle Bronze Age onwards, fewer complete vessels or vessel profiles are available, and so the relationships between vessel size, rim diameter, base diameter and sherd thickness have been examined, as during the analyses of Middle Bronze Age assemblages from Black Patch, Sussex (Ellison 1982) and Grimes Graves, Norfolk (Ellison in Longworth et al. 1988). Further research on the definition of ceramic size groupings, based on plots of rim diameter against height, was undertaken for Trevisker pottery (Parker Pearson 1995) and for vessels from a series of Deverel-Rimbury urnfields (Woodward 1995). For the Late Bronze Age period, Barrett defined a series of five functional size categories and investigated their characteristics in terms of estimated vessel capacity (Barrett 1980). In the case of most later Bronze Age groups, capacity can seldom be calculated, but confident assertions concerning the changing patterns of vessel size groupings through time can be made. In addition to the study of the Bronze Age pottery from the sites in East Anglia (above), the main presentation of this approach has been in relation to the sequence of Bronze Age assemblages excavated at Brean Down, Somerset (Woodward 1990). These studies suggest increasing sophistication through time in the definition of discrete size groupings, with a marked increase in functional diversity around the Early Bronze Age/Middle Bronze Age transition. This development is thought to be linked to a change from individual pottery vessels representing specific people, especially in funerary and ritual contexts, to groups of pottery representing social groups. The social groups represented may operate at the household, community or regional levels.

Within the Iron Age period, very few attempts to gather vessel size statistics have been made. It seems likely that that this line of research has been hindered by the lack of complete vessels or reconstructable profiles, and the overwhelming nature of the huge sherd assemblages from hillfort and settlement sites excavated in England during the last few decades. Moreover, the low incidence of complete vessel profiles, linked to the higher incidence of more curvaceous and complex outlines, means that it is very difficult to assess vessel capacity. During the selective study of the very substantial Iron Age pottery assemblage from Alcock's excavations at Cadbury Castle, Somerset (Woodward forthcoming), it was decided to consider the subject of vessel size in some detail. The main aim of this particular study was to investigate the variation in vessel size amongst individual form types and through time. In addition it has been possible to compare some of the results from these analyses with size data from a selection of other Iron Age sites in southern England (Woodward 1996).

Analysts of Romano-British pottery also have begun to address the question of vessel function and variations between different categories of site, such as the large assemblages from the west midlands and the north (Booth 1991, Evans 1993). However, in both cases, the main thrust of the arguments rests upon the analysis of the relative occurrence of fine and coarse ware form types, and there has been little consideration of the raw statistics of vessel size. Initial plotting of vessel height against rim radius for a series of coarse wares (Evans 1993, Fig. 1) does indicate that the size parameter is likely to be of paramount importance in the assessment of ceramic function in the Roman period, and future research no doubt will further the application of such analyses. Medieval pottery studies have been discussing and analysing specific vessel function for many years , but again the research has been based mainly upon the study of form type and occurrence of decoration. However, recent studies of some medieval pottery in the midlands has indicated that a detailed analysis of size parameters may throw up some very interesting patterns and conclusions. The analysis of ceramics from the deserted medieval village of West Cotton, Northamptonshire (Blinkhorn in print) indicated that the coarseware bowls from the site had capacities which closely correlated with their rim diameters. The distribution of the rim diameters of incomplete vessels, when extrapolated upon a rim diameter/volume correlation graph of the complete examples, suggested the commonest sizes of the bowls were in the ranges *c.* 2.0, 3.5–4.0 and 6.0–8.0 litres. The standard medieval dry measure, the bushel, at *c.* 35.2 1itres (Zupko 1968), had a sub-unit, the pottle, of *c.* 1.9 (*ibid*). Thus, the volume ranges of the medieval bowls could be seen to cluster around units of 1, 2 and 4 pottles. Such bowls are generally regarded as having functioned primarily in the skimming of milk, but organic residue analysis revealed a total absence of those or any other fats in the vessels (Charters *et al* 1994), despite the substances occurring in other contemporary vessel forms in the same fabrics within the settlement. However, many of the bowls occurred in and around the bakehouses at the settlement. Documentary evidence shows that a shallow wooden vessel known as a cantel, which was of a similar form to the pottery bowls, was used in medieval bakeries for measuring meal and flour. Since the pottle was a dry measure, it seems highly likely that the pottery bowls at West Cotton were designed primarily for measuring flour and meal for baking. It should be noted that some of the vessels showed signs of having been heated at some point during their use-life, illustrating some of the comments made above.

In the light of the results of these various avenues of research it was decided to use the methodology developed for the analysis of the Northamptonshire medieval material to investigate the potential presence of a correlation between rim diameter and capacity for jar forms from Iron Age assemblages in the south-east midlands. Similar tests were applied to the Iron Age vessel data derived from the Cadbury Castle study, and comparisons made of the degrees of size standardisation amongst the fine and coarse ware groups in the various regions.

The relationship between rim diameters and vessel volumes

Assemblages can be divided into fine and coarse ware components in several ways. The most common is by form, as in the Romano-British analyses cited previously, this being probably the most sensitive method when a wide range of form variation and of decorative technique is present. In the case of assemblages which show less variation and a general lack of decoration, this approach is less useful, but attempts at a fine/coarse definition can be made by considering variations in the fabric types and surface finishes. In southern England, Middle-Late Iron Age pottery is highly variable and it has proved possible to devise complex systems of form classification for the large assemblages from sites such as Danebury (Brown 1991). A similar classification has been applied to the recently analysed groups from Cadbury Castle, and selected data from the Middle-Late Iron Age (Middle Cadbury) phases will be drawn on in this analysis. In the midlands, Middle-Late Iron Age pottery is less diverse, both in terms of clearly diagnostic form type and degree of decoration. In this case we are depending on a detailed analysis of fabrics to indicate a simple bipartite division between fine and coarse ware groups.

Northamptonshire is particularly rich in Middle and Late Iron Age sites, many of which have been published. The data from two of these, Weekley (Jackson and Dix 1988) and Twywell (Jackson 1975) is examined here, as are two adjacent sites in the neighbouring county of Buckinghamshire, Pennyland and Hartigan's in Milton Keynes (Williams 1993). The Middle and Late Iron Age pottery of the south-east midlands appears fairly homogeneous in terms of the range of forms and fabric, with the main fabric being shell-tempered wares, which can usually be divided into two groups:

F1: 'Coarse Shell' Moderate to dense temper of angular coarse shell fragments up to 10mm, with sparse to moderate quartzite, grog, flint, organic material or ironstone, depending upon the local geology.

F2: 'Fine Shell' Sparse to moderate angular shell fragments up to 5mm, although most are usually below 2mm. Other materials occur as in F1.

When examining the published evidence from Weekley and Pennyland, Penelope Allison's comments (this volume)

were only too keenly appreciated: drawings of large numbers of rimsherds were present in the reports, but no indication was given as to whether these represented some or all of those found at the sites, despite there being a microfiche report in the Weekley volume. In both cases, consideration was given to the rim forms of the vessels, but no mention was made of the number of examples found, or their diameters (Foster and Aird 1988; Knight 1993, 222). As a result, the data presented below is based purely on published drawings. Similarly, there was no formalized fabric analysis of the Twywell material at publication, so the data has been omitted from the rim diameter analysis, although the complete vessels have been included in the volumetric study. The rim diameter data from two presently unpublished sites in Northamptonshire, Wollaston Quarry and the Daventry International Rail Freight Terminal site (Blinkhorn forthcoming (a) and (b)) is included to increase the size of the dataset.

Both the fabrics are somewhat friable; the EVE tabulation from the Crick and Wollaston sites showed that in both cases, around 85% of the rim sherds recovered represented 15% or less of the complete rim. Similarly, vessels which survived as full profiles were rare: at Weekley, over 63 kg of pottery (2520 sherds) were recovered from Ceramic Phase 1 but only seven vessels were reconstructable to full profiles. Consequently, it was necessary to amalgamate the data from Pennyland, Twywell and Weekley to examine the correlation between vessel capacity and rim diameter (Table 1). The three complete vessels from the Northamptonshire sites of Brigstock and Hardwick Park (Jackson 1983) were also added. It was also decided to investigate the degree of correlation between rim diameter and capacity with a third parameter, namely vessel height, to test which provided the closest correlation.

In the Weekley report, it was noted that there was '*a tendency for larger jars to have been made in clay with coarser inclusions*' (Foster and Aird 1988, 73), although no detailed evidence for this was presented. Consequently, it was decided to test this assertion. The volume of each vessel was calculated by dividing it into a series of one centimetre cm thick frusta and summing their volumes. The rim diameter, vessel height and volume parameters are presented in Table 1. The calculation of the correlation coefficient, r, of two related variables, x and y, is a standard statistical operation (e.g. Hayslett 1978, 134). Computation of r gives a value between +1 and -1, where +1 is complete correlation i.e. any increase in one parameter results in an increase in the other, and -1 is an inverse correlation i.e. an increase in one parameter results in a decrease in the other. The closer the r value to zero, the less strong the correlation, with both values changing independently of each other.

Computation of the correlation between rim diameter and volume values listed in Table 1 gives a result of $r = 0.91$, indicating that there is a strong correlation between rim diameter and volume for these Iron Age jars. When the same operation is carried out to test the correlation between height and volume, the result is $r = 0.90$. This indicates that

Table 1. Volume, rim diameter and height of Iron Age jars from the east midlands.

Site	Fig. No	Diameter (mm)	Height (mm)	Capacity (litres)
Weekley	29.10	100	144	1.01
Weekley	30.26	88	104	0.47
Weekley	30.27	160	132	1.96
Weekley	30.37	148	128	1.60
Weekley	30.41	168	184	2.81
Twywell	21.1	138	92	0.72
Twywell	21.2	164	108	1.22
Twywell	21.3	152	124	1.57
Twywell	21.11	136	88	0.73
Twywell	21.17	129	128	0.98
Twywell	24.4	158	144	1.85
Brigstock	7.21	152	148	1.77
Brigstock	7.29	320	292	19.74
Hardwick Park	11.1	136	130	1.37
Pennyland	91.11	120	112	0.84
Pennyland	92.21	180	124	1.99
Pennyland	92.25	284	272	10.29
Pennyland	94.58	164	168	2.78
Pennyland	94.61	160	120	1.59
Hartigan's	97.86	140	140	1.65
Hartigan's	98.106	160	152	1.77
Hartigan's	98.107	220	164	4.52

Table 2. Volume, rim diameter and height of Iron Age vessels from Early and Middle Cadbury.

Form	Rim Diameter (mm)	Height (mm)	Capacity (litres)
JA1	220	210	6.87
JB2	150	175	3.33
JB2	76	135	0.64
JB4.2	102	120	0.92
JC1	128	156	1.53
JC1	240	258	11.95
JC2	132	170	2.46
JC2	210	206	5.93
JC2	120	175	2.18
JC2	156	160	2.38
JC3	178	205	4.70
JC3	134	160	2.17
JC3	120	175	2.36
JD3	110	220	4.88
PA1	232	235	7.58
PA1	210	278	6.13
PA2	118	118	0.98
PA3	128	128	1.18
PA3	138	170	2.24
PB1	140	120	0.69
PB1	120	95	0.76
BD6	136	132	1.94
BD6	94	126	1.04
BD6	142	120	1.85
BD6	156	128	2.22

rim diameter measurement is as accurate a representation of vessel volume as height. Calculation of *r* for rim diameter and height gives a value of *r* = 0.87, thus suggesting that the Iron Age potters in the south-east midlands increased the volume of vessels by increasing both the height and the rim diameter.

Similar calculations were computed for the commonest ceramic forms represented in the Early and Middle Cadbury phases at Cadbury Castle (Table 2). For the coarse ware jar forms JA/JB/JC the correlation coefficient for rim diameter and volume is 0.89 and that for height and volume is 0.85. The corresponding values of *r* for the short jar/bowl forms PA/PB are seen to be even more significant: 0.98 and 0.93. For the fine bowls of form BD6 the correlation between rim diameter and volume is highly significant (*r* = 0.99), although there was no clear correlation between height and volume in this case. Thus, for the main ceramic types current in the Middle Cadbury phase, the close correlation between rim diameter and vessel volume matches the pattern established for the east midlands assemblages. However, there are indications that this direct relationship begins to break down in the Late Cadbury period (from the early first century A.D.) when more curvaceous profiles and complex forms become more common.

Rim diameter ranges amongst coarse and fine wares

In each region, we are interested in studying the occurrence of different vessel sizes and capacities amongst the various groups of fine and coarse ware. Such a study compares the ranges of rim diameter occurrence exhibited by the different form or fabric groups, the results being presented in Table 3 and Fig. 1.

Coarse wares

At Cadbury Castle rim diameter data for the two main form groups of Middle-Late Iron Age coarse ware are presented. These are the barrel-shaped jars (form group PA) and the slack- to round-bodied profile jars with proto-bead or bead rim forms (form groups JC and JD). Both form groups display major concentrations of small vessels, with marked peaks in the 121–140mm rim diameter range. Larger vessels, however, are present in both groups and minor peaks may be observed in the 281–300 and >400 mm ranges, with the addition of another peak at 341–360 mm for the JC/JD form group only.

In the east Midlands, all four site assemblages show a broadly similar range of rim diameters, with peak values clustering around the same sizes. Combining the data from the sites suggests two main peaks, one around 141–160mm, and the other around 261–280 mm. Extrapolating these values graphically suggested capacitance modes around 1.5 and 10 litres. The two rimsherds of 500mm diameter suggest a third possible mode, although no vessels of such a rim diameter have yet been reconstructed, and thus the situation will only become clear as more data is collected. Despite the variation in the population sizes of the four sites, there is a standard deviation of only 21.95 mm in the mean rim diameter, suggesting a very similar range of vessel sizes in this fabric group.

The percentage histograms show that, as at Cadbury, most of the coarse ware vessels are small, although the peak here lies in a slightly larger rim diameter range, 141–160 mm. Also, there are several minor peaks for the larger vessels, one at >400 mm, as at Cadbury, and another at 261–280 mm. Thus, all the coarse ware groups show three rim diameter peaks, which relate to volume size. These may

Table 3. *Cadbury and Northamptonshire/Buckinghamshire: rim diameter occurrence at 20 mm intervals, expressed as a percentage of each assemblage.*

	Coarse Wares			Fine Wares		
Rim Dia (mm)	PA	JC/D	NA/BK	PB coarse	BD6	NA/BK fine
80-99	4.5%	1.4	4.5	0	0	3.4
100-119	17.8	13.1	9.1	7.1	4.8	12.0
120-139	**40.6**	**31.1**	11.4	**53.6**	31.0	**15.5**
140-159	20.3	26.1	**19.3**	32.1	**40.5**	13.8
160-179	7.3	10.4	9.1	7.1	19.0	**21.6**
180-199	3.5	3.6	9.1	0	4.8	12.9
200-219	2.1	2.7	5.7	0	0	6.0
220-239	1.7	2.7	5.7	0	0	**9.5**
240-259	0.7	2.3	3.4	0	0	1.7
260-279	0	0.9	**8.0**	0	0	1.7
280-299	**0.3**	2.7	5.7	0	0	1.7
300-319	0	0	0	0	0	0
320-339	0	0.5	2.3	0	0	0
340-359	0	**1.8**	1.1	0	0	0
360-379	0	0.5	2.3	0	0	0
380-399	0	0	0	0	0	0
400-419	**1.0**	0.5	**2.3**	0	0	0
Total No	286	222	88	28	42	116

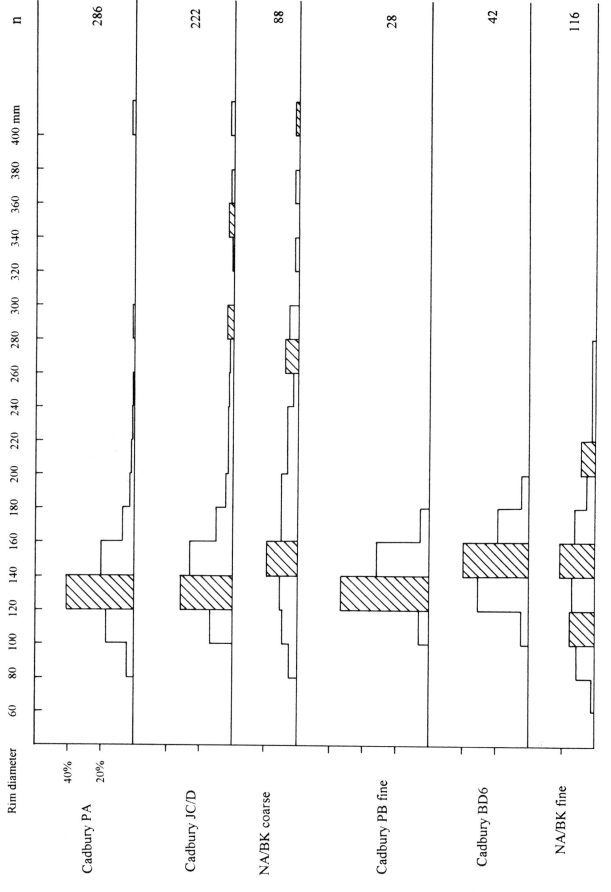

Fig. 1. The occurrence of rim diameters amongst six regional types of decorated bowl.

reflect generalized functional roles such as storage, liquid containment, food processing, cooking and serving. However, some interesting contrasts may be highlighted. Firstly the east Midlands coarseware vessels appear to have a more generalised size and volume range than the Cadbury assemblage, and, secondly, the smaller and medium-sized concentrations in the East Midlands examples are closer to each other in size than at Cadbury. In other words, the different postulated functional size types at Cadbury seem to have been both more standardised and more discretely defined.

Fine wares

The rim diameter spreads for the two main groups of decorated bowls found at Cadbury were compared with those obtained for the fine shelly fabric vessels from Northamptonshire. The Cadbury bowl groups analysed are the saucepan pots (form PB) and the Glastonbury jars and bowls of form BD6. In both cases the size ranges of the vessels, as displayed by rim diameter counts, are tightly defined with clear peaks. However, the saucepan pots show a marked concentration of vessels with rim diameters in the 121–140 mm range, compared with a less marked peak of Glastonbury jar rim diameters in the larger 141–160 mm range.

The pattern displayed by the fine shelly ware vessels from the east Midlands is even more interesting. The rim diameters of the fine shelly vessels show clustering around three values: 101–120 mm, 141–160 mm and 201–220 mm., suggesting modal volumes of 0.5, 1.5 and 5.0 1itres. As with the coarse shelly fabric example, the four site groups show very similar mean rim diameters, there being only a 29.2 mm standard deviation. This suggests a similar range of vessel sizes at each of the four sites.

The two main Middle-Late Iron Age fine ware forms at Cadbury are equally standardised, but they occur in two different size groups, perhaps indicative of varying functions in the sphere of the serving and consumption of food and drink. In Northamptonshire, although the general range of fine ware vessel size is more generalised, there are three peaks of size distribution, suggesting the operation of a more complex system of vessel allocation according to function. The medium peak equates roughly to that of the Cadbury bowls, but the presence of distinct groups of both smaller vessels, cups, and larger serving vessels is of particular interest.

Rim diameter ranges amongst decorated bowl groups

Previous research has indicated that the size ranges of specific decorated bowl types, as represented by rim diameter statistics, vary from site to site and region to region (Woodward 1996, Fig. 4.2). In the context of the present study it seems appropriate to extend this approach by comparing some of the results from southern England with some data-sets from central and eastern sectors of the country. The assemblages to be compared comprise regional groups of round-bodied necked bowls carrying curvilinear decoration of La Tène type. These include two major types of Glastonbury Ware, the La Tène decorated pottery of the Nene valley and decorated bowls from the middle and upper Thames region: the Stanton Harcourt-Cassington and Southcote-Blewburton types as defined by Cunliffe (1991). The percentage occurrences of rim diameter ranges for these regional groups is shown in Fig. 2; the data for the Glastonbury Ware groups has been listed elsewhere (Woodward 1996, Appendix) whilst that for the Thames and Nene valley groups is listed below (Appendix). The totals of vessels with measurable rim diameters within each regional group is rather low, but the distinctive patterns are suggestive of some clear regional diversity, or show remarkable similarities. Whilst the size ranges of the Glastonbury Group 4 Wares from Cadbury and Meare are basically similar, the larger sub-peak at 201–220 mm occurs only at Meare East. Furthermore, the main cluster of vessels at Meare tends to include rather more vessels with rim diameters of <140 mm than those of 161–180 mm. In other words, the Meare assemblage shows a very clear bimodal pattern whilst the distribution of bowl sizes at Cadbury is much more standardised. The Group 1 Glastonbury Wares of the Cornish peninsula show a different pattern again. Although with the same peak as the Meare and Cadbury groups, the main cluster contains vessels mainly of rim diameter 140 mm and above, while a clearly defined discrete cluster of very large vessels peaks in the 221–240 mm rim diameter range.

It was suggested that such regional and inter-site differences may be reflecting deliberate but embedded traditions of vessel standardisation, mental templates, which serve to signify the cohesion of social groups at site or regional level. It is interesting therefore to investigate how these patterns from the south-west compare with those for some of the ceramic groups in central England. At first sight the Thames valley groups, when combined to give a population of 33, show a slightly less standardised pattern than those obtained for the south-western groups, although the generalised peak occurs at more or less the same point. However, when the data is broken down into the two sub-styles, Stanton Harcourt-Cassington and Southcote-Blewburton, an interesting result emerges. The total is very low, but it does seem that the Stanton Harcourt-Cassington bowls were larger in size than the general run of Southcote-Blewburton vessels (peak at 161–180 mm cf. 121–140 mm rim diameters respectively). In addition, the Southcote-Blewburton group shows a discrete occurrence of larger vessels, equivalent in size range to the larger sub-peak visible within the data from Meare East. It seems that these two Thames ceramic groups were characterised by very clear contrasting size parameters, in addition to their distinct repertoires of decorative motifs. The Nene valley La Tène decorated wares show a size distribution which is dissimilar from both of the Thames valley groups, although the main unimodal distribution of rim diameters is remarkably similar to that obtained for the Glastonbury bowls from Cadbury. The occurrence of a few vessels in the 261–280 mm rim diameter range is remarkable: These decorated bowls are larger than any from all

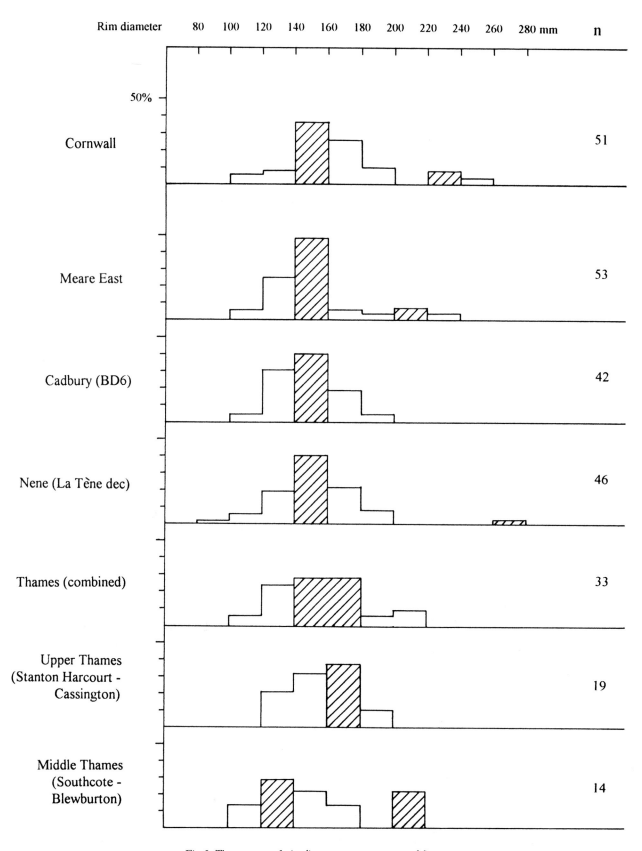

Fig. 2. The occurrence of rim diameters amongst coarse and fine wares.

the other regional groups so far surveyed. The distinct similarity between the Somerset and Nene valley histograms may be more than coincidental. Attention has been drawn previously to the occurrence of Glastonbury Ware sherds, in south-western fabrics, amongst Iron Age assemblages in the Nene Valley. In particular, we note the substantial fragments of a decorated bowl from Weekley (Jackson and Dix 1988, Fig. 36, 91). Although the Nene Valley La Tène decorated bowls are of slightly different shape, generally having a less well developed neck zone than the Glastonbury vessels, it does seem possible that the Nene valley pottery was strongly influenced by the Glastonbury forms in terms of size, and probably therefore of function. Thus it may be than the connections with the south-west were more far-reaching that the result of sporadic trade or long-distance inter-community exchange. Social interaction at a kinship or ideological level may in fact have been involved.

Conclusions

These detailed investigations began with analysis of the relationships between vessel volume, height and rim diameter for various groups of Middle to Late Iron Age pottery from central and southern England. Having established that these parameters co-vary at a significant level, it is possible to use rim diameter data from sherd collections to portray the varying size ranges of contemporary ceramic forms and groups. The rim diameter ranges for fine and coarse wares were compared using the data from two contrasting areas. This involved pottery from a series of sites in the east midlands and the large assemblage excavated at Cadbury Castle on the west margins of Wessex (Fig. 1). We may conclude that, although the Cadbury assemblage, with its tightly defined, standardised and easily recognisable form groups, appears most obviously to be an assemblage which reflected clear functional ascriptions, and controlled production and use of different vessel types in prescribed activities and locations, the apparently uniform and amorphous plain ware assemblages of the east Midlands may have been produced under similar constraints. The three-fold size grouping of the coarse wares is roughly equivalent to that detected at Cadbury, although the overall distribution of small, medium and large vessels is more even. Amongst the east Midlands fine wares, the triple size grouping may even suggest a more complex patterning of serving, eating and drinking vessels than is evidenced by the two standardised but slightly contrasting bowl groups at Cadbury.

Finally, a specific analysis of the size ranges, as represented by rim diameters, of various regional groupings of decorated bowls was undertaken. This showed that the regional bowl styles are characterised not only by specific sets of decorative motifs, but also by specific ranges of capacity (Fig. 2). In some cases, the bowls appear to have been multi-functional and preferred modal size varies. It is particularly interesting to observe that, whilst the Thames groups show size ranges quite different from those in the south, the pattern found in the Nene valley is markedly

similar to that obtained for the Cadbury assemblage. Bearing in mind the existence of occasional Glastonbury ware sherds from sites in the east Midlands, a theory of close social interaction between these areas may be advanced.

The main problem associated with these analyses involves the low numbers of complete profiles and reconstructable rim diameters that are currently available for Iron Age sites in Britain. Neither groups of such data become common until the very final phases of the period, around the turn of the millennium. Owing to the low populations available, the numerical patterns obtained must be treated with extreme caution, and their preliminary status must be stressed. However, it is hoped that two major aims have been achieved. Firstly, it is intended that this study should stimulate the systematic collection of rim diameter data in the future, the searching of existing archives which already contain previously unused data of this nature, and the measuring of rim diameters for all possible sherds in large curated assemblages which did not receive this treatment during primary analysis. Secondly, we stress that, during many decades of detailed analysis of Iron Age ceramics, a major theoretical approach has been ignored. Whilst the vicissitudes of form and decorative style are an essential component of meaningful analysis, it is studies of vessel capacity that now hold the key to significant progress in interpretation. For insights into the mechanisms of production, economy and social identity at a whole series of levels, size is important.

Appendix

Data used in Figure 2.

Nene Valley La Tène decorated wares:
Aldwincle, Wakerley, Hunsbury, Moulton Park, Blackthorn, Hardingstone (Elsdon 1993); Weekley (Jackson and Dix 1988); Wollaston (Blinkhorn in prep.)

Southcote-Blewburton Hill style:
Blewburton Hill, Theale (Cunliffe 1991); Southcote (Piggott and Seaby 1937)

Stanton Harcourt-Cassington style:
Hatford, Cassington, Frilford, Iffley/Rose Hill, Cherbury Camp, Blewburton Hill (Harding 1972); Boxford Common, Wokingham (Cunliffe 1991); Appleford (Hinchliffe and Thomas 1980)

Bibliography
Barrett, J.C. 1980 The pottery of the later Bronze Age in lowland England. *Proceedings of the Prehistoric Society* 46, 297–319.
Barrett, J., Bradley, R. and Hall, M. (eds.) 1991 *Papers on the Prehistoric Archaeology of Cranborne Chase.* Oxbow Monograph 11.
Booth, P. 1991 Inter-Site Comparisons Between Pottery Assemblages in Roman Warwickshire: Ceramic Indicators of Site Status. *Journal of Roman Pottery Studies* 4, 1–10.
Blinkhorn, P. in print The Post-Roman Pottery. In: A. Chapman, *West Cotton: A Study in Settlement Dynamics. Excavations at West Cotton, Raunds, Northamptonshire, 1985–9.* English Heritage.

Blinkhorn, P. forthcoming (a) The Pottery. In: A. Chapman *Excavations at the Daventry International Rail Freight Terminal, Northamptonshire, 1994–5.*

Blinkhorn, P. forthcoming (b) The Pottery. In: I. Meadows *Excavations at Wollaston Quarry, Northamptonshire.*

Brown, L. 1991 The Iron Age pottery. In: B.W. Cunliffe and C. Poole (eds.) *Danebury: an Iron Age hillfort in Hampshire. Volume 5. The excavations 1979–1988: The Finds.* Council for British Archaeology Research Report 73, 277–319.

Charters, S., Evershed, R.P., Goad, L.J., Leyden, A., Blinkhorn, P.W. and Denham, V. 1993 Quantification and distribution of lipid in archaeological ceramics: implications for sampling potsherds for organic residue analysis and the classification of vessel use. *Archaeometry* 35: 211–223.

Cunliffe, B. 1991 *Iron Age Communities in Britain.* Routledge and Kegan Paul.

Ellison, A.B. 1982 Middle Bronze Age pottery. In: P. Drewett Later Bronze Age downland economy and excavations at Black Patch, East Sussex. *Proceedings of the Prehistoric Society* 48, 361–368.

Elsdon, S.M. 1993 *Iron Age Pottery in the East Midlands: A Handbook.* Unpublished, Department of Classics and Archaeology, University of Nottingham.

Evans, J. 1993 Pottery function and finewares in the Roman north. *Journal of Roman Pottery Studies* 6, 95–118.

Foster, P.J. and Aird, P. 1988 Appendix: the ceramic succession. In D. Jackson and B. Dix Late Iron Age and Roman Settlement at Weekley, Northants. *Northamptonshire Archaeology* 21, 73–90.

Harding, D.W. 1972 *The Iron Age in the Upper Thames Basin.* Oxford University Press.

Hayslett, H.T. 1978 *Statistics Made Simple.* W.H. Allen.

Howard, H. 1981 In the wake of distribution: towards an integrated approach to ceramic studies in prehistoric Britain. In: H. Howard and E.L. Morris (eds.), *Production and Distribution: a Ceramic Viewpoint.* British Archaeological Reports International Series 120, 1–30.

Hinchliffe, J. and Thomas, R. 1980 Archaeological Investigations at Appleford. *Oxoniensia* 45, 9–111.

Jackson, D. 1975 An Iron Age Site at Twywell, Northamptonshire. *Northamptonshire Archaeology* 10, 31–93.

Jackson, D. 1983 The Excavation of an Iron Age Site at Brigstock,

Northamptonshire, 1979–81. *Northamptonshire Archaeology* 18, 7–32.

Jackson, D. and Dix, B. 1988 Late Iron Age and Roman Settlement at Weekley, Northants. *Northamptonshire Archaeology* 21, 41–94.

Knight, D. 1993 Late Bronze Age and Iron Age Pottery from Pennyland and Hartigans (MK 19). In: R.J. Williams *Pennyland and Hartigans. Two Iron Age and Saxon Sites in Milton Keynes.* Buckinghamshire Archaeological Society Monograph 4, 219–37.

Longworth, I.H. 1984 *Collared Urns of the Bronze Age in Great Britain and Ireland.* Cambridge University Press.

Longworth, I, Ellison, A. and Rigby, V. 1988 *Excavations at Grimes Graves, Norfolk 1972–1976. Fascicule 2. The Neolithic, Bronze Age and Later Pottery.* British Museum Press.

Miller, D. 1985 *Artefacts as Categories: a study of ceramic variability in central India.* Cambridge University Press.

Parker Pearson, M. 1995 Southwestern Bronze Age pottery. In: I. Kinnes and G. Varndell (eds.), *'Unbaked Urns of Rudely Shape'. Essays on British and Irish Pottery for Ian Longworth.* Oxbow Monograph 55.

Piggott, C.M. and Seaby, W.A. 1937 Early Iron Age site at Southcote, Reading. *Proceedings of the Prehistoric Society* 3, 43–57.

Richards, J.D. 1987 *The significance of form and decoration of Anglo-Saxon cremation urns.* British Archaeological Reports, British Series 166.

Thomas, J. 1991 *Rethinking the Neolithic.* Cambridge University Press.

Williams, R.J. 1993 *Pennyland and Hartigans. Two Iron Age and Saxon Sites in Milton Keynes.* Buckinghamshire Archaeological Society Monograph 4.

Woodward, A. 1990 The Bronze Age Pottery. In: M. Bell, *Brean Down Excavations 1983–1987.* English Heritage Archaeological Report no. 15.

Woodward, A. 1995 Vessel Size and social identity in the Bronze Age of southern England. In: I. Kinnes and G. Varndell (eds.), *'Unbaked Urns of Rudely Shape'. Essays on British and Irish Pottery for Ian Longworth.* Oxbow Monograph 55.

Woodward, A. 1996 Size and style: an alternative study of some Iron Age pottery in southern England. In: C. Haselgrove and A. Gwilt (eds.) *Reconstructing Iron Age Societies.* Oxbow Monograph 71.

Zupko, R.E. 1968 *A dictionary of English weights and measures from Anglo-Saxon times to the nineteenth century.*

— SPECIAL EVENTS —
INSIDE AND OUT

SECOND EDITION

Steven Wood Schmader, CFE
Robert Jackson

SAGAMORE PUBLISHING
Champaign, IL 61820

©1997   Steven Wood Schmader
and Robert Jackson

Book Design, editor: Susan M. McKinney
Cover Design: Deborah Bellaire

ISBN:1-57167-128-5

Printed in the United States.